D1448264

EXPLORING
Antiques
IN BRITAIN

EXPLORING ANTIQUES IN BRITAIN
By Carol Fisher

First published in Great Britain in 2002 by Miller's,
a division of Mitchell Beazley, imprints of Octopus
Publishing Group Ltd, 2–4 Heron Quays,
London E14 4JP

Commissioning Editor Anna Sanderson
Executive Art Editor Rhonda Fisher
Editorial Assistant Rose Hudson
Designer Peter Gerrish
Jacket Designer Victoria Bevan
Copy-Editor Claire Musters
Proofreader Selina Mumford
Indexer Sue Farr
Production Angela Couchman

ISBN 1 84000 504 1

Set in Arial MT
Produced by Toppan Printing Co., (HK) Ltd.
Printed and bound in China

MILLER'S

EXPLORING
Antiques
IN BRITAIN

Carol Fisher

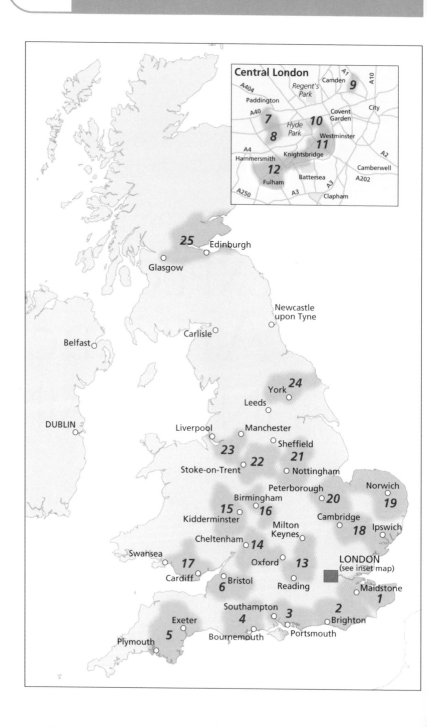

Contents

In 1990, I decided to produce my own book on antiques shops. I had been involved in antiques publishing since 1979, and I thought that a book organized into antiques buying tours would be useful for dealers. The first edition of *Touring British Antiques Shops* was published in 1991. It was quite a slim volume but the second edition, published two years later, more than doubled in size. I was surprised at how popular it was with private buyers as well as dealers, and the number of books we sold to overseas visitors to Britain was amazing. A third edition proved to be even more successful than the previous ones. Although an updated edition was planned, I just ran out of time. Running my own business, an antiques website, and writing for specialist magazines meant that producing a book on my own again was just not possible – there were not enough hours in the day. I was delighted when Miller's asked me to write a similar book for them and the result is *Miller's Exploring Antiques in Britain*. I hope everybody who enjoyed the previous books, finds this one is even better and just as useful.

THE ROUTES

The 25 routes are spread around Great Britain – inevitably there are excellent antiques shops to be found outside these routes but the ones here provide an excellent selection. Each of the 25 routes has a map locator highlighting key roads, towns, and villages. These maps should be used as a guide only, as they are not to scale. Do consult a detailed road map if you are unfamiliar with an area. All the road names are included within the route.

PREPARING YOUR VISIT

Each route opens with listings which give contact details for relevant trade organisations, places of interest, tourist information offices, etc. These can provide information on accommodation and transport as well as more details on what stock individual dealers or antiques centres carry. In addition, many of the antiques websites listed opposite include calendars of fairs and auctions. (Please note that while all website addresses have "http://" in front of them, it is not necessary to type this into the address bar, your computer should do this automatically, and we have not added these into the addresses given. However, not all sites begin with "www" and we have only added this prefix when it is actually part of the address.)

The colour illustrations provide a taster of the type of antiques you might find on the different routes or else represent through their decoration or subject, some link with the different locations.

A good tip if you are visiting a new area is to consult the local press for details of everything from top antiques shows to local fairs. Don't forget to buy the national antiques newspapers and magazines, too, and use information from all these sources to plan your trip and make the most of any antiques-related events, fairs, or auctions.

OPENING HOURS

Dealers are listed under their speciality so you can see at a glance whether there is something of interest to you in a particular location. The length of time each route takes will vary according to your interests. Most antique shops and

▶ ▶ USEFUL WEBSITES

www.artizania.co.uk
Details of specialist costume & textile fairs

www.antiques-web.co.uk/fairs.html
Fairs through UK

www.dmgantiquefairs.com
Over 60 fairs a year are organized by DMG at eight different venues throughout the UK including Newark International Antiques & Collectors Fair. Tel: 01636 702 326

www.penman-fairs.co.uk
Penman Antique Fairs organize good quality antiques and art fairs in London, Chester, Bath and Petersfield (Hampshire).
Tel: 01444 482 514

www.antiques-uk.co.uk
This site includes a searchable database with links to dealers, fairs, antiques centres, auctions and other antiques-related services.

www.antiquesbulletin.com
This site covers many areas of interest within the antiques world.

http://artantiques.allinfo-about.com
Carol Fisher's antiques site with features, and book reviews.

www.antiquesworld.co.uk
Packed with information for everyone with an interest in antiques and collectables.

▶ ▶ USEFUL WEBSITES

Publications

www.antiques-info.co.uk
Website of *Antiques Info* magazine published six times a year. The site includes listings of UK fairs and auctions, plus dealers.

www.antiquecollectorsguide.co.uk
Website of Britain's largest-selling monthly magazine *Antique Dealer & Collectors Guide* devoted to antiques and the fine and decorative arts. Online site includes information on forthcoming sales and fairs plus useful links.

www.antiquesmagazine.com
Antiques Magazine is published weekly and the online site is available to all except the auction and fair databases which are accessible to Antiques Magazine subscribers only.

www.antiquestradegazette.com
The online site of the *Antiques Trade Gazette* the weekly newspaper of the antiques trade.

National Trade Organisations

www.bada.org
British Antique Dealers' Association

www.lapada.co.uk
London & Provincial Antique Dealers' Association

---

centres are open from Monday to Saturday, so where this is the case, opening times have not been stated. Offices are generally open from Monday to Friday, and so if an office also opens on Saturday, for example, this will be indicated. If opening hours are irregular, i.e. outside of the conventional hours of approximately 9am–5.30pm/10am–6pm, this will be specified. (For example, a number of shops shut at 4pm). Many smaller establishments shut for lunch, and this is not specified. Some shops are open by appointment only and a telephone number has been provided so you can make arrangements in advance. Shops do change their opening times and while all information was correct at the time of going to press, there could be subsequent changes. A key to the trade associations listed in the book is on page 200. Antiques centres and auction houses are listed separately within each location. Also included are places of interest to visit – some of these include wonderful collections of antiques, others will appeal to the whole family.

CAROL FISHER

1 The Garden of England

Kent is a great county for buying antiques. There are numerous antiques shops scattered among towns and villages as well as concentrations of shops in places like Canterbury.

Kent's long history has left it with a magnificent heritage of cathedrals, churches, castles, and great houses as well as picturesque villages and busy market towns. It is also a county of beautiful countryside. Orchards, market gardens, and hopfields gave Kent the name "The Garden of England". Right up until the late 1950s/early 1960s, families came from the East End of London in September to pick hops. Not only did this give them a holiday, it was also a source of extra income. This custom stopped when hop picking became mechanized.

The county has many areas of outstanding natural beauty. One way to enjoy them is to walk parts of the North Downs Way, a National Trail that runs from Farnham in Surrey to Dover.

As the closest point to continental Europe, Kent has always been in the front line of wars. The Romans built fortresses along the coast, as did the Normans. During World War II the Battle of Britain took place from the 10th July to 31st October 1940 in the skies above Kent. If you want to know more about this, visit the Battle of Britain Museum located at the former RAF Hawkinge, on the A260 between Canterbury and Folkestone. You can also visit the Battle of Britain Memorial at Capel-le-Ferne on the A2 between Folkestone and Dover.

Websites

www.canterbury.co.uk
This website is run by Canterbury City Council to provide visitors to the Canterbury, Herne Bay and Whitstable area with guides to accommodation, events, local attractions, and much more.

www.canterbury-cathedral.org
Canterbury Cathedral's official website has all the information you need to make your visit enjoyable.

www.dmgantiquefairs.com
Look at this website for more information on the Detling International Antiques & Collectors Fairs and other DMG events.

www.leeds-castle.co.uk
The well illustrated official site for Leeds Castle gives information on opening hours, directions, events, and attractions, as well as providing a history of the castle.

Tourist Information Centres

Ashford 18 The Churchyard.
Tel: 01233 629165

Canterbury 34 St Margaret's Street.
Tel: 01227 766567

Dover Townwall Street. Tel: 01304 205108

Maidstone The Gatehouse, Palace Gardens, Mill Street. Tel: 01622 602169

Rochester 95 High Street.
Tel: 01634 843666

Sevenoaks Buckhurst Lane.
Tel: 01732 450305

ROCHESTER

Rochester was originally built as a Roman fortress to protect the crossing of the River Medway, and the Medieval castle follows the line of this ancient fortress. Although not as famous as Canterbury, the city's cathedral received so many pilgrims that its steps have been worn down by their feet. Charles Dickens lived at Gads Hill from 1857 to 1870 and used the area for the setting of *Great Expectations*. There is a Charles Dickens Centre at Eastgate House in the High Street today.

BOOKS
The city's two bookshops are both situated in the High Street and are open 7 days a week. **Baggins Book Bazaar** and **Baggins Too** sell antiquarian, rare, and second-hand books.

COLLECTABLES
Also in the High Street, **Collectables** has a large selection of collectables and curios including badges, glass, and ceramics. Nearby Frindsbury is home to **Cottage Style Antiques** in Bill Street Road. The shop has a large stock of collectables, architectural salvage, fireplaces, and many other interesting pieces.

FURNITURE
Rochester has two specialist furniture dealers, both in the High Street. **Cathedral Antiques** has an extensive range of antique furniture from the 17thC–1910. **City Antiques Ltd** also has a large range of Georgian, Victorian, and Edwardian furniture, as well as clocks and barometers. It is closed on Sundays and some Wednesdays.

GENERAL ANTIQUES
All four of Rochester's general antiques dealers are conveniently located in the High Street. **Castlebridge Antiques** has a large stock of antiques and collectables, and is open 7 days a week. **Field, Staff & Woods** sell furniture, small items, clocks, collectables, and silver. **Hard Times Antiques Centre** sells general antiques. Lastly, **Memories** has small furniture, china, and general antiques, and is open 7 days a week.

AUCTION HOUSES
Both of the city's salerooms, again in the High Street, hold regular sales. The first, **Amhurst Auctions**, has weekly auctions of antiques, collectables, and general household effects on Saturdays at 12 noon. There is viewing on Fridays from 2–5pm and Saturdays from 9am–12 noon. The office is open Monday–Saturday. **Medway Auctions** have a variety of sales: there are general sales on the first and second Wednesday of each month, specialist monthly sales (each month apart from in December), and quarterly sales of antiques and collectables.

▶ Join the M2 at Junction 2 and travel along it for 42km (26 miles) to Junction 6. Come off the motorway and turn left into Faversham.

FAVERSHAM

This town was once a busy port and market town and contains many interesting and historic buildings. If you are visiting during the summer on a weekend, it is well worth making a slight detour south along the A251 to Badlesmere and then follow the signs to Belmont, which is an 18thC historic house containing a very fine collection of clocks.

COLLECTABLES
Collectors Corner, in East Street, Crescent Road, has a selection of second-hand tools, brassware, door knobs, furniture, coins, pictures, and cigarette cards. It is closed Thursdays and Sundays.

GENERAL ANTIQUES
Faversham Antiques and Collectables, located in Court Street, has a large stock of general furniture, collectables, blue and white china, and Osborne plaques. Squires Antiques of Jacob Yard, Preston Street also has an extensive range of general antiques. It is shut on Wednesdays and Sundays.

▶ Leave Faversham eastbound on the A2, then, after just 3.2km (2 miles), take the A299 to Whitstable, which is about 8.5km (5 miles) away.

WHITSTABLE

This town has been famous for its oysters since Roman times. It is also the home of one of the country's oldest railway bridges, built in 1834.

BOOKS
Book & Pieces in Oxford Street has some antiquarian books and general second-hand books. It is open until 4pm every day except Wednesdays and Sundays.

GENERAL ANTIQUES
There are three antiques shops in Whitstable. The first, Heather's Antiques, is situated in Oxford Street. It has a large range of small antiques and collectables and is open until 4pm. Next, Laurens Antiques in Harbour Street also has a large stock of general antiques. It is closed on Wednesdays and Sundays. Tankerton Antiques of Tankerton Road sells antiques, 18th and 19thC clocks, watches, china, furniture, fabrics, and ceramics. Its opening hours are Tuesday and Wednesday 10am–1pm and Thursday–Saturday 10am–5pm.

ANTIQUES CENTRES
Boulevard Antiques, in Tankerton Road, has five dealers selling china, Art Deco, glass, furniture, postcards, books, records, Osborne plaques, dolls, toys, silver, and silverplate.

AUCTION HOUSES
Christopher Hodgson, again of Tankerton Road, is the regional representative of London auctioneers, Bonhams & Brooks.

▶ Canterbury, the next stop, is just 8.5km (5 miles) away on the A290.

CANTERBURY

There has been a human settlement at Canterbury since prehistoric times. It began as a Roman administrative settlement and the existing Medieval city walls follow the lines of the earlier Roman ones. St Augustine built his priory here, which is now the site of the present great Cathedral. To truly appreciate its beauty and historic significance, take a guided tour or buy a guidebook.

Apart from the city's Medieval crooked streets with timber-framed houses and the remains of the city walls, Canterbury has much to offer the visitor, including numerous historic buildings and museums. The Canterbury Tales Visitors Attraction in St Margaret's Street is one of the most popular. Here five of Chaucer's Tales are recreated and visitors are taken back, through smell and sounds as well as the displays, to Medieval Canterbury. In contrast, St Augustine's Abbey Museum, 0.4km (¼ mile) from the city centre in Longport, dates from AD 598 and is one of the oldest monastic sites in the country. Its museum charts the history of the abbey and displays many of the historic finds from the site, including the early 16thC burial mitre of Abbot John Dugon.

ARCHITECTURAL ANTIQUES
Bygone Reclamation (Canterbury) Ltd of Nackington Road has thousands of reclaimed

items including Victorian fireplaces, cast-iron radiators, building materials, and architectural salvage. It is open 7 days a week.

BOOKS

The Canterbury Bookshop in Palace Street has antique and second-hand books and is open Thursday–Saturday 10am–5pm. The Chaucer Bookshop is in the curiously named Beer Cart Lane. It has an extensive stock of antiquarian and out-of-print books.

COLLECTABLES

There are two contrasting shops in the city selling collectables. The first, Whatever Comics in Burgate Lane, has a large stock of die-cast cars, *Star Trek* and *Star Wars* toys, movie-related items, sci-fi collectables, Beanie Babies, and action figures. World Coins in Broad Street specializes in coins, medals, militaria, bank notes, stamps, medallions, and tokens. The shop is closed on Thursday afternoons and Sundays.

FURNITURE

Canterbury is blessed with several antique furniture dealers. Antique & Design at The Old Oast, Hollow Lane has a large stock of English and Continental pine furniture and is open 7 days a week. Located in Palace Street, Conquest House Antiques sells Georgian and Victorian furniture as well as small items, paintings, chandeliers, and rugs. Housepoints in The Borough has antique French country pine furniture and Edwardian and Victorian pieces. Also in The Borough, Michael Pearson has early oak, country furniture, and clocks. Pinetum located at Oaten Hill sells antique, pine, and country furniture. It is open 7 days a week, closing at 3pm on Sundays.

GENERAL ANTIQUES

W J Christophers, another antiques shop located in The Borough, has an extensive range of general antiques, 1720s–1950s, which include pottery, porcelain, clocks, furniture, prints, and books. Located in St Radigunds Street, Maddisons & Luckhurst sell mirrors, antiques, and collectables.

ANTIQUES CENTRES

The Coach House Antique Centre in Duck Lane, Northgate, has ten dealers selling general antiques and collectables. It is open until 4pm.

AUCTION HOUSES

The Canterbury Auction Galleries, in Station Road West, has monthly sales of Victorian and later furniture and bi-monthly specialist sales. G W Finn and Son Auctioneers at Canterbury Auction Market, Market Way, has monthly sales of general household effects as well as antiques and fine art sales. The regional office of Phillips International Auctioneers & Valuers is in Watling Street.

▶ Take the A257 for 19.25km (12 miles) to its junction with the A256. Turn right and follow that road for about 1.6km (1 mile). Turn left onto the A258 to Deal, which is a distance of about 10km (6 miles).

DEAL

The treacherous Goodwin Sands lie just 8.5km (5 miles) offshore from Deal so ships come relatively close to land to avoid them. The town itself has many Georgian houses, a pebble beach, and a castle built by Henry VIII as part of coastal defences against French invasion. Walmer Castle, on the southern edge of the town, was built at the same time. Both castles were erected in the shape of Tudor roses.

COLLECTABLES

Rons Emporium in Church Lane, Sholden, has an extensive range of unusual items, clocks, telephone boxes, antique furniture, snooker tables, and other collectables. The shop is open every day except Thursdays and Sundays. Toby Jug Collectables, located at South Toll House, Deal Pier Beach Street sells Royal Doulton, discontinued Toby, and other character jugs and china collectables. The shop is open all week apart from Mondays.

GENERAL ANTIQUES

The remaining seven antiques shops in Deal all sell a general range of antiques. Decors in Beach Street has 17th–19thC antiques, modern St Louis, Baccarat, non-renewable pieces, and textiles and is open 7 days a week. In the High Street, Delpierre Antiques sells individual and specialist pieces, lighting, Art Deco, Art Nouveau, Oriental, and French furniture. It is closed on Sundays and Mondays. Fordhams, located in Alfred Square, has silver, furniture, general antiques, and antiquities and is open all week except Thursdays and Sundays. Mulbery Antiques, in St George's Passage, has general antiques, furniture, glass, china, textiles, lamps, lighting, and jewellery, and is open Tuesdays and Thursday–Saturday, 10am–4pm. Quill Antiques, in Alfred Square, sells general small antiques. In Dover Street, R S B Antiques sells general antiques and decorative items. In the High Street, Serendipity has a large stock of small furniture, ceramics, and pictures. It is closed on Thursdays and Sundays.

▶ Take the A258 for 13km (8 miles) until you reach Dover.

DOVER

Once the Roman town of *Dubris*, Dover is probably most famous for its white cliffs, which were immortalized in the World War II song by Vera Lynn. The 12thC Dover Castle, built on the site of an Iron Age fort, survived the Civil War because it was held for Parliament. Crabble Corn Mill gives visitors the chance to see a genuine early 19thC mill grinding corn into flour.

ARCHITECTURAL ANTIQUES
Situated in Queens Gardens, **The Warehouse** sells architectural antiques and old metal toys. It is open Thursday–Saturday.

BOOKS
The town's only antiquarian bookshop, **Preface & Prints Bookshop** in London Road has a large range of antiquarian, military, and cinema books and prints.

FURNITURE
Alexandra's Antiques, situated in The Droveway, St Margaret's Bay, sells antique furniture as well as paintings.

▶ Now take the A20 along the coast, signposted Folkestone, which is about 13km (8 miles).

FOLKESTONE

Until the railway reached Folkestone in 1843 it was just a quiet fishing village. But then the railways brought holiday makers from London, attracted by the safe sandy beaches. Since then the town has grown into a major ferry point. Today it is also the Channel Tunnel terminus. Folkestone was a major embarkation point for troops in World War II and rosemary bushes, for remembrance, have been planted along the road running from The Leas (a clifftop walk and gardens) to the harbour. The Folkestone Museum and Sassoon Gallery, in Grace Hill, relates the history of the town through audio-visual displays as well as through more traditional exhibitions.

BOOKS
Situated in Tontine Street, **Bookstop** sells a selection of antiquarian and second-hand books. It is closed on Wednesdays and Sundays. The town's other bookshop, **G & DI Marrin & Son** (ABA, PBFA) specializes in books on the topography of Kent, history, literature of World War II, prints, and maps. The shop is open Tuesday–Saturday.

FURNITURE
Also in Tontine Street, **Alan Lord Antiques** has a warehouse with unrestored furniture and a shop selling antiques that range in price from £10 to £6,000. The shop shuts at 1pm on Saturdays.

GENERAL ANTIQUES
Lawton Antiques, in the Canterbury Road, sells general antiques.

AUCTION HOUSES
The town's only saleroom, **Hogben Auctioneers & Valuers Ltd**, has regular sales. On Saturdays fine art and collectables are sold and on Sundays, Victorian and later items. Viewing takes place on Thursdays 10am–6pm and Fridays 10am–8pm. They also have specialist jewellery, ephemera, books, and Art Deco sales taking place throughout the year.

▶ Take the A259 through Folkestone to Sandgate, which is located on its western edge.

SANDGATE

This small town has now become part of Folkestone itself but, even so, it has one of Kent's most intense concentrations of antiques shops.

EPHEMERA
Like all the other antiques shops in Sandgate, **Collectables** is located in the High Street. It sells old postcards and prints and is open until 4pm each day.

FURNITURE
The town has a good selection of specialist furniture dealers. **Bespoke Furniture** sells chairs, tables, and cabinets and opens 8.30am–5pm on weekdays and 9am–2pm on Saturdays. **Christopher Buck Antiques** (BADA) has a good range of 18thC and early 19thC English furniture and associated items. **Emporium Antiques** has antique and decorative furniture. It is open by appointment only – ring 01303 244430. **Freeman and Lloyd Antiques** (BADA, LAPADA) has a large collection of 18th and early 19thC furniture as well as accessories, pictures, clocks, and bronzes. It is open Tuesdays and Thursday–Saturday. **David Gilbert Antiques**

specializes in Edwardian and Victorian Arts and Crafts furniture and other objects. Nearby, **David M Lancefield** (LAPADA) sells 17th–20thC furniture, other antiques, and decorative arts. The shop is open 7 days a week, and Bank Holidays 11am–5pm. **John McMaster** has an extensive range of 18th and early 19thC English furniture and engravings.

GENERAL ANTIQUES

The following dealers in the town, again in the High Street, sell a wide general range of antiques. **Jonathan Greenwall Antiques** (LAPADA) has a large stock of jewellery, clocks, watches, furniture, pictures, and prints and is open 7 days a week (until 4pm on Sundays).**Robin Homewood Antiques** sells general antiques, furniture, and Art Deco. **Nordens** has a wide range of general antiques, Georgian and Victorian furniture, china, glass, silver, and silverplate. The shop is open by appointment only – ring 01303 248443.

HYTHE

The adjoining town of Hythe is another well-known holiday resort and is also the terminus of the Romney, Hythe, and Dymchurch narrow gauge railway.

GENERAL ANTIQUES

La Brocante in Bank Street has an extensive stock of furniture, china, glass, and jewellery. The shop shuts at 2pm on Wednesdays. Situated in the High Street, **Second Treasures** has a large range of general antiques, clocks, and collectables.

SILVER & JEWELLERY

Owlets, in the High Street, has a large selection of antique and estate jewellery and silver. The shop is closed Wednesdays and Sundays.

ANTIQUES CENTRES

The Malthouse Arcade in the High Street has 37 dealers. It is open Fridays and Saturdays.

▶ Take the A20 for about 19.25km (12 miles) from Hythe to the next stop, Ashford.

ASHFORD

Ashford owed its prosperity in the Middle Ages to its cattle and sheep market. Then, in the 19thC, the railways brought industry to the town as it did to so many others round the country. Today, there are no antiques shops but there are two auctioneers.

AUCTION HOUSES

Established since 1850, **Hobbs Parker** in Monument Way, Orbital Park, has regular sales of antiques and collectables in the Amos Hall. **Parkinson Auctioneers** in Beaver Road has monthly sales of general antiques on Mondays at 10am with viewing on Saturdays 9am–1pm.

▶ Leave Ashford on the M20 and continue for 21km (13 miles), coming off at Junction 7 for Maidstone. Alternatively, leave the motorway at Junction 8 and take the A20 southbound to visit Leeds Castle (see below).

▶ To get from the castle to Maidstone, you can either retrace your steps and take the M20 for 6.5km (4 miles) or you can continue into Maidstone on the A20.

MAIDSTONE

From Saxon times the county town of Maidstone was the location of the "shire moot" or county assembly. From the Middle Ages onwards the town was the most important market for produce from the surrounding area. Maidstone's long

▶ ▶ LEEDS CASTLE

The first royal palace was built here in AD 857 and then rebuilt in 1119. It continued as a royal palace for more than 300 years. It is set on an island in a lake and has 500 acres of beautiful gardens and parkland, making it a popular venue for concerts and other special events. There is an unmissable museum for all dog lovers: the Dog Collar Museum has collars covering 500 years including ones with spikes to protect a dog's throat from wild boar. Still on an animal note, the castle's aviary, housed in a walled garden, has 100 species of parrots, parakeets, softbills, and waders. The house itself contains outstanding collections of fine English and French furniture, tapestries, paintings, and 18thC Chinese porcelain.

history has left it with a large number of historic buildings including the late 14thC Church of All Saints which has, at 28m (93ft), one of the widest naves in the country. There is also the 14thC bridge in Mill Street and the 15thC mansion, Mote Park, which is situated close to the town centre. The Elizabethan Chillington Manor, in St Faith's Street, houses the Maidstone Museum and Art Gallery. As well as a wide collection of archaeological finds ranging in date from prehistoric times to the Middle Ages, it also houses a collection of Japanese Edo period ceramics, lacquer, prints, and metalwork – said to be one of the finest outside London. It also has collections of British and European paintings, glass, furniture, ceramics, and 17th–19thC costume.

COLLECTABLES
Located in Middle Row in the High Street, **Whatever Comics** has a selection of second-hand comics, *Star Trek* and *Star Wars* toys, movie-related items, sci-fi collectables, Beanie Babies, and action figures.

FURNITURE
Becky's Attic is situated in Loose Road, in the village of Loose, 3.2km (2 miles) south of the town centre on the A229. It has a large stock of antique pine furniture and china. The shop is open 7 days a week (until 1pm on Sundays). In the same village, **Loose Valley Antiques** of Scriba House, also in Loose Road, has an extensive range of oak and pine furniture and collectables. It is open every day except Monday and closes at 4pm on Sunday.

JEWELLERY
Gem Antiques of Gabriels Hill sells jewellery, pocket watches, and objets d'art.

ANTIQUES CENTRES
The first of the town's two antiques centres, the **Garden of England Antique Centre** in Bank Street has 20 dealers selling a wide range of good-quality antiques. It is open 7 days a week. The other centre, **Newnham Court Antiques** in the Newnham Court Shopping Village, Bearsted Road, Weavering, is much smaller. It has just three dealers but still boasts an extensive stock of collectables, ceramics, and dining furniture. It is also open 7 days a week.

ANTIQUES FAIRS
The Kent County Showground at Detling, just off the A249, is home to the **Detling International Antiques & Collectors Fairs**, organized by DMG Antiques Fairs. It has up to 600 inside and outside stalls selling a wide range of antiques and collectables and takes place six times a year.

▶ Take the A26 from the town centre for 21km (13 miles) to reach Tonbridge.

TONBRIDGE
A 13thC gatehouse is all that remains of Tonbridge Castle, which was built to defend the ford of the River Medway.

CLOCKS & BAROMETERS
Derek Roberts Antiques (BADA) of Shipbourne Road is one of the best-known dealers in the country. He specializes in 17th and 19thC clocks, barometers, and books about clocks.

GENERAL ANTIQUES
Lawson Antiques Ltd, in the High Street, has a large range of general antiques and is open Thursday–Saturday. **Greta May Antiques** in The New Curiosity Shop, Tollgate Buildings, Hadlow Road sells furniture, silver, silverplate, china, and glass. Its opening days are Tuesdays and Thursdays–Saturdays.

ANTIQUES CENTRES
Located in Priory Street, **Barden House Antiques** has four dealers with a large selection of general antiques, prints, watercolours, jewellery, china, and small pieces of furniture.

▶ Take the A21 direct to Sevenoaks, which is about 11.25km (7 miles) away.

SEVENOAKS
The poet John Donne was rector of this charming town of half-timbered buildings from 1616–31 and there is a memorial to him in the church of St Nicholas. Nearby Knole, standing just over 1.6km (1 mile) east of the town, is the largest private house in England with 365 rooms and 52 staircases. It houses a fine collection of 17thC furniture. Ightham Mote, another notable property in the area, is one of the most complete Medieval

moated manor houses in the country. Combe Bank House, also nearby, has attractive gardens and pleasure grounds.

GENERAL ANTIQUES

The first of Sevenoaks' dealers is **Amherst Antiques**, which is open by appointment only. It sells 19thC English ceramics, coloured glass, and silver and the telephone number is 07850 350212. Next, **Emma Antiques** in Holy Bush Lane has general antiques, furniture, china, silver, pictures, and tapestry cushions. The shop is open Mondays and Fridays 2–5.15pm, Tuesdays and Thursdays 10am–5pm, and Saturdays 10am–1pm. The last of the general dealers is **Furniture and Effects** in St Botolph's Road, which sells a large stock of general antiques and furniture.

JEWELLERY

Gem Antiques in London Road has a selection of clocks and jewellery.

ANTIQUES CENTRES

Roundabout Antiques, in London Road, Riverhead, has six dealers selling collectables and general antiques. It is open every day except Wednesdays and Sundays.

AUCTION HOUSES

Ibbett Mosely in the High Street has nine sales of general antiques a year. **Phillips International Auctioneers & Valuers** have their regional office in London Road.

▶ Follow the A25 from Sevenoaks for just 3.2km (2 miles) to Brasted.

BRASTED

This picturesque village is best known for its comparatively large number of antiques shops.

FURNITURE

Brasted's five specialist furniture dealers all have their shops in the High Street. **Bigwood Antiques** sells antique furniture and is open 7 days a week (from 1.30pm on Sundays). **Peter Dyke** at Kentish House sells 18th–19thC furniture together with works of art. At the Coach House, **Roy Massingham** (LAPADA) also has 18th and 19thC furniture with pictures and other objects. He is open by appointment only – ring 01959 562408. Still in the High Street, **Southdown House Antique Galleries** again has 18th and 19thC furniture together with textiles, porcelain, glass, and metalware. Finally, **Dinah Stoodley** has a selection of early oak and country furniture.

GENERAL ANTIQUES

Again in the High Street, **David Barrington** has general antiques and is open 7 days a week. **Cooper Fine Arts** in Swan House, also in the High Street, sells paintings, sculpture, and decorative items from all periods. Still in the High Street, **Courtyard Antiques** has a large stock of silver, jewellery, ceramics, 19thC furniture, Tunbridge ware, glass, copper, brass, and pictures. It is open 7 days a week (Sundays and Bank Holidays from 12.30–4.30pm). The last of the general dealers, **WW Warner Antiques** (BADA), is located at the Old Forge, The Green. The shop has a good range of 18th and 19thC porcelain, glass, pottery, and furniture.

SCULPTURE

Celia Jennings, in the High Street, has early European wood carvings and sculpture.

ANTIQUES CENTRES

Again in the High Street, the **Village Antiques Centre** has 25 dealers selling a wide range of antiques up to the 1930s including jewellery, pictures, country oak, teddy bears, mirrors, and porcelain. It is open 7 days a week.

▶ The final stop on this tour, Westerham, is just 3.2km (2 miles) further west along the A25.

WESTERHAM

Westerham has even more antiques shops than Brasted, and some good attractions. Quebec House, at the eastern end of the town, was the birthplace of General Wolfe, famous for storming the Heights of Abraham to take Quebec in Canada from the French (although he lost his life in the attempt). A statue of Sir Winston Churchill stands on the green. His house, Chartwell, now owned by the National Trust, is just a couple of miles south on the B2026. Sir Winston lived there for over 40 years, from 1922 to 1964. His own paintings still hang in the house, some of them depicting the beautiful scenery surrounding Chartwell while others show the countries he visited. His study is essentially the same as it was when he worked there, with family photographs and other mementos.

COLLECTABLES

Selling by appointment only, **More Than Music Collectables** has vinyl, books, magazines, and posters etc. Its telephone number is 01959 565514. It is open mornings, Monday–Saturday.

FURNITURE

Situated in the Market Square, **20th Century Marks** has an extensive range of classic 20thC designed furniture and effects. It is open every day apart from Monday (on Sundays it is open from 12 noon–6pm). **Apollo Galleries** (LAPADA), also in the Market Square, has a large stock of mainly Georgian, Victorian, and Edwardian furniture as well as bronzes, oil paintings, watercolours, mirrors, and objets d'art. **Aquarius Antiques** (LAPADA), again in Market Square, sells period furniture, high-quality bronzes, and pictures.

This time in The Green, **Brazil Antiques Ltd** (LAPADA) has predominantly 19thC furniture. **Anthony Hook Antiques**, also in The Green, has period furniture, shipping goods, and reproduction garden statuary. Another dealer in The Green is **Marks Antiques**, which has fine 18th and 19thC furniture and objets d'art. In Vicarage Hill, **Westerham House Antiques** (LAPADA) has a large stock of Georgian, Victorian, and Edwardian furniture as well as decorative items.

GENERAL ANTIQUES

London House Antiques in Market Square has an extensive range of furniture, clocks, bears, dolls, porcelain, and glass. Also in Market Square, **Regal Antiques** (WKADA) has antique jewellery, portrait miniatures, porcelain, watches, and fine paintings. Its opening days are Wednesday–Saturday.

GLASS

D H Sargeant, situated in The Green, has a large selection of chandeliers, table glass, and glass wall lights.

ANTIQUES CENTRES

Castle Antique Centre Ltd is on the London Road and has eight dealers in four showrooms selling linen, tools, silver, jewellery, china, glass, books, 19thC clothing, kitsch, retro-clothing, and small furniture.

TUNBRIDGE WELLS ▶ CRANBROOK ▶ RYE ▶ BATTLE ▶ HASTINGS ▶ ST LEONARDS ▶
BEXHILL ▶ HAILSHAM ▶ EASTBOURNE ▶ SEAFORD ▶ LEWES ▶ BRIGHTON ▶ HOVE ▶
SHOREHAM-BY-SEA ▶ WORTHING ▶ HORSHAM

There are numerous antiques shops on this tour, which includes many towns famous for their antiques such as Brighton. This area has a large number of antique furniture dealers.

Although Sussex has a variety of scenery ranging from Georgian towns to beautiful countryside dotted with pretty villages, it is most famous for its Victorian seaside resorts like Brighton and Eastbourne. These were both made popular by their association with royalty in the early 19thC.

There is more to Sussex than the seaside, though. One of its most famous features, the South Downs, is a designated Area of Outstanding Natural Beauty. It is a steep chalk ridge running from Eastbourne, Sussex to Winchester, Hampshire, and encompasses many habitats important for conservation, including lowland heath and chalk grassland. The area is also rich in archaeological remains with prehistoric field patterns, hill forts, barrows, Roman roads, and deserted Medieval villages.

The Romans grew grape vines in Sussex 2,000 years ago and today the county is once again becoming famous for its vineyards and wine. Many of the vineyards encourage visitors. The Sedlescombe Organic Vineyard, for example, is the oldest organic vineyard in England (established in 1979). It is located about 6.5km (4 miles) north of Hastings. Why not visit it and others in the county to find out just how good English wine can be?

▶ ▶ USEFUL CONTACTS

Websites

www.brighton.co.uk
This site describes itself as "Virtual Brighton and Hove" and provides a wealth of information on both towns.

www.rye-tourism.co.uk
Find out more about the picturesque and historic town of Rye.

www.sussextourism.org.uk
On this web page you can learn the top 50 attractions in Sussex.

Tourist Information Centres

Brighton 10 Bartholomew Square.
Tel: 0906 711 2255

Folkestone Harbour Street.
Tel: 01303 258594

Hastings Old Town The Stade.
Tel: 01424 781111

Horsham 9 The Causeway.
Tel: 01403 211661

Rye The Heritage Centre, Strand Quay.
Tel: 01797 226696

Tunbridge Wells The Old Fish Market, The Pantiles. Tel: 01892 515675

Worthing Marine Parade.
Tel: 01903 210022

TUNBRIDGE WELLS

The town's mineral spring was discovered in 1606 and was given the royal seal of approval in 1630 when the wife of Charles I, Henrietta Maria, came here to recuperate after the birth of their son. In the 18thC the town became so fashionable that Beau Nash, usually associated with Bath, visited. So many royal personages followed that it received the name of Royal Tunbridge Wells. The town's most famous area, the Pantiles, was so named because the roofing tiles used locally were laid to make a pavement. Tunbridge Wells Museum & Art Gallery, in the Civic Centre, Mount Pleasant, has displays of Tunbridge

ware, local history, dolls, and toys. As well as touring exhibitions, the art gallery has collections of Victorian oil paintings, cartoon collages, early photographs, and pictures by local artists.

ARCHITECTURAL ANTIQUES

Architectural Emporium (SALVO), in St John's Road, has a large collection of decorative architectural salvage, 18th and 19thC fireplaces, garden statuary, and door furniture. The shop is open Tuesday–Saturday.

CLOCK & WATCHES

The Vintage Watch Company (WKADA), in the High Street, has a selection of antique watches and jewellery. It is open Wednesday–Saturday.

COLLECTABLES

Sporting Auctions in Union Square, part of the Pantiles, has an impressive assortment of sporting antiques, arms, armour, technical instruments, and tools. The shop is closed on Wednesdays and Sundays.

FURNITURE

Tunbridge Wells has a dozen specialist furniture dealers with greatly varying stock. In the famous Pantiles, **Beau Nash Antiques** has a large range of Georgian, Victorian, and Edwardian pieces plus associated items. It is open Tuesday–Saturday. **Pamela Goodwin** has a wide selection of 18th–20thC furniture plus clocks, silver, English porcelain, Moorcroft, Doulton, glass, and sewing collectables. Her shop is open from 8.30am weekdays and shuts at 12 noon on Saturdays. **Pantiles Antiques** has Georgian–Edwardian furniture, porcelain, and decorative pieces. **John Thompson** also has 18th–19thC furniture as well as 17th–20thC paintings, glass, and porcelain. In Crescent Road, **Calverley Antiques** has an extensive range of pine, decorative, and painted furniture. The shop is open 7 days a week. In Church Road, long-established dealer **Henry Baines** (LAPADA) has a wide selection of both oak and country furniture. St Johns Road is home to five of the town's specialist dealers. **Claremont Antiques** has a broad choice of pine, hardwood, painted, and country furniture. **Culverden Antiques** stocks 19thC furniture and decorative pieces. **Old Colonial** has painted furniture, large country antiques, and decorative items. **Phoenix Antiques** (WKADA) has a variety of 18th and 19thC English and French furniture with overmantel mirrors and associated decorative items. **Up Country** also has a selection of antique and decorative country furniture and rural artefacts. In the London Road, **Robert Dove Antiques**, open every day except Wednesday, has period furniture.

GENERAL ANTIQUES

Aaron Antiques (RADS), in St Johns Road, has a large stock of coins, medals, clocks, china, silver, paintings, prints, scientific and musical instruments, furniture, and Chinese porcelain. Also in St Johns Road, **Junk & Disorderly** has a myriad of antiques, country furniture, jewellery, and collectables. In the Pantiles, **Reflections Antiques'** stock includes furniture, paintings, silver, jewellery, clocks, and watches. The shop is open every day except Wednesday. **Tunbridge Wells Antiques** in Union Square, part of the Pantiles, boasts an extensive selection of Tunbridge ware, Staffordshire figures, watches, clocks, silver, porcelain, pottery, and furniture.

SILVER & JEWELLERY

Chapel Place Antiques, unsurprisingly in Chapel Place, has a wide choice of new silver, hand-painted Limoges boxes, Arabic jewellery, silver photo frames, old silverplate, and claret jugs. In Union Square, **Glassdrumman** has an extensive range of Georgian, Victorian, and second-hand jewellery as well as silver, pocket watches, decorative items, and furniture. The shop is open Tuesday–Saturday.

ANTIQUES CENTRES

In the Pantiles, **Corn Exchange Antiques Centre** houses 11 dealers that sell a range of antiques including pictures, tapestries, glass, silver, furniture, musical boxes, and china.

AUCTION HOUSES

Bracketts Fine Arts in Linden Park Road has two monthly antiques sales on Friday at 10am with viewing Thursday 9am–7pm. **Gorringe's** (SOFAA) in the Pantiles has quarterly sales of fine art and antiques at the Spa Hotel on Tuesday at 11.30am with viewing on Monday 12 noon–8pm. The office opens at 8.30am during the week and shuts at 12 noon on Saturdays.

▶ Leave Tunbridge Wells on the A264 eastbound to its junction with the A21 where you should turn right. Take this road for just 8.5km (5 miles) then turn left onto the A262. After about 11.25km (7 miles) the road will meet the A229 where you can turn right into Cranbrook.

Hever Castle
Alternatively, while you are in Tunbridge Wells you might take the opportunity to visit Hever Castle (see below), which is about 13km (8 miles) south-west of the town. Take the A264 westbound out of Tunbridge Wells for about 11.25km (7 miles) then turn right onto the B2026 and look for signposts within 5km (3 miles) of the junction. Once you have visited the castle, retrace your route back to Tunbridge Wells and follow the directions above.

CRANBROOK

Sited on a hill above the Kentish Weald, Cranbrook has many charming and historic buildings, including an Elizabethan Cloth Hall.

FISHING TACKLE

The Old Tackle Box sells antique fishing tackle and is open by appointment only – ring 01580 713979.

FURNITURE

There are three specialist antique furniture shops in Cranbrook. The first, **Swan & Foxhole Antiques** in Stone Street, has country decorated furniture. **Vestry Antiques**, also in Stone Street, has a large stock of 18th–early 19thC pine, oak, and mahogany furniture with decorative items. **Douglas Bryan Antiques** (BADA, LAPADA), St David's Bridge, has a selection of 17th and 18thC oak furniture with decorative items. It is open Thursday–Saturday.

GENERAL ANTIQUES

Also in Stone Street, **Berry Antiques** sells furniture, textiles, and decorative items. Nearby **Tudor House Antiques** has a large selection of 18thC oak and general furniture with decorative items.

ANTIQUES CENTRES

In the High Street, **Cranbrook Antiques Centre's** ten dealers sell 19thC country antiques, silver, small furniture, ceramics, and prints.

AUCTION HOUSES

Bentleys Fine Art Auctioneers (RADS) in Waterloo

▶ ▶ **HEVER CASTLE**

This romantic 13thC castle was the home of Anne Boleyn, Henry VIII's tragic queen. It was at the castle that he first courted her. At the beginning of the 20thC the castle was bought by the American William Waldorf Astor. He restored the property to its former glory and his collections of furniture, tapestries, and paintings may now be seen here. He has even built an Italian garden, in which to display his antique statuary.

Road has sales of antiques and fine art on the first Saturday of each month at 11am, with viewing three days prior from 10am–6.30pm. The office is open on Saturday mornings too.

▶ Leave Cranbrook on the A229 for about 11.25km (7 miles) to its junction with the A21 where you should turn left and follow the A21 for about 8.5km (5 miles). Turn right onto the A2100 and within 8.5km (5 miles) you will arrive in Battle.

▶ Alternatively, you may include the town of Rye in the itinerary. Leave Cranbrook on the A229 for 6.5km (4 miles). Turn left onto the A268 and follow this road for 8.5km (5 miles) to reach Rye.

RYE

It may seem unbelievable today but in Elizabethan times Rye was a busy port on the coast. Unfortunately, the harbour silted up and now Rye is 3.2km (2 miles) from the sea. Today it is a picturesque town with Elizabethan and Georgian buildings and it has a good selection of antiques shops. Rye Castle Museum in the Ypres Tower, once part of the town's defensive fortifications, tells the story of Rye's 700 year history. There are also displays of Rye pottery, toys, and dolls and it has one of the oldest fire engines in the world. Lamb House, a Georgian mansion, has interesting literary associations. It was the home of the American author Henry James from 1898 to his death in 1916. Between the two World Wars an English author took up residence there. E F Benson, most famous for his *Mapp* and *Lucia* novels was also the Mayor of Rye in the 1930s.

BOOKS

Chapter & Verse Book Sellers, situated in the High Street, sell antiquarian and out-of-print books. They are open every day except Tuesday. Landgate Books, Hilders Cliff, has general second-hand and antiquarian books. The shop is open Monday, Wednesday, Friday, and Saturday. Situated in Lion Street, Rye Old Books sells antiquarian and second-hand books, illustrated books, and fine bindings. It is open 7 days a week (afternoon only on Sundays).

COLLECTABLES

In Market Road, Corner Collectables has a large stock of antiques, collectables, china, pistols, militaria, and oil lamps. The shop is open 7 days a week.

FURNITURE

Open by appointment only, Bragge & Sons has 18thC English furniture and works of art (tel: 01797 223358). In Lion Street, Herbert G Gasson offers an extensive range of early oak, country, walnut, and mahogany furniture. In Wish Street, Masons Yard has a broad selection of antique furniture, 1920s artefacts, and lighting. It is open 7 days a week. Mint Antiques, in The Mint, sells antique furniture and decorative items. Wish Barn Antiques, again in Wish Street, has a wide selection of 19thC pine and country furniture and 19thC mahogany furniture. It is open 7 days a week.

GENERAL ANTIQUES

Ann Lingard Rope Walk Antiques (LAPADA), in the Ropewalk, has a wide selection of English antique pine furniture, glass, copper, wooden items, garden and kitchen items. In the High Street, Rye Antiques sells silver, copper, brass, pewter, and jewellery. It is open every day except Tuesday and Sunday.

TEDDY BEARS

Bears Galore, in the High Street, sells handmade collectable teddy bears and is open 7 days a week (from 12 noon on Sundays).

ANTIQUES CENTRES

In Cinque Ports Street, Needles Antique Centre's five dealers sell small antiques and collectables. The centre is open 7 days a week. The second of the town's two centres, Strand Quay Antiques on The Strand, has 12 dealers selling Victorian and Edwardian furniture, porcelain, glass, pictures, and collectables. It is also open 7 days a week.

AUCTION HOUSES

Rye Auction Galleries in Rock Channel has twice monthly antique and general sales on the first and third Friday of each month at 9.30am. Viewing takes place on Thursdays from 9am–5pm. The office opens at 8.30am each day.

▶ Take the A259 for about 16km (10 miles) to the junction with the B2093. Turn right onto that road till it crosses the A21 and becomes the A2100. Just 3.2km (2 miles) further on is Battle.

BATTLE

Although always called the Battle of Hastings, William the Conqueror actually vanquished the Anglo-Saxon King Harold and his army here, 11.25km (7 miles) north of the town. William built Battle Abbey as a thanksgiving for his victory and, it is said, the High Altar stands on the spot where King Harold died.

DOLLS & TOYS
Annie's Dolls/Teddies in Upper Lake has teddies, dolls, Steiff bears, and Sigikid dolls. It is open Thursday–Saturday until 3pm.

FURNITURE
Barnabys of Battle in the High Street sells old pine, oak, and hardwood furniture. Also in the High Street, Lavande has French 18th and 19thC furniture and accessories.

SILVER & JEWELLERY
Spectrum Fine Jewellery Ltd in the High Street has a selection of antique jewellery and silver. The shop is open Tuesday–Saturday.

AUCTION HOUSE
Burstow & Hewett in Lower Lake have monthly sales of general antiques.

▶ Leave Battle on the A2100 then take the A21 southwards to Hastings, which is a distance of about 11.25km (7 miles).

HASTINGS

In Saxon times this was an important harbour and port and its castle, now mostly in ruins, was built soon after the Norman invasion. Although the old part of the town retains some of its Medieval character, Hastings also has many of the attractions of a traditional English seaside resort. The Hastings Museum and Art Gallery in John's Place, Bohemia Road, has a collection of fine paintings and ceramics as well as exhibitions on dinosaurs and the Hastings-born naturalist, Grey Owl. John Logie Baird made his first television transmission from the town and the museum has an exhibition about his life and work. The White Rock Theatre is the home of the Hastings Embroidery – made by the Royal School of Needlework, it is 74m (243ft) long and depicts 81 events in British history from 1066 onwards.

ANTIQUITIES
K M & J Garwood in George Street have Oriental and tribal antiquities as well as art and antiques. It is open 7 days a week.

BOOKS
Hastings is generously supplied with bookshops. The first, the Book Centre in West Street, has an impressive stock of antiquarian and second-hand books and is open 7 days a week. In Bohemia Road, Bookman's Halt has what they describe as a "low-key" general stock of antiquarian and second-hand books. They are closed Wednesdays and Sundays. Open by appointment only, Helgate sells antique books about art, architecture, china, glass, and objets d'art – ring 01424 423049. Howes Bookshop (ABA, PBFA) in Braybroke Terrace has an extensive range of antiquarian and second-hand books and specializes in books on arts and humanities. The shop is open Tuesday–Saturday. Located in George Street, the Old Hastings Bookshop sells antiquarian, rare, and second-hand books. The shop closes at 4pm each day, and all day Wednesday and Sunday. The last of the town's booksellers, John & Shahin Wilbraham are situated in George Street. They sell antiquarian and second-hand books, with literature and children's books being their specialities. The shop is closed on Wednesdays and Sundays.

EPHEMERA
Movie Finds in George Street sells movie-star portraits from the Golden Age of Hollywood to the present day, together with a range of pop and movie merchandise.

GENERAL ANTIQUES
John & Noel Connell in George Street sell furniture, silver, and glass and are open Thursday–Saturday 11am–4pm. Situated in Courthouse Street, Nakota Curios has an excellent stock of ornate chandeliers, decorative china, silverware, rugs, pictures, and mirrors.

MILITARIA
Reeves & Son in Courthouse Street has an extensive range of military collectables, china, smalls, and books.

ANTIQUES CENTRES
The 12 dealers in the George Street Antiques Centre, which is open 7 days a week, have an impressive range of collectables. The Queen's Road Antiques & Flea Market has 25 dealers selling antiques, bric-a-brac, clocks, toys, pictures, furniture, collectables, metalware, Art Deco, and 1950s–70s collectables.

▶ Just follow the coast road, the A259, to the western edge of the town in order to reach the next stop, St Leonards.

ST LEONARDS

This quiet, genteel town has now been overtaken by Hastings and stands on its western flank.

ARCHITECTURAL ANTIQUES

Woodstock Antiques, situated in Norman Road, sells architectural and garden antiques as well as contemporary garden ornaments.

BOOKS

The Book Jungle in North Street has antiquarian and second-hand books.

FURNITURE

In Grand Parade, Nicholas Cole Antiques has an extensive selection of French and English oak from Victorian times to the 1920s. Also in Grand Parade, Monarch Antiques has Victorian and Edwardian furniture, pine, bamboo, and decorative items. Lloyd Owen Antiques in Norman Road also sells antique furniture and is open until 4pm on weekdays and 1pm on Saturdays.

▶ Continue along the A259 westward for about 5km (3 miles) to Bexhill.

BEXHILL

Bexhill is a very popular resort with families because it has excellent, safe, sandy beaches. It also boasts the fascinating Museum of Costume & Social History in Manor Gardens, Upper Sea Road. The exhibitions of clothes, embroidery, lace, dolls, and other memorabilia range from the 18th–early 20thC. The displays include a special exhibition of costumed, full-size models showing clothes from Medieval times right up to the 19thC.

FURNITURE

Acme Inc. in Wickham Avenue has a large stock of 19th and 20thC furniture and decorative arts, and is open Monday, Thursday, and Friday 11am–12 noon and 2.30–4pm, Saturday 3–5pm, and Sunday 3–4pm. Located in Turkey Road, Bexhill Antique Exporters has an extensive range of Spanish, Italian, and French market furniture. To visit at the weekend, make an appointment – ring 01424 225103. Springfield Antiques in Ninfield Road has a wide selection of original old English pine furniture together with kitchenware. The shop is open 7 days a week.

GENERAL ANTIQUES

At Little Common on the west side of town, Annie's, in Bixlea Parade, Little Common Road, has a broad range of small pieces of furniture and collectables. It is closed on Wednesdays and Sundays. Val & Tyne in London Road sells antiques, collectables, and ephemera. It is also closed Wednesdays and Sundays, and shuts at 1.30pm on Saturdays.

AUCTION HOUSES

Gorringe's Auction Galleries (SOFAA, ISVA) in Terminus Road has fine art, antiques, and collectables sales every six weeks. They take place on Tuesdays and Wednesdays and start at 10am each day. There is viewing on Fridays 10am–5pm and Saturdays 9.30am–4pm. The office itself opens until 12 noon on Saturdays, as well as weekdays.

▶ Take the A269 for 11.25km (7 miles) until it meets the A271. Turn westward onto the A271and drive to the next stop, Hailsham, which is a distance of another 11.25km (7 miles).

HAILSHAM

Situated just below the Sussex Downs, Hailsham is a typical, pleasant, English market town.

FURNITURE

Sunburst Antiques & Art Furniture, in Carriers Path, High Street, has a wide selection of late 19thC furniture.

GENERAL ANTIQUES

Hawkswood Antiques, located in Carew Court, Hawkswood Road, offers general antiques and collectables. It is closed on Wednesday and Saturday afternoons as well as Sundays. In Market Street, Stable Doors has a large range of antiques and collectables.

PAPERWEIGHTS

In Market Street Wealth of Weights has the largest selection of paperweights in Southern England. It is open 7 days a week.

▶ The A22 southbound will take you straight to Eastbourne, which is just 13km (8 miles) away.

EASTBOURNE

Although Eastbourne was first established in the late 18thC when George III's children visited for their summer holidays, it was the Victorians who laid out its many parks and gardens. The Towner Art Gallery and Local Museum in the High Street has a fine collection of 19th and 20thC art and also covers the history of Eastbourne. The displays include Bronze Age axes, Roman artefacts, and an original Victorian kitchen range.

BOOKS

Camilla's Bookshop in Grove Road has a large stock of antiquarian and second-hand books, postcards, ephemera, children's books, and needlework. Military and nautical topics are their specialities. In South Street, A & T Gibbard (PBFA) offers a wide selection of antiquarian and second-hand books specializing in natural history, travel, topography as well as leather-bound books.

COLLECTABLES

Francois Celada in South Street has a large stock of stamps, cigarette cards, medals, coins, silver, and collectables (on Wednesdays it is open from 1pm). Pharoahs Antiques, also in South Street, has a wide selection of collectables including lighting, linen, china, furniture, medical instruments, "the bizarre", and architectural ironmongery.

DOLLS & TOYS

Crest Collectables in Grove Road sells teddy bears, dolls, soft toys, and collectables. It is open every day except Wednesdays and Sundays.

FURNITURE

Seaside Antiques, located in a street just called Seaside, has a large stock of old and new pine and oak.

GENERAL ANTIQUES

Cornfield Antiques & Collectables, located in Cornfield Terrace, has an extensive range of paintings, furniture, silver, crystal, glass, jewellery, porcelain, pottery, perfume bottles, and collectables. In South Street, John Cowderoy Antiques (LAPADA) has a wide selection of general antiques, collectables, clocks, and musical boxes. It is open at 8.30am each day but is closed on Wednesdays and Sundays. Charles French, in Kings Drive, sells general antiques. (The shop is shut at weekends.) Situated in Grove Road, Inta Design Sea Antiques has an extensive range of objects of interest, furniture, paintings, woodcarvings, prints, and Art Deco. It is open until 7pm each day. Timothy Partridge Antiques, situated in Ocklynge Road, offers general pre-war goods, furniture, and smalls. It is also shut at weekends.

ANTIQUES CENTRES

With five antiques centres, visitors to Eastbourne are spoilt for choice. Antique Grove, in Grove Road, has 17 dealers selling glass, silver, ceramics, jewellery, Hornby and Dinky toys, furniture, perfume bottles, embroidery, and paintings. Eastbourne Antiques Market, Seaside, has 25 dealers offering a range of antiques and collectables. In Station Parade, The Enterprise Collectors Market's 15 dealers sell antiques and collectables. The Old Town Antiques Centre in Ocklynge Road has 16 dealers with mixed antiques, furniture, fine porcelain, glass, silver, and Beswick and Copenhagen figures. Seaquel Antiques & Collectors Market in Seaside Road is home to 18 dealers selling furniture, collectables, and bric-a-brac. It is open 7 days a week. Also in Seaside Road, South Coast Collectables has 18 dealers too. They sell antiques, collectables, and Georgian, Victorian, and Edwardian furniture.

AUCTION HOUSES

Edgar Horn's Fine Art Auctioneers, Eastbourne's only saleroom, is situated in South Street. On Tuesdays, there are weekly general sales with viewing Saturday 9am–12.30pm and Monday 9am–7pm. There are also six antiques sales a year. These take place on Wednesdays at 10am with viewing at the same time as for the weekly sales, plus Tuesday at 9am–5pm.

▶ Take the A259 westbound to the next stop in Seaford, approximately 16km (10 miles) away.

SEAFORD

Until the 16thC the River Ouse met the sea at Seaford, which gave the town a good natural harbour and made it a busy and prosperous port. In 1579 the river was diverted to Newhaven. It wasn't until the 19thC that Seaford gained popularity again – this time as a holiday resort.

CLOCKS

J R Clocks, situated in the High Street, has restored antique clocks. It is shut Wednesdays and Sundays.

COLLECTABLES

The Barn Collectors Market & Bookshop in Church Lane sells collectables, books, militaria, as well as jewellery.

FURNITURE

In the High Street, Colonial Times II has a large range of furniture imported from India, China, and the Far East.

GENERAL ANTIQUES
Again in the High Street, **Masthead Antiques** sells a wide selection of general curios and collectables.

▶ Leave Seaford on the A26 for 11.25km (7 miles), then take the A27 westbound for about 3.2km (2 miles) to reach Lewes.

LEWES

Lewes is located at a gap in the rolling Sussex Downs, which made it a natural defensive position. King Alfred established a fort here, and later the Norman William de Warenne built a castle on two artificial mounds that are now the home of the Lewes Castle & Barbican House Museum. The Anne of Cleves Museum in Southover High Street is situated in a typical Tudor Wealden hall-house, and was part of Anne of Cleves' divorce settlement from Henry VIII. Exhibitions of local history and crafts are housed in the museum.

BEDS
For a large stock of antique beds, visit **Bedtimes Past Ltd** in Malling Street.

BOOKS
Bow Windows Bookshop (ABA, PBFA), in the High Street, has general antiquarian books on all subjects. Also in the High Street, A & Y Cumming (ABA) has a large selection of antiquarian and second-hand books on travel, natural history, and colour plate books, as well as first editions and leather-bound titles. Nearby, The Fifteenth Century Bookshop (PBFA), also in the High Street, has a general stock together with collectable children's books. It is open 7 days a week. Lewes Book Centre in Cliffe High Street offers antiquarian and second-hand books to suit all tastes with military topics being their speciality.

FURNITURE
Ashcombe Coach House Antiques (BADA, CINOA), in the Brighton Road, has been selling 18th and early 19thC furniture and decorative objects since 1953. It is open by appointment only – ring 01273 474794. Castle Antiques in the High Street has antique pine furniture and is open 7 days a week. Bob Hoare Antiques in Phoenix Place, North Street, also has a large selection of antique pine furniture, linen presses, and pine dressers as well as

decorative objects. The shop is open from 8am during the week, but shuts at 1pm on Saturdays. In the High Street, School Hill Antiques sells Victorian and Edwardian furniture and decorative items. Peter Thacker Antiques and Restorations, located in Lansdown Place, has mahogany and walnut furniture. It is open from 7am during the week and shuts at 1pm on Saturdays.

GENERAL ANTIQUES
Situated in Malling Street, Antique Interiors for Home & Garden sells general antiques, decorative items, garden furniture, and country pine. Curiously named, The Elephants Trunk in West Street has a broad range of antiques, collectables, furniture, lighting, and mirrors. It is open 7 days a week and shuts at 4pm on Sundays. Lewes Flea Market, situated in Market Street, boasts a large selection of antiques, collectables, and bric-a-brac. It is open 7 days a week. Finally, The Treasury in the High Street sells collectables, small antiques, and out-of-production figurines. The shop is open Thursday–Saturday.

ANTIQUES CENTRES
The first of the town's five centres is the Churchill Antique Centre in Station Street. It has 60 dealers selling a wide range of art and collectables. Next, the Cliffe Antiques Centre, in Cliffe High Street, has 15 dealers offering antiques and collectables. Also in Cliffe High Street, The Emporium Antiques Centre is home to 40 dealers with a large stock of general antiques, collectables, studio ceramics, toys, textiles, silver, jewellery, books, and clocks. It is open 7 days a week (from 12 noon on Sundays). The largest of the town's centres, The Emporium Antiques Centre Too, in the High Street, has 100 dealers selling antiques, collectables, and furniture and it is also open 7 days a week (from 12 noon on Sundays). Finally, the Lewes Antique Centre, also in Cliffe High Street, has in excess of 60 dealers over four floors. They sell furniture, architectural salvage, bric-a-brac, china, clocks, metalware, and glass. They are open 7 days a week (Sundays and Bank Holidays from 12.30–4.30pm).

AUCTION HOUSES
Lewes has three auction houses, all established in the 1920s. The first, Gorringes Auction Galleries (SOFAA, ISVA) in North Street has fine art and antiques sales every six weeks. They take place Tuesday–Thursday and start at 10am each day. There is viewing on Friday, 9.30am–5pm and Saturday 9.30am–4pm. The office opens at 8.30am during the week and is open Saturday mornings until 12 noon. In the High Street, Lewes Auction Rooms has weekly sales of antiques, general furniture, and collectables every Monday at 11am with viewing on Saturdays 9am–12.30pm and the morning of a sale from 8am. They also have special sales of 18th and 19thC furniture and

effects every six weeks on Thursdays at 10.30am. Viewing for these is Friday 10am–4pm, Saturday 9am–12.30pm, and Wednesday 9.30am–7.30pm. The office is open weekdays and Saturday mornings. Finally, every six weeks **Wallis & Wallis** at the West Street Auction Galleries have specialist sales of militaria, medals, coins, arms, and armour taking place on Tuesdays and Wednesdays at 11am. They also have eight sales a year of die-cast and tinplate toys taking place on Mondays at 10.30am. Viewing is on the previous Friday, 9am–10.30pm and the morning of the sale from 9–10.30am.

▶ Still on the A27 westbound, the next stop of Brighton is just 13km (8 miles) away.

BRIGHTON

Perhaps the most famous of the South Coast seaside resorts, Brighton's early popularity began with the Prince Regent's visit in 1783 to what was then the small fishing village of Brighthelmstone. He originally built the Royal Pavilion to a much more traditional design. The architect, John Nash, added the flamboyant Oriental style, including the famous onion domes, in the early 19thC. Although the Royal Pavilion is now such a well-known symbol of the town, during Queen Victoria's reign it was left to decay and was to have been demolished in 1850. It was saved by the town's residents, who raised £50,000 to buy it. The Pavilion has now been restored to all its Regency glory and contains beautiful furniture and antiques.

Brighton Museum & Art Gallery, in Church Street, houses outstanding collections of Art Nouveau and Art Deco furniture, glass, and ceramics; 18th–20thC clothes; and extensive paintings, watercolours, and prints. There are also ceramics galleries containing English pottery and porcelain, non-western art, and a collection of historic toys.

ARCHITECTURAL ANTIQUES
Brighton Architectural Salvage in Gloucester Road has a large stock of restored architectural antiques.

BOOKS
Brighton has a good selection of antiquarian bookshops. **The Bookmark** in Dyke Road sells antiquarian and second-hand books. On Mondays the shop opens at 1pm. Situated in St James's Street, **Borus Snorus** has a large selection of antiquarian books as well as collectables. **Brimstone's**, also in St James's Street, has a good selection of antiquarian and second-hand books. **Colin Page Antiquarian Books** (ABA) in Duke Street offers an extensive collection of antiquarian and second-hand books, antiquarian literature, natural history, plate books, and bindings. In Ditchling Road, **Savery Books** sells second-hand books and is open Wednesday–Saturday 10am–4.30pm. **Studio Bookshop** in St James's Street sells reference books on glass, art, and antiques.

CERAMICS
Memories (LAPADA) in Dukes Lane has a large selection of 18th and 19thC china and porcelain and is open until 7pm.

COLLECTABLES
Located in Cavendish Street, **Enhancements** sells kitchenware, tools, beds, pine, and shabby chic furniture. **Oasis**, in Kensington Gardens, has period lighting, telephones, gramophones, furniture, Art Deco, Art Nouveau, watches, lighters, glass, textiles, and 1920s–30s clothes. In North Road, **Rin-Tin-Tin** (ESoc) sells old advertising and promotional matter, magazines, early glamour, games, toys, plastics, and 20thC fixtures and fittings. **Valelink Ltd**, in Queens Road, sells collectables.

COSTUME & CLOTHING
Jezebel, in Prince Albert Street, has a good range of Art Deco, Art Nouveau, costumes, vintage clothing, and costume jewellery. In Upper North Street, **Wardrobe** sells vintage clothing and accessories, textiles, jewellery, and Art Deco. It is open Wednesday–Saturday.

DOLLS & TOYS
Situated in Prince Albert Street, **Sue Pearson Antique Dolls & Teddy Bears** has a large selection of antique and modern bears, soft toys, and dolls.

EPHEMERA
Brighton Postcard Shop of Beaconsfield Road has postcards, ephemera, and vintage glamour magazines. It is open Tuesday–Saturday until 4pm.

FURNITURE
Bright Helm Antiques & Interiors in Sydney Street, North Laines, has a large range of antique pine furniture, painted pine furniture, and architectural salvage. It is open 7 days a week. **Tony Broadfoot Antiques**, of Upper Gardner Street, has a wide choice of commercial and antique furniture. In Queens Road, **Clock Tower Antiques** has an

extensive selection of antique pine furniture. The shop is open 7 days a week. The long established **Alan Fitchett Antiques** in Upper Gardner Street has a large variety of antique furniture. In Prince Albert Street, **Julie Goss Antiques** sells antique, reproduction, and reclaimed pine furniture as well as decorative mahogany pieces. **Dudley Hume**, situated in Upper North Street, sells 18th–19thC furniture and decorative items. The shop is open weekdays and Saturday mornings until 12 noon. **Patrick Moorhead Antiques** in Spring Gardens, Church Street, has an extensive choice of 18th and 19thC furniture together with European and Oriental ceramics, paintings, and clocks. The shop is open Monday–Friday. In Preston Street, **Odin Antiques** sells antique furniture as well as maritime items and telescopes. **Dermot & Jill Palmer Antiques** in Union Street has been selling mainly 19thC French and English furniture for over 30 years. **Ben Ponting Antiques**, located in Upper North Street, has an extensive range of Georgian, Victorian, and Edwardian antique furniture and is open Monday–Friday. **Wilkinsons** in Church Street sells antique furniture as well as decorative objects and lighting. They are open 7 days a week (from 12 noon on Sundays). **Wish**, in Gloucester Road, has early 20thC furniture and Arts and Crafts and is open 7 days a week. In Upper North Street, **Pamela Wright** sells period furniture, metal, light fittings, and paintings and is open Monday–Friday.

GENERAL ANTIQUES

The town has a large choice of antiques shops. **Alexandria Antiques**, in Hanover Place and also in Upper North Street, has eight showrooms selling 18th and 19thC furniture, porcelain, bronzes, paintings, and decorative objects. In Upper Gloucester Road, **Art Deco Etc** sells 1860s–1980s pottery (specializing in Poole), glass, lighting, small furniture, and metalwork. It is open by appointment only – ring 01273 329268. At **Bear Antiques**, in Trafalgar Street, there is a good range of Georgian, Edwardian, Art Deco, brass, copper, and steel fittings, embellishments, small pieces of furniture, and collectables. **Brighton Flea Market**, Upper St James's Street, has a large stock of antiques, bric-a-brac, and collectables and is open 7 days a week. The small village of Rottingdean, just east of Brighton along the coast road, is the home of **Georgina's Antiques** (in the High Street), which sells a selection of antiques and collectables and is open 7 days a week (from 12 noon on Sundays). **The House of Antiques** (LAPADA) in Upper North Street has general antiques, furniture, bronzes, porcelain, and clocks and is open Monday–Friday. In Gloucester Road, **Luckpenny Antiques** sells pine furniture, kitchenware, curtains, mirrors, and collectables. It is closed on Wednesdays and Sundays. In Ditchling Road, **Savery Antiques** has small furniture, porcelain, glass, and metalwork. It is also closed on Wednesdays and Sundays.

MAPS & PRINTS

In Meeting House Lane, **The Witch Ball** has a large range of antique prints and maps, dating from 1550 to 1850.

MILITARIA

The **Lanes Armoury** in Meeting House Lane specializes in arms, armour, and militaria from pre-Christian times to World War II.

MUSICAL BOXES

Graham Webb Musical Boxes in Ship Street has a large selection of antique musical boxes.

PICTURES

Established in 1959, and with a stock of paintings and watercolours as well as period furniture, **The Old Picture Shop** in Nile Street is aptly named.

SILVER & JEWELLERY

Hallmarks in Union Street, within the famous Brighton Lanes, has a broad collection of antique silver, silver collectables, and jewellery.

ANTIQUES CENTRES

There are between 60 and 70 dealers in **Snooper's Paradise**, Kensington Gardens, selling a large range of collectables, furniture, kitsch, and 1970s items. It is open 7 days a week (from 11am–3pm on Sundays).

AUCTION HOUSES

The town's only saleroom, **Raymond P Inman** in Temple Street, has 10 sales a year that each sell general antiques.

▶ Take the seafront road, the A259, westward for around 0.8km (½ mile) to arrive in Hove.

HOVE

While Brighton has always had a racy image, adjoining Hove is much more genteel. Located in a Victorian house, the Hove Museum and Art Gallery in New Church Road displays the South East Arts and Crafts Collection started in 1981, with pieces commissioned from leading local craftsmen. There is a Childhood Room with a fine collection of dolls, games, books, puzzles, and dolls' houses. There are also exhibitions of 18th–20thC decorative art, English pottery, and porcelain and paintings from the 18th–20thC.

FURNITURE

J S Carter in Boundary Road sells Georgian, Victorian, and Edwardian furniture. In Western Road, Michael Norman Antiques (BADA) has a large stock of 18th–19thC English furniture. Shirley-Ann's Antiques and Decorative Furniture, situated in Church Road, sells Georgian, Victorian, and Edwardian furniture and antiques.

GENERAL ANTIQUES

In Portland Road, Antiques et Cetera has an extensive range of porcelain, gold, silver, glassware, pictures, furniture, chandeliers, lighting, and costume jewellery. The shop shuts at 4pm during the week and 1pm on Saturdays. Seymour Antiques in Blatchington Road sells Georgian and Victorian furniture, collectables, and curiosities. It is open from 8.30am.

MAPS & PRINTS

A large selection of antique maps can be found in St John's Road at Simon Hunter Antique Maps. The shop is open by appointment only – ring 01273 746983.

AUCTION HOUSES

The regional representative of Bonhams & Brooks (SOFAA) may be found in Palmeira Square and is open Monday–Friday. In Hove Street, every five to six weeks Graves Son & Pilcher have regular sales of general antiques on Thursdays and Fridays, with viewing on Tuesdays and Wednesdays 10am–4.30pm. There are also special sales.

> Take the coast road, the A259, westbound to the next stop, Shoreham-by-Sea.

SHOREHAM-BY-SEA

Although part of the Brighton and Hove conurbation, Shoreham still retains some of its original character. To learn about the town's history, from prehistoric burials to Shoreham Airport, visit Marlipins Museum in the High Street, which is located in a beautiful old building with a 'chequer board' façade.

BOOKS

In the High Street, Bookworms of Shoreham has a stock of rare, second-hand books and its specialities are military, modern art, and Sussex topography. Opening hours are Tuesday–Saturday 10am–5pm.

> Back on the A259 westbound, the next stop at Worthing is only 6.5km (4 miles) away.

WORTHING

Made famous by Amelia, sister of the Prince Regent, Worthing is nowhere near as dashing as Brighton – it is much quieter and more refined. Its development as a seaside resort was set back when there was a cholera outbreak in the 1850s and then a typhoid epidemic in the 1890s. Between the two World Wars the town managed to solve its public health problems and regained its popularity as a seaside resort. Worthing Museum & Art Gallery in Chapel Road has award-winning exhibitions, including the latest dated hoard of Roman gold found in Britain, a 1,600-year-old Egyptian glass goblet, and a reconstructed Victorian nursery. There are also two galleries of costume.

BOOKS

Badgers Books in Gratwicke Road has a very large selection of rare, antiquarian, and second-hand books.

COLLECTABLES

Postcard Cabin of West Buildings sells postcards, coins, medals, and banknotes. It is closed on Wednesdays and Sundays.

FURNITURE

The town has two specialist furniture dealers who have both been established for more than 50 years. The first, R Warner and Son, situated in South Farm Road, has a large selection of antique furniture. The shop is closed on Wednesday afternoons and Sundays. The other, Wilson's Antiques of New Broadway, Tarring Road, has an extensive range of Georgian, Victorian, and Edwardian formal English furniture.

GENERAL ANTIQUES

The remaining six antiques shops in Worthing all offer a general range of antiques. Acorn Antiques, situated in Rowlands Road, has Georgian–Edwardian furniture, china, silver, and jewellery. Chloe Antiques of Brighton Road has a good selection of small collectables, jewellery, china, and glass. The shop is open every day except Wednesdays and Sundays. In North Street, Corner Antiques has general antiques, textiles, and collectables. Interiors and Antiques, located in Findon Road, sells furniture, china, glass, garden statues, and bird baths. Opening times are Tuesday–Sunday 10am–6pm. Situated in the village

of Findon on the edge of Worthing, **The Nutshell** in
the High Street has small collectables, furniture,
and clocks. The shop is open Thursday–Sunday
11am–5pm. Finally, **Past Times Antiques** in Brighton
Road sells porcelain, china, furniture, and jewellery.

AUCTION HOUSES
Both of the town's auctioneers hold regular sales.
R H Ellis and Son Auctioneers and Valuers in the
High Street have monthly auctions of Victorian and
Edwardian furniture and collectables and quarterly
ones of silver, paintings, Oriental antiques, and
rugs. **Worthing Auction Galleries Ltd** of Teville Gate
has monthly sales of general antiques.

▶ For the final visit of the tour, take the A24 for
29km (18 miles) to reach Horsham.

HORSHAM

Horsham has been a borough and
market town since the 13thC. Its most
interesting street, The Causeway, is
quiet and lined with timber-framed
and Georgian houses and it leads to
the town's 12thC church. One of The
Causeway's Medieval timber-framed
houses is also the location of Horsham
Museum, which has exhibitions ranging
from bicycles to dinosaur bones. There
are also displays about local, social, and
farming history.

BOOKS
The first of the town's two bookshops is **The
Horsham Bookshop** in Park Place. They stock rare,
antiquarian, and second-hand books and cricket
and aviation are their specialities. The shop is
open Tuesday–Saturday. The second, **Murray
and Kemmett in Bishopric**, sells rare and second-
hand books and specializes in crime fiction and
religious books.

ANTIQUES CENTRES
The **Horsham Antiques Centre**, again in Park Place,
has a large stock of furniture, pictures, pottery,
toys, porcelain, glass, silver, jewellery, and other
collectables. It is open Tuesday–Saturday and
Sunday until 4pm.

ANTIQUES FAIRS
The **Ardingly International Antiques and Collectors
Fairs** takes place six times a year at the
South of England Showground, near the village
of Ardingly. To reach the showground, take the
A281 southbound from Horsham for about 5km

(3 miles) then turn left onto the B2110 for about
11.25km (7 miles). Follow signposts for the last mile
or so. The fair has up to 1,500 stallholders and is
organized by DMG Antiques Fairs Ltd. (for contact
details, see page 7).

AUCTION HOUSES
There is a local saleroom, **Denham's**, in the village
of Warnham, just 1.6km (1 mile) from the town on
the A24 northbound and they have sales of
antiques and collectors' items every four weeks.
The office is open weekdays and Saturday until
12 noon.

NEW ALRESFORD ▶ PETERSFIELD ▶ MIDHURST ▶ PETWORTH ▶ ARUNDEL ▶
CHICHESTER ▶ SOUTHSEA ▶ PORTSMOUTH ▶ SOUTHAMPTON ▶ ROMSEY ▶
WINCHESTER

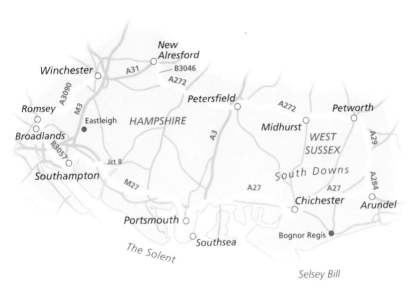

Selsey Bill

Hampshire has a wide selection of antiques shops but only one specialist dealer in maritime antiques, surprising for a county with such a strong nautical tradition. Great oaks from the New Forest, which is just to the west of Southampton, were used to build the ships that were captained by the likes of Horatio Nelson and Sir Walter Raleigh. Portsmouth has a long association with the navy and Southampton was the departure point for luxurious blue-riband ocean liners – the *Queen Mary*, *Queen Elizabeth*, and others.

When you want a break from antique hunting this area also has a host of attractions and activities. The Solent, the area of sea between the Isle of Wight and the mainland, is famous for its sailing and the annual Cowes Week in August is a highpoint on the national sailing calendar. It started in 1812 and within three years had become an annual event, making it the longest running regular regatta in the world.

There are also numerous museums to visit as well as attractions like the Manor Farm Country Park, between Fareham and Southampton, where you can experience life on a farm before the 1950s with traditional working animals and vintage machinery. The Marwell Zoological Park near Winchester has a thousand rare and endangered animals within its 100 acres. In Southampton, the Hawthorns Urban Wildlife Centre has different wildlife habitats where native animals may be seen.

Websites

www.chichesterweb.co.uk
Learn more about all aspects of life in
Chichester including pubs, shops, hotels and
B & Bs, restaurants, and events.

www.flagship.org.uk
If you want to know more about Portsmouth's
naval history and its historic ships, visit this
website.

www.southampton.gov.uk
Southampton's official website has all the
information a visitor to the city could want,
including what's on, trips and tours, and lists
of restaurants and hotels.

www.winchester.gov.uk
Another official website, this time for
Winchester, gives a wealth of useful and
historic information.

www.winchester-cathedral.org.uk
It might be a good idea to find out more about
Winchester Cathedral so that you can make
the most of your visit. This, the Cathedral's
official site, will help you.

Tourist Information Centres

Chichester 29a South Street.
Tel: 01243 775888

Petworth Market Square.
Tel: 01798 343523

Portsmouth The Hard.
Tel: 02392 826722

Romsey 13 Church Street.
Tel: 01794 512987

Southampton 9 Civic Centre Road.
Tel: 02380 833333

Winchester Guildhall, The Broadway.
Tel: 01962 840500

NEW ALRESFORD

Often referred to as just Alresford, this
small country town once had one of the
top ten wool markets. Since the 16thC it
has also been famous for its watercress.

FURNITURE
Two of the town's furniture dealers are located in
West Street. The first, **Artemesia**, has an extensive
range of English and Continental furniture together

with ceramics and works of art. The other,
Underwood Oak in West Street, sells 17th–19thC
country furniture. It is closed on Wednesdays and
Sundays. **Tudor Antiques and Fine Arts Ltd**, in
Station Road, has a wide selection of 17th–19thC
English, French, and Oriental furniture and objets
d'art. The shop is open until 4pm.

PICTURES
Laurence Oxley in Broad Street has a good
selection of Victorian watercolours, old maps,
and antiquarian books.

▶ Leave New Arlesford on the B3046 for about
3.2km (2 miles) and then turn left at the junction
with the A272, which takes you straight to
Petersfield, a distance of approximately 17.75km
(11 miles) away.

PETERSFIELD

Set on the River Rother, this handsome
market town has some splendid
Georgian buildings.

BOOKS
The Petersfield Bookshop in Chapel Street has a
large stock of antiquarian and modern books.

GENERAL ANTIQUES
In College Street, **Antique Collectiffs** has a wide
selection of furniture, silver, porcelain, glass,
pictures, and collectables.

ANTIQUES CENTRES
Folly Antiques Centre, College Street, has a large
range of gold and silver jewellery, silver cutlery,
furniture, and collectables.

AUCTION HOUSES
Jacobs and Hunt Fine Art Auctioneers in Lavant
Street have been a fixture in the town since 1895.
They have sales of general antiques every six to
eight weeks with viewing the day before the sale
from 10am–6.30pm and the morning of sale from
9am. The office is open weekdays as well as
Saturday mornings.

▶ Continue on the A272 eastbound for 16km
(10 miles) to reach the next stop of Midhurst.

MIDHURST

As well as its half-timbered and Georgian
buildings, Midhurst also has a large
coaching inn, The Spread Eagle, which
dates from 1430.

CLOCKS

Churchill Clocks (BHI), in Rumbolds Hill, sells all kinds of antique clocks including longcase, mantel, French, and bracket. The shop is closed Wednesday afternoons and Sundays.

ANTIQUES CENTRES

Situated in the Market Square, the Old Town Antiques Centre has furniture, glass, and porcelain.

▶ Still travelling on the A272 eastbound, the next stop, Petworth, is just 10km (6 miles) away.

PETWORTH

This town is dominated by the magnificent 17thC Petworth House. A manor house owned by the Percys has stood here since the 13thC. When Elizabeth Percy married the Earl of Somerset in 1682 the house was rebuilt, causing streets in the town to be diverted and houses demolished. Set in parkland designed by Capability Brown, this National Trust property contains a wealth of sculptures and paintings, including works by Turner, Titian, and Gainsborough. The famous "Carved Room" is a showcase for the genius of Grinling Gibbons and the Grand Staircase has, as a backdrop, the world-famous murals by Louis Laguerre.

BOOKS

Petworth Collectables and Bookshop, situated in Middle Street, has a large collection of rare, second-hand, and out-of-print books.

CLOCKS & BAROMETERS

In Saddlers Row, Baskerville Antiques, Antiquarian Horologist, (BADA) has clocks and barometers. It is open Tuesday–Saturday.

FURNITURE

There are five specialist furniture dealers in Petworth High Street. BADA member Granville Antiques has a large stock of furniture together with fine art and decorative antiques. The French Room (PADA) has an extensive selection of French period furniture and decorative wares. Lesley Bragge Antiques (LAPADA, PADA) sells 18th and 19thC decorative furniture as well as lighting, silver, and porcelain. Riverbank Gallery Ltd (PADA) has 18th and 19thC furniture and garden furniture,

decorative items, and paintings. The last of the High Street furniture dealers, Stewart Antiques, sells Victorian and Edwardian stripped pine and fruitwood furniture, kitchenware, and Continental decorative items. In New Street, Antiquated (PADA) has 18th and 19thC painted furniture and 19thC rocking horses. Also in New Street, Red Lion Antiques (LAPADA) has a large stock of 17th–19thC furniture. Madison Gallery (PADA), located in Market Square, sells oak, walnut, mahogany, and country furniture together with silver, porcelain, decorative items, and paintings. It is open 7 days a week. Also in the Market Square, H G Saunders (LAPADA) has 18th and 19thC furniture along with paintings, objets d'art, and jewellery. It is open 7 days a week. In East Street, Elliott's (PADA) has a large stock of Georgian–Edwardian furniture and is open Wednesday–Saturday. Du Cros Antiques, situated in Pound Street, has 17th–19thC English furniture and metalware. J C Tutt Antiques in Angel Street has a large stock of mahogany and country furniture and accessories. Finally, T G Wilkinson Antiques Ltd (BADA), in Lombard Street, sells 18th and 19thC furniture and related items.

GENERAL ANTIQUES

Back in the High Street, Bradley's Past and Present Shop sells antiques, collectables, and decorative items. It is open Tuesday–Saturday. Octavia Antiques (PADA) in East Street has decorative antiques, small furniture, mirrors, lamps, chairs, and china. It is open every day except Fridays and Sundays. Richard Gardner Antiques (LAPADA, CINOA, PADA), in the Market Square, has an extensive range of fine period furniture, works of art including bronzes, Staffordshire figures, paintings, silver, mirrors, 18th and 19thC porcelain, and etchings. The shop is open 7 days a week. Also in the Market Square, Ronald G Chambers Fine Antiques (LAPADA, CINOA, PADA) has a large selection of fine-quality antique furniture and objets d'art 1700–1910, paintings, longcase clocks, gilded mirrors, bronze statuary, decorative items, as well as jewellery.

ORIENTAL ANTIQUES

In the Market Square, John's Corner Allsorts has a selection of netsuke, okimonos, ivory, small bronzes, and silver.

WINE-RELATED ANTIQUES

A must for all wine lovers, Bacchus Gallery in Lombard Street has a collection of decanters, glasses, and corkscrews.

ANTIQUES CENTRES

In East Street, Petworth Antique Market has a large range of English oak furniture, silver, linen, books, soft furnishings, porcelain, glass, fans, as well as general antiques.

Take the A283 for 3.2km (2 miles) eastbound then turn right onto the B2138. Follow that road for another 3.2km (2 miles) to the A29 southbound. Take that road for about 5km (3 miles) to a roundabout where you should take the A284 to Arundel, which is about another 3.2km (2 miles).

a large stock of furniture, clocks, jewellery, brass, silver, porcelain, and French antique furniture. The centre is open 7 days a week.

Leave Arundel on the A27 and, after 16km (10 miles), you will arrive in Chichester.

ARUNDEL

Arundel Castle, built soon after the Norman Conquest, dominates the town. It has been owned by the Dukes of Norfolk since the mid-16thC and they have lived there ever since, apart from during the Civil War. The castle contains fine collections of furniture and paintings. Arundel Museum and Heritage Centre in the High Street has a wide-ranging collection of artefacts, from flint tools to models of ships.

BOOKS
The Arundel Bookshop in the High Street has rare, antiquarian, and second-hand books.

FURNITURE
Arundel Galleries in Castle Mews, Tarrant Street, has Georgian–Edwardian furniture and is open 7 days a week (Sundays from 2.30–4.30pm). The long-established Wilson's Antiques (LAPADA) in the High Street also sells Georgian–Edwardian furniture together with paintings, china, glass, and silver. It is open Tuesday–Saturday.

GENERAL ANTIQUES
Situated in Tarrant Street, Antiquities has a large stock of 19thC English and French furniture, decorative items, majolica, blue and white, pond boats, and French mirrors. In the High Street, The Jolly Pedlars has general antiques, toys, and dolls. It is open 7 days a week. Passageway Antiques, also in the High Street, has a large range of antiques and collectables and is open 7 days a week. Again in the High Street, Charles Ralph Antiques has an extensive selection of general antiques. Maureen Rees in Tarrant Street sells small silver, cranberry glass, and small collectors' items. It is closed on Wednesdays and Sundays. Whitehouse Antique Interiors in Tarrant Square sells general antiques.

ANTIQUES CENTRES
Arundel Antiques Centre in the High Street has 30 dealers selling furniture, china, silver, porcelain, and general antiques. It is open 7 days a week. Tarrant Street Antique Centre, in Tarrant Street, has

CHICHESTER

Chichester has been the administrative centre for West Sussex since Roman times and follows the street pattern of a typical Roman town – four main streets within a walled enclosure. The city is the home to an annual festival of arts and its cathedral, completed in 1123, combines the best of the new with the old. There are numerous places of interest, galleries, and museums to visit in the city, including the Pallant House Gallery in North Pallant where there is a good collection of mostly modern British paintings, drawings, and sculpture. Chichester District Museum, Little London, tells the story of the city from earliest times. The Mechanical Music and Doll Collection in Church Road has a demonstration of mechanical music from the last 100 years. There are also collections of gramophones and phonographs and over 100 dolls, ranging in date from 1830 to 1930.

BOOKS
The Chichester Bookshop in Southgate has rare and second-hand books and specializes in railway books, Sussex books, maps, and prints. In South Street, Canon Gate Bookshop (PBFA) has rare, antiquarian, and second-hand books.

FURNITURE
Heirloom Antiques, situated in Pound Farm Road, has an extensive selection of furniture, collectables, and curios. It is open 7 days a week (until 4pm on Sundays). In St Pancras, Heritage Antiques sells Georgian–Edwardian and 1920s furniture. Situated just 1.6km (1 mile) south of the city centre in the village of Runction, The Pine Place has original pine furniture, decorative items, French garden furniture, and French kitchenware. Additionally, furniture and kitchens are made to order from church pews. It opens at 8.30am each day and

shuts at 1pm on Saturdays. **W D Priddy Antiques**, Chichester Furniture Warehouse, in Terminus Road, has Victorian, Edwardian, and pre-World War II furniture. Another village to the south, Hunston, is home to **J and M Riley** at Frensham House, which has 18thC English furniture.

GENERAL ANTIQUES

Antiques and Bygones, in The Buttermarket, North Street, sells china, glass, and collectors' items. It is open Tuesday–Saturday until 4pm. In Southgate, **Philip Baker Antiques** has small Victorian and Edwardian antiques. **Barnett Antiques**, in the Almshouse Arcade, The Hornet, has furniture, china, and toys. **St Pancras Antiques** is situated, appropriately enough, in St Pancras. The shop has pre-1800 furniture, arms, armour, ceramics, numismatics, and militaria. It closes at 1pm on Thursdays.

ANTIQUES CENTRES

Chichester Antiques Centre, The Hornet, has 40 dealers selling a large range of general antiques, collectables, and 18th–20thC furniture. It is open 7 days a week.

AUCTION HOUSES

The regional office of **Phillips International Auctioneers & Valuers** is in Baffins Lane. **Stride & Son** in St John's Street has been in business for over 100 years and has monthly sales of general antiques with periodic book auctions.

> Continue westward on the A27 for 16km (10 miles) until you reach the A2030 where you should turn left to visit Southsea and Portsmouth.

SOUTHSEA

As part of coastal defences, Henry VIII built a castle here and a dry dock. Today, the town has a wide range of antiques shops offering an extensive choice.

ARCHITECTURAL ANTIQUES

Ian Parmiter, in Albert Road, specializes in architectural antiques and unusual items and is open Fridays and Saturdays.

BOOKS

In Marmion Road, the **Book Academy** (ABA) has a large stock of antiquarian and new books, particularly reformed theology books including bibles, prayer, and hymn books. Dickens and Hampshire are also specialities.

CLOCKS & WATCHES

The Clock Shop, in Highland Road, has a large range of clocks, watches, and general antiques.

FURNITURE

Open by appointment only, **Karen Dalmeny Antiques** in Highland Road has a wide selection of furniture, porcelain, copper, brass, clocks, paintings, and collectables (ring 02392 870364). **A Fleming** (BADA), in The Clock Tower, Castle Road, sells 18th and 19thC English and Continental furniture together with silver, boxes, and barometers. It closes at 1pm on Saturdays.

GENERAL ANTIQUES

Design Explosion, located in Exmouth Road, sells 1950s–70s china, glass, lighting, and furniture. It is open on Saturdays only. **Langford Antiques**, Albert Road, has Victorian, Edwardian–20thC furniture, collectables, silver, and costume jewellery. It is open every day except Wednesdays and Sundays.

AUCTION HOUSES

The long-established **D M Nesbit & Co** in Clarendon Road has monthly antiques sales.

> Less than 0.4km (¼ mile) westbound on the A288 will bring you to Portsmouth.

PORTSMOUTH

In the 12thC Portsmouth was built around a natural harbour by the lord of the manor of nearby Titchfield, who later rebelled against King Richard I. The king confiscated the town and harbour and so Portsmouth became a Royal borough. As an important naval base, even in the time of Henry VIII, the docks covered an area of 8 acres, now they cover approximately 300 acres. It was from here that Nelson embarked to fight in the Battle of Trafalgar in 1805. Much of the old town was destroyed in the extensive bombing during World War II but what remains is a fashionable and picturesque area of the city. There is much to see in Portsmouth, not least the famous HMS Victory. During its sea-going days it carried 821 officers and was Nelson's flagship at the Battle of Trafalgar. The *Mary Rose* Museum and Ship Hall displays another of the city's famous vessels. When the *Mary Rose* was raised from the Solent it presented historians with a wealth of information on shipboard life in Tudor times and many of the artefacts raised from the seabed are on display. Continuing the maritime theme, the Royal Navy Submarine Museum in Haslar Jetty Road, Gosport, has a museum showing the history of the submarine. The highlight of the museum is probably the HMS Alliance, a post-World War II submarine that visitors can tour. Moving away from things nautical, the Gosport Museum and Gallery in Walpole Road recounts the history of the area from earliest times.

FURNITURE

Alexandra Gray, Havant Road in Drayton, to the north of the A27, has a large stock of Georgian, Regency, Victorian, Edwardian, and pine furniture together with pictures. It is open all week, from 12 noon on Sundays, apart from Wednesday.

GENERAL ANTIQUES

Good Day Antiques and Décor, The Green, Rowlands Castle, has Victorian furniture, small cabinets, jewellery, silver, porcelain, pottery, and pictures and is open Thursday–Monday.

▶ Travel along the M275 then the M27 until you reach Junction 8, where you should take the A3024 into Southampton.

SOUTHAMPTON

Used for 2,000 years as a port, Southampton has been the landing and embarkation point for armies during the whole of its history. It is also the harbour used by the great liners crossing the Atlantic including the *Queen Mary* and the *Queen Elizabeth*.

Traces of the Medieval town can be seen in a remaining section of the city walls in the Western Esplanade, although the wall towers have all survived. Southampton City Art Gallery in the Civic Centre, Commercial Road, contains a good collection of works of art including French Impressionists, 18thC portraits, and 17thC Dutch landscapes.

BOOKS

Amazingly, H M Gilbert (PBFA) of Portland Street has been selling books since 1859. Its specialities are British topography, English literature, military, and maritime books. It opens early on Saturdays, at 8.30am. Situated on the edge of the New Forest, 10km (6 miles) from the city centre in Ashurst, Nova Foresta Books (PBFA) in the Lyndhurst Road has antiquarian, rare, and second-hand books, especially on the New Forest, 20thC literature, and art. It is open Tuesday–Saturday. Open Hand Books and Crafts in Portswood Road has a large stock of antiquarian, rare, and second-hand books – architecture, art, design, and illustrators are their specialities.

FURNITURE

In the Portswood area, Amber Antiques in Portswood Road has a large stock of furniture and opens 7 days a week. Pennyfarthing Antiques in Rumbridge Street, Totton, has Georgian–Edwardian furniture as well as clocks, Oriental items, and watches. It is open Thursday–Monday. K Standrin, Northam Road, sells antique furniture, mirrors, and decorative items. Also in Northam Road, Mr Toby has Georgian and later furniture, collectables, and Toby jugs. The shop shuts at 4pm.

GENERAL ANTIQUES

Curios in Canute's Pavilion, Ocean Village, has a large range of china, glass, jewellery, and furniture. Highfield Antiques, located in Highfield Lane, sells Georgian–1930s furniture, pictures, prints, garden furniture, ceramics, glass, and toys. Getty's Antiques in Northam Road has a wide choice of furniture, ceramics, collectables, silver, copper, and brass. Memory Lane, Manor Farm Road, in the Bitterne area of Southampton, has furniture, pictures, and collectables. It is closed Wednesdays and Sundays. In Bedford Place, Moody Antiques is another long-established dealer that has been in business since 1890. Stock consists of furniture, silver, pictures, and porcelain. On Wednesdays and Saturdays It shuts at 12 noon.

MARITIME ANTIQUES

Again in Northam Road, Cobwebs has a large stock of ocean liner memorabilia, including items relating to the *Titanic* and *White Star Line* as well as Royal Naval and aviation items. It is open every day except Wednesdays and Sundays.

PAINTINGS

The Brompton Gallery, in Old Northam Road, has contemporary paintings, sculpture, ceramics, etchings, and prints.

RAILWAYANA

Athena Antiques of Newtown Road, Warsash, has railwayana as well as china, glass, figurines, and chandeliers. Ring 01489 584633 before you visit.

ANTIQUES CENTRES

Southampton has four antiques centres. The first is **The Antique Centre** in Britannia Road where 40 dealers sell furniture, porcelain, jewellery, pictures, glass, medals, ocean memorabilia, and Clarice Cliff. The centre is open 7 days a week (until 4pm on Sundays). There are 15 dealers selling a wide range of antiques and collectables in **The Antiques Quarter**, Old Northam Road. **The Clocktower Antiques Centre** in Manor Farm Road, Bitterne, has 20 dealers with furniture, porcelain, brass, silver, and clocks. Finally, the 14 dealers at **Roberta's Relics**, Rumbridge Street, sell furniture, silver, glass, porcelain, curios, and collectables.

▶ Take the A3057 from Southampton to Romsey, a distance of about 13km (8 miles).

ROMSEY

The pleasant riverside town of Romsey is probably best known for Broadlands, the home of the late Lord Mountbatten. The 18thC house is set in parkland laid out by Capability Brown and it contains an exhibition devoted to the life and achievements of Lord Mountbatten. Romsey was also the site of a 10thC abbey but now all that remains on the site is the 12thC abbey church.

FURNITURE

F E A Briggs Ltd on Plaza Parade, Winchester Road, has a large range of Victorian and Edwardian furniture and textiles.

GENERAL ANTIQUES

Open by appointment only, **Antique Enterprises** in Cavendish Close has furniture, china, glass and collectables – ring 01794 515589. **Bell Antiques** (GA), in Bell Street, has an extensive range of jewellery, silver, glass, china, small furniture, maps, and topographical prints. It is closed on Wednesdays in winter, as well as Sundays all year round. Open by appointment only, **Cambridge Antiques** (LAPADA) has general antiques, furniture, porcelain, clocks, and paintings – ring 01794 324499 or 322125 (evenings). On Plaza Parade, Winchester Road, **Eddison Antiques** sells Victorian furniture, copper, brass, linen, and jewellery. It is open Tuesday–Saturday.

MEDALS

Another shop selling by appointment only, **Romsey Medals** (OMRS, LAPADA) has a large stock of British orders, gallantry/campaign groups, British cap badges, and medals – ring 01794 324488 or 322125 (evenings).

AUCTION HOUSES

Romsey Auction Rooms, The Hundred, has sales on the first or second Tuesday of the month. They have five silver sales and three toy sales a year. Viewing is held the day before from 12 noon–7.30pm.

▶ Take the A3090 to Winchester, which is 16km (10 miles) away.

WINCHESTER

The county town of Hampshire, Winchester was for centuries one of the most important cities in England. It was built by the Romans alongside an earlier settlement and they called it *Venta Belgarum*. The High Street and city walls still follow the Roman lines. Before the Norman invasion it was the capital of the kingdom of Wessex. After the Conquest, it remained important as the site of the Royal Treasury until the 12thC.

Wolvesey Castle, built by Bishop Henry Blois, has been largely destroyed except for its Great Hall, said to be the finest aisled Medieval hall in England. Winchester Cathedral, the second longest in Europe, was started in 1079 and has many notable features including 14thC carved stalls and coffers containing the bones of Saxon and Danish kings. It also contains the tombs of Jane Austen, Izaak Walton (author of *The Compleat Angler*), and King William Rufus who was killed by an arrow in the New Forest. When visiting the cathedral, look up at the pillars and you will see the hooks that held the decorations for the wedding of Queen Mary Tudor and Philip of Spain in 1554.

BOOKS

The Winchester Bookshop (PBFA) in St George's Street has antiquarian, rare, and second-hand books with topography, archaeology, travel, and literature being specialities.

CLOCKS

In Parchment Street, **The Clock-Work-Shop**
(BHI, AHS) has clocks, barometers, and furniture.
G E Marsh Antiques Clocks Ltd (BADA, CINOA,
CC, BHI, NAWCC) in The Square specializes in
carriage clocks, English longcase clocks, and
Continental clocks.

COINS

Open by appointment only, **Studio Coins** (BNTA)
of Kilham Lane sells old English coins – ring
01962 853156.

FURNITURE

Burns and Graham (BADA), in St Thomas Street,
has 17th–19thC furniture and decorative items. **The
Pine Barn** is situated at Folly Farm in the village of
Crawley, which is about 6.5km (4 miles) north-west
of Winchester just off the B3049. It has a large
stock of furniture made from reclaimed pine,
antique, and reproduction pine furniture. It is
open 7 days a week (closes at 4pm on Sundays).
The Pine Cellars in Jewry Street, has an extensive
selection of antique pine and country furniture.
The village of Hursley, on the A3090 about 8.5km
(5 miles) south-west of Winchester, is home to
Seymour's Antiques. They have a large stock of
decorative French, country, and 18thC oak furniture
as well as textiles, lighting, and carpets. The shop
is open Tuesday–Saturday.

GENERAL ANTIQUES

West and Wills Corbett in Stockbridge Road have
eccentric decorative pieces, 18th–20thC furniture,
objects of interest, and contemporary pieces. They
are open Tuesday–Saturday (mornings only, until
1pm, on Saturdays).

SILVER & JEWELLERY

Christopher Barbour (The Silvershop) in the Antique
Market, Kings Walk sells a range of antique silver
and jewellery.

ANTIQUES CENTRES

In Jewry Street, **Winchester Antiques** has 20
dealers selling a large range of furniture, silver,
jewellery, glass, porcelain, and pine. The six
dealers in **The Old Blacksmith's Shop**, Hursley,
sell general antiques, lighting, silver, glass, and
small furniture.

AUCTION HOUSES

The regional office of **Phillips International
Auctioneers & Valuers** is located at The Red
House, Hyde Street.

Ancient Forest to Heathland

4

FORDINGBRIDGE ▶ RINGWOOD ▶ CHRISTCHURCH ▶ BOURNEMOUTH ▶ POOLE ▶
WEYMOUTH ▶ DORCHESTER ▶ SHERBORNE ▶ SHAFTESBURY ▶ SALISBURY

Starting in Hampshire, progressing into Dorset, and ending in Wiltshire, this tour takes in several towns with large concentrations of both general and specialist antiques dealers. At the beginning the tour skirts the New Forest, the largest area of lowland common land in the country. There is a theory that some areas were part of the original primeval forest once covering most of Britain after the last Ice Age. Since Norman times it has been a legal forest,

ie an area, not necessarily wooded, in which Forest Law protects animals to preserve them for hunting by royalty or licensees. Now it is extremely important for wildlife as it provides a continuous range of habitats from dry heathland to forest bog. Halfway through the tour, the heathland near Poole is another wildlife and conservation area, as it has many species of flora and fauna that are endangered or extinct in other areas of the country.

▶ ▶ USEFUL CONTACTS

Websites

www.bournemouthandpoole.co.uk
If you want to know where to go, what to see, or where to stay in Bournemouth or Poole, then this site has all the information you need.

www.thenewforest.co.uk
What do you want to know about the New Forest? Its official website will answer all your questions whether they are on places to visit, entertainment, or the Forest's history.

www.poolepottery.co.uk
Poole Pottery is very popular with collectors. The company's website has information for visitors and collectors alike.

www.eng-h.gov.uk/stoneh
English Heritage's website has much authoritative scientific and historic information about Stonehenge with data from recent archaeological research that has been carried out on the ancient monument.

www.stonehenge.co.uk
This site gives an easy-to-understand and straightforward history of Stonehenge.

www.tankmuseum.co.uk
Not only does the museum's website give information on admission prices, how to get there, and opening times, it also has online pictures of some of its exhibits.

www.wiltonhouse.com
Wilton House's own website gives detailed information on all its attractions.

FORDINGBRIDGE

Set on the River Avon and on the edge of the New Forest, Fordingbridge makes a good base for exploring the Forest. Just off the A338, 5km (3 miles) north of the town, the Elizabethan manor Breamore House has a fine collection of paintings, tapestries, and furniture. There is also a Countryside Museum where visitors can see exhibitions showing village life in days gone by. About 5km (3 miles) west of Breamore, Rockbourne Roman Villa has a museum with displays of objects excavated from the site as well as the mosaics and foundations of the villa itself.

▶ ▶ USEFUL CONTACTS

Tourist Information Centres

Bournemouth Westover Road.
Tel: 0906 802 0234 (Calls charged at 50 pence per minute)

Christchurch High Street.
Tel: 01202 471780

Dorchester Antelope Walk.
Tel: 01305 267992

Fordingbridge Salisbury Street.
Tel: 01425 654560

Poole High Street. Tel: 01202 253253

Ringwood The Furlong.
Tel: 01425 470896

Salisbury Fish Row. Tel: 01722 334956

Shaftesbury Bell Street.
Tel: 01747 853514

Sherborne Tilton Court, Digby Road.
Tel: 01935 815341

Weymouth The Esplanade.
Tel: 01305 785747

BOOKS

Bristow and Garland in Salisbury Street has antiquarian, rare, and second-hand books as well as manuscripts and ephemera. It is open all week apart from Wednesdays and Sundays.

COINS

West Essex Coin Investments are located in Station Road, in the village of Alderholt, which is about 3.2km (2 miles) west of Fordingbridge on the B3078. It sells English coinage from Medieval to the present day, including English milled, British colonial, and coins of the USA. The shop is open by appointment only – ring 01425 656459.

AUCTION HOUSES

The regional office of **Bonhams & Brooks** is located at Frogham Mount in the village of Frogham, just 1.6km (1 mile) south-east of the town.

▶ Take the A338 south for 10km (6 miles) to arrive in Ringwood.

RINGWOOD

The market town of Ringwood is also set on the Avon and on the edge of the New Forest. Its claim to fame, apart from its relatively large number of antiques dealers, is that the Duke of Monmouth stayed in a house here, which is now called Monmouth House, after his defeat at the Battle of Sedgemoor in 1685.

BOOKS

Booksellers E Chalmers Hallam, in Post Office Lane in St Ives, is situated about 3.2km (2 miles) west of Ringwood on the A31. It is open by appointment only – ring 01425 470060 – and sells antiquarian, rare, and second-hand books. Specialities include angling, field sports, travel, and Africana.

COLLECTABLES

Lister Hugh and Favia are also situated outside Ringwood, this time in Ringwood Road, Burley, 6.5km (4 miles) to the south-east and within the perambulation of the New Forest. It has porcelain and small collectables and is open 7 days a week, 10am–5pm. Another shop that sells by appointment only, The Old Toyshop, has a large stock of old collectables and vintage toys – ring 01425 476899. Sci-Fi World in Lynes Lane sells cards, badges, mugs, videos, books, and toys.

FURNITURE

Lorraine Tarrant Antiques in the Market Place has furniture in oak and old pine, as well as bears, collectors' items, and tapestry cushions. It is open Tuesday–Saturday. Millers Antiques Ltd (LAPADA), in Christchurch Road, has an extensive range of English and Continental country furniture as well as 19thC majolica, Quimper, treen, and decorative items. On Saturdays it is open until 4pm.

GENERAL ANTIQUES

Also in Christchurch Road, Robert Morgan Antiques has small furniture, unusual items, medals, and coins.

AUCTION HOUSES

The regional office of Phillips International Auctioneers & Valuers is in Southampton Road.

▶ Leave Ringwood on the A31 but turn left onto the A338 once you are about 1.6km (1 mile) from the town. Follow this road for approximately 8km (5 miles) then turn left onto the B3073 for 3.2km (2 miles) until you reach Christchurch.

CHRISTCHURCH

Set on both the Rivers Stour and Avon, this town was originally called *Twynham*. The name was changed to Christchurch after its famous church was built – this was originally part of Christchurch Abbey

and, at 95m (311ft), is the longest parish church in England. It stands on the site of a 7thC church, and building began in 1094. In Quay Road, the Red House Museum has exhibits on local and natural history, archaeology, and costume.

ANTIQUITIES

Open by appointment only, Chris Belton Antiquities (ADA) sells prehistoric, ancient, and Medieval antiquities – ring 01202 478592.

COLLECTABLES

In Castle Street, Classic Pictures (Postcard Traders Association) has a wide range of old postcards, Edwardian pictures, and prints. H L B Antiques in Barrack Road has general collectables, gramophones, postcards, walking sticks, Art Deco, and ivory. It is open Saturday 10am–4pm. Past 'n' Present in St Catherine's Parade, Fairmile Road, has a large selection of collectables.

GENERAL ANTIQUES

Situated in the Lymingon Road, Highcliffe, just to the east of Christchurch on the A337, Tudor House Antiques (LAPADA) sell a range of general antiques. They are open Tuesdays and Thursday–Saturday.

▶ Travel on the A35 westward for just 8.5km (5 miles) and you will then be in the centre of Bournemouth.

BOURNEMOUTH

Among the ancient towns and villages of Dorset and Hampshire, Bournemouth is a relative newcomer. The first house wasn't built until 1810, on the site of the present Royal Exeter Hotel. However, the sandy beaches and wooded chines guaranteed the town's quick success as a holiday resort. The Russell-Cotes Art Gallery and Museum on East Cliff has collections of 19th–early 20thC paintings, sculpture, decorative art, and furniture, and a collection of Modern Art.

ARCHITECTURAL ANTIQUES

Southern Stoves & Fireplaces Ltd, in the Christchurch Road, Pokesdown, has architectural antiques, stoves, and fireplaces.

BOOKS

Located in Cardigan Road, Winton, Books & Maps

has a large stock of antiquarian, rare, and second-hand books and maps. Books on Africa and dogs are specialities. **H Rowan**, Christchurch Road, Boscombe, has a broad range of antiquarian and second-hand books, maps, and prints and specializes in local interest and art and antiques topics. Again in Christchurch Road, **Volume One Books and Records** (NMTA) has a large stock of books, LP records, cassettes, and CDs (classical, easy listening, jazz, stage and screen, country, rock, and pop). It is open every day except Thursdays and Sundays, until 1pm on Wednesdays, and until 2pm on Saturdays. (It is also closed the third Saturday of each month.) Situated in Cecil Avenue, **Yesterday's Books** (PBFA) has antiquarian books and specializes in African topics. The shop is open by appointment only – ring 01202 522442.

CERAMICS
Hengistbury Antiques & Collectables, in Broadway, Southbourne, has Meissen porcelain and Edwardian and Victorian furniture. It is open Tuesday–Saturday.

COINS & MEDALS
Sterling Coins and Medals (OMRS), in Somerset Road, Boscombe, is open until 3.30pm Monday, Tuesday, Thursday–Saturday. It is shut on Wednesday afternoons and Sundays.

COLLECTABLES
Hardy's Collectables, situated Christchurch Road, Boscombe, has an extensive range of 20thC collectables – mainly smalls, toys, metalware, and ceramics. **Recollections**, in the Royal Arcade, Boscombe, sells collectables, china, Poole Pottery, commemoratives, Beatrix Potter figures, and Art Deco. The shop is open Monday and Thursday–Saturday. **Selection**, also in the Royal Arcade, sells collectables, antiques, teapots, tea services, and Carlton ware. Still in Boscombe but this time in Christchurch Road, **Wonderworld** has modern collectables, *Star Wars*, comics, and Beanie Babies.

FURNITURE
All of the town's antique furniture shops are located in Christchurch Road, Boscombe on the eastern side of Bournemouth. Among these, **Anna's Attic** sells furniture and some smalls. The shop is open until 4pm. **Brian A Jones Esq Antiques** sells mostly furniture, 1820–early Victorian together with reproduction. Still in Christchurch Road, **Chorley-Burdett Antiques** has Victorian, Edwardian, oak, mahogany, and antique furniture plus new and reclaimed pine. **Lionel Geneen Ltd** (LAPADA), established in Boscombe in 1902, has 19thC English, Continental, and Oriental furniture together with porcelain, bronzes, glass, ornamental decorative pieces as well as dessert, tea, and dinner services. The shop shuts on Saturday afternoons and Sundays. **Portabellows**, still in

Christchurch Road, sells mainly furniture with general antiques. It is closed on Wednesdays and Sundays. **S A Antiques** sells mainly furniture. **Sandys Antiques** sells Victorian, Edwardian, and shipping furniture.

GENERAL ANTIQUES
Still in the Christchurch Road, Boscombe, **The Antiques Exchange** has furniture, glass, china, collectables, and reproduction Tiffany lamps. It is open 7 days a week. On the other side of Bournemouth, in Westbourne, **Arcade Antiques**, Westbourne Arcade, sells general antiques and Poole pottery. It shuts at 2pm on Wednesdays and all day Sundays. **Rawlinsons**, Christchurch Road, Boscombe, has general antiques, smalls, furniture, glass, china, metalware, clocks, and Art Deco. **Carole Russell Antiques**, in Westover Road, has objets d'art, jewellery, clocks, silver, porcelain, and paintings. The shop is open Thursday–Saturday.

LIGHTING
Allegras Lighthouse Antiques (LAPADA) in Poole Road, Westbourne has a large stock of antique ceiling, wall, and table lighting, as well as 19thC furniture and mirrors. It is open all week apart from Wednesdays and Sundays. **Peter Denver Antiques**, situated in Calvin Road, sells general antiques, collectables, and furniture and is open Tuesday–Saturday.

MILITARIA
Specialist dealer **Boscombe Militaria**, in Palmerston Road, has 20thC militaria, uniforms, medals, and badges. It is open every day except Wednesdays and Sundays. **Norman D Landing Militaria** in Alma Road, Winton, has a large range of US uniforms and equipment from 1900–45. The shop is open Thursday–Saturday.

ORIENTAL ANTIQUES
Back in Boscombe, **Pennywise** in the Royal Arcade sells Oriental pieces and Chinese snuff bottles.

TOOLS
Situated in Wimborne Road, Moordown, **Woodies Tools** has a selection of antique and collectable tools with some modern ones and is open 7 days a week until 4pm.

TOYS
Abbey Models in Littledown Drive, Littledown, sells old toys, including Dinky, Corgi, and Matchbox, by appointment only – ring 01202 395999.

ANTIQUES CENTRES
All the centres are situated in Christchurch Road, Boscombe. The 10 dealers in **The Emporium Antiques Centre** sell general antiques and decorative arts. **Kebo Antiques Market** has 5

dealers selling general antiques. **Pokesdown Antique Centre's** 10 dealers sell decorative antiques, wristwatches, lighting, pine, collectables, and paintings.

AUCTION HOUSES

Dalkeith Auctions Bournemouth, Christchurch Road, Boscombe, has regular collectors' sales of ephemera and other collectors' items on the first Saturday of the month at 11am. Viewing takes place the week before, 9am–3pm. **Riddetts of Bournemouth**, in Holdenhurst Road, has sales every two weeks, usually on Tuesdays and Wednesdays.

▶ It is difficult to see where Bournemouth ends and Poole begins but if you travel 8.5km (5 miles) westward on the A338 you will be in the centre of Poole.

POOLE

In contrast to Bournemouth, Poole's history goes back to at least the 13thC. Set by a large natural harbour, it was a thriving port in the 17th and 18thC when it specialized in trading with Newfoundland. There are five islands inside Poole harbour, which is one of the largest natural harbours in the world. The biggest island is Brownsea – this has one of the few surviving viable populations of red squirrels in the country and it is also where Lord Baden-Powell held his first camp for boys – a pre-curser to the Scout movement.

Poole has several museums including the Royal National Lifeboat Museum on West Quay and the Waterfront, in the High Street, which is devoted to the town's nautical history. Perhaps of most interest to many antiques enthusiasts is Poole Pottery on East Quay, where innovative, striking pottery has been made for 125 years. As well as the factory shop, there is a display of the company's history and a "Have a Go" area where children can try making and painting pots.

BOOKS

Situated in North Street, **Castle Books** has a selection of antiquarian, modern, second-hand, and collectable books. **W A Howe**, in Merrow Avenue, Branksome, sells antiquarian and second-hand books and specializes in children's illustrated books, modern first editions, cookery, and golf titles. The shop is open 7 days a week, 8am–8pm. **Christopher Williams** (PBFA) in Morrison Avenue sells by appointment only – ring 01202 743157. He has antiquarian and fine modern books with art, lace-making, needlework, cookery, antiques, collecting, and local history being specialities.

COINS & MEDALS

Located in Ashley Road, Parkstone, **Dorset Coin Company** (BNTA, IBNS) has a large stock of coins, medals, and banknotes and is open Monday–Friday until 4pm.

DOLLS & TEDDY BEARS

Down To The Woods Ltd, in The Dolphin Centre in the middle of Poole, has a wide selection of bears, soft toys, beanbag collections, and dolls' houses.

FIREPLACES

Fireplaces 'n' Things, Alder Road, Parkstone, has an extensive stock of antique and reproduction fireplaces. It is closed on Wednesday afternoons and Sundays.

FURNITURE

Again in Parkstone on the eastern side of Poole, **A Berry** in Ashley Road has French furniture and decorative beds. The shop is open 7 days a week. **Laburnum Antiques** in the Bournemouth Road has Georgian, Victorian, and Edwardian furniture as well as accessories, ottomans, stools, and cushions. It is open Tuesday–Saturday. **Pedlars Tray** in the High Street sells furniture and is open until 4pm. **Stocks and Chairs** in Bank Chambers, Penn Hill Avenue, has 18th and 19thC furniture with some smalls. It is closed Wednesdays and Sundays.

GENERAL ANTIQUES

Black Dog Antiques (RADS), located in Ashley Road Parkstone, has World War I and II telescopes, furniture, decorative items, silver, jewellery, and marine items. It is closed Wednesdays and Sundays. **Grandad's Attic** in Ringwood Road has a wide range of antiques, collectables, Poole Pottery, and corkscrews. It is open Tuesday–Saturday (from 2pm Tuesday–Friday).

AUCTION HOUSES

The regional office of **Bonhams & Brooks** is situated in Parkstone Road. **Davey & Davey** (NAVA) in St Peters Road, Parkstone, has sales of general antiques and collectables every two months on Tuesdays at 10am. Viewing takes place on Mondays 10am–4pm.

▶ Leave Poole on the A35 westbound. Just after Lychett Minster, about 5km (3 miles) from Poole town centre, turn left onto the A351 towards Wareham. Continue through Wareham and, just to the west of the town, take the A352 to the village of Watercombe, which is about 19.25km (12 miles) away. Immediately after Watercombe, turn left onto the A353 and travel to Weymouth, approximately another 10km (6 miles) away.

▶ You can break your journey at the Tank Museum, which is located about 11.25km (7 miles) west of Wareham just off the A352.

WEYMOUTH

George III once lived in Gloucester House, now a hotel, in the holiday resort of Weymouth. It has some fine Georgian buildings as well as a good sandy beach. The Deep Sea Adventure on Custom House Quay tells the story of underwater exploration and maritime events from the 17thC onwards. It has an outstanding *Titanic* exhibition. There are also special activities for children.

In Barrack Road, a Victorian fortress, Nothe Fort, is now the Museum of Coastal Defence. It has 70 rooms of guns, weapons, and other military equipment as well as exhibitions of the life of soldiers in a garrison.

CERAMICS

Paddy Cliff's Clarice, in Coombe Valley Road, sells his large range of Clarice Cliff pieces by mail order, via the Internet, or by appointment – ring 01305 834945.

COLLECTABLES

The Curiosity Shop on the Quay, Trinity Road, is a general collectors' shop with Victoriana,

collectables, Moorcroft, Poole Pottery, and Pendelfin. It is open 7 days a week.

DOLLS & TOYS

The Shrubbery in The Colwell Centre has an extensive selection of collectable dolls, dolls' houses, and toys.

GENERAL ANTIQUES

Situated in East Street, P Barrett sells curios, coins, medals, local prints, brass, copper, china, and army badges. It is closed on Wednesday afternoons and Sundays. The Crows Nest in Hope Square has a wide range of china, glass, pictures, farming, ships' lamps, nautical items, and collectables. It is open 7 days a week.

MARITIME ANTIQUES

Books Afloat in Park Street has a large stock of antiquarian, rare, and second-hand books with shipping and naval antiques and memorabilia as well as old postcards. They also have ship models and paintings. The Nautical Antique Centre in Old Harbour Passage, Hope Square, has a wide range of original maritime equipment, ships' souvenirs and instruments, nautical collectables, and memorabilia. The shop is open Tuesday–Friday.

AUCTION HOUSES

The town's only auctioneer, Hy Duke & Son (SOFAA), in St Nicholas Street, has two sales a month of general antiques and household effects. They take place on Tuesdays at 10.30am with viewing on the previous Monday.

▶ Go due north on the A354 for 13km (8 miles) to arrive at the next stop of Dorchester.

DORCHESTER

Once the Roman town of *Durnovaria*, present-day Dorchester is a busy market town, and it provided the setting for Thomas Hardy's great novel *The Mayor of Casterbridge*.

The town has two outstanding museums. The first, the Tutankhamun Exhibition in West Street, recreates the discovery of the Pharaoh's famous tomb by Howard Carter. It also has facsimiles of the treasures found there. The second is the Dinosaur Museum, in Icen Way, which contains life-size replicas of many well-known dinosaurs like tyrannosaurus rex. Maiden Castle, just 3.2km (2 miles)

▶▶ THE TANK MUSEUM

This museum has over 300 exhibits of tanks from 26 countries ranging in date from World War I to the British Army's current Challenger tank. Some of the more recent examples were captured in the Gulf War. There are also prototypes that never made it to production.

to the south-west of Dorchester, is one of the finest earth fortresses in Europe. Although Stone Age remains have been found there, it was the Iron Age inhabitants who expanded the settlement into a great fortress. It covers about 120 acres and could once accommodate 5,000 people. Although only using a simple ditch and bank system, the fortifications became more complex as banks and ditches were added. When the Romans invaded they had to take Maiden Castle. Although it had been virtually impregnable to attack by local bands, the Romans' superior weapons and military skills quickly subdued the fortress and its inhabitants. Without its defensive role, Maiden Castle was abandoned completely by AD 70.

BOOKS
Dorchester Bookshop in Nappers Court, Charles Street, has a range of second-hand and antiquarian books.

CERAMICS
The Box of Porcelain in Icen Way has a large stock of Doulton, Beswick, Royal Worcester, and Spode. It is closed Thursdays and Sundays.

CLOCKS
Time After Tyme Antiques (AHS) in the De Danann Antique Centre, London Road, sells longcase, English, and bracket clocks.

FURNITURE
Legg of Dorchester, in the High East Street, has an extensive range of mostly furniture and some general antiques. BADA member, John Walker Antiques in High West Street, has early oak together with textiles, ceramics, and metalwork.

MAPS & PRINTS
Located in the village of Puddletown, just 8.5km (5 miles) north-east of Dorchester on the A35, Antique Map and Bookshop (PBFA, ABA), in the High Street, sells antique maps as well as antiquarian and second-hand books.

ANTIQUES CENTRES
The six dealers that can be found in Colliton Antique Centre, Colliton Street, have a wide selection of general Victorian, Georgian, and Edwardian furniture as well as jewellery, silver, old pine, and a range of general antiques.

AUCTION HOUSES
Hy Duke & Son (SOFAA) in Weymouth Avenue has been established since 1823 and has another saleroom in Weymouth. It has sales of paintings, furniture, ceramics, silver, and jewellery. Viewing the week before the sale occurs on Saturday 9.30am–12 noon, Monday 9.30am–5pm, Tuesday 9.30am–7pm, Wednesday 9.30am–5pm, and the morning of the sale. The office is open some Saturdays.

▶ Continuing northward, now on the A352, Sherborne, is 30.5km (19 miles) away.

SHERBORNE
Set on the River Yeo Sherborne is a pleasant town and has many Georgian, Regency, and Victorian buildings. The focus of the town is Sherborne Abbey, which has a magnificent roof of golden Ham stone. The town has two castles because Sir Walter Raleigh was given a 12thC castle there by Elizabeth I and he built a new one close by on the site of a former hunting lodge. After he was executed, the castle passed into the hands of the Digby family. The castle was enlarged and, in the 18thC, Capability Brown laid out the grounds. It is now the home of fine collections of furniture, porcelain, and pictures.

Sherborne Museum Association in Church Lane has over 15,000 exhibits relating to local history including costume from 17th–20thC, a Medieval wall painting, and artefacts from the town's 8thC Saxon abbey.

BOOKS
Chapter House Books (PBFA, BA), Trendle Street, has antiquarian books, out-of-print books, paperbacks, and pictures.

CLOCKS
Arnold Dick Antiques, located in Newland, sells clocks and general antiques. Timecraft Clocks (BHI) in Cheap Street has clocks, barometers, and musical boxes and is open Tuesday–Saturday.

FURNITURE
Antiques of Sherborne (SAADA), The Green, has a range of town and country, Georgian, Victorian, and Edwardian furniture, period soft upholstery,

pottery, chess sets, and games. In South Street, **Heygate Browne Antiques** has an extensive selection of English 18th and 19thC furniture, pottery, and porcelain. **Phoenix Antiques** (SAADA) in Cheap Street sells 18th and 19thC English and Continental furniture including mahogany, rosewood, painted country furniture, furnishings, and lighting. **Piers Pisani Antiques** (SAADA), The Green, has a stock of English and French furniture and upholstery.

GENERAL ANTIQUES
Geometrica (SAADA) in Westbury has decorative arts, 20thC ceramics, furniture, and studio pottery. It is open Friday–Saturday until 4pm. **Keeble Antiques** in Tilton Court, Digby Road, has eclectic pieces, pictures, mirrors, clocks, boxes, and antique and fine art books. The shop is open 7 days a week. The **Nook Antiques** (SAADA) in South Street has small, useful, refurbished furniture as well as china, glass, brass, copper, and collectables. It is open Tuesday–Saturday.

    Victor & Co (SAADA) in Trendle Street has a wide selection of furniture, china, glass, rugs, curtains, and domestic furnishings. BADA member, **John Walker Antiques** in Cheap Street, has early oak, textiles, ceramics, and metalwork, and is open Tuesday–Saturday.

SILVER
Greystoke Antiques in Swan Yard, Cheap Street, has a large stock of Georgian and Victorian silver and is closed Wednesdays and Sundays.

AUCTION HOUSES
The regional office of **Phillips International Auctioneers & Valuers** is located in Cheap Street.

▶ Leave Sherborne on the A30 eastward and continue for 25.75km (16 miles) to reach the next stop of Shaftesbury.

SHAFTESBURY
Set on a plateau overlooking the Blackmore Vale, Shaftesbury was founded in AD 880 by King Alfred. Its picturesque Gold Hill, a steep cobbled street lined with cottages, has been a popular location for period films.

    The town's museum, which is situated at the top of Gold Hill, has exhibits ranging from Shaftesbury's earliest days to more recent farming and dairying implements. It includes a fire engine dating from 1744.

FURNITURE
Shaston Antiques in Bell Street has Georgian, Regency, and Victorian quality furniture. It closes Wednesday afternoons and Sundays.

GENERAL ANTIQUES
Dairy House Antiques, Station Road, Semley, has a large stock of 17th–19thC paintings, furniture, ceramics, and textiles.

ANTIQUES CENTRES
In Bell Street, **Mr Punch's Antique Market** has 20 dealers with a large range of general antiques, furniture, and collectables, as well as a Punch museum and militaria.

AUCTION HOUSES
Chapman, Moore & Mugford, in the High Street, have sales of antiques and collectables every six to eight weeks on Fridays at 6pm. They also have two sales per year of musical instruments on a Friday at 6pm, with viewing for all sales taking place on Fridays from 10.30am–6pm.

    Semley Auctioneers of Station Road, Semley, have fortnightly sales on Saturdays at 10am with viewing Fridays 9am–9pm and the morning of the sale. They say that items of higher quality appear in these sales about every six weeks.

▶ Continue eastward along the A30 for 32km (20 miles). At the small town of Wilton take the A36 into Salisbury.

▶ Alternatively, instead of passing through Wilton, stop and visit Wilton House first (see page 45).

SALISBURY
Approaching Salisbury the first thing that a visitor usually sees is the elegant spire of the city's cathedral. This is a scene so beautiful and quintessentially English that it has attracted many artists, including Constable and Whistler, to paint it. The first settlement in the area was located at Old Sarum, a natural defensive position above the river. Evidence of human habitation has been found here going back to the Iron Age. The settlement continued until the Norman time, when a castle and cathedral were built together on the hill. In the 13thC the clerics moved down to the valley where they built the magnificent cathedral.

Situated just 5km (3 miles) west of Salisbury, Wilton House originated in Tudor times but the building we see today is largely the design of Inigo Jones as a disastrous fire in 1647 destroyed much of the original. The house is said to contain the most perfect rooms in England – the Cube and Double Cube Rooms, both of which have magnificently painted ceilings. The art collection here, which includes work by Van Dyck, Rubens, and Reynolds, is also thought to be one of the best private collections in the whole of Britain.

The building of Salisbury Cathedral was started in 1220, although its famous 22m (400ft) spire was not added until the 14thC. By the following century, strainer arches were added to prevent its collapse. The cathedral contains many treasures including an original copy of the *Magna Carta*, which is one of only four that survive. The Cathedral Close, containing buildings ranging in date from the 14th–18thC, is said to be one of the finest in England.

The award-winning Salisbury and South Wiltshire Museum, in The Close, has a wide range of exhibits from the earliest times of the city onwards. Also situated in The Close, the Redcoats in the Wardrobe shows the history of the Royal Berkshire and Wiltshire regiments over 250 years.

BOOKS

John & Judith Head, of **Barn Book Supply** (ABA) in Crane Street have a range of antiquarian books on fieldsports and they are open Monday–Friday. **Trevan's Old Books**, in Catherine Street, has some antiquarian books.

COINS

In Castle Street, **Castle Galleries** (OMRS) has a selection of coins, medals, small items, and jewellery and is open Tuesday, Thursday, Friday, and Saturday until 1pm.

FURNITURE

Specialist dealer, **Robert Bradley Antiques** in Brown Street, has a range of 17th–18thC furniture. **Pennyfarthing Antiques**, Winchester Street, sells country furniture. It is open 7 days a week (until 4pm Sundays). **Steven Shell** at Old Sarum Airfield has a selection of Indonesian furniture and accessories. It opens at 8am.

GENERAL ANTIQUES

The Antiques Market in Catherine Street has general antiques. In Fisherton Street, **Fisherton Antiques Market** has Victorian and Edwardian furniture, jewellery, modern first editions, and collectables. Situated in West Street, Wilton, 5km (3 miles) from Salisbury, **Carol Musselwhite Antiques** has china, glass, linen, lace, and out-of-production Derby. The shop is open Tuesday–Saturday.

Chris Watts Antiques (LAPADA) in the Salisbury Antiques Warehouse, Wilton Road, has 18th and 19thC furniture, paintings, clocks, bronzes, and barometers. The shop is open the first Saturday of every month.

AUCTION HOUSES

Woolley and Wallis Salisbury Salerooms Ltd (SOFAA) in Castle Street has household sales. These occur fortnightly on Fridays at 10am, with viewing on Thursdays 10am–7pm. There are also 30 specialist sales a year including furniture, ceramics, rugs and textiles, silver and jewellery, wine, books and maps, and paintings. The office is open on Saturdays until 12 noon as well as during weekdays.

▶ You cannot finish the tour without visiting the impressive Stonehenge, which is very nearby. To reach it, take the A360 northbound from Salisbury until it meets the A303, which is a distance of about 13km (8 miles). Then you should turn right and travel for about 1.6km (1 mile) and Stonehenge will appear on your right.

Believed to have been started 5,000 years ago, Stonehenge is one of the best-known ancient monuments in the world. Some of the stones were carried 320km (200 miles) from Wales, which is an amazing feat – especially considering that a recent attempt to re-enact the achievement failed dismally. On Midsummer's Day Stonehenge attracts present-day Druids who are eager to see the sun rise exactly in line with its stone avenue.

5 Beaches to Moorland

HONITON ▶ TOPSHAM ▶ EXETER ▶ NEWTON ABBOT ▶ TORQUAY ▶ PAIGNTON ▶ TOTNES ▶ ASHBURTON ▶ PLYMPTON ▶ PLYMOUTH ▶ TAVISTOCK ▶ OKEHAMPTON ▶ CREDITON ▶ TIVERTON ▶ SOUTH MOLTON

Devon is a good hunting ground for antiques buyers, having numerous shops concentrated mostly in the towns and cities. Also, by its location in the far south-west of England, it presents the visitor with contrasting scenery. There are the good safe beaches of South Devon and the wilder, surfing beaches on the North Devon Atlantic coast. In between are picture postcard villages with thatched cottages, busy market towns, and pretty country lanes. Dartmoor dominates the south-west of the county with its stark beauty, rocky tors, and infamous prison. In contrast, Exmoor is a softer, less fierce moorland.

This is also the county of great sailors and maritime adventure. Sir Francis Drake, Sir Walter Raleigh, and Sir Richard Hawkins were born here and the Pilgrim Fathers set sail from Plymouth for a new life in America.

▶ ▶ USEFUL CONTACTS

Websites

www.beautiful-devon.co.uk
The Beautiful Devon website is well illustrated and packed with useful information about the county.

www.bbc.co.uk/devon
Listening to the local radio is a good way to get to know a place. This BBC Devon website will give you a taste for the county before you arrive.

www.devon-cc.gov.uk
Devon County Council's website gives some useful visitor information on tourist attractions, beaches, Dartmoor, fishing, gardens, and leisure amenities.

Tourist Information Centres

Dartmoor Leonards Road
Tel: 01752 897035

Devon Exeter Services, Sandygate, M5 Junction 30, Exeter South

Plymouth Plymouth Discovery Centre, Crabtree
Tel: 01752 266030/266031

Torquay Vaughan Parade
Tel: 01803 297428

HONITON

The tour starts in Honiton, which is famous for its lace-making industry. Although the trade has now largely died out in the area, demonstrations of lace-making may be seen during the summer at the Allhallows Museum in the High Street. The museum also houses a collection of different types of lace made in the town over the centuries, and displays of other types of trades and crafts once prevalent. Those interested in prehistory might like to visit the Murch Gallery in the museum, which has fossils of hippos' bones and elephants' teeth found in the area.

BOOKS & PRINTS

There are two specialist antiquarian bookshops in Honiton High Street. One is called, quite appropriately, **High Street Books** (PBFA) and it sells antiquarian books, maps, and prints. The other bookshop, **Honiton Old Book Shop** (ABA, PBFA), can be found at Felix House and has stock of antiquarian, rare, and second-hand books as well as leather bindings, West Country antiquarian maps, and prints. British topography, travel, and natural history topics are specialities here. **Geoffrey M Woodhead**, situated at Monkton House in the High Street, has a large stock of general antiques and books.

COLLECTABLES

Another appropriately named shop, **Collectables**, is also on the High Street. It has a large selection including ceramics, Wade, cameras, railwayana, toys, militaria, annuals, telephone cards, cigarette cards, breweriana, commemorative, games, postcards, and crested china.

DOLLS & TOYS

Honiton Antique Toys has a large stock of antique toys and dolls. It is open Tuesday, Wednesday, and Friday–Saturday.

FURNITURE

Honiton High Street has a good selection of furniture dealers. BADA member **Roderick Butler** at Marwood House has a large stock of 17th–18thC Regency furniture, works of art, and metalwork. In August he is open by appointment only – ring 01404 42169. In contrast, **Colystock Antiques**, Rising Sun Farm, Stockland (a village about 10km/ 6 miles north-west of Honiton), has a large stock of 18th and 19thC pine and reproduction furniture. Reclaimed pine kitchens can also be bought here. It is open 7 days a week from 8.30am (Sunday from 1–4pm). Back in Honiton High Street, **Kingsway House Antiques** deals in Georgian furniture, china, and clocks.

Various other treasure troves can be found in the High Street. **Maya Antiques** has a large stock of furniture including Georgian, Victorian, and Edwardian. Not far away, **Merchant House Antiques** has a broad range of fine furniture, general antiques, and collectables. As well as having a large stock of 17th and 18thC English and French oak and country furniture, **Pilgrim Antiques** also sells longcase clocks. **Plympton Antiques** sells mostly mahogany furniture, copper, brass, and porcelain. **Wickham Antiques** sell mainly 18th and 19thC mahogany furniture. It is open every day except Thursdays and Sundays.

The village of Offwell stands 1.6km (1 mile) outside Honiton, eastbound on the A35, and is where **Ray Poole Antiques and Recycling** can be found. The shop is at Unit 3, The Stables Workshop, Mount Pleasant. It has a large stock of French furniture, beds, small items, and general antiques and is open Monday–Friday 9am–3pm.

Pughs Antiques at Pughs Farm is also situated in a small village, Monkton, again about 1.6km (1 mile) from Honiton on the northbound A30. They sell to trade only and have a large stock of Victorian and Edwardian furniture in mahogany, oak, walnut, and pine, as well as French furniture and antique beds.

GENERAL ANTIQUES

Although some of the specialist furniture dealers above also sell general antiques, there are some true general dealers in Honiton whose stock often contains unusual and fascinating objects. Along the High Street, **Jane Barnes Antiques and Interiors** has Victorian and Edwardian general antiques. It is closed on Wednesdays and Sundays. **Hermitage Antiques** also has a large stock of general antiques including furniture. Finally, **Marchant Denman Antiques** sells general antiques, porcelain, period furniture, jewellery, light fittings, door furniture, brass, and copper.

SILVER

Otter Antiques on the High Street is Honiton's only silver dealer and it has a wide range of fine and antique silver and silverplate.

ANTIQUES CENTRES

There are three antiques centres in Honiton, and all of them are based in the High Street. The first, **Abingdon House Antique Centre**, has a good stock of general antiques, Arts and Crafts, country antiques and collectables, tools, and prints. **The Grove Antique Centre**'s stock includes teddy bears, silver, porcelain, 18th and 20thC furniture, collectables, paintings, clocks, barometers, rugs, and decorative items. It is open 7 days a week (until 4pm on Sundays). Finally, the **Kings Arms Antiques Centre** has a large stock of general antiques as well as early oak through to reproduction furniture. It is closed on Thursday afternoons and Sundays.

AUCTION HOUSES

Honiton has two auction houses. The regional branch of Bonhams & Brooks, known as **Bonhams & Brooks West Country**, is located in Dowell Street. This particular branch serves the Devon and West Country area. The other auction house, **Taylors**, at Honiton Galleries on the High Street, has bi-monthly sales of antiques and collectables, taking place on Fridays at 10.30am. They also have bi-monthly sales of oils, watercolours, and prints, again on Fridays but starting at 11am. Viewing for both types of sale is the day before and from 9–10.30am on the day of the sale.

Leave Honiton on the A30, following signs for Exeter. When the road reaches the M5 at Junction 29, take the motorway following signs for Torquay. Come off at the next junction, 30, and take the A376 for about 5km (3 miles) turning right for Topsham, which is about 1.6km (1 mile) further on.

TOPSHAM

Situated on the River Exe, Topsham was once a thriving port because a weir upstream denied large ships entry to Exeter. Its role came to an end in the mid-16thC when a canal was built to take ships right into the city centre. Topsham's prosperous past can still be seen in the riverfront warehouses and merchants' houses. Topsham Museum, at 25 The Strand, is a 17thC furnished house, and its displays trace the town's history, particularly its role as a major Medieval port. All the antique shops and centres are based in Fore Street.

BOOKS

Joel Segal Books has a large stock of antique, rare, and second-hand books.

GENERAL ANTIQUES

Pennies sell general antiques.

PORCELAIN

Specialist dealer, **Mere Antiques**, has a stock of 18th and 19thC porcelain and Japanese Satsuma ware as well as small period furniture.

ANTIQUES CENTRES

Topsham Antiques Centre is on the First Floor at 76 Fore Street.

Take the main road through Topsham northwards to Exeter. About 1.6km (1 mile) after it passes under the motorway it joins with the A3015, which will take you into the heart of Exeter.

EXETER

As might be expected in such an historic city, Exeter boasts a wealth of antiques shops and centres selling pieces ranging from collectables to fine antiques that complement the city's historic attractions.

Exeter's long history goes all the way back to Roman times when it was known as *Isca Dumnoniorum*. Parts of the Roman walls, strengthened by the Normans, may still be seen in Southernhay. Although the city lost a large number of historic buildings in German air raids during World War II, many do still survive. The most impressive of the buildings is the cathedral, which dates from the late 13th–mid-14thC. On its west face it has the largest collection of 14thC sculpture in Britain and, inside, the longest stretch of 13thC Gothic vaulting in the world. Exeter has a number of interesting museums including the Royal Albert Memorial Museum and Art Gallery in Queen Street. Its displays include West Country silver, clocks, and watches as well as fine art and a world cultures collection. The city also has a most unusual museum, believed to be the only one of its kind in the country: Exeter's Underground Passages, which has its entrance in Romangate Passage off the High Street. The passages were built in the 13thC to bring water into the city and they have remained largely unchanged since then. Visitors first see an exhibition and video before being taken on a guided tour of the passages.

ARCHITECTURAL ANTIQUES
Tobys (SALVO) is at Station House, Station Road, Exminster, a village about 1.6km (1 mile) from Exeter on the A379 to Dawlish. It has a large stock of architectural antiques, sanitary ware, fireplaces, and reclaimed building materials. The shop is open 7 days a week, including Bank Holidays.

BOOKS
The city offers two antiquarian bookshops. The first is **Exeter Rare Books** (ABA, PBFA) at Guildhall Shopping Centre, which sells antiquarian, rare, second-hand books. It also specializes in West Country books. The other, **Isabelline Books** on Victoria Park Road, has a small stock of antiquarian books on ornithology. They are only open by appointment – ring 01392 201296.

EPHEMERA
Lisa Cox Music (ABA) on Old Tiverton Road has a large stock of antiquarian music, pictures, ephemera, and autographs. The shop is open by appointment only – ring 01392 255776.

FURNITURE
The first of the furniture dealers, **Fagins Antiques**, is located at the Old Whiteways Cider Factory in the village of Hele. Hele is situated about 10km (6 miles) north of Exeter just off the B3181, which runs alongside the M5 in this area. It has a large stock of stripped pine, dark wood, general antiques, china, and architectural antiques. **McBains Antiques** (LAPADA), at Exeter Airport Industrial Estate, also has a large stock of furniture including Georgian, Victorian, and Edwardian with a selection of French and Continental furniture. It is open Monday–Saturday (until 1pm on Saturday). **Tredantiques** is adjacent to Exeter Airport. It sells good-quality furniture and decorative items and is open from Monday–Friday and Saturday by appointment (tel: 01392 447082). **A E Wakeman and Sons Ltd** is situated about 14.5km (9 miles) from Exeter on the A30 to Okehampton, and it specializes in 19thC furniture. The address is Newhouse Farm, Tedburn St Mary, and it is open Monday–Friday from 8.30am.

GENERAL ANTIQUES
Brook Antiques is situated at The Courtyard, Thorndon House, Rewe, which is a small village about 8.5km (5 miles) from Exeter on the northbound A396. It has a large range of general antiques and furniture and is open 7 days a week. Back in the centre of Exeter, **Eclectique** is at 26–27 Commercial Road, The Quay. The stock includes antique and painted furniture, ceramics, lamps, objets d'art, and collectables. Located about 5km (3 miles) south-east of Exeter on the B3181, **Broadclyst** is the home of Foxglove Antiques and Interiors in Clystia House. It has a small stock of general antiques and furniture. Lastly, **Pennies Antiques** at Unit 2, Wessex Estate, Station Road, St David's, has a large stock of general antiques and second-hand furniture. It is open 7 days a week (until 4pm on Sundays).

JEWELLERY
Mortimers of Queen Street has a large selection of antique jewellery, watches, clocks, and silver. **Victoriana Antiques and Kents Jewellers** on Sidwell Street sells jewellery and silver, general antiques, and porcelain. It is closed Wednesdays and Sundays.

LIGHTING
Exeter Antique Lighting, in Cellar 15, The Quay, has a large stock of antique lighting, fireplaces, and iron beds. It is open by appointment only – ring 01392 490848.

ANTIQUES CENTRES

The city's antiques centres are all located on the Quay. The first, **Exeter's Antiques Centre**, has 21 dealers selling general antiques, collectables, books, postcards, jewellery, tools, and cameras. The centre is open 7 days a week. **Phantique** has nine dealers selling general antiques and collectables, prints, and books. **The Quay Gallery Antiques Emporium** at 43 The Quay, has a large stock of fine mahogany and oak furniture, maritime, porcelain, silver, glass, paintings, prints, general antiques, antiquities, and clocks. It is open 7 days a week. With 60 dealers, the largest antiques centre in Exeter is definitely the **Quay Centre**. Stock includes furniture, collectables, ephemera, Exeter silver, Torquay ware, studio pottery, jewellery, and tools. The centre is open for business 7 days a week.

ANTIQUES FAIRS

Westpoint Antiques Fairs is held bi-monthly at the Westpoint Exhibiton Centre, at the Devon County Showground, Clyst St Mary, about 5km (3 miles) from Exeter. It has about 500 stands and is organized by **Devon County Antiques Fairs**. The same organizers also hold a regular fair at the Exeter Livestock Market. This takes place almost monthly but there are breaks in the summer and in the New Year.

AUCTION HOUSES

Exeter has two auction houses, which are both well-known names in the antiques trade. The first, **Bearne's** (SOFAA), located at St Edmund's Court, Okehampton Street, has a fortnightly general sale on Tuesdays with viewing on Saturday morning and all day Monday. It also has specialist sales three times a year.

The city's other saleroom is **Phillips International Auctioneers & Valuers**, Alphin Brook Road, Alphington. They are the regional office for the London auction house.

▶ Leave Exeter on the A377, then at the junction with the A30 turn left until you reach junction 31 of the M5. Turn right at this junction onto the A38. Follow that road for about 3.2km (2 miles) until it forks. Take the left-hand fork, the A380, to reach Newton Abbot.

NEWTON ABBOT

The town got its name because, in the 13thC, it was a new town that belonged to the Abbot of Torre Abbey. In the 19thC the railways brought great prosperity to the town. As well as having railway workshops, the town also became a very busy centre for the surrounding area. Now the workshops have gone but the town still remains a good centre for visitors to Dartmoor to the north or the coastal towns to the south.

COLLECTABLES

Little Shop Antiques in East Street has collectables and ephemera. It is open Monday–Wednesday 10am–3pm and 10am–12 noon Saturday.

FURNITURE

Bonstow and Crawshay Antiques are located halfway between Newton Abbot and Torquay on the A380 at 12a Torquay Road, Kingskerswell. The stock is pre-1830 period English furniture and decorative items and it is closed on Tuesdays and Sundays.

GENERAL ANTIQUES

Newton Abbot boasts four general antiques shops. The first is **The Attic** on Union Street, which has a large selection of general antiques and small furniture. It is closed Monday, Thursday, and Sunday. **The Jolly Roger** at 4 Western Units, Pottery Road, also has a large stock of general and nautical antiques. It is open Monday–Friday until 4pm and Saturday 9am–12 noon but telephone first (01626 835105). Another large stock of general antiques, furniture, and jewellery can be found at **St Leonards Antiques and Craft Centre**, St Leonards, Wolborough Street. They are open 7 days a week. The last of the general antiques shops is **Tobys** (SALVO) in Brunel Road, which also has a shop near Exeter selling architectural antiques. Here in Newton Abbot there is a large stock of general antiques as well as reclaimed material.

ANTIQUES CENTRES

The town's only antiques centre is **Newton Abbot Antique Centre** on East Street. It has 40 dealers selling a large range of general antiques, collectables, Staffordshire figures, Victorian furniture, jewellery, pottery, and porcelain. It is open on Tuesdays 9am–3pm.

ANTIQUES FAIRS

Hyson Fairs Ltd hold a number of specialist fairs at the Tote Hall, Newton Abbot Racecourse. These include Art Deco, glass, ephemera, and decorative antiques fairs.

AUCTION HOUSES

Michael J Bowman of Haccombe House, Netherton, has seven sales a year of antiques and effects. They are held at 2pm on Saturdays at Chudleigh Town Hall with viewing the previous day from 4.30–8.30pm. They also provide free valuations at the same venue on Mondays from 2–5pm, otherwise by appointment – ring 01626 872890.

▶ Leave the town following the signs for Torquay. This will bring you to the A380 just outside Newton Abbot. Stay on this road for about 5km (3 miles) then take the A3022 to Torquay.

TORQUAY

Virtually synonymous with South Devon, Torquay is famous for its palms, sandy beaches, and luxury hotels and apartments. The town got its name from the 12thC Torre Abbey and a quay that the monks built. Now all that remains of the abbey are some ruins set in a park on the seafront. Torquay Museum, at 529 Babbacombe Road, was built in 1876 and is reputed to be Devon's oldest museum. Its displays include an Agatha Christie Exhibition, the Devon and Dorset Regimental Museum, and archaeological exhibits from Kents Cavern where evidence of human habitation in the area dates back to the Stone Age, 40,000 years ago. The museum recreates a late 19th/early 20thC Devon kitchen and it also has a good exhibition of Victoriana and World War II memorabilia.

BOOKS

The town's only antiquarian bookshop is **West Country Old Books** (PBFA) on Perinville Road. It has a small stock of antiquarian and good-quality second-hand books and specializes in topography and literature. It is open by appointment only – ring 01803 322712.

GENERAL ANTIQUES

Torquay's remaining antiques shops all have general stock. The first is **Curiosity Corner** at Foxlands Walk Street, Marychurch, which has a large stock of antique and modern jewellery, glass, rocking horses, paintings, china, and furniture. It is open Tuesday–Saturday. **The Old Cop Shop** is on Castle Lane while **Redwood Antiques** is situated on South Street (it is open until 4pm). Lastly, **Tobys** (SALVO) has branches near Exeter and also in Newton Abbot. In Newton Abbot its address is Torre Station, Newton Road, and it has a large

stock of general antiques, furniture, architectural antiques, and gifts. It is open 7 days a week, including Bank Holidays.

AUCTION HOUSES

The town's only auction house, **West of England Auctions** on Warren Road has sales every three weeks on Mondays at 11am. Viewing takes place on Saturdays 9am–12 noon, Sundays 2–6pm and on the day of sale 9–11am.

▶ Follow the coast road south to reach the next stop, Paignton, about 1.6km (1 mile) away.

PAIGNTON

Situated in the centre of Torbay, Paignton is another popular holiday resort with beautiful beaches. The steam railway from Paignton to Kingswear and Dartmouth is a very popular attraction for visitors.

BOOKS

The Pocket Bookshop on Winner Street has a large stock of antiquarian, second-hand, and out-of-print books. It is closed on Mondays in winter.

GENERAL ANTIQUES

Paignton's only antiques shop is **Hyde Road Antiques** at 23 Hyde Road. It has a large stock of general antiques and collectables.

▶ Take the main road out of Paignton following the signs for Totnes, which is 6.5km (4 miles) away. Less than 1.6km (1 mile) from Paignton town centre take the A385 direct to Totnes.

TOTNES

The ancient town of Totnes stands on a hill above the River Dart and was first settled in Saxon times. In the Middle Ages, when the wool trade was important, the town prospered. At that time Totnes was a walled town but just two gateways remain today. The High Street contains a number of 16th–18thC houses, among which is the Tudor Merchant's House, at 43 High Street, where there is a themed costume exhibition including items from the mid-18thC onwards.

BOOKS

Pedlar's Pack Books (PBFA) of 4 The Plains sells antiquarian, second-hand, rare, and modern books. It specializes in art and history books. It is open 7 days a week in the summer (until 4pm on Sundays) but is closed Sundays in winter.

COLLECTABLES

In the centre of Totnes, The Exchange on the High Street sells collectables including books, printed ephemera, tools, brass, African collectables, china, stamps, toys, and much more.

FURNITURE

Past and Present James Sturges Antiques is located on the High Street, The Narrows. The shop has a small stock of Victorian, Georgian, and early 20thC furniture as well as small items. Nearby Vine Antiques has a large stock of Victorian furniture, brass, copper, and general antiques. It is closed on Mondays during the winter months.

GENERAL ANTIQUES

There are just two general antiques dealers in Totnes. The first is Bogan House Antiques on the High Street, selling a wide range including silver, wood, brass, glass, and Japanese woodblock prints. The shop is open on Tuesdays, Fridays, and Saturdays (from 12 noon on Tuesdays). The other one is Rotherfold Antiques at 2 Rotherfold, which

sells interesting antiques, ceramics, pictures, rugs, furniture, lights, objets d'art, and fabrics. It is closed on Thursday afternoons and Sundays.

▶ Take the A384 from Totnes to its junction with the A38, where you should turn right to reach Ashburton, which is about 10km (6 miles) from the junction.

ASHBURTON

Standing within the boundaries of the Dartmoor National Park, the historic town of Ashburton was the centre of the local wool trade. It was also a Stannary town – the centre for weighing and stamping tin for the tin mines on Dartmoor. The 15thC parish church of St Andrews has several notable features including two Italian brass candelabras from the 18thC and an oak chest dating from 1482.

BOOKS

The Dartmoor Bookshop (PBFA) at 2 Kingsbridge Lane has a large stock of antiquarian, second-hand, rare, and out-of-print books.

▶ ▶ BUCKFAST ABBEY

If you have time on your way to or from Ashburton, stop at Buckfastleigh (at the junction of the A384 from Totnes and the A38 to Ashburton), to visit Buckfast Abbey. With almost half a million visitors a year, Buckfast Abbey is one of the most popular attractions in the West Country. It was founded in 1018 by Benedictine monks, but the site of the original building is uncertain. The Abbey's fortunes improved when it was taken over and rebuilt by the Cistercians in 1147. During Medieval times it prospered by trading in wool until, in the 15thC, it became a major landowner. In the 16thC came the Dissolution of the Monasteries and Buckfast Abbey was closed in 1539. All of the Abbey's land went to the King and some was sold. The Abbey buildings were stripped of everything of value and left to decay.

Little happened until the 1800 when the site was bought by Samuel Berry who demolished all the ruins, except the Abbot's Tower and the 12thC undercroft, to build a mansion. The property was bought and sold several times until 1872 when Dr James Gale bought it. In 1882 he wanted to sell it to a monastic order so that it

would revert to its original purpose. Within six weeks of an advertisement appearing in a Catholic newspaper, monks were again making Buckfast Abbey their home. Over the following years the monks uncovered the original foundations and rebuilt what was, effectively, a 12thC Cistercian abbey and restored the two surviving buildings.

The beautiful Abbey Church has many things in it worth seeing: stained glass windows made in the Abbey's own workshops and marble mosaic pavements made with marble taken from Greek and Roman buildings. Most striking of all, the *Corona Lucis* (the light of the world), is a huge circular candelabra hanging above the High Altar. There are many other notable and beautiful features in the church and so it is well worth a visit.

The Abbey has good facilities for visitors including an audio-visual exhibition, a gift shop, restaurant, bookshop, and a monastic produce shop selling a wide range of stock from candles to chocolate, perfume to pottery, beer to biscuits. For more information visit the website – www.buckfast.org.uk or ring 01364 645500.

ARCHITECTURAL ANTIQUES

Ashburton Antiques at The Great Hall, North Street, specializes in marble fireplaces, furniture, carpets, lighting, and garden statuary. It is open from 8am during the week and until 1pm on Saturdays.

FURNITURE

Specialist furniture dealers, Kessler Ford Antiques, on North Street, has a selection of 17th and 18thC English oak and mahogany furniture. It is open on Tuesdays and Thursday–Saturday, or by appointment – ring 01364 654310.

GENERAL ANTIQUES

There are two general antiques shops in Ashburton, both on North Street. The first, Mo Logan Antiques, has a range of stock including small furniture, decorative items, textiles, and Oriental rugs. It is open Tuesdays and Thursday–Saturday until 4pm. The other, Moor Antiques, sells 18th and 19thC furniture, silver, glass, porcelain, clocks, and jewellery. On Wednesdays it is open until 1pm.

AUCTION HOUSES

Rendells at Stonepark is the only auctioneer in the town. It holds monthly antiques sales on Thursdays and Fridays with viewing on Tuesday 10am–7pm and Wednesday 10am–5pm.

▶ If you have time, it is worth stopping at Buckfast Abbey (see box, below left). Whether or not you stop there, you should take the A38 to Plympton, which is on the outskirts of Plymouth.

PLYMPTON

This town is now almost part of the Plymouth conurbation. It is just 3.2km (2 miles) from the Dartmoor Wildlife Park and only 10km (6 miles) from Dartmoor. The ruins of the motte of Plympton Castle are worth a look, and in the summer months you can visit Saltram House, a beautiful Georgian mansion.

ARCHITECTURAL ANTIQUES

Plympton Reclamation and Architectural Salvage Ltd (SALVO) in Huxley Close, Newnham Industrial Estate, has architectural antiques including granite and slate flooring. It is open all week, including Sunday mornings.

AUCTION HOUSES

Eldreds Auctioneers and Valuers on Ridge Park

Road have fortnightly sales of 19th and 20thC items, with specialist sales every six to eight weeks.

PLYMOUTH

The city of Plymouth is renowned for its maritime history. It was from here that the world-famous Elizabethan captains – Sir Francis Drake, Sir Walter Raleigh, Sir Richard Hawkins, and Sir Martin Frobisher – sailed forth in search of treasure and Spanish galleons. It is also the home of the Royal Navy's Devonport Dockyard, which was built at the end of the 17thC.

Much of historic Plymouth was destroyed in the bombing raids of World War II but some of the old town survives, particularly around the harbour. There are numerous places of interest to visit. The Plymouth Dome on the Hoe, where Sir Francis Drake famously played bowls, recounts the history of the city from Elizabethan times to World War II. There is also the Merchant's House at 33 St Andrew's Street. This 18thC building contains a local history museum.

There are also cruises on the River Tamar or sea trips to the River Yealm. If you want panoramic views of the city go to the Hoe and visit the 17thC fortress, the Royal Citadel, and view the waterfront from the ramparts. Also on the Hoe, Smeaton's Tower, an 18thC lighthouse, was originally 22.5km (14 miles) out to sea but has been rebuilt on dry land. It gives panoramic views across the city and surrounding countryside.

ARCHITECTURAL ANTIQUES

Grosvenor Chambers Restoration on Rendle Street has a large stock of general architectural antiques.

BOOKS

Frederick Harrison on Bridwell Road, Weston Mill, has a large selection of antiquarian, rare, and second-hand books, particularly on diving,

Dartmoor, and local topography. It is open by appointment only – ring 01752 365595.

COLLECTABLES

Skwirrels on Beauchamp Road has a varied stock of old, new, and reproduction general collectables as well as ceramics, glassware, prints, lace, linen, general antiques, and toys. Woodford Antiques & Collectables on New Street, The Barbican, sells ceramics, kitchenware, general antiques, and Torquay pottery. It is open 7 days a week (from 1pm on Sundays).

FINE ART

Michael Wood Fine Art of Southside Ope, The Barbican, has 1850 to present-day oils, watercolours, original prints, sculptures, and ceramics.

FIREPLACES

If you are looking for fireplaces or associated antiques, this is the shop for you. The Antique Fireplace Centre on Molesworth Road, Stoke, has a large stock of 18th–20thC fireplaces, fire irons, spark guards, overmantels, fenders, and helmet coal skuttles.

FURNITURE

Annterior Antiques on Molesworth Road, Stoke, specializes in 19th–early 20thC country furniture, stripped pine, and small accessories.

GENERAL ANTIQUES

Of the five dealers in general antiques in Plymouth, three of them are located in the Stoke area of the city. One of the exceptions is Anita's Antiques on New Street, which has a large stock of furniture, silver, china, jewellery, lighting, glass, clocks, barometers, and general antiques. During May–September the shop opens on Sundays. The other exception is Parade Antiques at The Parade, The Barbican. This shop has a large stock of general antiques and militaria, and is open 7 days a week. The first of the Stoke dealers is C Garreta at Molesworth Road, which sells general antiques and is open Tuesday and Wednesday 2–5pm and Thursday–Saturday 12 noon–5pm. Nearby Sunshine Antiques has a small stock of antique furniture, decorative items, and collectables. Opening times are Friday and Saturday, 10am–5pm or by appointment – ring 01752 607271. Close by, Brian Taylor Antiques has a good range of clocks, mechanical music, brass, copper, and Oriental country furniture.

ANTIQUES CENTRES

The largest of Plymouth's two antiques centres is the Barbican Antique Centre on Vauxhall Street. It has 60 dealers selling silver, jewellery, porcelain, glass, pictures, furniture, and collectables. In contrast New Street Antique and Craft Centre, on New Street, The Barbican, has only 13 dealers but still has a large stock of general collectables, books, stamps, postcards, and craft materials. It is open 7 days a week during the holiday season.

AUCTION HOUSES

There are two auctioneers in Plymouth. Eric Distin Auctioneers & Chartered Surveyors (RICS), 72 Mutley Plain has fortnightly sales of antiques and collectables on Saturdays at 10.30am with viewing Friday afternoon or before the sale. It also has monthly specialist coins and stamps sales on the second Monday of each month. The other saleroom is G S Shobrook and Co, incorporating Fieldens (RICS), at 20 Western Approach. It has monthly sales of antiques and collectables on a Wednesday at 1.30pm with viewing on Tuesday 9am–5pm or by appointment – ring 01752 663341. There is also a weekly general household sale on a Wednesday at 10am, also with viewing Tuesday 9am–5pm. The office is open weekdays and Saturday mornings.

▶ Take the A386 northwards from the centre of Plymouth and follow it for about 19.25km (12 miles) until it arrives in Tavistock.

TAVISTOCK

Standing on the River Tavy, Tavistock is nowadays a quiet country town ideally situated for exploring Dartmoor. It grew up around a great 12thC Benedictine abbey, which was later destroyed during the famous Dissolution of the Monasteries. The town became very prosperous as a woollen centre and also as a Stannary town, an administrative centre for copper-mining, as one of the largest copper mines in the world is situated nearby.

BOOKS

Tavistock has three bookshops. The first, Books and Antiques Too at The Old Wine Centre, Russell Street, has a mixture of books, furniture, and smalls and is open Tuesday–Saturday. J J Books and Antiques, on Mount Tavy Road, sells antiquarian books and smalls and is closed Tuesdays, Wednesday afternoons, and Sundays. The last of the bookshops is Tavistock Books at 5 Pepper Street, where the stock includes antiquarian, second-hand, and out-of-print books and the speciality is books on the history of ideas. Open Tuesdays and Thursday–Saturday.

FURNITURE

Tanglewood at 7 Pixon Lane, Crelake Industrial Estate, has a large stock, mainly furniture.

GENERAL ANTIQUES

The first of Tavistock's two general dealers is Archways of Court Gate, Bedford Square. The shop has a medium-sized stock of general antiques, small items, and clocks. It is open Tuesday, Wednesday, Friday, and Saturday until 4pm. The second is C J Poole, also at 7 Pixon Lane, Crelake Industrial Estate, who has general antiques, furniture, and architectural antiques. It is open 7 days a week (from 2pm on Sunday).

AUCTION HOUSES

The town also has two auctioneers. Robin A Fenner and Co are located at the Stannary Gallery, Drake Road. Each year they have eight antiques sales as well as three of vintage toys and models, one of books and ephemera, and one of postcards and cigarette cards. Sales take place on Mondays at 11am with viewing Friday–Sunday 12 noon–5pm. The other auction house is Ward and Chowen Auction Rooms in Market Road. It has fortnightly sales of household items on Thursdays at 10am with viewing on Wednesday 1–6pm. It also holds quarterly antiques sales. The office opens at 8.30am.

▶ Follow the A386 from Tavistock to the next town, Okehampton, which is a distance of about 21km (13 miles).

OKEHAMPTON

There has been a settlement at Okehampton since the Iron Age although the present town was founded in the 11thC by a Norman knight, Baldwin de Brionne. There are still substantial ruins of a Norman castle, reputed to have been one of the strongest in the country.

The town's 15thC church was destroyed by fire in 1842 and its Victorian replacement has windows designed by William Morris. Two of the highest tors on Dartmoor, High Willhays and Yes Tor, lie within 8.5km (5 miles) of the town.

FURNITURE

The town's only specialist furniture dealer, Alan Jones Antiques is situated at Fatherford Farm. It has a large range of furniture up to the Edwardian period. The shop opens at 8.30am.

GENERAL ANTIQUES

Okehampton's only other dealer, Tarka Antiques at Red Lion Yard also has a large stock, this time of traditional upholstery, porcelain, glass, lighting, furniture, Lloyd Loom, and decorative items. It is open all week apart from Wednesday and Sunday.

▶ Take the B3215 eastbound from Okehampton. After about 6.5km (4 miles) it will join the A3072, which you should follow to the village of Copplestone at the junction with the A377. Then turn right to Crediton.

CREDITON

This town was the birthplace of St Boniface in AD 674. Because of this, Crediton was the seat of the first Bishop of Devon and Cornwall.

CLOCKS & BAROMETERS

Specialist dealers Musgrave Bickford Antiques, at 15 East Street, sells clocks, barometers, and small furniture and is open by appointment only – ring 01363 775042.

MARINE ANTIQUES

Woods Emporium on Exeter Road is another specialist dealer, with a large stock of marine

▶ ▶ MORWELLHAM AND TAMAR VALLEY

Situated about 6.5km (4 miles) from Tavistock (follow the A390 westbound then take the B3257 at Gullworthy), this AA award-winning "living history" village is well worth a detour to visit before going on to Okehampton.

There is a train ride into a real copper mine with displays of mining techniques and visible seams of copper. (Please note: this ride is not suitable for anyone who suffers from claustrophobia.) There are also rides on wagonettes pulled by Shire horses as well as video shows, demonstrations, and activities.

All the staff wear 19thC costume and visitors can try on replica period costumes in the Limeburners Cottage. There is a restaurant in the 16thC Ship Inn.

antiques. They also have another shop at 32 Exeter Road, with Government surplus navy equipment. Both shops are open until 3.30pm on Sundays.

▶ Take the A3072 for about 14.5km (9 miles). When it joins the A396 take that road and follow it, northbound, for approximately 6.5km (4 miles) to arrive in Tiverton.

TIVERTON

This is another town that achieved prosperity from the Medieval wool trade. The local church, St Peter's, was enlarged in the 15th–16thC and it was wool trade money that paid for the alterations. The town's pink sandstone castle was built in the 12thC but it is now in ruins. In spite of this, it is the home of the town's excellent museum. The displays include a Civil War armoury as well as a small but interesting Napoleonic exhibition.

FURNITURE
Bygone Days Antiques of Gold Street has a large stock of James II–Edwardian furniture. It is open every day except Thursdays and Sundays, and closes at 4pm on Saturdays.

GENERAL ANTIQUES
The town's other dealer, **Judith Christie**, is also found on Gold Street. This shop has a medium-sized stock of general antiques, porcelain, and glass. It is open Tuesday, Friday, and Saturday.

▶ Although South Molton is not part of the tour it is well worth visiting before returning home. From Tiverton take the A361 for about 21km (13 miles) and you will arrive in South Molton.

SOUTH MOLTON

Because it was ideally situated close to iron and copper mines, the town enjoyed considerable prosperity from Medieval times until the 19thC. It was a woollen trade centre and also on the main coach road to Barnstaple. As these industries died out, so it became a quiet rural town. The award-winning South Molton and District Museum recounts the history of

the area through its excellent displays. As well as a unique collection of pewter, the museum has two fire engines, one from 1736 and the other from 1886, and two original charters. The first charter, from Elizabeth I, is dated 9th May 1590 and the second, from Charles II, is dated 24th December 1684.

BOOKS
South Molton's only antiquarian bookseller, **R M Young Bookseller**, is on Broad Street. It has a very large stock of antiquarian, second-hand, rare, and out-of-print books and specializes in countryside topics.

FURNITURE
C R Boumphrey at Finehay, Mariansleigh, sells 17th and 18thC furniture and is open by appointment only – ring 01769 550419.

GENERAL ANTIQUES
The town has three general dealers. The first, **The Dragon** at George Arcade, Broad Street, sells general antiques, furniture, books, and collectables. **Memory Lane Antiques**, on East Street, has furniture, smalls, china, silver, and glass and is closed Wednesday afternoons and Sundays. The last of the general dealers is **Snapdragon** on South Street. This shop has a medium-sized stock of general antiques, pine furniture, books, farming bygones, and kitchenware.

Kent is famous for its country houses and gardens, such as Knole House and Leeds Castle. Combe Bank House is shown on the 18thC blue-and-white plate above. The area also has something to offer the literary visitor. Charles Dickens' house can be visited at Gads Hill, Rochester and this area was used as a setting for his book *Great Expectations*.

The South Coast is jewelled with seaside towns and villages packed with antique shops. Search out items to buy that have a particular link to the area, such as Tunbridge ware from Tunbridge Wells or the distinctive Rye pottery vase – you can see a collection of this in the Rye Castle Museum. Alternatively, look for topical souvenirs such as the postcard illustrating the famous Royal Pavilion at Brighton, or other seaside trinkets.

This area is a treat for those with a nautical or military bent. It has museums dedicated to Britain's great seafaring tradition – from the 16thC *Mary Rose* to *HMS Victory* – as well as the submarines of the 20thC. You can also visit the Tudor House Museum, which is a restored late 15thC house as shown in the Goss model below.

H.M.H.S. ANGLIA

E.9.

Evidence of ancient Roman settlers remains at the site of Rockbourne Roman villa. A visit to the magnificent Stonehenge monoliths should not be missed. This route has museums serving a range of interests, from old seafaring relics at the Royal National Lifeboat Museum to modern warfare at the Tank Museum. Within easy reach of the coast, you can relax at the quintessential British resort of Bournemouth. You may want to buy some Poole pottery, such as the vase illustrated, as a souvenir.

Many of us have happy childhood memories of holidays on the beaches of Devon, watching Punch and Judy shows. Visits to the most south-westerly areas of Devon often include day trips into Cornwall as well. Torquay is probably the most famous of the South Devon resorts, and is also home to the Aller Vale pottery. Further east, Honiton is famous for its lace. If you visit Allhallows Museum you can see lace from different periods as well as view demonstrations of the various techniques.

While you are on this tour, look out for the famous Bristol Blue and Nailsea Glass, which is still being made today. Bath is one of the jewels of the south-west and, as such, has a large number of places of interest. Two of the more unusual are the Postal Museum and the American Museum in Britain. The latter has a stunning collection of quilts. While you are visiting Warminster, why not see the ruins of Fontwell Abbey, which is situated 13km (8 miles) south of the town. This enormous folly was built in the early 1800s – it is pictured on the blue-and-white plate below.

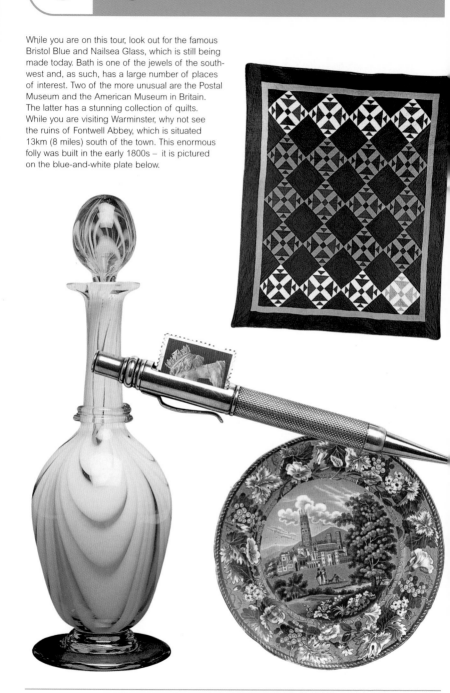

You cannot visit London without going to the world-famous antiques market in and around Portobello Road on Saturday. You can buy everything there, from furniture to small collectables. You will also find all kinds of needlework, like the slippers or sampler shown above, as well as glass, porcelain, pictures, and much more. Nearby Kensington Church Street also offers a good selection of antiques but it is particularly famous for its fine pottery and porcelain dealers.

Camden Passage, near the Angel tube station in Islington, is another of London's renowned antiques markets. It offers a vast selection of antiques and collectables, like Lalique glass and Arts & Crafts silver, but there is a particular emphasis on decorative pieces like this Chinoiserie-style cabinet.

DEVIZES ▶ MELKSHAM ▶ BRADFORD-ON-AVON ▶ WESTBURY ▶ WARMINSTER ▶
FROME ▶ RADSTOCK ▶ MIDSOMER NORTON ▶ SHEPTON MALLET ▶ WELLS ▶
CHEDDAR ▶ AXBRIDGE ▶ WESTON-SUPER-MARE ▶ CLEVEDON ▶ BRISTOL ▶ BATH ▶
CORSHAM ▶ CHIPPENHAM

Somerset and Wiltshire have a vast range of antiques shops. Bath and Bristol, in particular, have an enormous selection. This tour also has an above average number of shops selling architectural antiques: Somerset and Wiltshire seem to be the counties to visit when restoring an old house.

Outside the towns and cities both counties are predominantly agricultural, providing a landscape of typically English fields, hedges, and drystone walls. Most of the towns are small, some still with weekly markets, and the cities all have historic buildings from a long and varied past. The basis of the economy for the two counties over the centuries has largely been based on wool. However, Wiltshire is noted as a pig-rearing county – to such an extent that there is a statue of a bronze pig in Calne, which is near Devizes.

Wiltshire is dominated by Salisbury Plain in the centre of the county, which covers 775 sq km (300 sq miles). The army has used Salisbury Plain for exercises since the early Napoleonic Wars and this continues today. Perhaps surprisingly, this has had some positive benefits for conservation. Rare species of flora and fauna have been found in the areas the army use.

Websites

www.bristol-cathedral.co.uk
Take a look at Bristol Cathedral's website and you will see from the pictures of the exterior and interior why it is well worth a visit.

www.bristol-city.gov.uk
Bristol City Council's website gives useful information for both visitors and residents.

www.r-cube.co.uk/fox-talbot
Before you visit the Fox-Talbot Museum in Lacock, why not find out more about the man and his work?

www.longleat.co.uk
Longleat House has an enormous amount to see and do. Here you can find out more about the full range of attractions in the house and grounds.

www.romanbaths.co.uk
Bath's most famous attraction is probably its Roman Baths. Learn more about them and their history here.

www.henry-aldridge.co.uk
Check out dates and viewing times of sales at this long-established auction room.

Tourist Information Centres

Bath Abbey Churchyard.
Tel: 01225 477101

Bristol Wildscreen Walk, Harbourside.
Tel: 0117 926 0767

Cheddar The Gorge. Tel: 01934 744071

Devizes Cromwell House, Market Place.
Tel: 01380 729408

Frome The Round Tower, Justice Lane.
Tel: 01373 467271

Shepton Mallet 70 High Street.
Tel: 01749 345258

Westbury The Library, Edward Street.
Tel: 01373 827158

Weston-super-Mare Beach Lawns.
Tel: 01934 888800

DEVIZES

Set in the heart of rich farming country, Devizes is on the Kennet and Avon Canal. Here the canal rises through 29 locks. The Devizes Museum in Long Street is the home for the Wiltshire Archaeological and Natural History Society's collections. Its exhibitions cover the county's history from its prehistoric stone circles to recent agricultural and social history.

FURNITURE

Julia's, in the High Street, has antique, second-hand, and new pine furniture as well as bric-a-brac. It is open Tuesdays and Thursday–Saturday until 4pm. In Northgate Street, St Mary's Chapel Antiques (BABAADA) sells original painted and country furniture, garden antiques, and accessories. It closes Wednesdays and Sundays.

GENERAL ANTIQUES

Also in Northgate Street, **Margaret Mead Antiques** has general antiques; Georgian, Edwardian, and Victorian furniture; clocks; and china. It is open Tuesdays and Thursday–Saturday.

AUCTION HOUSES

The first of the town's two auctioneers is **Henry Aldridge & Son**, located in Bath Road Business Park, Bath Road. They have two maritime sales a year on Saturdays at 12 noon, furniture sales on alternate Saturdays at 10am, and six fine furniture sales a year also on Saturdays at 10am. The office is open until 4pm. In New Park Street, **Devizes Auction Centre** has weekly sales on Tuesdays at 10am with viewing on Mondays 4–7pm. Again, the office is open until 4pm.

▶ Take the A365 direct to Melksham, which is a distance of about 11.25km (7 miles).

MELKSHAM

Once a stop on the coaching road to Bath, this town has several fine 18thC inns. Melksham's oldest houses are situated in Canon Square and Church Walk, many of which date back to the 16th and 17thC.

FURNITURE

Located in Bath Road, in the village of Atworth just 5km (3 miles) from Melksham, **Peter Campbell Antiques** (BABAADA) has country furniture and decorative items. **Dann Antiques Ltd** (BABAADA), in New Broughton Road, has English mahogany furniture and furniture accessories. It is open at 8.30am on weekdays and until 1pm on Saturdays. In the heart of the town, **Jaffray Antiques** (BABAADA), in the Market Place, has a wide selection of 18th and 19thC furniture including allboys, desks, bamboo, dining tables, and chests of drawers; also linen presses, Staffordshire, and metalware.

GENERAL ANTIQUES
King Street Curios, unsurprisingly in King Street, has a large stock of general antiques and collectables. Almost next door, **Polly's Parlour** also has a large selection of general antiques, collectables, and decorative items. It is open Monday–Saturday and Bank Holidays.

> Travel for 10km (6 miles) on the B3107 to Bradford-on-Avon.

Lacock
Alternatively, you could take the opportunity to visit the National Trust Village of Lacock (see below), which is about 5km (3 miles) north of Melksham just off the A350. Afterwards, return to Melksham and then follow the directions to Bradford-on-Avon.

BRADFORD-ON-AVON

The next town, Bradford-on-Avon, was mentioned in the *Domesday Book* but its history goes back before the Norman invasion. As proof of this, a Saxon chapel was discovered here in the 1850s. The local vicar, Canon William Jones, noticed that some cottages under repair made a curious cruciform shape. Then the workmen discovered two carved angels, so confirming the Canon's suspicions that the cottages were, in fact, a Saxon church. Adjoining cottages were demolished in the 1870s

making the church clearly recognizable. It is one of the most complete Saxon churches in the country.

BOOKS
Roundabout Shop in Silver Street has literally thousands of antiquarian books, literature, and modern first editions especially on sports, art, history, travel, and military. It also has prints of most subjects, but particularly topographical, costumes, and period and it is open 7 days a week (although out of season it does close on Wednesday afternoons).

FURNITURE
Audley House Antiques (BABAADA), Wooley Street, has a large range of Victorian and Edwardian furniture together with silver, pictures, and porcelain. **Avon Antiques** (BADA) in Market Street has a wide selection of 17th–mid-19thC English furniture, clocks, barometers, metalwork, needlework, and treen. **No. 32**, which is situated in Silver Street, sells antique pine and collectables and the shop is open Tuesday–Sunday. **Granary Antiques** (BABAADA), which is located in Pound Lane, has an extensive selection of country pine furniture and collectables. It is open 7 days a week.

In Woolley Street, **Mac Humble Antiques** (BADA) has 18th and 19thC furniture as well as needlework, samplers, metalware, and decorative items. **Town & Country Antiques** (BADA, BABAADA) in Market Street has a wide range of fine Georgian and Regency English furniture, tea caddies, and snuff shoes. The shop shuts at 1pm on Saturdays. **Moxhams Antiques** (LAPADA, BABAADA), Silver Street, has a large stock of good 17th–early 19thC mahogany and oak furniture, ceramics, tapestries, and objects.

> Leave Bradford-on-Avon on the A363 southbound. Follow it through Trowbridge until

Pronounced "Laycock", this village has had a prosperous history, first from the Medieval wool trade and then, when that declined, as a stop on the London to Bath coaching road. It was only in the 19thC that it became less popular. The Talbot family, local landowners, refused to allow the railways into the village so development went to nearby towns. Because of this, it still looks like a charming Medieval village, which makes it a favourite not only with tourists but also with film makers. *Pride and Prejudice* and *Emma* are among the many costume dramas shot here.

Lacock Abbey lies at the heart of the village. Founded in the 13thC by the Countess of Salisbury as a nunnery, it became a private house in the mid-16thC during the Dissolution of the Monasteries. Luckily, the house was sympathetically converted from a convent to a private home and many of its original Medieval and Renaissance features were kept.

There is a museum at the Abbey gates that is dedicated to one of its 19thC residents, William Fox Talbot, who was one of the pioneers of photography.

▶ ▶ LONGLEAT HOUSE

This house has been in the Thynne family since it was built in 1580. Said to have been the first magnificent Elizabethan house to be built, it certainly was the first to open its doors and grounds to the public in 1949. It was also the first of the big estates to install a safari park in its grounds and it is still one of the best. The animals have the freedom to roam while it is the visitors who are kept in cages (their cars of course)!

Take a ride on the Safari Boat on the lake where you can feed the sealions and maybe catch a glimpse of two gorillas who live on an island there. They have their own house, complete with a television that the gorillas are said to enjoy watching!

The house itself is a jewel of a building, both compact and elegant. The interior is a treasure house containing furniture, pictures, ceiling paintings, rare books, Victorian kitchens, and much more besides.

There are numerous other attractions in the grounds like the Butterfly Garden, the Maze, Pets Corner, and a Historic Vehicles Exhibition. All this is set in extensive parkland designed by Capability Brown.

---

it meets the A350 where you should turn right. Westbury, which is the next stop on the tour, is approximately 3.2km (2 miles) from the last junction you turned off of.

WESTBURY

Clearly visible for miles on the approach to Westbury from the north, the eerily eye-catching White Horse, cut into the green hillside near the village of Bratton, is perhaps the town's best-known landmark.

FURNITURE

Westbury's only dealer, **Ray Coggins Antiques** in Fore Street, has a large stock of antique, country, and decorative furniture as well as architectural antiques. The shop is open Monday–Thursday.

▶ Continue southwards on the A350 direct to Warminster, which is a distance of about 5km (3 miles).

WARMINSTER

The town's prosperous past as a centre for wool and, later, as a stop on the coaching road is reflected in the local stone houses from the 18th and 19thC and in its 14thC church that contains an organ originally designed for Salisbury Cathedral. With just one exception, all of the town's antiques shop are situated in Silver Street.

FURNITURE

In East Street, **Bishopstrow Antiques** (BABAADA) has 17th and 19thC oak, mahogany, and country furniture as well as small items. **Cassidy Antiques and Restorations** (BABAADA) sells Georgian and Victorian furniture. It shuts at 4pm on Saturdays. **Isabella Antiques** (BABAADA) has 18th and 19thC mahogany furniture with chests of drawers a speciality. **Obelisk Antiques** (LAPADA, BABAADA) has 18th and 19thC French, English, and Continental furniture.

GENERAL ANTIQUES

Choice Antiques has small antiques, the unusual, furniture, and decorative objects.

PICTURES

Giltsoff and Maxwell (BABAADA) sell paintings and furniture.

ANTIQUES CENTRES

The 15 dealers in **Warminster Antique Centre** sell a wide range of antiques and collectable items, including furniture, clocks, models, linens, etc.

▶ Take the A362 for 13km (8 miles) to Frome.

Longleat House

Alternatively, you can stop off about halfway between Warminster and Frome to visit Longleat House (see above). Afterwards, you should continue on the A362 to Frome.

FROME

Much of the centre of the historic market town of Frome (pronounced "Froom") is a conservation area that is aimed at preserving the many Medieval and later buildings. Make sure you take a look at Cheap Street, where a watercourse still runs down the centre.

ARCHITECTURAL ANTIQUES
In Station Approach, **Frome Reclamation** (SALVO) has a large selection of architectural antiques including roofing, flooring, period fireplaces, doors, bathrooms, etc. It opens at 8am.

COLLECTABLES
Steve Vee Bransgrove Collectables of Catherine Hill sells a range of collectables, advertising material, vintage magazines, ephemera, and nostalgia. In the winter the shop is closed on Thursdays, but it is open from 10am–2pm on that day during the summer months.

GENERAL ANTIQUES
Also located in Catherine Hill, the **Green Man Antiques** has an extensive range of 15th–19thC furniture, ceramics, glass, marble, and silks. **Valentine Antiques**, this time in Catherine Street, has a wide selection of furniture, collectables, small items, radios, gramophones, kitchenware, and general antiques.

ANTIQUES CENTRES
The town's only antiques centre, **Antiques and Country Living** in Vallis Way, has four dealers boasting an impressively large range of 18th–19thC pottery and porcelain, Georgian–Edwardian furniture, and books.

AUCTION HOUSES
Cooper and Tanner Chartered Surveyors in The Agricultural Centre, Standerwick, have regular weekly sales of furniture, fine art, and antiques on Wednesday at 10.30am with viewing from 7.30am on the day of the sale.

▶ Take the A362 again, this time for about 13km (8 miles), until you arrive in Radstock.

RADSTOCK
Located on the Roman Fosse Way, Radstock's historic buildings reflect its past life as a Victorian mining and railway town.

FURNITURE
The town's only furniture dealer is **Nott Pine** in Coombend, whose speciality is stripped antique pine furniture.

▶ The next stop of Midsomer Norton actually adjoins Radstock.

MIDSOMER NORTON
This ancient market town's Medieval and later buildings include a 15thC tithe barn that is now being used by the local Catholic Church.

GLASS
Somervale Antiques in Radstock Road is open by appointment only – ring 01761 412686. It has English 18th and 19thC drinking glasses, decanters, cut and coloured, Bristol and Nailsea glass, and scent bottles. The proprietors will meet trains in Bath by arrangement to take people to their shop.

▶ Now take the A367 southward for about 11.25km (7 miles) where it joins the A37. Continue south on the A37 for another 3.2km (2 miles) into the centre of Shepton Mallet.

SHEPTON MALLET
Shepton Mallet is another of the towns in the region whose former prosperity was based on wool.

ARCHITECTURAL ANTIQUES
MJM's in F Block, Anglo Trading Estate in Commercial Road, has general antiques, period bathrooms, architectural antiques, and collectables.

FURNITURE
Parkways Antiques in the High Street has period and Victorian furniture and reproduction pine. It is open until 4pm (1pm on Saturdays) but is closed on Wednesdays and Sundays. About 8.5km (5 miles) south of the town, the village of East Pennard is home to **Pennard House Antiques** (LAPADA, BABAADA), which is open by appointment only – ring 01749 860266. It has a large range of French and English country furniture and decorative items.

GENERAL ANTIQUES
Edward Marnier Antiques in Forum Lane, Bowlish, Shepton Mallet, has 17th–20thC furniture, pictures, mirrors, interesting items, antique rugs, and carpets and is open 7 days a week.

ANTIQUES FAIRS
The three-day **Shepton Mallet Antiques & Collectors Fair** takes place bi-monthly at the Royal Bath & West Showground, which is about 5km (3 miles) to the south of the town on the A371. It usually has around 600 exhibitors housed in four halls as well as outdoor shopping arcades. The event is organized by **DMG Antiques Fairs Ltd**.

▶ Take the A371 for 10km (6 miles) direct to the next stop, Wells.

WELLS

This town is named after the holy wells that were situated here in Saxon times. The present cathedral was started in the late 12thC, and has many beautiful and historic features including a 24-hour dial clock from 1390. The West Front of the cathedral was designed as a sculpture gallery containing 293 Medieval statues, two-thirds of which are life-size. The Bishop's Palace is also a splendid building set within a moat.

The Wells Museum on Cathedral Green has exhibits relating to the Mendip caves, archaeology, geology, mining, samplers, Medieval statuary, and the legendary Witch of Wookey Hole.

ARCHITECTURAL ANTIQUES
Wells Reclamation Company in Coxley has a large range of architectural antiques, bricks, tiles, slates, fireplaces, doors, finials, pews, etc. It opens at 8.30am on weekdays.

BOOKS
In Southover, **Kym Grant Bookseller** is open by appointment only – ring 01749 675618. It has antiquarian and second-hand books, as well as children's annuals and books.

CLOCKS
Bernard G House Longcase Clocks, in the Market Place, has a selection of longcase clocks, barographs, barometers, clocks, telescopes, as well as scientific instruments.

GENERAL ANTIQUES
Alcove Antiques in Priest Row has china, brass, copper, and a range of pine, Victorian, Edwardian, and mahogany furniture. The shop is closed on Wednesdays and Sundays.

AUCTION HOUSES
Wells Auction Rooms in Southover has been established since 1845. It has monthly sales on Wednesdays at 1.30pm with viewing on Tuesday 12 noon–5pm and from 9am on the day of the sale.

▶ Take the A371 westward direct to Cheddar, a distance of about 14.5km (9 miles).

Wookey Hole
Alternatively you can take the opportunity to visit Wookey Hole (see below), which is just 1.6km (1 mile) from Wells off the A371. Afterwards, continue westward on the A371 to Cheddar.

CHEDDAR

The approach to Cheddar on the A371 is quite spectacular. The road begins a gradual descent into the Gorge but, as you get closer, it takes a breathtaking plunge to the valley floor with the cliffs rising to 137m (450ft) above you.

The village of Cheddar is very commercialized but nothing can spoil the exquisite beauty and wonder of the famous Cheddar Caves, which man is said to have inhabited some 10,000 years ago. Visitors to the caves can see a whole range of dramatic and beautiful rock formations including numerous stalagmites and stalagtites.

GENERAL ANTIQUES
There is just one antiques dealer here, **Matthew Bayly Antiques** in The Cliffs. He sells general antiques by appointment only – ring 01934 743990.

▶ Continue on the A371 for about 1.6km (1 mile) to Axbridge.

▶ ▶ WOOKEY HOLE

Wookey Hole is a great cavern carved into a number of chambers by the action of water in the carboniferous limestone. There is evidence that there was human habitation in the cavern between about 250 BC and 450 BC. Above ground, there is a museum and a papermill with an exhibition of handmade paper and another of fairground figures.

AXBRIDGE

Another Medieval wool centre, Axbridge has inherited many historic buildings. The best known is the misnamed King merchant's house and dates from around AD 1500. It now houses a small museum.

GENERAL ANTIQUES

The Old Post House is situated on Turnpike Road, Lower Weare, just 1.6km (1 mile) out of town on the A38 northbound. It has general antiques, country pine furniture, and paintings and the shop is open Tuesday–Saturday.

▶ Turn north onto the A38 for just 1.6km (1 mile) then turn left at Sidcot. After about another 1.6km (1 mile) this will join the A371, which will take you straight to Weston-super-Mare.

WESTON-SUPER-MARE

A popular holiday resort on the Bristol Channel, Weston-super-Mare has two piers, donkey rides, and long sandy beaches. You can actually drive your car onto the southern end of the beach, although you will have to pay a parking charge to do so.

BOOKS

Sterling Books (ABA, PBFA) in Locking Road has a large stock of antiquarian and second-hand books on every subject. It is closed on Thursday afternoons and Sundays.

COLLECTABLES

Collectors Corner, in Jubilee Road, has a range of collectables including Wade, stamps, coins, and pottery.

FURNITURE

Clifton House Furniture, Clifton Road, sells furniture – mainly pine. In Severn Road, Purely Pine sells old English pine furniture.

GENERAL ANTIQUES

Baytree Antiques, located in Severn Road, has a selection of general antiques, collectables, oak, mahogany, satinwood, and 1950s–60s furniture. David Hughes Antiques in Baker Street has a stock of general antiques plus Arts and Crafts and Art Nouveau. Opening hours are Monday and Saturday, 9am–1pm and Tuesday and Friday 2–4pm. Severn Antiques (RADS), again in Severn

Road, also has a variety of general antiques and is open until 4pm on weekdays and until 2pm on Saturdays.

SCIENTIFIC INSTRUMENTS

Richard Twort, in Sand Road, Sand Bay, to the north of the town, is open by appointment only – ring 01934 641900. He sells barographs, thermographs, rain gauges, and all types of meteorological instruments.

ANTIQUES CENTRES

The 27 dealers in Weston Antique Centre, in the High Street, have a selection of general antiques. The centre is open 7 days a week.

▶ Take the A371 out of Weston-super-Mare then, just outside of the town, take the A370 that arrives at the northbound M5 at junction 21. Follow the motorway for 10km (6 miles), before coming off at junction 20 at Clevedon.

CLEVEDON

Also set on the Bristol Channel, this pleasant seaside resort is the burial place of Arthur Hallam whose death inspired the poem *In Memoriam*, by Alfred Lord Tennyson.

BOOKS

Clevedon Books (PBFA) in Copse Road sells antiquarian books, maps and prints, as well as second-hand books. History, science, and technology are the shop's particular specialities and it is open Thursday–Saturday.

COLLECTABLES

The Collector, The Beach, has smalls and collectables including Beatrix Potter figures. It is closed on Thursdays but open from 12 noon on Sundays.

GENERAL ANTIQUES

Located in Hill Road, Nostalgia has a varied range of general antiques including linen, furniture, and china. The shop is open Tuesday–Saturday.

AUCTION HOUSES

Clevedon Salerooms in Herbert Road has monthly sales of Edwardian, Victorian, and post-Victorian furniture on Thursdays at 10am. Viewing takes place on Wednesdays 10am–7.30pm. There are also quarterly fine art sales on Saturdays at 10.30am with viewing on Tuesdays 2–5.30pm and Wednesdays 10am–6.30pm. On Saturdays following sales, the office is open in the morning until 12 noon.

▶ Return to the M5 at junction 20 and continue
north for 14.5km (9 miles) to Junction 18, where
you should come off the motorway and take the
A403 into Bristol.

BRISTOL

Bristol's history as a busy and successful
port stretches back over 800 years.
Initially ships from the city traded with
Europe but it was the trade with the
Americas that brought enormous
prosperity to Bristol. John Cabot left
Bristol in 1497 to discover the Northwest
Passage to the Indies. Instead he arrived
in North America, near Newfoundland.
The Cabot Tower, on Brandon Hill, was
erected in the 19thC to commemorate
his achievement. Just over 50 years after
Cabot set sail, Bristol merchants formed
the Society of Merchant Venturers to
take advantage of trade with the new
colonies. The city supplied the colonies
with the necessities and luxuries
unavailable there and, shamefully, it was
also a major contributor to the slave
trade. In exchange, tobacco, cocoa
beans, and other commodities were
imported into Bristol, forming the basis
of local industries.

Famous engineer, Isambard Kingdom
Brunel, had strong links with Bristol. He
designed the SS *Great Britain* (now
moored by Gas Ferry Road), the first
iron, steam-driven passenger vessel. The
ship was launched in 1843 and was in
service for over 40 years before being
used as a store. In 1970 the rotting hulk
was towed back to Bristol to be restored,
a process that is still continuing.

Among the city's other attractions,
Harvey's Wine Cellars in Denmark Street
are housed in the 13thC cellars of the
Monastery of St Mark and have been
used by John Harvey & Sons since 1796.
The exhibitions there tell the story of
wine through the ages. There are

displays of antique silver, Georgian
furniture, and rare glass – including
a very fine collection of early English
lead crystal drinking glasses.

ARCHITECTURAL ANTIQUES
Robert Mills Architectural Antiques (SALVO) in
Narroways Road, Eastville, has architectural
antiques including Gothic church fittings, stained
glass, and pub interiors and is open Monday–Friday.

BEDS
Bedsteads (BABAADA), Regent Street in the Clifton
area of the city, have antique bedsteads.

BOOKS
Bishopston Books, in Gloucester Road, Bishopston,
has antiquarian and second-hand books and is
open Thursday–Saturday. Chandos Books in,
appropriately enough, Chandos Road sells
antiquarian books including those on travel,
transport, natural history, Bristol, and the south-
west as well as illustrated books. In North Street,
Bedminster, Circle Books sells antiquarian and
second-hand books, specializing in history and
health. The shop is closed Tuesdays and Sundays.
Cotham Hill Bookshop (PBFA) in Cotham Hill has
antiquarian and second-hand books as well as a
range of antiquarian prints.

CERAMICS
Located in the village of Abbots Leigh, just off the
A359 on the south-western edge of Bristol, David
and Sally March Antiques (LAPADA, CINOA)
specializes in 18thC porcelain and is open by
appointment only – ring 01275 372422. In the Mall,
Clifton, Porchester Antiques has Moorcroft, enamels,
pottery, Okra glass, Sally Tuffin pottery, and
jewellery. It is open Tuesday–Saturday until 4pm.

CLOCKS
A & C Antique Clocks in Bryants Hill, Hanham,
has a large stock of clocks, furniture, ceramics,
and Winstanley cats. It is open Tuesdays and
Thursdays–Saturdays 10am–4pm.

COINS
The Coin Cabinet, located in Lower Park Row,
has Roman and Greek coins and curios.

FRENCH ANTIQUES
Bristol Brocante, located in St George's Road,
Hotwells, has a large stock of French antiques.
It opens at 11am.

FURNITURE
Bristol Trade Antiques in Cheltenham Road sells
Victorian and Edwardian furniture. The Antiques
Warehouse Ltd (RADS) in Gloucester Road,
Horfield, has Georgian–post-Edwardian furniture

as well as carpets and mirrors. The warehouse is open 7 days a week. **Hotwell Antiques** in St George's Road, Hotwells, sells furniture and silver – it is closed Tuesday, Thursday, and Sunday. On the western side of the city in Westbury-on-Trym, **Angel Antiques** in Stoke Lane has Victorian mahogany furniture, general antiques, china, and glass. The shop is closed Wednesday, Saturday afternoons, and Sundays.

GENERAL ANTIQUES
The Antique and Classic Collection (SBA) in Coldharbour Road, Redland, sell antiques and replicas – everything, they say, from lighting to wallpaper. In Boyces Avenue, Clifton, **Arcadia Antiques** has furniture, collectables, upholstery, prints, and paintings. It is open Tuesday–Saturday. **Paula Biggs**, again in Boyces Avenue, Clifton, sells antiques, collectable silver, and objets de vertu. The shop is also open Tuesday–Saturday. **Cotham Antiques** in Cotham Hill sells general antiques, and is open Tuesday–Saturday. **Cotham Galleries**, also in Cotham Hill, sells general antiques. On Saturday it is open until 12 noon. Located in the Mall, Clifton, **Terry M Cox** has a large stock of general antiques, clocks, silverplate, and silver. It is shut on Mondays and Sundays. Still in Clifton, **Focus on the Past** in Waterloo Street has an extensive range of furniture, pine, kitchenware, china, glass, books, jewellery, and 20thC collectables. Also in Waterloo Street, **Margaret R Jubb** has general antiques. **Raw Deluxe**, in Gloucester Road, Bishopston, has general antiques and collectables. The shop is closed Tuesdays and Sundays.

MILITARIA
Grimes Militaria in Lower Park Row sells militaria, scientific instruments, and nautical memorabilia. **Pastimes** (OMRS), also in Lower Park Row, has an extensive range of militaria.

MUSICAL INSTRUMENTS
Piano Export in Bridge Road, Kingswood, has a range of Steinways, Bechsteins, grand pianos, and decorative pianos. The shop is open Monday–Friday.

PICTURES & PRINTS
Gloria Barnes of Clifton Antiques Centre, the Mall in Clifton, has Sir William Russell Flint prints, paintings, Indian art, and jewellery. It is open Tuesday–Saturday.

SILVER & JEWELLERY
Caledonia Antiques, also in the Mall, has a selection of jewellery and silver. Again in Clifton, this time in Princess Victoria Street, **Grey-Harris & Co** have an extensive range of jewellery and silver. Back in the Mall, Clifton, **Marlene's** has silver and jewellery and is open Tuesday–Saturday. **Jan Morrison** in Boyces Avenue, Clifton, sells silver,

jewellery and 18th–19thC glass. The shop is open Tuesday–Saturday. **Vincent's of Clifton**, also in the Mall, has jewellery, silver, and gold and is also open Tuesday–Saturday.

TEXTILES
Still in Clifton, **Clifton Hill Antiques** in Lower Clifton Hill has a large stock of textiles, buttons, and buckles. The shop opens at 11am.

ANTIQUES CENTRES
Clifton Antique Centre, again in the Mall in the Clifton area, has six dealers that sell a large range of silver, silverplate, paintings, clocks, ceramics, and Moorcroft. The centre is open Tuesday–Saturday.

AUCTION HOUSES
Bristol Auction Rooms has two salerooms. Baynton Road, in the Ashton area, has fortnightly sales of Victorian and modern effects on Thursdays at 10.30am with viewing on Wednesdays 11am–6pm and on the day of sale from 9am. The other saleroom is in Apsley Road, Clifton. Here, monthly sales of antiques and decorative items take place on Tuesdays at 10.30am. Viewing is on Saturdays 9.30am–1pm, Mondays 9.30am–7pm, and on the day of sale from 9am.

▶ Take the A4 from the centre of Bristol straight to Bath, a distance of 21km (13 miles).

BATH

Even in Roman times Bath, then called *Aqua Sulis*, was famous for its mineral spa, and elaborate baths were built here dedicated to the Celtic god Sul and the Roman goddess of healing, Minerva. In the 18thC the town became extremely fashionable and the distinctive Georgian architecture dates from this time. One of Bath's most famous characters was Beau Nash, the city's Master of Ceremonies, and he was instrumental in giving Bath its social cachet among the aristocracy.

The city has numerous interesting and historic places to visit. Most famous are the almost 2,000-year-old Roman baths and the adjoining Pump Room. The present building was built in 1797 and was the social centre of Bath. The world-famous Royal Crescent is a perfect example of a Georgian crescent built as a wide arc looking onto parkland.

The Holburne Museum & Crafts Study Centre in Great Pulteney Street is located in a most elegant Georgian hotel, the focal point of the street. It contains collections of English and European silver, majolica, bronzes, furniture, old master paintings, portrait miniatures, bronzes, and glass all collected by Sir William Holburn in the 19thC. The collections have been augmented by later pieces, including paintings by Gainsborough and Turner and the work of 20thC British artists and craftsmen.

The Bath Postal Museum in Broad Street is housed in the very building where the first ever stamped letter was posted. There is a full-sized Victorian post office there, and displays of postal uniforms and other post-related exhibits.

On the edge of the city in Claverton Manor, Claverton, the American Museum has displays showing life in the American colonies with realistic room settings as well as individual exhibits. One of its most popular and interesting displays is its collection of over 200 American patchwork and wholecloth quilts, although only a proportion of the collection is on display to the general public.

ARCHITECTURAL ANTIQUES

Source (BABAADA) in Walcot Street has a selection of architectural antiques and lights including 1950s aluminium kitchens. It is open Tuesday–Saturday. One of the best known of the architectural antiques dealers, Walcot Reclamation Ltd (BABAADA), also in Walcot Street, has a substantial range of architectural antiques including bathrooms, radiators, fireplaces, garden furniture, and reproductions of hard-to-find items. It is shut at weekends.

BEDS

Located in London Road, Bedsteads (BABAADA) sells antique bedsteads in iron, brass, and exotic woods.

BOOKS

Bath Old Books (PBFA) in Margaret's Buildings sells antiquarian and second-hand books. George Bayntun (ABA) in Manvers Street has been established since 1894. The shop has a large stock of antiquarian and rare books and specializes in English literature first editions and fine bindings. It shuts at 1pm on Saturdays and is closed all day Sunday. Camden Books (PBFA), situated in Walcot Street, has an extensive range of antiquarian books, specializing in architecture, philosophy, and science. George Gregory in Manvers Street is another long-established bookseller and also has a large range of antiquarian books and prints. It also shuts at 1pm on Saturdays.

CERAMICS

Andrew Dando (BADA, LAPADA) in Wood Street is a well-established dealer known for his large selection of pottery and porcelain from 1750–1870. He is shut Saturday afternoons and Sundays. Located in the Bartlett Street Antiques Centre, Peter Scott has an extensive range of white transfe ware and early English pottery including Mason's.

COSTUMES & CLOTHING

Julia Craig (BABAADA), also in the Bartlett Street Antique Centre, has an extensive range of antique lace and linen, costumes, and costume accessories. Ann King Antique Clothes, Belvedere, Lansdown Road, sells antique clothes, quilts, and lace.

EPHEMERA

Michael Saffell Antiques (BABAADA) in London Road sells advertising items, British tins (biscuit, tobacco, confectionery, mustard, etc), and decorative items.

FURNITURE

In Broad Street, A J Antiques (BABAADA) has Georgian–1950s furniture. The Antiques Warehouse (BABAADA) in Walcot Street has a selection of Georgian, Victorian, and early 20thC furniture and collectables. Arkea Antiques in Monmouth Place opens at 11am. Situated in George Street, Geoffrey Breeze (BABAADA, LAPADA) sells 19thC furniture. Mary Cruz Antiques (LAPADA, CINOA, BABAADA) in Broad Street has an extensive range of large 18th and 19thC English and French furniture, 18th–20thC paintings, and bronze and marble statues. The shop is open until 7pm.

Indigo, another antiques shop in Walcot Street, has Indian and Chinese antique furniture, small handicraft and decorative items, and furniture from Indonesia made from recycled teak. In Mount Road, Southdown, Simon and Frauke Jackson sell antique furniture by appointment only – ring 01225 422221. Jadis Antiques Ltd (BABAADA), again in London Road, has a large stock of French furniture and decorative items. Lansdown Antiques (BABAADA) in Belvedere, Lansdown Road has a variety of painted pine and country furniture, metalware, and decorative items. The shop is open from 8am on Wednesdays. **T J Millard Antiques** (BABAADA) in Saville Row has a wide range of 18th–19thC decorative furniture, boxes, tea caddies, and chess sets. On Wednesdays it is open from 7.30am. **Montague Antiques** (BABAADA), London Road, has a large stock of general furniture from the 18thC–1920s, as well as decorative and collectors' items. It is open every day except Thursdays (until 4pm on Sundays). **Orient Expressions Ltd** (BABAADA), also in Saville Row, has predominantly early 19thC provincial Chinese furniture and accessories. **Tim Snell Antiques** (BABAADA) in Cleveland Terrace has an extensive stock of 19th and 20thC oak furniture and Arts and Crafts. Back in Saville Row, **James Townshend Antiques** (BABAADA) has 19thC furniture, decorative items, and mirrors.

GENERAL ANTIQUES

Alderson (BADA, CINOA) in George Street has 18th and 19thC furniture and works of art. It shuts at 1pm on Saturdays. **Antiques of Bath** (BABAADA) in Brock Street sells furniture, clocks, paintings, silver, and decorative items and is open Wednesday–Sunday. **Bath Galleries** (BABAADA), Broad Street, sells furniture, silver, pictures, barometers, and clocks. The shop is shut Thursday afternoons and Sundays. **Lynda Brine Antiques**, Saville Row, has a large selection of perfume bottles, vinaigrettes, pomanders, and objets de vertu. **Brian and Caroline Craik Ltd** in Margarets Buildings sells general portable items, china, and metalwork and shuts at 4pm. **Quiet Street Antiques** (BABAADA), located in John Street, has an extensive range of 18th and 19thC furniture, clocks, tea caddies, boxes, mirrors, and Royal Worcester, and works of art. **Susannah** (BABAADA, The Textiles Society) in Walcot Street has general antiques, decorative items, and textiles. Please telephone in advance of visiting – ring 01225 445069.

GLASS

Back in Belvedere, Lansdown Road, **Antique Glass** (BABAADA) sells Georgian glass, collectors' drinking glasses, rummers, ales, friggers, decanters, and other curiosities. It is open Tuesday–Saturday. **Frank Dux Antiques** (BABAADA), also in Belvedere, Lansdown Road, has 18th and 19thC glass and country oak furniture and is also open Tuesday–Saturday.

LINEN

Antique Linens & Lace (BABAADA) on Pulteney Bridge has tablecloths, bed linen, cushions, baby bonnets, wedding veils, shawls, christening gowns, textiles, quilts, and bead bags. **Penny Philip** in Great Pulteney Street sells dyed antique linen sheets by appointment only – ring 01225 469564.

SILVER & JEWELLERY

Abbey Galleries (NAG, NPA) in Abbey Church Yard has a large range of jewellery, Oriental porcelain, and silver. **Bryers Antiques** in the High Street sells silver, silverplate, china, and antique glass. **D & B Dickinson** (BADA, BABAADA) in New Bond Street has a large stock of silver, jewellery, and silverplate. It is shut Saturday afternoons and Sundays. **The Galleon** in Monmouth Street sells Georgian–1950s jewellery, silver, and general smalls.

TEXTILES

Antique Textiles (BABAADA) in Belvedere, Lansdown Road, has a large stock of tapestries, samplers, wall and ceiling lighting, Paisleys, fans, and beadwork. It is open Tuesday–Friday.

ANTIQUES CENTRES

The Assembly Antiques Centre (BABAADA) in Saville Row has an extensive range of 18th and 19thC furniture, lighting, chess sets, tea caddies, jewellery, scent bottles, and porcelain. On Wednesdays the centre opens at 8am. **Bartlett Street Antiques Centre** (BABAADA), in Bartlett Street, has 50 dealers and 160 showcases selling antiques and collectables. Again, it opens early (8am) on Wednesdays. **Bath Antiques Market** in Guinea Lane has small items, jewellery, copper, brass, fabrics, and small furniture. The market takes place on Wednesdays 6.30am–2.30pm. The 10 dealers in the **Fountain Antiques Market** (BABAADA), The Paragon, sell a large range of general antiques, toys, porcelain, silver, antiques, costume and textiles, costume jewellery, militaria, 1950s, as well as late 19thC and early 20thC furniture. On Wednesdays it opens at 7am.

AUCTION HOUSES

Aldridges of Bath in Cheltenham Street has been established since 1740. It has fortnightly sales of Victorian and general items on Tuesdays at 10am. There are specialist antiques sales every 6–8 weeks, also on Tuesdays at 10am. The office opens on Saturday mornings. **Phillips International Auctioneers & Valuers** have their regional office in Old King Street.

▶ Take the A4 from Bath direct to Corsham, which is about 14.5km (9 miles) away.

CORSHAM

There is evidence that there was a settlement here in pre-Roman times. Over the centuries, it grew into a thriving market town and Medieval weaving centre. Weavers' cottages may still be seen in the High Street. Built on the site of a Saxon manor, the Elizabethan Corsham Court contains fine 18thC furniture as well as Old Master paintings.

COLLECTABLES
Automatic Dream Comics in Pickwick Road has a large stock of American import comics, old and new action figures, and Star Wars figures. Opening hours are Monday and Tuesday 12 noon–5pm and Thursday–Saturday 10am–5pm.

GENERAL ANTIQUES
Matthew Eden in Pickwick End has general antiques including garden furniture.

▶ Still on the A4, Chippenham is just 5km (3 miles) away.

CHIPPENHAM

Chippenham has a long history; it has been a market town since the 14thC. However, the actual town does not have any antique shops – they are all located in nearby villages.

CERAMICS
Heirloom & Howard Ltd on Manor Farm, West Yatton, is about 6.5km (4 miles) west of Chippenham on the A420. It has Chinese armorial and other porcelain, armorial paintings, coach panels, hall chairs, and portrait engravings.

FURNITURE
Cross Hayes Antiques (LAPADA) at Westbrook Farm, in Draycot Cerne is situated on the B4122, just 730m (800 yards) from junction 17 of the M4. It has a large stock of furniture.

GENERAL ANTIQUES
Harley Antiques is on the Main Road of Christian Malford, which is just off the B4069 about 10km (6 miles) from Chippenham. It has an extensive range of general antiques including decorative and unusual items, conservatory furniture, and objects. The shop is open 7 days a week.

GLASS
Just off the A4 westbound, about 10km (6 miles) from Chippenham, Delamosne & Son Ltd (BADA) is located at Court Close, North Wraxall. Established since 1905, it sells 18th–19thC English and Irish glass, English porcelain, treen, and needlework.

AUCTION HOUSE
Atwell Martin (RICS), New Road, have sales every 3 weeks of general antiques on Saturdays at 10am. They also have 5 sales a year of selected antiques.

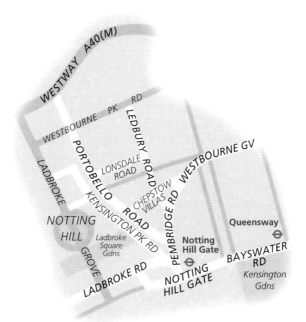

The closest tube station to Portobello Road is Notting Hill Gate on the Circle, Central, and District lines. When you exit the station you will find that you are on the corner of Notting Hill Gate and Pembridge Road. Turn into Pembridge Road past the fork with Kensington Park Road and the first turning on the left is Portobello Road. However, there are only a few antiques shops here. You need to walk for 5–10 minutes to reach the main concentration.

Almost synonymous with antiques, Portobello Road comes alive on Saturday when all the antiques shops, centres, and arcades are open. Although many of the shops open during the rest of the week, the majority of antiques centres and arcades are closed until the

weekend. There is an enormous variety to be found here; everything from inexpensive collectables to high-quality antiques. The dealers in the centres and arcades come from all over the country to sell at Portobello on Saturday. This is not like an antiques fair, though, as the dealers here rent their space on a long-term basis so that they can use it most weeks. Many of them drive hundreds of miles to get to Portobello Road just to drive home again in the late afternoon.

The Notting Hill Carnival is the most famous event that occurs in the area. Taking place annually on the last weekend of August, it was started in 1964 by Caribbean immigrants. It has now grown into one of the biggest and most publicized events in London.

Websites

www.medicalmuseums.org/museums/alex.htm
Learn how Alexander Fleming discovered
penicillin on the website of this museum
in Paddington.

www.nottinghillcarnival.ukgateway.net
The Notting Hill Carnival is the biggest annual
event in the area. Find out more about it here
and see pictures from the last Carnival.

www.portowebbo.co.uk
This local website contains all the information
on Notting Hill and Portobello Road that you
will ever need.

www.portobelloroad.co.uk
Check out the Portobello Road Antique
Dealers' Association website before visiting to
see the scope of antiques and collectables
that are for sale here.

Tourist Information Centres

There are no centres in the Notting Hill area
but if you want information the following
central offices below should be able to help.

London: British Visitor Centre 1 Regent Street,
Piccadilly Circus
Heathrow Airport Underground Station
Concourse
Victoria Station Forecourt
London Waterloo International Arrivals Hall

The telephone number for all of these
is 09068 663344. (Calls are charged at
60 pence per minute.)

There are not many visitor attractions
in the area apart from the antiques
market. However, there is an unusual
museum not far away at St Mary's
Hospital, Paddington – the Alexander
Fleming Laboratory. Here you can learn
how Fleming discovered penicillin in
1928 in a reconstruction of his
laboratory. Paddington is just two
stations north of Notting Hill Gate and
is on the Circle, District, Bakerloo, and
Metropolitan lines. To reach the hospital,
come out of the station on Praed Street.
You should see the mainline station

immediately to your right. Turn left along
Praed Street and the hospital is just a
few minutes away.

If you walk east along Notting Hill Gate
it becomes the Bayswater Road, running
along the north side of Kensington
Gardens and Hyde Park. Every Sunday
around 250 artists of all kinds display
their work, hanging them from the
railings. The artists range from those
highly established to those just out of
art school. All the paintings and other
art are for sale but normally at studio
prices. This art market has been running
for about 50 years and is the largest of
its type in the world.

ANTIQUITIES
Helios Gallery (ADA, PADA, BABAADA) Westbourne
Grove sells Roman, Greek, Egyptian, and Chinese
ancient art. It is open on Saturdays 8am–4pm.

BOOKS
Book and Comic Exchange, Pembridge Road, sells
modern first editions, cult books, and comics. It is
open 7 days a week until 8pm. **Simon Finch** (ABA,
PBFA) in Ledbury Road has modern first editions,
as well as books on art and photography.

CERAMICS
51 Antiques in Ledbury Road sells Italian ceramics
from 1500–1900, together with Venetian glass.
The shop is open all week (until 1pm on
Saturdays). **Mercury Antiques** (BADA), in Ladbroke
Road, has 18th–early 19thC pottery, porcelain,
Delft, and glass. On Saturday it is open until
12.30pm. In Westbourne Grove, **Aurea Carter**
(LAPADA) sells 18th–early 19thC English pottery
and porcelain and is open Saturdays
7.30am–2.30pm.

CLOCKS & WATCHES
Atlam Sales and Service (PADA) in Portobello Road
has a large range of silver and antique pocket
watches. The shop is open Fridays and Sundays
11am–3pm and Saturdays 6am–5pm. **Chamade
Antiques**, also in Portobello Road, sells antique
Rolex watches and is open Saturday 7am–3pm.

COLLECTABLES
Mayflower Antiques (PADA), in Portobello Road, has
music boxes, clocks, dolls, scientific instruments,
pistols, and collectable items. It is open Saturday
7am–4pm. **Mimi Fifi** of Pembridge Road has a large
stock of collectors' and vintage toys, Coca Cola
memorabilia, Pokemon, perfume-related items,

vintage badges, tobacco memorabilia, Michelin memorabilia, Kewpie dolls, and Astro Boy. The shop is open until 7pm. **Visto**, also in Pembridge Road, sells 1950s and 1960s collectables, lighting, textiles, furniture, ceramics, and glass.

COSTUME & CLOTHING
In Westbourne Grove, **Sheila Cook Textiles** has mid-18thC–1970s European costume, textiles, and accessories. The shop is open Tuesday–Saturday. **Virginia**, Portland Road, sells vintage clothes from the late 19thC–late 1930s by appointment only – ring 020 7727 9908.

DECORATIVE ANTIQUES
B and T Antiques Ltd (LAPADA, PADA) in Ledbury Road has decorative antiques and arts, Art Deco furniture, and objects as well as mirrored Art Deco items. In Westbourne Grove, **Solaris Antiques** sell decorative antiques from France and Sweden, covering all periods up to the 1970s.

FURNITURE
Alice's, Portobello Road, has been established since 1887. The shop has a large stock of painted furniture, decorative items, and general antiques and is open Tuesday–Saturday (until 4pm on Saturdays). **P R Barham** (LAPADA), also in Portobello Road, has a wide range of Victorian and decorative furniture, clocks, paintings, and objets d'art. **Trude Weaver** (LAPADA), still in Portobello Road, sells 18th and 19thC English and Continental furniture and complementary accessories. It is open Wednesday–Saturday. In Westbourne Grove, **Butchoff Antiques** (LAPADA) has an extensive selection of English and Continental furniture, decorative items, porcelain, and mirrors. **Canonbury Antiques Ltd**, again in Westbourne Grove, has 18th and 19thC furniture, reproduction furniture, and accessories. **Terence Morse & Son**, still in Westbourne Grove, has 18th–19thC fine English and Continental furniture, linen presses, and library furniture. It is open Monday–Saturday (on Saturdays until 2pm).

Myriad Antiques, this time in Portland Road, has French painted furniture, garden furniture, bamboo, Victorian/Edwardian upholstered chairs, mirrors, and objets d'art and it is open Tuesday–Saturday. **Nicholas Chandor Antiques** in Ladbroke Grove, has an eclectic range of Continental furniture and is open Tuesday–Saturday. **Hirst Antiques**, Pembridge Road, sells general antique furniture, antique beds, bronzes, sculpture, and pictures. Also in Pembridge Road, **Caira Mandaglio** has 14th–20thC furniture, lighting, glassware, objets d'art, and chandeliers. The shop is open Tuesday–Saturday. **M & D Lewis** have three shops in the area. One is in Ledbury Road, one in Lonsdale Road, and the third in Westbourne Grove. They all sell English and Continental furniture as well as Oriental porcelain. The Ledbury Road and Lonsdale Road shops open

until 4pm on Saturday, while the Westbourne Grove one closes at 3pm. **Robin Martin Antiques** is also located in Ledbury Road. The shop has mirrors, Regency furniture, Continental furniture, works of art, and lighting. On Saturdays it is open until 1pm. In Ledbury Mews North, **Arenski Fine Art** (BADA, LAPADA) sells exotic, unusual, and colonial furniture as well as sculpture and animals in art by appointment only – ring 020 7727 8599. **Peter Petrou** (BADA, LAPADA) again in Ledbury Mews North also sells exotic, unusual, and colonial furniture, sculpture, and animals in art by appointment only. His number is 020 7229 9575.

GENERAL ANTIQUES
In Portobello Road, **Barham Antiques** (PADA) sells boxes, caddies, inkwells, clocks, glassware, inkstands, small furniture, and silverplate. On Saturday it opens at 7am. **Kleanthous Antiques Ltd** (LAPADA), also in Portobello Road, has jewellery, wristwatches, furniture, clocks, pocket watches, porcelain, china, silver, works of art, and 20thC decorative items. The shop is open Saturdays 8am–4pm. In Westbourne Grove, **Butchoff Interiors** (LAPADA) sells one-off items, textiles, collectables, dining tables, chairs, consoles, and accessories. **Cura Antiques**, Ledbury Road, has Continental works of art, furniture, and old master paintings. On Saturday it is open until 1pm.

GLASS
Anthea's Antiques in Westbourne Grove sells 19thC English and Continental glass and ceramics and is open Saturdays 7am–4pm.

METALWARE
In Pembridge Road, **Jack Casimir Ltd** (BADA, LAPADA) sells 16th–19thC British and European domestic brass, copper, pewter, and paktong.

ORIENTAL
Sebastiano Barbagallo Antiques, located in Pembridge Road, has a large stock of Chinese furniture, Indian, and Tibetan antiques and crafts. The shop is open 7 days a week (until 7pm on Saturdays). **Beagle Gallery and Asian Antiques**, in Westbourne Grove, sells Oriental furniture and sculpture and is open by appointment – ring 020 7229 9524. Again in Westbourne Grove, **MCN Antiques** has Japanese porcelain and works of art. On Saturdays it shuts at 3pm. **Cohen & Cohen** (BADA), in Portobello Road, has Chinese export porcelain and works of art. It is open Friday 9am–4pm and Saturday 8am–4pm. **Ormonde Gallery** (LAPADA), also in Portobello Road, sells 19thC Chinese and Indonesian furniture, ceramics, 2000 BC-Ching Dynasty, Oriental art, jade, and snuff bottles. **David Wainwright** has two shops in Portobello Road both selling antique, old furniture and decorative items from India, Indonesia, and China. The shops are open 7 days a week.

SILVER & JEWELLERY

Arbras, situated in Westbourne Grove, has a large range of silver picture frames and giftware. On Saturdays it opens at 7am. **Tony Booth Antiques** (PADA), back in Portobello Road, sells silver photograph frames and is open Saturdays 7am–5pm. Still in Portobello Road, **J Freeman** (LAPADA) sells Victorian and Edwardian silver as well as silverplate. **Henry Gregory** (PADA), also in Portobello Road, sells silverplate, silver, sporting goods, and decorative antiques. On Saturdays it opens at 8am. **Portobello Antique Store**, in Portobello Road, has silver, silverplate, decorative items, and flatware. The shop is open Tuesday–Friday 10am–4pm and Saturday 8.15am–4pm. **Schredds of Portobello** (LAPADA, CINOA, PADA), again in Portobello Road, has small pieces of pre-1880 silver and is open Saturday, 7am–2.30pm.

ANTIQUES CENTRES

Apart from the arcade listed in the final paragraph, all of the following antiques centres, galleries, and arcades are in Portobello Road. **75 Portobello Road** is an architect-designed antiques gallery with four specialist dealers under one air-conditioned roof. One dealer specializes in 18th and 19thC continental clocks, decorative gilt bronze, porcelain, and bronzes. Another specializes in antique boxes, tea caddies, writing slopes and desks, humidors etc. 19th and 20thC animal subjects, Vienna and French bronzes, porcelain, and Staffordshire make up the stock of the third while the last dealer has antiques, fine chess sets, and glass paperweights. On Saturday the centre opens at 7.30am. **The Admiral Vernon Antiques Market** has 190 dealers offering a complete range of antiques including Art Deco, boxes, metalware, collectables, clocks, etc. The market is open on Saturdays only. **Chelsea Gallery** has a good range of antiques and collectables including 17th–19thC samplers and needlework, silver and jewellery, ceramics, glass, metalware, and collectables. It is open Saturday only, from 7am. **Crown Arcade** has dealers selling 18th and 19thC glass, treen, boxes, 19th and 20thC pictures, bronzes, sculpture, silver, jewellery, Arts & Crafts, Art Nouveau, and Art Deco. This is another of Portobello Road's centres that only opens on a Saturday. **The Geoffrey Van Arcade**, again open on Saturdays only, has over 20 dealers selling furniture, books, silver, jewellery, treen, tartenware, and collectables. **Good Fairy Antiques Market** has 50 covered market stalls in a yard selling a variety of antiques and collectables and is open on Saturday only. **The Portobello Green Market**, with over 100 stalls, is open Fridays selling designer clothes, Art Deco, and collectables from the 1950s and 1960s. On Saturdays and Sundays it has a selection of antiques and collectables. **Portobello Market** has dealers selling collectables, hip flasks, Art Deco, jewellery, pictures and prints, books, dolls, teddies, and toys. Again, it is open on Saturdays only. The dealers at the **Port Wine Galleries**, open on Saturdays, sell jewellery, paintings, prints and photographs, ceramics, walking sticks and umbrellas, pens, pond yachts, clocks, lace and linens, bags, and collectables. **Red Lion Antiques Market**, again only open on Saturdays, sells a range of antiques and collectables. **Roger's Antiques Gallery**, open Saturday only, has specialist dealers in most fields.

Moving to Westbourne Grove, the **Lipka Arcade** has specialist dealers selling scientific instruments, small furniture, Oriental art, books, paintings, and works of art. It is open Saturday 7am–12.30pm.

Outside of the City area, London was just a collection of villages until the 18th and 19thC and we can still see signs of its ancient history today. For example, Oxford Street, which is Mayfair's northern boundary, was a Roman road. Mayfair itself took its name from the annual fair held in May in the late 17th and early 18thC. Perhaps there were lavender sellers there, like the one illustrated on the powder compact below. While you are in the area, take the opportunity to visit the Duke of Wellington's home, Apsley House, where you will see a fine collection of furniture, porcelain, statues, and paintings.

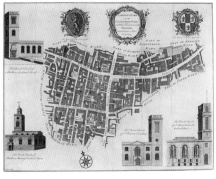

You can see some of the most famous of London's attractions within and just outside this area. For example, view the Changing of the Guard at Buckingham Palace, and at Horseguards Parade on Whitehall, attempt to make one of the soldiers in the sentry boxes change expression – you won't succeed! At the bottom of Whitehall you will find the Houses of Parliament – will you catch a glimpse of the Prime Minister?

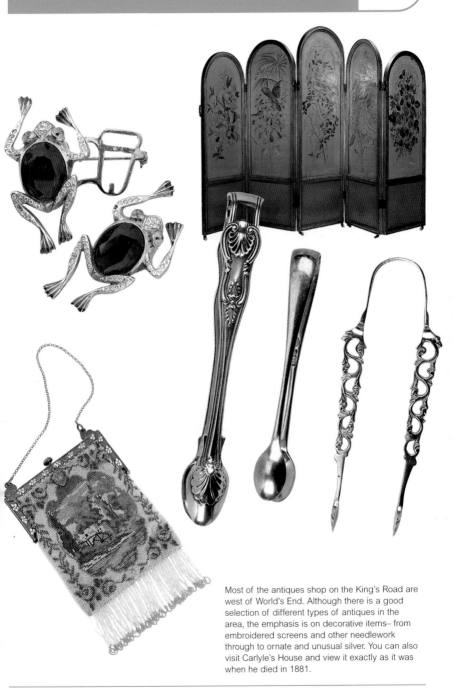

Most of the antiques shop on the King's Road are west of World's End. Although there is a good selection of different types of antiques in the area, the emphasis is on decorative items– from embroidered screens and other needlework through to ornate and unusual silver. You can also visit Carlyle's House and view it exactly as it was when he died in 1881.

Windsor Castle and royalty are the predominant features of the southern part of this tour and you will probably find many souvenirs like the plate and postcard here with pictures of the Castle or jewellery with a regal theme. Take the opportunity to visit Windsor Castle and see the State Rooms and the charmingly named Exhibition of the Queen's Presents and Royal Carriages. Henley-on-Thames, north west of Windsor, is the scene of another great British tradition, the Henley Regatta. When you get weary from antiques hunting, take a stroll alongside its lovely river illustrated on this collectable postcard.

The Cotswolds probably has the greatest concentration of antiques shops in England outside of London. Here you can find everything from fine furniture to Old Master and contemporary paintings. Other treasures include decorative objects like the piano powder compact below, and textiles such as the Adam and Eve sampler. The tour ends in the historic university town of Oxford, which has its own associated memorabilia, for example the print showing Christchurch College and the Oxford College bottle.

This area saw a lot of fighting between the English and Welsh before the two countries united, and the famous Marcher castles all along the border are a legacy from those troubled times. Hartlebury Castle, near Kidderminster, houses the Worcestershire County Museum with its excellent collections of archaeology, costume, and toys as well as everyday items shown in recreated Victorian rooms. All bibliophiles will want to take the side trip to Hay-on-Wye at the end of the tour. This town is known as the book capital of England, with about 40 antiquarian and other bookshops and an annual Book Festival.

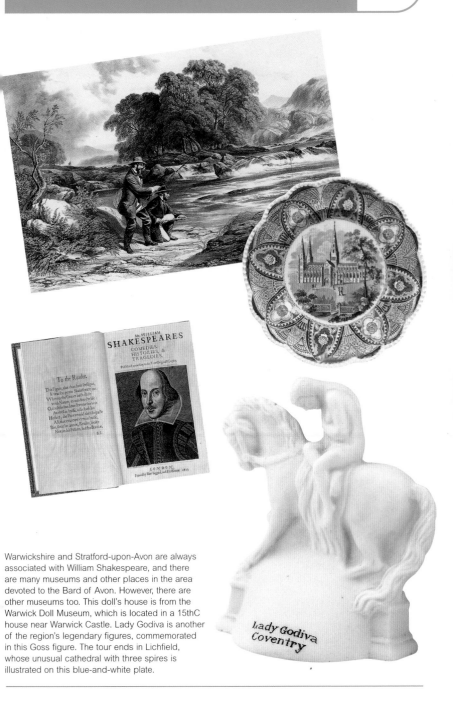

Warwickshire and Stratford-upon-Avon are always associated with William Shakespeare, and there are many museums and other places in the area devoted to the Bard of Avon. However, there are other museums too. This doll's house is from the Warwick Doll Museum, which is located in a 15thC house near Warwick Castle. Lady Godiva is another of the region's legendary figures, commemorated in this Goss figure. The tour ends in Lichfield, whose unusual cathedral with three spires is illustrated on this blue-and-white plate.

The Welsh national costume, as worn by this Goss figure, is one of the most famous in the world. The Morton Nance Collection of Welsh Pottery and Porcelain, bequeathed to the Cardiff National Museum and Gallery in 1952, tells the story of pottery and porcelain production in Wales, particularly Cardiff and Swansea. A spoon rack like the one illustrated here would have been found in a traditional Welsh kitchen, such as the recreated example found in Swansea Museum's 'Cabinet of Curiosities', which is furnished and equipped in 19th century style.

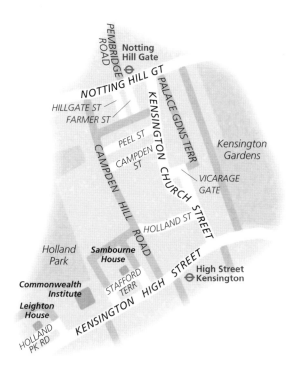

The closest tube station to the southern end of Kensington Church Street is High Street Kensington on the Circle and District lines. When you come out of the station, just look across the road to your right to see the street. However, you can also approach from the northern end via Notting Hill Gate, which is on the Circle, District, and Central lines. Cross over the main road and then turn left. You will see Kensington Church Street with Waterstones Bookshop on the corner.

This street, which is in the western part of Central London, is famous for the concentration of high-quality antiques shops, particularly those selling furniture, pottery, and porcelain, although there are antiques of all kinds to be found here.

The area around Kensington Church Street is a wealthy residential one and has had many famous people living in it. Number 16, Phillimore Place was once the home of *Wind in the Willows* author, Kenneth Grahame, and Victorian painter, Frederic, Lord Leighton, lived in Leighton House in Holland Park Road. The latter house is now a museum. It was built in the 1860s although its centrepiece, the Arab Hall, was not added until the 1870s. It was built specifically to display Leighton's astounding collection of tiles. They have been used to recreate a Moorish palace and now constitute the most important collection of 16th and 17thC Damascus tiles in the country. The house contains many treasures including paintings by Millais, Burne-Jones, and

▶▶ USEFUL CONTACTS

Websites

www.thehalcyon.com/Halcyon/exit_two.asp
You can take a "virtual" walk around Holland Park via this website.

www.antiques-london.com
The Kensington Church Street Antique Dealers' Association has its own website that includes lists of all its members.

www.hrp.org.uk/ken/indexken.htm
Kensington Palace contains some magnificent collections of furniture, pictures, and costume. Find out more here.

www.rbkc.gov.uk/leightonhousemuseum
The Royal Borough of Kensington & Chelsea's website gives some basic information on a room by room basis (as well as floor plans) about Leighton House. On the opening page, there is also a picture of the magnificent Arab Hall.

www.rbkc.gov.uk/linleysambournehouse
Take a look at another house owned by the Royal Borough of Kensington and Chelsea that was also owned by a Victorian artist.

www.olympia-antiques.com
To find out dates, opening times, exhibitors, and much more information, visit the Olympia Fair's website.

www.royal.gov.uk/palaces/index.htm
If you want to know more about the Royal Palaces or to visit them, this official website gives you all the information you need.

Tourist Information Centres

There are no centres in the Kensington Church Street area but if you want information the central ones below should help.

London: British Visitor Centre
1 Regent Street, Piccadilly Circus
Heathrow Airport
Underground Station Concourse
Victoria Station Forecourt
London Waterloo International Arrivals Hall

The telephone number for all of these is 09068 663344 (calls charged at 60 pence per minute).

Leighton himself. To reach Leighton House, walk west along Kensington High Street. When you have just passed the Commonwealth Institute, turn right into Melbury Road and then first left into Holland Park Road.

Another artist attracted by the area's Bohemian atmosphere in the late 19thC was Edward Linley Sambourne, a leading cartoonist for the humorous magazine *Punch*. His home in Stafford Terrace is also open for visitors. It contains a wide and interesting collection of furniture, Oriental porcelain, pictures, stained glass, and much more. To visit the house, walk west from Kensington Church Street along Kensington High Street and take the fourth turning on the right, Argyle Road. Stafford Terrace is then the second turning on the left.

If you visit the area in fine weather, you might also like to see Holland Park, the largest park in the borough of Kensington and Chelsea. It came into the borough's ownership after the Jacobean mansion set in the middle was bombed during World War II. The area contains parkland, wooded areas, an ecology visitor centre, and wildlife pond as well as the remains of the original house, partly used as a restaurant, the Orangery, and the Ice House. To reach the park, walk west along Kensington High Street and turn right just before the Commonwealth Institute onto a path that leads directly into it.

The home of Diana, Princess of Wales at the time of her death, Kensington Palace, has seen some momentous events. Queen Anne died here and Princess Victoria was given news of her accession to the throne here in 1837. Parts of the palace are still used as royal apartments but other areas are open to the public, including the magnificently decorated State Apartments and the

Royal Ceremonial Dress Collection, which has an exhibition of royal, court, and ceremonial dress from the 18thC to the present day. While visiting Kensington Palace you can also visit Kensington Gardens, once the palace grounds. To visit the Palace and Gardens from Kensington Church Street, turn left along Kensington High Street. The entrance to the Palace and Gardens is just past Kensington Palace Hotel.

Unless mentioned, all the shops below are in Kensington Church Street.

ARMS & ARMOUR
Michael German Antiques (BADA, LAPADA) sells antique walking canes, arms, and armour. On Saturdays it is open until 1pm. Robert Hales Antiques sells Oriental and Islamic arms and armour ranging in date from Medieval times–19thC. The shop is open Tuesday–Friday.

BOOKS
Adrian Harrington Antiquarian Bookseller (ABA, PBFA) has a large stock of antiquarian, rare, and second-hand books on literature and travel, as well as children's illustrated books.

CARPETS & RUGS
In nearby Kensington High Street, Isaac Carpets has an extensive range of antique Oriental carpets, European carpets, and tapestries.

CERAMICS
Garry Atkins has a large stock of English and Continental pottery, from the 18thC and earlier. The shop is open Monday–Friday. Nicolaus Boston Antiques sells an extensive selection of majolica, Christopher Dresser, and aesthetic pottery and is open Fridays and Saturdays. David Brower (KCSADA) has a wide range of Meissen, K P M, European and Asian porcelain, French bronzes, and Japanese works of art. The shop is open Monday–Friday. Cohen & Cohen (BADA, KCSADA) sell a large variety of Chinese export porcelain and works of art. On Saturday, the shop is open until 4pm. Davies Antiques (LAPADA) has a wide range of Continental porcelain dating from 1710 to the Art Deco period as well as Meissen porcelain. On Saturdays the shop shuts at 3pm. Richard Dennis Gallery sells antique and modern studio ceramics, ranging from 1850–present-day contemporary ceramics. Hope & Glory, still in Kensington Church Street but with its entrance in Peel Street, has a large stock of commemorative ceramics ranging from Royal to political, etc. The well-known dealer, Jonathan Horne (BADA, CINOA), has early English

pottery, from Medieval times–1820. His shop is open Monday–Friday. Valerie Howard (LAPADA), located in Campden Street, is famous for her Mason's Ironstone, other English ironstone, Miles Mason porcelain from 1796–1840, and Quimper pottery from the 19thC–1920.

Roderick Jellicoe (BADA, KCSADA), also in Campden Street, is a well-known and respected figure at major British antiques fairs. He sells 18thC English porcelain. On Saturday the shop is open until 1pm. Peter Kemp has a large stock of 18thC Oriental and European porcelain and works of art and is open Monday–Friday. Libra Antiques sells a wide range of English blue and white pottery from 1790–1820 and creamware. On Saturday, the shop shuts at 1pm. The London Antique Gallery sells Meissen, Dresden, Worcester, Minton, Shelley, Sèvres, Lalique, and bisque dolls. Mah's Antiques has a large stock of Oriental and European porcelain and works of art. It is open Monday–Friday. E and H Manners (BADA) sells 18thC European porcelain and pottery and is also open Monday–Friday. Colin D Monk sells Oriental porcelain. Santos sells 17th and 18thC Chinese export porcelain by appointment only – ring 020 7937 6000. Simon Spero, much respected and established since 1964, sells 18thC English porcelain and enamels. The shop is open Monday–Friday. In Holland Street, Constance Stobo sells 18th and 19thC pottery, English lustreware, and Staffordshire animals. On Saturday, the shop is open until 2pm. Another well-known ceramics dealer, Stockspring Antiques (BADA, LAPADA, KCSADA) has a wide range of English porcelain from 1745–1835, figures, tea ware, dinnerware, and decorative ware. On Saturday it is open until 1pm. Jorge Welsh (BADA) sells Chinese porcelain and on Saturday is open until 2pm. The Woolahra Trading Co Ltd (Syndicate des Antiquaires) sells European ceramics and oil paintings from the 16th–18thC by appointment only – ring 020 7727 6996.

CLOCKS
In Vicarage Gate, Roderick Antiques (LAPADA, KCSADA) has a large range of antique clocks from 1700–1900, including bracket, Vienna, longcase, carriage, English, French, and German. On Saturday it is open until 4pm.

COINS
In Hillgate Street, Michael Coins sells English and foreign coins and banknotes from Medieval times–present day. It is open Tuesday–Friday.

DECORATIVE ARTS
Abstract/Noonstar (LAPADA) has 20thC decorative arts, including Art Nouveau and Art Deco. Artemis Decorative Arts Ltd (LAPADA) also sells Art Nouveau and Art Deco including glass, bronze, ivory, furniture, and other decorative arts. Jag

Applied and Decorative Arts (Decorative Arts Society), has Liberty pewter/silver, Art Nouveau metal, and glass decorative items. **John Jesse** has 20thC decorative arts, sculpture, glass, ceramics, silver, and jewellery. On Saturday the shop shuts at 4pm. **Fay Lucas Gallery** (BADA, LAPADA, CINOA) sells fine 20thC English and Continental Arts and Crafts, Art Nouveau, Art Deco, silver, and applied arts. **New Century** sells 1860–1910 design. **Zeitgeist Antiques Dealer** has Art Nouveau, Art Deco, glass, ceramics, and metalware.

FURNITURE
Eddy Bardawil (BADA) sells 18th–19thC English furniture and works of art. On Saturday, the shop shuts at 1pm. **C Fredericks and Son** (BADA, KCSADA), established since 1947, has 18thC English furniture and is open Monday–Friday. **Lewis & Lloyd** (BADA) sells 18th–early 19thC English and Continental furniture. It is open Monday–Friday. **C H Major**, founded in 1919, has a large stock of 18th–19th century English furniture. On Saturdays it shuts at 2pm. **Reindeer Antiques Ltd** (BADA, LAPADA), who also have a shop in the Cotswolds, sell fine period English furniture – 17th–19thC mahogany, walnut, and oak – together with mirrors, paintings, and objets d'art. **Brian Rolleston Antiques Ltd** (BADA) has 18thC English furniture and is open Monday–Friday. **Patrick Sandberg Antiques** (BADA, CINOA) sells 18th and 19thC English furniture, mirrors, and accessories. On Saturdays the shop shuts at 4pm. **M & D Seligman** (BADA, CINOA) has vernacular furniture from the 16th–early 19thC, as well as treen and works of art. The shop is open Monday–Friday.

GENERAL ANTIQUES
The Lacquer Chest has a wide range of military chests, china, clocks, samplers, and lamps. On Saturdays, the shop shuts at 3pm. **Nassirzadeh Antiques** has an extensive range of porcelain, glass, and textiles. **Paul Reeves** sells a large selection of Victorian and Edwardian furniture, artefacts, textiles, glass, ceramics, metalwork, Arts and Crafts, aesthetic movement, and Gothic revival. On Saturdays, the shop shuts at 4pm. In Holland Street, **Mary Wise & Grosvenor Antiques** (BADA) has porcelain, small bronzes, works of art, and Chinese watercolours on pith paper. It is open Monday–Friday.

GLASS
Nigel Benson 20th Century Glass (KCSADA) has an impressive range of 1870–1980 British, post-war Scandinavian, and Continental glass. It is open Thursday–Saturday from 12 noon. **Jeanette Hayhurst** (BADA), another of the Street's well-known expert dealers, has an excellent selection of 18thC glass, specializing in English drinking glasses. On Saturdays, the shop opens at 12 noon.

LIGHTING
Denton Antiques and **Mrs Quick Chandeliers** are separate shops under the same ownership, selling French and English chandeliers, lighting, and 1750–1920 table lamps. They are open Monday–Friday.

MIRRORS
Through The Looking Glass has 19thC mirrors.

ORIENTAL
Antiquewest Ltd at **Patrick Sandberg Antiques** (CINOA) sells Oriental porcelain, pottery, Chinese carpets, and furniture. On Saturdays the shop shuts at 4pm. **Gregg Baker Asian Art** (BADA, LAPADA, CINOA) has Japanese, Chinese, and Asian works of art and is open Monday–Friday. **Berwald Oriental Art** (BADA, CINOA) has fine Chinese pottery and porcelain, Han to Qing, and also Chinese works of art. It opens Monday–Friday. **J A N Fine Art** (KCSADA) sells Japanese, Chinese, and Korean ceramics; bronzes; and works of art. It opens Monday–Friday. **The Japanese Gallery Ltd** (Ukiyo-e Society) has a wide range of Japanese woodcut prints, Japanese ceramics, sword armour, and Japanese dolls. **S Marchant & Son** (BADA, KCSADA) has Chinese porcelain, works of art, snuff bottles, and jade. It is open Monday–Friday.

OTTOMAN ANTIQUES
Dyala Salam Antiques (KCSADA) has a large stock of 18th and 19thC Ottoman antiques, textiles, Bohemian glass, and Islamic furniture. On Saturdays, the shop opens until 3.30pm.

SILVER & JEWELLERY
Didier Antiques (LAPADA) has late 19th–early 20thC Arts and Crafts and Art Nouveau jewellery and silver, as well as 1960s–70s designer jewellery. The shop is open Tuesday–Saturday from 12 noon. **Howard Jones Antiques** (LAPADA) sells antique and modern silver, trinket boxes, picture frames, and cufflinks. **Lev Antiques Ltd** (GMC) has jewellery, silver, paintings, objets d'art and antiquities. On Mondays, the shop opens at 12 noon.

ANTIQUES CENTRES
Kensington Church Street Antique Centre has 19th–20thC decorative arts, and Oriental and English ceramics.

ANTIQUES FAIRS
The Fine Art and Antiques Fair takes place at Olympia Exhibition Hall, Hammersmith Road three times a year, in February, June, and November. The June fair is often called the "barometer of the trade because a poor fair means the UK antiques trade is in for a bad time. **The West London Antiques Fair** at Kensington Town Hall is organized by one of the most well respected fairs organizers in the country, **Caroline Penman**. She also does another fair at Chelsea Town Hall in the King's Road.

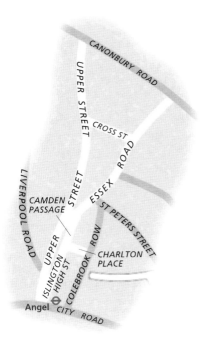

Situated in the borough of Islington, Camden Passage and the surrounding area is one of the most popular places in London for antiques buyers. Here you can find an enormous selection of antiques shops and centres with the stock ranging from collectables costing just a few pounds to fine antiques for many thousands. Antiques dealing is centred on Camden Passage itself and this is open on Wednesdays and Saturdays. Opening hours of other shops and centres vary so are listed below.

To reach the area, take the underground to Angel, on the City Branch of the Northern Line. When you come out of the station, turn right into Upper Street and the main antiques centres are a few minutes walk away.

It is hard to believe, looking at Islington today, but this area started as an Anglo-Saxon village called *Gislandune*, which means Gisla's Hill, and it was owned by the canons of St Paul's. From the Middle Ages onwards Islington was a place for royalty to break their journey to and from London. In the 16thC it was famous for its magnificent mansions including two owned by Henry VIII. Later, Sir Walter Raleigh had a house in Upper Street.

Until the early 19thC Islington was a pleasant place, full of dairy farms supplying milk to the capital. Its springs also provided the city with clean water. First the Regent's Canal and then the railways brought an end to the pastoral idyll. Although industry and slums were found in the area in the mid–late 19thC,

Websites

www.geffrye-museum.org.uk/
Not only does this website give useful information about the museum, it also has a good, clear map. Print it out before you visit.

www.islington.gov.uk/
If you decide to base your visit in Islington, this site will be useful as it lists places to stay and go, events taking place in the borough, and has a piece on its history too.

www.myislington.co.uk/
This commercial site gives a flavour of the borough. There is less official information than on the council website above but many of the subjects covered are just as useful for the visitor.

www.museum-london.org.uk/
The excellent pictures and descriptions here give you a good idea of what to expect from the Museum of London. There is also a map to help you find it.

Tourist Information Centres

There are no centres in the Islington area but if you want information the central ones below should be able to help.

London: British Visitor Centre
1 Regent Street, Piccadilly Circus
Heathrow Airport
Underground Station Concourse
Victoria Station Forecourt
London Waterloo International Arrivals Hall

The telephone number for all of these is 09068 663344. (Calls charged at 60 pence per minute.)

it was generally the more prosperous people who moved to Islington. With the advent of the 20thC, however, this changed and much of the area declined until it enjoyed a renaissance in the 1960s–80s when it became fashionable again. Now much of Islington has been gentrified and is the home of many rich and famous people, including Tony Blair and his family until they moved into an even more desirable address: 10 Downing Street.

There are a few visitor attractions in the area too. Canonbury Tower, a Medieval house altered and restored in the 18thC, has been home to Washington Irving and Oliver Goldsmith and it now houses a theatre company.

It is also worth taking a short journey to the Geffrye Museum in Kingsland Road, London E2. It specializes in the domestic interiors and furniture of the urban middle classes. Set in 18thC former almshouses and a Grade 1 listed building, the displays take the form of a series of rooms showing interiors from 1600–20thC. The museum is set in gardens and these show the changes in garden design over the centuries. It is just one stop away on the underground. Go to Old Street station, still on the Northern Line, and you can either walk (about 15 minutes) or take the number 243 bus. You need to exit the station so that you come out on the north side of Old Street. Walk east along Old Street to Kingsland Road, which is on the left. Turn into it and the museum is on the right.

The Museum of London, situated in London Wall (a street, not a wall), tells the story of the capital city from prehistoric times to the present day. Its displays include Roman Dining Rooms, Elizabethan jewellery and "Macabre London", which has Roman skulls, the death mask of Oliver Cromwell, and a reconstruction of part of Newgate Prison using the original iron doors from the gaol. To reach it from Camden Passage, go back to Angel tube station and travel to Moorgate, two stops away. When leaving the station, take Fore Street, a tiny street that will take you to London Wall, turn right there and the museum is at the end of the street on the right.

ART DECO
Camel Art Deco (LPTA) in Islington Green sells Art Deco ceramics, furniture, and lighting. It is open

Wednesday 9am–3.30pm, Thursday and Friday 12 noon–5pm, and Saturday 9am–6pm.

BOOKS
Upper Street Bookshop, in Upper Street, sells antiquarian and second-hand books on architecture and photography. It is open 7 days a week until 6.30pm.

CLOCKS
BADA member **Patric Capon** in Upper Street sells antique clocks, marine chronometers, and barometers. It is open Wednesday–Saturday.

COSTUME & CLOTHING
Cloud Cuckoo Land, Charlton Place, has vintage clothes and accessories. It is open 7 days a week.

FURNITURE
After Noah (LAPADA), in Upper Street, sells antique and contemporary furniture and houseware. It is open 7 days a week (from 12 noon on Sundays). At the **Sign of the Chest of Drawers** in Upper Street there is a large stock of soft and hardwood old furniture, wooden and metal beds, sofas, armchairs, chests of drawers, and wardrobes. The shop is open 7 days a week. **Castle Gibson**, also in Upper Street, has a wide range of 1800–1940s office furniture, polished metal items, 1930s leather chairs, sofas, early 20thC industrial furniture, 1920s–40s shop fittings, and garden furniture. The shop is open 7 days a week (from 12 noon on Sundays). The last of the specialist furniture dealers in Upper Street, **Woodage Antiques** (LAPADA) sells a wide range of 18th–20thC furniture. Opening days are Wednesdays from 7.30am and Saturdays. In White Conduit Street, **Metro Retro** has an extensive selection of industrial style and stripped steel furniture, as well as lighting and home accessories. It is open Tuesday–Saturday and Sunday until 2pm. **Regent Antiques**, York Way, has a large range of 18thC–Edwardian furniture. In Essex Road, **Keith Skeel Antiques** (LAPADA) has a wide and various stock of 18th and 19thC furniture and accessories. The shop is open 7 days a week.

LIGHTING
Rosemary Conquest, located in Charlton Place, has Continental and Dutch lighting and copper, brass, and decorative items. It is open 7 days a week.

MILITARIA
R J Tredwen, in Upper Street, has an extensive stock of helmets, uniforms, guns, caps, swords, and badges and is open Tuesday–Saturday.

SILVER & JEWELLERY
Eclectica, in Charlton Place, has a large stock of vintage costume jewellery from the 1920s–60s. In Upper Street, **John Laurie** (LAPADA) has a wide range of antique and modern silver and silverplate. The shop is open 7 days a week. **Leolinda**, Islington Green, sells old and new silver jewellery, gemstone necklaces, ethnic art, and jewellery. It is open Wednesday and Saturday.

TOOLS
In Cross Street, **The Old Tool Chest** has an extensive selection of ancient and modern tools for all trades – woodworking, dentistry, veterinary, and masonry – and books. It is open 7 days a week.

ANTIQUES CENTRES
Camden Passage Antiques Market, opened in 1960, is the oldest and largest of the centres. It has 300 dealers selling a wide range of general antiques and specialist antiques. It is open Wednesday and Saturday 8am–3pm (the stalls) and 8am–5pm (the shops).

The Camden Passage dealers cover a wide range of specialist antiques: architectural antiques, Art Deco and Art Nouveau, books, glass, and ceramics including Oriental, Continental, fine-quality 19thC porcelain, Meissen, and major English factories and Staffordshire. Decorative items are here, as well as 17th–19thC engravings. If you collect 20thC ephemera, you will be in your element with Disney, Warner Brothers, and McDonalds' items as well as egg cups, postcards, song sheets, and folk and fairground art. There is also a huge variety of furniture, including French, country, and decorative, garden furniture and statuary, Japanese antiques, kitchenware, lamps and lighting, lighters, linen, Georgian and Victorian mirrors, pens, and wrist- and pocket watches. For collectors there are marine antiques, metalware, 19thC musical boxes, shop fittings, toys, games and optical toys, textiles, and vintage costume, trade signs, and shop fittings.

The Georgian Village Antique Centre in Islington Green has 45–50 dealers. It is open Tuesday–Friday 9am–1pm, Wednesday 8.30am–4pm, and Saturday 1–4pm.

The Mall Antiques Arcade in Upper Street has 35 dealers. It is open Tuesday–Saturday (from 7.30am on Wednesdays). Clarice Cliff and other 20thC ceramics are among the most popular items here. You can also find antiquities, Victorian and Edwardian silver, jewellery and silver photograph frames, 19thC Continental works of art, cloisonné, and 18th–19thC brassware. For collectors, there are celluloid items, Bakelite radios and telephones, marine models, and pond yachts. Dealers in the Mall also sell decorative arts; glass; Japanese ivory and netsuke; English, European, and Japanese porcelain and pottery; and lighting.

AUCTION HOUSES
Criterion Auctioneers in Essex Road hold weekly sales of antiques and decorative furnishings with better-quality antiques sales held monthly.

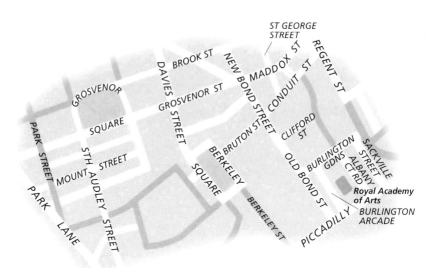

Bounded by Oxford Street, Regent Street, Park Lane, and Piccadilly, Mayfair in London W1 has an enormous selection and variety of antiques shops to offer the visitor. It abounds in those that sell antiquarian books, fine furniture, and Oriental antiques. This area is also home to world-famous auctioneers Sotheby's and Phillips, among others.

Mayfair received its name from the annual fair held here from the late 17th–early 18th century. As early as the 1660s development had started around the present-day Piccadilly Circus and spread north and west until, in less than 100 years, the whole area was built up. Right from the start, the area was fashionable, with a Grosvenor Square address carrying the greatest social cachet. The present American Embassy,

standing on the west side of the square, was built in 1961 and just a few years later was the focus for anti-Vietnam War demonstrations leading to scenes never before experienced by the residents.

Although Piccadilly is an ancient road, it only received its name from the first shop that opened here in the 17thC. Robert Baker sold ruffs, also called picadils, hence Piccadilly. During the 17th and 18thC the area was home to famous people like Lord Byron, the Duke of Wellington, and Nelson's mistress Lady Hamilton. Situated on the southern side of Piccadilly, the Ritz Hotel was completed in 1906 for Swiss hotelier César Ritz. At the eastern end, world-famous Piccadilly Circus was originally intended to be as elegant as Regent Street. The statue here, now called Eros, was erected as a

Websites

www2.vam.ac.uk/collections/apsley
This page from the Victoria & Albert
Museum's site gives an overview of the Duke
of Wellington's former home, Apsley House.

www.dnw.co.uk
Check out Dix Noonan Webb's site for their
programme of coins and medals auctions.

www.grosvenor-antiquesfair.co.uk
You can find everything you need to know
about the prestigious Grosvenor House Art
and Antiques Fair on its website.

www.haughton.com/ceram/ceram.html
Ceramics dealers, Brian and Anna Haughton,
organize the fine quality International
Ceramics Fair and Seminar. Find out more
about the annual fair here.

www.phillips-auctions.com
Phillips International Auctioneers list their
forthcoming auctions worldwide here together
with pictures of forthcoming lots, a history of
the auction house, and information on their
services. The site requires "Flash".

www.tao2000.net/pollocks
This website for Pollocks Toy Museum doesn't
only give you information, you get music to
accompany it.

www.royalacademy.org.uk
Check out this site for the Royal Academy's
programme of exhibitions.

www.sothebys.com
If you want to attend sales at Sotheby's in
London, their website gives their auction
programme among other information.

www.the-wallace-collection.org.uk
The Wallace Collection is one of the finest
collections ever bequeathed to the nation.
Find out more about it here.

www.graysantiques.com
The site for this well-known antiques centre
is packed with specialist dealers.

Tourist Information Centres

London: British Visitor Centre 1 Regent Street,
Piccadilly Circus. Tel: 09068 663344 (calls
charged at 60 pence per minute).

memorial to Lord Shaftesbury and in fact
represents the Angel of Christian Charity.

When you visit, take a good look at the
beautiful Regency terraces that form
Regent Street and were designed by
John Nash. Look above the shop fronts
to appreciate the beauty of their design
and the perfect arc they form.

The Duke of Wellington's home,
Apsley House, on Hyde Park Corner
at the western end of Piccadilly, is one
of London's lesser-known museums. It
is also called Number One, London,
because it was the first house after the
tollgate for travellers coming in from
the west. Many of the articles in its fine
collections were given to the "Iron Duke"
in gratitude from the nation for his defeat
of Napoleon at the Battle of Waterloo.
These include paintings by Goya,
Rubens, Correggio, Brueghel, Steen,
and de Hooch. There are a number of
statues including a huge one of a nude
Napoleon standing over 3.3m (11ft) high.
Among the 3,000 plus items in the
collections are fine porcelain services,
silver, ornate 19thC furniture, medals,
and memorabilia. To visit the house,
take the tube to Hyde Park Corner on
the Piccadilly line and you will see the
signposts to it on the north side.

The Royal Academy of Arts is located
in Burlington House, Piccadilly, on the
north side. It is one of the country's
premier art organizations and has a
permanent collection covering paintings,
sculpture, artists' memorabilia, prints,
and drawings from British artists ranging
from the 18thC–present day. The Royal
Academy also has a programme of fine
temporary exhibitions throughout the
year. Just walk down Piccadilly from
Piccadilly Circus and Burlington House is
about 5 to 10 minutes away on the right.

For more works of art visit the Wallace Collection in Manchester Square. One family, the Hertford-Wallaces, acquired all the works in the Collection during the 19thC, mostly in Paris and London. Bequeathed to the nation in 1897, it contains some magnificent items including works by Watteau, Fragonard, Rembrandt, Van Dyck, and Canaletto. The ceramics include stunning pieces by Sèvres, as well as Oriental porcelain, Italian majolica, and German earthenware. There are also fine collections of furniture, glass, gold boxes, metalwork, and miniatures. Manchester Square is located just north of the western end of Oxford Street. The closest tube is either Marble Arch or Bond Street. Both are on the Central Line, although Bond Street is also on the Jubilee Line. Whichever you use, walk towards the eastern side of Selfridges and turn into Duke Street, which runs alongside. It will take you directly to the Square, which is just a few minutes away.

Lastly, if you like toys, dolls, and teddy bears, visit Pollock's Toy Museum. It is named after Benjamin Pollock, a Victorian toy theatre maker so the museum concentrates on this aspect of the subject. Other exhibits include English tin toys, puppets, dolls, teddy bears, dolls houses, mechanical and construction toys, and lead miniatures. The closest tube station is Goudge Street on the Northern Line. Scala Street is immediately behind the station.

ANTIQUITIES

David Aaron in Berkeley Square has a large stock of ancient art and rare carpets. It is open Monday–Friday. Charles Ede Ltd (BADA, ADA, IADA), located in Brook Street, sells Egyptian, Greek, Roman classical, and pre-classical antiquities. Opening hours are Tuesday–Friday 12.30–4.30pm. In Davies Street, Hadji Baba Ancient Art Ltd (IADA) has Near and Middle East antiquities and is open Monday–Friday. Rupert Wace Ancient Art Ltd (ADA, IADAA, BADA), Old Bond Street, has a wide range of antiquities including Greek, Roman, ancient Egyptian, Near Eastern, Celtic, and Dark Ages. The shop is open Monday–Friday.

BOOKS

In Maddox Street, Simon Finch Rare Books (ABA, PBFA) has 15th–20thC books on art, architecture, literature, science, and medicine. It is open Monday–Friday. Maggs Bros Ltd (ABA, BADA) in Berkeley Square has a large stock of military history, travel, natural history, science, modern literature, early English, and Continental books as well as illustrated manuscripts and autographed letters. The shop is open Monday–Friday. New Bond Street has three booksellers. The first, Marlborough Rare Books Ltd (ABA) sells antiquarian and rare art books, architecture and illustrated books, colour plates, fine bindings, English literature, and books on topography. It is open Monday–Friday. The second, Jonathan Potter Ltd (ABA, BADA, LAPADA, PBFA), has an extensive range including books on the history of cartography, atlases, maps, and reproduction globes. The shop is open Monday–Friday. Sotheby's Bookshop has a stock that varies each month.

In St George Street, Pickering and Chatto (ABA, PBFA) have been in business since 1820. The shop stocks antiquarian, rare, and second-hand books on economics, philosophy, medicine, and general literature. It is open Monday–Friday. Bernard Quaritch Ltd (PBFA, ABA, BADA) in Lower John Street was founded in 1847. It has a wide selection of antiquarian books and is open Monday–Friday. Located in St George Street, Bernard J Shapero Rare Books (ABA, PBFA, BADA) has a large stock of 16th–20thC guidebooks, antiquarian and rare books, and English and Continental literature. It specializes in travel, natural history, and colour plates. Henry Sotheran Ltd (ABA, PBFA, ILAB), in Sackville Street, is the longest established of these booksellers as it opened in 1761. It sells antiquarian books on English literature, natural history, travel, children's illustrated, modern first edition, prints, art, and architecture. On Saturdays it is open until 4pm.

CARPETS, RUGS, & TAPESTRIES

C John Ltd (BADA) in South Audley Street has a wide range of Persian, French, Russian, and Caucasian tapestries and Indian, Turkish, and Chinese carpets, rugs, and textiles. Open Monday–Friday.

CERAMICS

In Burlington Gardens, Brian Haughton Antiques is the organizer of the International Ceramics Fairs and Seminars, among others. His shop has a large stock of 18th and 19thC English and European porcelain and pottery and is open Monday–Friday.

CLOCKS

Pendulum of Mayfair in Maddox Street has an

extensive selection of clocks, including longcase, bracket, and wall. The shop also sells Georgian period furniture.

COINS

Classical Numismatic Group Inc (BNTA), Old Bond Street, sells coins including Greek, Roman, Medieval, and European up to the end of the 18thC. It is open Monday–Friday.

ENAMELS

Halcyon Days (BADA) in Brook Street is famous for its 18thC English enamels, fans, objects of virtue, tortoiseshell, pique, and scent bottles.

FURNITURE

Adrian Alan Ltd (BADA, LAPADA) of South Audley Street has a large stock of furniture, light fittings, mirrors, objets d'art, paintings, statues, garden furniture, and pianos – 19thC Continental furniture is a speciality. It is open Monday–Friday. The Graham Gallery (LAPADA), also in South Audley Street, has 18th and 19thC furniture as well as 19thC oil paintings and objets d'art. The shop is open Monday–Friday. Still in South Audley Street, Claire Guest at Thomas Goode & Co. Ltd, has antique furniture, silver, silverplate, glass, and china.

There are four fine furniture dealers in Mount Street. The first, H Blairman & Sons Ltd (BADA) has a wide selection of 18th and 19thC furniture and works of art and is open Monday–Friday. Next, Leuchers & Jefferson sells 18thC English furniture and decorative items. The third, Stair & Company Ltd (BADA, CINOA) has fine 18thC English furniture and works of art. It is open Monday–Friday. Finally, Toynbee-Clarke Interiors Ltd has Continental furniture, works of art, 18th and 19thC Chinese hand-painted export wallpapers, and early 19thC French panoramic papers. It is also open Monday–Friday.

In Bruton Street, Antoine CheneviPre Fine Arts Ltd (BADA) sells 18th and 19thC Russian, Austrian, German, and Italian furniture as well as objets d'art. Ronald Phillips Ltd (BADA), also of Bruton Street, has a large stock of 18thC English furniture, glass, clocks, barometers, and mirrors. The shop is open Monday–Friday. Mallett (BADA), in Davies Street, sells fine antique furniture as well as works of art, glass, paintings, watercolours, and needlework. On Saturdays the shop is open until 4pm.

GENERAL ANTIQUES

Back in South Audley Street, the Mayfair Gallery Ltd has a wide range of 19thC antiques, decorative arts, bronzes, marbles, Continental porcelain, and furniture and is open Monday–Friday. Alistair Sampson Antiques Ltd (BADA), another of the Mount Street dealers, has English pottery, oak, country furniture, metalwork, needlework, pictures,

and 17th and 18thC decorative items. It is open Monday–Friday. In Burlington Arcade, the St Petersburg Collection Ltd has English and French objets d'art, boxes, 19th and 20thC silver, glass, and ormolu. Vinci Antiques in Avery Row sells objets d'art, objects of virtue, silver, porcelain, glass, paintings, Russian icons, and jewellery. The shop stays open until 7pm.

MAPS & PRINTS

Altea Maps and Books (ABA, PBFA), in Regent Street, sells 15th–19thC maps, atlases, and travel books by appointment – ring 020 7494 9060. Map World (IMCOS), Burlington Arcade, also sells 15th–19thC antique maps. In Mount Street, The O'Shea Gallery (BADA) again has 15th–19th century maps as well as decorative, natural history, sporting, and marine prints. It is also the publisher of Annie Tempest and Tottering-by-Gently cartoons. The shop is open Monday–Friday.

ORIENTAL

In New Bond Street, Brandt Oriental Antiques (BADA) sells Japanese metalwork and screens by appointment only – ring 020 7499 8835. Again open by appointment only, Nicholas S Pitcher Oriental Art, also in New Bond Street, has early Chinese ceramics and works of art – ring 020 7499 6621. Paul Champkins Oriental Art (BADA) in Dover Street is also open by appointment – ring 020 7495 4600. The shop stocks Chinese, Korean, Japanese porcelain, and works of art.

Barry Davies Oriental Art (BADA) in Davies Street has Japanese works of art and is open Monday–Friday. Jan Van Beers Oriental Art (BADA), also in Davies Street, has a large stock of Chinese and Japanese antiques, ceramics, and works of art. It is open Monday–Friday. John Eskenazi Ltd (BADA) in Old Bond Street sells South East Asian, Himalayan, and Indian works of art, as well as Oriental textiles and carpets. The shop is open Monday–Friday. Eskenazi Ltd (BADA), this time in Clifford Street, has early Chinese works of art and is open Monday–Friday. Also in Clifford Street, Robert Hall (BADA) sells 18th and 19thC Chinese snuff bottles. The shop is open Monday–Friday. Roger Keverne Ltd (BADA), still in Clifford Street, has Chinese ceramics, jade, lacquer, bronzes, enamels, hard stones, ivory, and bamboo. It is open Monday–Friday, and Saturday for exhibitions. In Old Burlington Street, Nicholas Grindley (BADA) has Chinese works of art, sculptures, wall paintings, furniture, etc. The shop is open Monday–Friday afternoons from 2–5pm. Gerard Hawthorn Ltd (BADA), Mount Street, sells Chinese, Japanese, and Korean ceramics and works of art. It is open Monday–Friday until late. Also in Mount Street, A and J Speelman Ltd (BADA) has a wide range of Oriental furniture, porcelain, and works of art. It is open Monday–Friday. Sydney

L Moss Ltd (BADA) in Brook Street has a large stock of Chinese and Japanese antiques, works of art, and paintings. The shop is open Monday–Friday. **Shiraz Antiques** (BADA) in Davies Mews sells Asian art, antiquities, glass, marble, and pottery and is open Monday–Friday.

SILVER & JEWELLERY
The Burlington Arcade, just off Piccadilly, is a popular location for silver dealers and has four different specialists. The first, **Daniel Bexfield Antiques** (LAPADA, CINOA) has fine-quality silver and objets de vertu from the 17th–20thC. The next, **Sandra Cronan Ltd** (BADA) has 18th–early 20thC jewellery and is open Monday–Friday. Still in Burlington Arcade, **Hancocks and Co. (Jewellers) Ltd** (BADA) sells jewellery and silver. On Saturday it is open until 4pm. Lastly, **Johnson Walker Ltd** (BADA) has jewellery and bijouterie.

One of London's best-known silver dealers, **Brand Inglis** (BADA) sells antique silver by appointment only – ring 01798 839180. In Davies Street, **Peter Edwards** has 20thC jewellery including signed pieces. The shop is open Monday–Friday. **Simon Griffin Antiques Ltd**, in Royal Arcade, Old Bond Street, has antique and modern silverware and old Sheffield plate. In Conduit Street, **D S Lavender Antiques Ltd** (BADA) has a large stock of gold, silver, fine enamel snuff boxes, and jewels, as well as 16th–early 19thC portrait miniatures. The shop is open Monday–Friday. **Marks Antiques** (BADA, LAPADA) of Curzon Street has a wide range of antique silver. **S J Phillips Ltd** (BADA), also in New Bond Street, has an extensive selection of silver jewellery and snuff boxes and is open Monday–Friday. Again in New Bond Street, **E Swonnell Ltd** has a big stock of 17th–19thC silver and silverplate together with large decorative items. It is open Monday–Friday.

TEXTILES
The Textile Gallery (BADA) in Queen Street sells textile art from China, Central Asia, India, and the Ottoman Empire – from 300BC–AD1800 – and classical carpets 1400–1700 by appointment only – ring 020 7499 7979). It is open Monday–Friday.

ANTIQUES CENTRES
The dealers at **The Bond Street Antiques Centre** in New Bond Street specialize in Victorian, Georgian, and Edwardian jewellery as well as silver and objets d'art and include famous names like **N Bloom and Son** and **Trianon Antiques Ltd**. The nearby **Bond Street Silver Galleries** have dealers selling antique and modern silver, silverplate, pocket watches, and jewellery. **Grays Antique Markets** have two separate establishments, one in Davies Street and another in the adjoining Davies Mews. The dealers in both centres sell a diverse range of antiques including Georgian, Victorian, Edwardian, Art Deco, and modern

jewellery. Oriental antiques are well represented too. Dealers also sell vintage wristwatches, clocks, silver and silverplate, English and Continental pottery, porcelain, glass, bronzes, sculpture, and works of art. Among the wide range of collectables are kitchenalia; antiquarian books; Judaica, 20thC drinking, smoking, and gambling items; vintage fashion accessories; handbags; perfume bottles; and powder compacts. You can also find medals, coins, toys, dolls, militaria, uniforms, badges, documents, and 20thC fine art monographs as well as illustrated books, exhibition catalogues, maps, and prints.

ANTIQUES FAIRS
Grosvenor House Art and Antiques Fair, the most prestigious fair in Britain, takes place annually in June at the Grosvenor House Hotel on Park Lane. It attracts the finest quality antiques dealers as well as some of the richest people in the world. The **International Ceramics Fair and Seminar** also occurs in June, this time at the Park Lane Hotel on Piccadilly. The exhibitors all have the finest quality ceramics and attract buyers from all over the world. There are also a number of regular one-day fairs in this area, taking place in the big hotels like the Hilton, the Park Lane, and the Inter-Continental. They are organized by **Heritage Fairs** and by **KM Fairs**.

AUCTION HOUSES
Dix Noonan Webb (BNTA, OMRS, OMSA), in Old Bond Street, has 10 sales a year of coins and military medals. They take place on Wednesdays with viewing on Tuesdays 12 noon–1pm as well as prior to the sale. Each year **Glendining's** (BNTA, SOFAA), New Bond Street, have four coin sales and three medal sales together with arms, armour, and militaria. The office is open from 8.30am.

Phillips International Auctioneers & Valuers, also in New Bond Street, has regular sales of art and antiques as well as many specialists ones including arms and armour, automobilia, and scientific and nautical instruments. **Sotheby's** of New Bond Street is probably one of the most famous auctioneers in the world with salerooms in European and American cities, as well as the original one here. It has numerous sales of art and antiques including specialist auctions like wine, musical instruments, and Asian Art. Sotheby's also provides specialist services, including restoration, valuation, financial service, picture library, and online auctions.

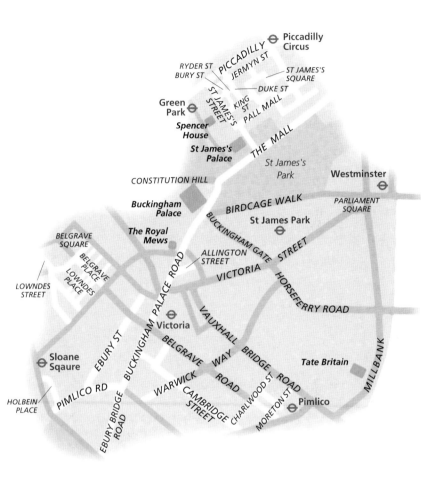

There are several tube stations serving this area as well as Victoria mainline railway station. For Belgravia, the nearest stations are Sloane Square, on the District and Circle Lines, and Victoria, which is also on those lines as well as the Victoria Line. The underground station is adjacent to Victoria mainline station. To get to the northern side of Belgravia, use either Knightsbridge or Hyde Park Corner, both on the Piccadilly Line. If you prefer to start in Pimlico, its tube station is also on the Victoria Line. For St James's, use either Piccadilly Circus, on the Bakerloo and Piccadilly Lines, or St James's Park, on the District and Circle Lines.

The dealers in Belgravia, Pimlico, and St James's are, generally speaking, in the highest echelons of the British

▶ ▶ USEFUL CONTACTS

Websites

www.royalresidences.com/frBPalace.htm
Check the opening times of Buckingham
Palace on its official website.

www.christies.com
If you want to attend sales at Christies, you
can see their auction calendar here.

www.mallgalleries.org.uk
Learn more about the Mall Galleries, which is
run by the Federation of British Artists.

www.the-royal-collection.org.uk
The Royal Collection does not belong to the
Queen personally. She is its trustee, holding
it for her successors and the nation. Learn
more about all the details on the official
Royal Collections website.

www.royal.gov.uk/palaces/stjamess.htm
Find out about St James's Palace, which was
built by Henry VIII and is now the London
home of the present Prince of Wales.

www.spencerhouse.co.uk
This house once belonged to the Spencer
family and has been recently restored to its
18thC grandeur. It is open most Sundays but
check here before visiting.

Tourist Information Centres

Victoria Station Forecourt. Tel: 09068
663344 (calls are charged at 60 pence
per minute).

antiques trade. They deal in the finest
quality, whether furniture, paintings,
ceramics, or other antiques. Specialist
dealers in fine furniture predominate
although there is a good selection of
other antiques too.

The district of St James's lies between
St James's Palace and Piccadilly. Henry
VIII built St James's Palace, off the Mall,
in the 16thC. For the following 300 years
it remained one of the principal palaces
of the sovereign. Queen Mary and
Elizabeth I both held court here, Charles
I was taken from here for his execution,
and nearly all of Queen Anne's children
were born in this palace. Even today,
it is the official London residence of the
Prince of Wales.

Nearby, Buckingham Palace now
opens its doors to visitors. Its Royal
Mews are open all year round but the
State Rooms and Queen's Gallery has
more restricted opening times so check
before visiting. The State Rooms are
furnished in the most opulent style with
the finest French and English antique
furniture. There are paintings by Masters
like Rembrandt, Rubens, and Vermeer as
well as beautiful Sèvres porcelain. The
Royal Gallery draws on an enormous
collection of paintings, watercolours,
drawings, and sculpture.

Spencer House in St James's Park
is one of London's lesser-known
attractions. It was the home of the late
Princess of Wales' family, the Spencers.
It was built in the mid-18thC and is one
of the great houses of the area. Now
owned by RIT Capital Partners plc, under
the Chairmanship of Lord Rothschild, it
has undergone extensive work to restore
it to its former glory. Take a look at the
magnificent ceiling in the Great Room
and the beautiful Painted Room.

This area is famous for its exclusive
gentlemen's clubs. They were featured
in much 19th and early 20thC fiction,
including that of P G Wodehouse, and
have become something of a joke among
those not privileged to be members.
However, if you would like to see inside
one of these enclaves, the Travellers
Club at 106 Pall Mall does conduct
guided tours.

The Mall Galleries, run by the
Federation of British Artists, in Carlton
House Terrace, has exhibitions of work
by both established and new artists.
The exhibitions held here are very
varied. They range from watercolours
to embroideries, and from marine to

Chinese art. You can check up on exhibitions on their website (see left).

Belgravia is owned by the Grosvenor Estate – the family trust of the Duke of Westminster, which is one of the wealthiest families in the country. Development here only started in about the 1820s and, like Mayfair, it has always been a fashionable address. It is full of grand houses, many of which are now embassies, and small mews cottages – once stables for the big houses.

Much of Pimlico is also owned by the Grosvenor Estate. Once an area of market gardens and reed beds for basket making, development started here in earnest in the 1840s. Although it has never been as fashionable as Belgravia, some of its terraces are delightful.

While in Pimlico, you can also visit the world-famous Tate Gallery on Millbank, which is applauded or derided for its exhibitions of avant garde art depending on the taste of the critic. The area is also ideally situated for making visits to the Houses of Parliament, Westminster Abbey, and the Roman Catholic Westminster Cathedral.

You might also like to cross the river and visit an unusual museum, the Florence Nightingale Museum, which is at the southern end of Westminster Bridge. It celebrates the life and achievements of Florence Nightingale, probably the most famous nurse in the world. It contains a unique collection of her personal possessions including clothes, furniture, books, letters, and portraits. As might be expected, there is a good section of exhibits relating to her role in the Crimean War and the Scutari Hospital there. Take the tube to Westminster then turn left over Westminster Bridge. When you have crossed the bridge, the museum is on the right – it is part of St Thomas' Hospital.

ARCHITECTURAL ANTIQUES

Crowther (SALVO) in Pimlico Road has decorative, period, garden ornaments, sculptures, urns, chimneypieces, paintings, and mirrors. On Saturdays it closes at 3pm. Nicholas Gifford-Mead (BADA, LAPADA), again in Pimlico Road, sells pre-1840 English and European chimneypieces and sculpture and is open Monday–Friday.

ARMS & ARMOUR

Peter Dale in Royal Opera Arcade sells antique arms and armour and is open Monday–Friday.

BOOKS

Classic Bindings, Cambridge Street, has general antiquarian books and classic bindings. The shop is open Monday–Friday. Thomas Heneage Art Books (ABA, LAPADA), in Duke Street, sells art reference books and is open Monday–Friday. Also in Duke Street, Sims Reed Ltd (ABA) has antiquarian, rare, and second-hand books, including books illustrated by artists and books on fine and applied arts. It is open Monday–Friday.

CARPETS & RUGS

Keshishian, (BADA) in the Pimlico Road sells Aubussons, British Arts and Crafts, Art Deco, antique, and modernist carpets and tapestries.

CERAMICS

One of the best-known dealers in fine ceramics, Albert Amor (RWHA) is located in Bury Street and sells 18thC English porcelain. The shop is open Monday–Friday.

CLOCKS & WATCHES

John Carlton-Smith (BADA), Ryder Street, has fine antique clocks and barometers and is open Monday–Friday. Somlo Antiques Ltd (BADA) in the Piccadilly Arcade sells vintage wristwatches and antique pocket watches.

COINS

Knightsbridge Coins (BNTA) in Duke Street has English and foreign Medieval–present-day coins. It is open Monday–Friday.

COLLECTABLES

Pullman Gallery Ltd, 14 King Street, has very up-market collectables including cocktail shakers, bar accessories, smoking accessories, automobilia, vintage Louis Vuitton and Hermès luggage, motor racing posters, and René Lalique glass from 1900–40. It is open Monday–Friday.

FURNITURE

There are a host of dealers in Pimlico Road. Among them, Anno Domini Antiques (BADA) has a large range of 18th and 19thC furniture, mirrors, pictures, and porcelain. The shop is open Monday–Friday until 3pm. Blanchard Ltd (LAPADA) sells

English and Continental furniture, decorative items, and works of art. On Saturday it closes at 3pm. Still in Pimlico Road, **Ciancimino Ltd** has Art Deco furniture, Oriental furniture, and ethnography. It is open Monday–Friday. **Ross Hamilton (Antiques) Ltd** (LAPADA, CINOA) in Pimlico Road, sells 17th–19thC fine English and Continental furniture as well as 16th–20thC paintings, Oriental porcelain, objets d'art, and bronzes. On Saturday it closes at 4pm. **John Hobbs Ltd** (BADA) has an extensive selection of 18th and 19thC Continental and English furniture, objets d'art, and statuary. On Saturday it closes at 4pm. **Christopher Hodsoll Ltd** (BADA), still in Pimlico Road, has 18th and 19thC furniture as well as works of art. **Christopher Howe Antiques** sells English Regency–20thC modern design classic furniture. **Anthony Outred Antiques Ltd** (BADA) has 18th and 19thC English, Irish, and Continental furniture as well as sculptures, lighting, and oil paintings. **Hermitage Antiques plc** has Biedermeier and Russian furniture and chandeliers, oil paintings, decorative arts, and bronzes. **Humphrey-Carrasco** sells English furniture, and objects from the 18th and 19thC. **Mark Ransom Ltd** has Russian and French Empire furniture, decorative items, objets d'art, prints, and pictures. **Rogier Antiques** has French and Continental 18th and 19thC decorative furniture, unusual lamps, reproductions, and lighting. On Saturday it closes early, at 4pm. **Westenholz Antiques Ltd**, in Pimlico Road, has 18th and 19thC English furniture and decorative items. It is open Monday–Friday from 8.30am.

In Bury Street, **John Bly** (BADA, LAPADA, CINOA), well known from his television appearances, sells 18th and 19thC English furniture as well as works of art, objets d'art, paintings, silver, glass, porcelain, and tapestries. The shop is open Monday–Friday. **Didier Aaron (London) Ltd** (BADA), in Ryder Street sells 18th and early 19thC Continental furniture as well as old master drawings and paintings and is open Monday–Friday by appointment only – ring 020 7839 4716. **Hotspur Ltd** (BADA), in Lowndes Street, has 18thC quality furniture and works of art. On Saturday it is open until 1pm. Also in Lowndes Street, **Jeremy Ltd** (BADA) has 18th–early 19thC English and Continental furniture, works of art, clocks, and antiques. It is open weekdays from 8.30am and on Saturday closes at 1pm. **Odyssey Fine Arts Ltd** (LAPADA), Holbein Place, sells 18th and 19thC French and English painted furniture, engravings, and Chinese watercolours. On Saturday the shop closes early, at 3.30pm. **Un Francais à Londres**, Ebury Street, sells French and Continental furniture and works of art from the 17th–19thC. On Saturday the shop shuts at 4pm.

GENERAL ANTIQUES

John King (BADA), in Pimlico Road, has a large stock of period furniture, associated items, and 20thC items. It is open Monday–Friday. **M & D Lewis**, also in Pimlico Road, sells English and Continental furniture and Oriental porcelain. On Saturday the shop is open until 12 noon.

LIGHTING

Still in Pimlico Road, **McClenaghan** has period lighting and English country house furniture.

MAPS & PRINTS

J A L Franks and Co., 7 Allington Street, has 16th–19thC antique maps and is open Monday–Friday.

MARINE ANTIQUES

Trevor Philip & Son Ltd (BADA), in 75a Jermyn Street, has ships' models, marine, and navigation instruments. On Saturday the shop shuts at 4pm.

MIRRORS

Back to Pimlico Road, **Chelsea Antique Mirrors** sells 18th and 19thC mirrors and furniture. On Saturday the shop shuts early, at 2pm. **Ossowski** (BADA), also in Pimlico Road, has a large range of 18thC English giltwood mirrors, tables, and decorative wood carving. On Saturday it is open morning only, until 1pm.

ORIENTAL

Brian Harkins, Bury Street, sells Chinese and Japanese antiques, scholars' items, furniture, decorative items, ceramics, bronzes, rocks, and baskets. The shop is open Monday–Friday. **Jeremy Mason**, 145 Ebury Street sells Oriental works of art from all periods by appointment only – ring 020 7730 8331. **Rossi & Rossi Ltd** in Jermyn Street has Asian art, sculpture, paintings from India and the Himalayas, and Chinese textiles. It is open Monday–Friday.

PAINTINGS & SCULPTURE

Victor Franses Gallery (BADA), in Jermyn Street, has 19thC animalia sculpture, paintings, drawings, and watercolours. It is open Monday–Friday. **Daniel Katz Ltd** (SLAD), also in Jermyn Street, has an extensive selection of European sculpture, works of art, and old master paintings. It is open Monday–Friday. **Peter Nahum** (BADA), one of the BBC's *Antiques Roadshow* experts is located in Ryder Street. The shop has 19th and 20thC paintings, drawings, and sculpture and is open from Monday–Friday.

ROYAL MEMORABILIA

The Armoury of St James (OMRS, GOMC) in Piccadilly Arcade specializes in royal memorabilia and model soldiers. On Saturday it opens at 12 noon.

SILVER & JEWELLERY

In Charlwood Street, **ADC Heritage Ltd** (BADA) sells antique English silver and old Sheffield plate by appointment only – ring 020 7976 5271. **Kenneth Davis (Works of Art) Ltd**, King Street, has antique English and Continental silver and works of art. The shop is open Monday–Friday. In Jermyn Street, **Alastair Dickenson Fine Silver Ltd** (BADA) sells 16th–19thC fine, rare English silver and is open Monday–Friday. **J H Bourdon-Smith Ltd** (BADA, CINOA), Masons Yard, Duke Street, has a large range of Georgian and Victorian silver and modern reproduction silver. It is open Monday–Friday. **Harvey & Gore** (BADA), Duke Street, sells jewellery, bijouterie, snuff boxes, old Sheffield plate, and miniatures. The shop is open Monday–Friday. In Bury Street, **N & I Franklin** (BADA) have 17th–18thC English domestic silver. It is open Monday–Friday.

The Silver Fund Ltd (LAPADA), also in Bury Street, has Georg Jensen, Tiffany, Martele, and Puiforcat silver and is open Monday–Friday.

TEXTILES

Peta Smyth Antique Textiles (LAPADA, CINOA) in Moreton Street sells early European textiles, needlework, silks, tapestries, and hangings. The shop is open Monday–Friday.

AUCTION HOUSES

International auctioneers, **Christie's of King Street** have a huge variety of sales of fine art and antiques throughout the year, except in August and January, with viewing four days prior to sales and during weekends and evenings. They also give free verbal auction estimates. As well as their salerooms in other countries, they have another one in London – Christie's South Kensington, in the Old Brompton Road, London SW7, where there are weekly specialist sales with a particular emphasis on collectables.

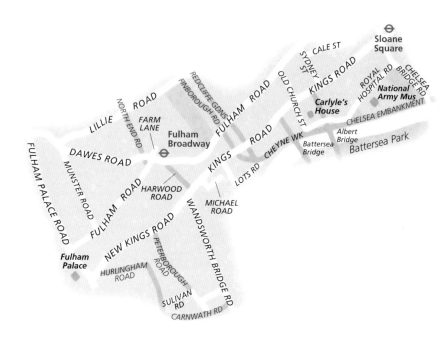

With most antiques dealers located towards the western end of the King's Road, if you want to start in Chelsea use the Sloane Square tube station on the Circle or District Lines and then get a bus down the King's Road. Alternatively, start in Fulham using Fulham Broadway tube station on the District Line. You can then catch a bus or walk to Chelsea.

The adjoining areas of Fulham and Chelsea have a profusion of antiques shops, especially those specializing in furniture. The dealers here have a reputation for finding antiques that are unusual and, in some cases, bizarre, which makes this a Mecca for interior designers looking for extraordinary

pieces. In Chelsea, the shops tend to be on the western side, past World's End on the King's Road. This area was the home of the Chelsea Porcelain Works in the middle of the 18thC. It was a relatively short-lived venture – Chelsea Porcelain is now rare and very collectable.

The village of Chelsea was mentioned in the *Domesday Book*, although it was another 500 years before it became fashionable. In 1520 Sir Thomas More, eventually executed by Henry VIII for his faith, built a country house here. In the same century Chelsea became known as the Village of Palaces when Henry VIII and other members of the aristocracy built palaces around the village. One of the area's most famous landmarks

▶ ▶ USEFUL CONTACTS

Websites

www.adams-antiques-fairs.co.uk
Adams Antiques Fairs hold regular Saturday events at Chelsea Old Town Hall. The website gives future dates and other information about all the fairs.

www.bonhams.com
If you want to attend auctions at Bonham & Brooks, you can find a full calendar of sales on their website.

www.penman-fairs.co.uk
Check out the dates of the forthcoming Chelsea Antiques Fairs and read information on exhibitors and vetting.

www.cpgarden.demon.co.uk
www.cpgarden.demon.co.uk/cpg.html
Both of these websites belong to the Chelsea Physic Garden. The first is the "Flash" version, which is very pretty but requires a "Flash" plugin and takes a while to load. Even then it is quite an effort to find any information. The second URL is a plain text version and tells you everything you need to know.

www.netcentral.co.uk/steveb/mark/c/chelsea.html
If you want to know more about Chelsea Porcelain, look at this specialist site, which gives a brief history of the factory together with illustrations of the marks that were used on the porcelain.

www.decorativefair.com
If you want to visit the Decorative Antiques & Textiles Fair, you will find all the information you need here together with pictures from past fairs.

www.towy-fairs.co.uk
Take a look at Towy Fairs site for the future dates of the Little Chelsea Fair.

www.lotsroad.com
Believe it or not, buyers at this auction house once had to use umbrellas when it rained because the owners could not afford to repair the fire-damaged building. Read more about the history of this independent auctioneer and also check on the dates of forthcoming sales.

www.national-army-museum.ac.uk
The National Army Museum in Chelsea is a "must" for anybody interested in militaria or military history. Find out more on its website.

▶ ▶ USEFUL CONTACTS

Tourist Information Centres

There are no centres in the Chelsea and Fulham area but if you want information, the central ones below should be able to help.

London: British Visitor Centre
1 Regent Street, Piccadilly Circus.
Heathrow Airport
Underground Station Concourse.
Victoria Station Forecourt.
London Waterloo International Arrivals Hall.

The telephone number for all of these is 09068 663344 (calls charged at 60 pence per minute).

is Chelsea Hospital, which was built by Charles II and designed by Sir Christopher Wren as a home for veteran soldiers. Nearly 500 years later, it still serves its original purpose and the "Chelsea Pensioners" can be seen around in the area in their distinctive navy blue uniforms. The grounds of the Hospital are host to the world-famous Chelsea Flower Show in May and, more recently, Decorex, which is the annual interior design show.

Founded at the end of the 17thC, Chelsea Physic Garden also continues its original work, which has now been expanded to include education and to ensure it is a visitor attraction. It contains in excess of 6,000 plants and also holds a seed bank of global importance. It has areas devoted to the history of plants in medicine as well as tender species benefiting from the urban microclimate and southern hemisphere species grown in greenhouses. The garden is situated in Royal Hospital Road, but has its entrance in Swan Walk. To get there, take the tube to Sloane Square. Come out of the station and walk straight ahead along the southern side of the square. Turn left at the traffic lights into Lower Sloane Street and walk down there to the next major junction. Turn right into Royal Hospital Road and Swan Walk is the last turning on the left. This walk should take no more than 10–15 minutes.

If you are interested in militaria or military history, do not miss the National Army Museum, which is also in Royal Hospital Road. It covers the history of the British Army from the 15th–21stC, and its displays include paintings, equipment, and the largest collection of military uniforms in the world. To visit the museum, follow the directions above for the Chelsea Physic Garden. Halfway down Royal Hospital Road the museum is on the left, just past the hospital.

If you are visiting the Chelsea Physic Garden or the National Army Museum, continue walking to the bottom of Royal Hospital Road and you will see Cheyne (pronounced "chainey") Walk opposite. This is the location of Carlyle's House, a National Trust property and once the home of the Victorian writer and historian, Thomas Carlyle, known as the Sage of Chelsea, who died in 1881. The Queen Anne house contains his original furniture and possessions and the rooms remain as they were when he died.

Neighbouring Fulham developed more slowly than Chelsea and still had farmland and market gardens until the latter half of the 19thC. From the 8thC, Fulham was owned by the Bishops of London and, until 1973, it was here they had their official residence, at Fulham Palace. Although a Grade 1 listed building, it is one of London's least known historic attractions. Parts of it date back to the early 16thC, although there have been alterations and additions throughout the centuries. It is set in 13 acres of beautiful gardens.

ART DECO
Gordon Watson Ltd (LAPADA) in Fulham Road sells Art Deco furniture and lighting.

BOOKS
Chelsea Gallery and Il Libro (LAPADA) in the Plaza King's Road, sells antique illustrated books, literature, prints, and maps, and specializes in natural history, travel, architecture, and history. It is open until 7pm. Peter Herington Antiquarian Bookseller (ABA, PBFA), in Fulham Road, sells antiquarian books – illustrated, fine bindings, English literature, travel, and children's as well as modern first editions. Also in Fulham Road, John Thornton has antiquarian and second-hand books, especially on Catholic/Anglo Catholic theology. World's End Bookshop, in the King's Road, has antiquarian, rare, and second-hand books on art, non-fiction, literature, etc. It is open 7 days a week.

CERAMICS
Jacqueline Oosthuizen Antiques (LAPADA), located in Cale Street, has a large stock of Staffordshire animals, cottages, and figures as well as a range of jewellery.

CLOCKS
Big Ben Clocks and Antiques, in New King's Road, has an extensive range of longcase, mantel, Grandfather, and traditional reproduction clocks. It is open Tuesday–Saturday. Roger Lascelles Clocks Ltd, in Carnwath Road, sells antique and reproduction clocks and is open Monday–Friday.

COLLECTABLES
Rogers de Rin (BADA), located in Royal Hospital Road, has collectors' items, snuff boxes, enamels, Vienna bronzes, and Staffordshire and Scottish Wemyss ware. On Saturday it is open until 1pm.

DECORATIVE ITEMS
H R W Antiques Ltd (LAPADA) at 26 Sulivan Road has a wide selection of decorative items and is open Monday–Friday. In the Fulham Road, Judy Greenwood Antiques sells 19th–20thC French decorative items, beds, textiles, lighting, furniture, mirrors, and quilts. L'Accademia Antiques, also in Fulham Road sells antiques, decorative items, chandeliers, bedroom furniture, mirrors, and French and Italian furniture. Nimmo & Spooner in Lillie Road sell decorative antiques, unusual objects, and 18thC French furniture.

FIREPLACES
Old World Trading Co., on the King's Road, have a large range of 18th–19thC English and French chimney places, fire dogs, and grates. On Saturday the shop shuts at 3pm. H W Poulter & Son in the Fulham Road, has 18th and 19thC marble, wooden, and stone fireplaces and accessories. On Saturday it is open until 12 noon.

FURNITURE

There is small concentration of dealers in Lillie Road, to the north of Fulham Broadway. The first, **275 Antiques**, sells 1880s–1930s furniture, decorative items, American Lucite furniture, and lighting from the 1930s–70s. Nearby, **Marc Costantini** Antiques has a large stock of English and Continental antique furniture. Still in Lillie Road, **Decorative Antiques** (LAPADA) has 18th and 19thC French provincial furniture and Irish furniture. **Jackdawes** (LAPADA), just along the road, sells decorative French, Italian, and English painted furniture together with lighting and gilded mirrors. The last of the Lillie Road shops, **Stephen Sprake Antiques** sells 18th–20thC English and French furniture, lighting, and unusual architectural pieces.

The King's Road is another area popular with antiques dealers. The first of the shops there, located near Chelsea Old Town Hall, is **After Noah**, which sells antique and contemporary furniture and housewares. It is open 7 days a week (from 12 noon on Sunday). Near World's End on the King's Road, **L'Encoignure** has 18th and 19thC French furniture, decorative items, and other Continental furniture. Towards the Fulham end of the road, **Nicole Fabre French Antiques** (LAPADA) has French Provençal furniture, beds, quilts, linens and textiles, and 18th and 19thC toiles and decorative items. **Ena Green** sells 18th–20thC painted furniture, lighting, mirrors, and decorative items. **L & E Kreckovic** has early 18th and 19thC furniture. Still in the King's Road, **M Luther Antiques** has 18th and 19thC English and Continental furniture, tables, chairs, mirrors, lighting, etc. **I and J L Brown Ltd** have a large stock of English country and French provincial antique and reproduction furniture as well as an extensive range of decorative items. **David Martin-Taylor Antiques** (LAPADA) has a wide range of 18th and 19thC Continental and English furniture, objets d'art, and decorative art – from the eccentric to the unusual. The last of the King's Road dealers, **Mora & Upham Antiques**, sells gilded French chairs, antique chandeliers, 18th and 19thC English and Continental furniture, and mirrors.

The Fulham Road runs parallel with the King's Road for part of its length and is home to many antiques dealers, including **Apter-Fredericks Ltd** (BADA). They specialize in 18thC English furniture and are open Monday–Friday. **Richard Courtney Ltd** (BADA) sells finest early 18thC English walnut furniture and is also open Monday–Friday. **Robert Dickson and Lesley Rendall Antiques** (BADA) has antique furniture, English and French works of art, and English Regency. Still in the Fulham Road, **Stephen Long** has painted furniture, small decorative items, and English pottery from 1780–1850. On Saturday the shop is open until 12.30pm. **Michael Foster** (BADA) sells fine 18th–early 19thC furniture and works of art. The shop is open Monday–Friday. **Anthony James & Son Ltd** (BADA, CINOA) specializes in fine 18th and 19thC English and Continental furniture and decorative items. It is open Monday–Friday. Continuing on the Fulham Road, **Christopher Jones Antiques** has French furniture, mirrors, screens, and 1860–90 Chinese porcelain. **Peter Lipitch Ltd** (BADA) sells 18thC English furniture and on Saturday shuts at 2pm. Nearby, **Michael Lipitch** (BADA) has an extensive range of 18th and 19thC fine furniture, mirrors, and objets d'art. **Michael Marriott** specializes in English 18th and 19thC furniture and antiquarian prints. On Saturday he is open mornings only, until 1pm. Finally in the Fulham Road, **Mark Maynard** sells painted French furniture and decorative items.

Moving now to Michael Road, just off the western end of the King's Road, **Alasdair Brown** has 19th and 20thC furniture, lighting, upholstery, and unusual items. The shop is open Wednesday and Thursday 10am–6pm. **Birdie Fortescue Antiques** (LAPADA), also in Michael Road, sells 18th–early 19thC Continental furniture by appointment only – ring 01206 337567. **Fulham Antiques**, in Munster Road, has antique and decorative furniture, lighting, and mirrors. **Lini Designs**, Sydney Street, sells antique Indian furniture, cushions, artefacts, and Christmas decorations. It is open 7 days a week (from 12 noon on Sunday). On the Wandsworth Bridge Road, **Ann May** has painted French furniture and decorative items. **O F Wilson Ltd** (BADA, LAPADA), in Old Church Street, sells Continental furniture, French chimney pieces, English painted decorative furniture, and mirrors. On Saturday the shop is open morning only, until 1pm.

GENERAL ANTIQUES

Back in the King's Road, **Joanna Booth** (BADA, CINOA) has a large stock of master drawings, early sculptures, tapestries, oak furniture, and textiles. **Nigel Hindley**, Lillie Road, has an extensive range of English period antiques, French furniture, and eccentricities. **No. 12**, Cale Street, sells French country antiques. **Christine Schell** (LAPADA) in Cale Street has tortoiseshell, ivory, silver, Arts and Crafts, decorative items, and mirrors.

LIGHTING

Fergus Cochrane, Leigh Warren, King's Road, sells 19th and 20thC lighting. On Saturday it shuts at 4pm. In Wandsworth Bridge Road, **Hector Finch Lighting** is a specialist period lighting shop with a large range of antique and contemporary decorative lighting. **Rainbow Antiques**, Lillie Road, has Italian and French 1880–1940 period lighting, chandeliers, lamps, and lanterns. **Rainbow Too Interiors**, this time in Munster Road, sells Italian and French period and decorative lighting. **Charles Saunders Antiques**, Fulham Road, has antique lighting as well as offering a variety of English and Continental 18th and 19thC furniture, objects, and decorations.

MAPS & PRINTS

In the King's Road, **Classic Prints** has a large range of antique prints of all ages as well as maps. The shop is open 7 days a week (from 12 noon on Sunday). **King's Court Galleries**, Fulham Road, sells antique maps, engravings, and sporting and decorative prints. **York Gallery Ltd**, located in the King's Road, specializes in antique prints.

MARITIME ANTIQUES

Langfords Marine Antiques (BADA, LAPADA), located in the Plaza, King's Road, is one of the world's leading dealers in nautical artefacts and maritime antiques.

MIRRORS

The Antique Mirror Gallery, in New King's Road, has an extensive stock of 18th and 19thC gilt mirrors and gilt furniture. **Through The Looking Glass**, King's Road, has a wide range of 19thC mirrors.

ORIENTAL ANTIQUES

Sebastiano Barbagallo Antiques, in the Fulham Road specializes in Chinese furniture, in addition to Indian and Tibetan antiques and crafts. The shop is open 7 days a week. **Snap Dragon**, also in the Fulham Road, has a selection of 18th and 19thC Chinese furniture and chairs. **Indigo**, in New King's Road, has a wide range of Indian and Chinese furniture, decorative items, handicrafts, and Indonesian furniture made from recycled teakwood. In the King's Road, **Daphne Rankin & Ian Conn Oriental Antiques** (LAPADA) has an extensive stock of 17th–19thC Japanese imari, Chinese export porcelain, Rose Mandarin, Blue Canton, and tortoiseshell tea caddies. **Soosan**, still in the King's Road, specializes in Asian interiors. **Orient Expressions Ltd** (BABAADA), Michael Road, sells mostly early 19thC provincial Chinese furniture and accessories by appointment – ring 020 7610 9311. **Red Room**, Farm Lane, just behind Fulham Broadway station, has 18th and 19thC Chinese decorative antique furniture. It is open Wednesday–Saturday (closing at 3pm on Saturday).

PAINTINGS

Rupert Cavendish Antiques, King's Road, has a large stock of European 20thC paintings.

RELIGIOUS ANTIQUES

Whiteway & Waldron Ltd of Munster Road specialize in religious Victoriana, statues, chalices, sanctuary lamps, crucifixes, and candlesticks. On Saturday, the shop shuts at 4pm.

SILVER & JEWELLERY

Giovanna Donoghue, back in the Kings Road, sells jewellery, silver, fans, amber, and coral. It is open Tuesday–Saturday.

ANTIQUES CENTRES

Antiquarius Antique Centre, on the King's Road near Chelsea Town Hall, has over 100 dealers selling general and specialist antiques of all periods. Among the antiques to be found there are Sabino glass, drinking glasses, decanters, scent bottles, and ceramics such as majolica, Moorcroft pottery, Staffordshire, Chinese export porcelain, famille rose, famille verte, Chinese Imari, blue and white porcelain, and Limogès boxes. Among the collectables you can find fountain pens, writing materials, scales, militaria, edge weapons, as well as British and foreign campaign and gallantry medals. There are also antique clocks, silver and jewellery, costume jewellery, photograph frames, and much more.

Bourbon Hanby Antiques Centre, located on the corner of the King's Road and Sydney Street, has 30 dealers selling 18thC textiles, scientific instruments, Georgian–Edwardian jewellery, Vienna bronzes, and decorative antiques. It is open 7 days a week.

The Furniture Cave, still on the King's Road but this time up by Lots Road, has a good selection of antiques. It is open 7 days a week (from 12 noon on Sunday). Included among the specialist antiques are many different types of furniture such as English and Continental 18th–20thC leather armchairs and bookcases. In spite of its name, there is more than just furniture here. You can find sculpture, bronzes, tapestries, paintings, works of art, chandeliers, lighting, antiquarian books, and prints by Simon Hatchwell

ANTIQUES FAIRS

Chelsea Antiques Fair has been established since 1950. It takes place twice a year at Chelsea Old Town Hall, on the King's Road. It is a well respected vetted fair. Although also held in the Old Town Hall and taking place twice a year, **Little Chelsea Antiques Fair** is quite different. This is the fair where the middle- to top-quality dealers go to buy. **The Decorative Antiques & Textiles Fair**, just across the Chelsea Bridge in Battersea Park, attracts buyers from all over the world. It was this fair that put decorative antiques on the map and led to scores of copycat events. While most of those have disappeared, the original goes from strength to strength. There are two other organizers who hold antiques and collectors' fairs at Chelsea Old Town Hall, but these are one-day events – **Adams Antiques Fairs** has a fair on Saturdays about once a month and **Mainwarings Antiques Fairs** has monthly Sunday fairs.

AUCTION HOUSES

Bonhams & Brooks in Lots Road is one of the "Big Four" London auction houses. Here it holds regular sales of furniture, carpets, ceramics, glass, Oriental works of art, 19thC oils, watercolours, modern pictures, prints, frames, toys, dolls, textiles, rock/pop, tribal art, and decorative arts. On Sunday the office is open 11am–3pm (viewing only). The main office is in Montpelier Street, SW7, where they hold sales of the finest antiques. They also have regular house and attic sales across the country. On Sunday the SW7 office is also open 11am–3pm. **Lots Road Galleries**, in Lots Road, has two sales each week on a Sunday. The first is a sale of contemporary items and the second of a selection of furniture, paintings, rugs, needlework, and decorative items. They also have a fine antiques sale each month. **Onslow Auctions Ltd**, Michael Road, has four collectors' sales per year and they include vintage travel, aeronautical, posters, railways, motoring, and ocean liners.

Francis Smith Ltd, again in Lots Road, has fortnightly antique and general sales on Tuesday at 6pm, with viewing Sunday 11am–4pm, Monday 9am–7pm, and the day of the sale 9am–6pm.

WALLINGFORD ▶ READING ▶ HENLEY-ON-THAMES ▶ WINDSOR AND ETON ▶
AMERSHAM ▶ TRING ▶ AYLESBURY ▶ LEIGHTON BUZZARD ▶ WOBURN

This tour goes through three counties: Oxfordshire, Berkshire, and Buckinghamshire. The scenery in this region shows England at its most civilized – neat fields and chocolate box villages are the typical views. The Thames runs through the southern part of the tour and here it becomes a wide but calm river, ideal for boating, and it also provides the backdrop to one of

Berkshire's most famous landmarks, which is of course Windsor Castle.

The famous Chiltern Hills, which have become a designated Area of Outstanding Natural Beauty, lie between Goring to the south-west and Luton in the north-east. This is an area of chalk hills and beech and bluebell woods. It contains 63 sites of special scientific interest and 3 national nature reserves.

▶▶ USEFUL CONTACTS

Websites

www.windsor.gov.uk
This official site for the Royal Borough of Windsor and Maidenhead is packed with information on the area.

www.windsor-tourism.co.uk
More directly aimed at visitors, this site provides information on places to visit, restaurants, shopping, transport, art, and antiques in the area.

www.woburnabbey.co.uk
Everything you want to know about Woburn Abbey, whether it is the history of the house and Russell family, the grounds, safari park, or the important collections of art and antiques, can be found on the official website.

www.tvada.co.uk
Check out this site for more information on the Thames Valley Antiques Dealers' Association and its members. You may also telephone them on 01865 341639.

Tourist Information Centres

Aylesbury 8 Bourbon Street.
Tel: 01296 330559

Henley-on-Thames King's Arms Barn, Kings Road. Tel: 01491 578034

Reading The Town Hall, Blagrave Street.
Tel: 0118 956 6226

Windsor 24 High Street.
Tel: 01753 743900

WALLINGFORD

The tour begins in this charming Oxfordshire, Georgian town, which is situated on the River Thames. The town grew up around a ford across the river, and the town's 275m- (900ft-) long bridge still has remnants of its original 13thC stonework.

BOOKS
The only antiquarian bookshop in Wallingford, **Toby English Antique & Secondhand Books** (PBFA), in St Mary Street, specializes in books on art, architecture, and Renaissance literature.

FURNITURE
There are three furniture dealers in the town, all located in the High Street. **M & J De Albuquerque** have 18th–19thC French and English furniture as well as other objects of the same period. Also selling 18th–19thC furniture, **Otter Antiques** specializes in antique boxes too, and they are open 7 days a week. **Summers Davis Antiques Ltd** (LAPADA, TVADA) has a large stock of 17th–19thC English and Continental furniture displayed in 11 showrooms. They are open 7 days a week.

GENERAL ANTIQUES
O'Donnell Antiques, again in the High Street, has a large stock of general antiques including Georgian–early 20thC furniture, taxidermy, rugs, English pine, and Oriental items.

MAPS
Tooley, Adams and Co. (IMCOS, ABA) specializes in antiquarian maps and atlases. It is open by appointment only – ring 01491 838298.

SILVER
Alicia Antiques in the Lamb Arcade sells silver and silverplate together with glass and small furniture. It also offers a silver repair service.

ANTIQUES CENTRES
The Lamb Arcade (TVADA) in the High Street is the town's only antiques centre. It has 39 dealers selling everything from period furniture to small items.

AUCTION HOUSES
Bonhams & Brooks' regional representative, **Tony Guy**, can be found at Moat Cottage in the nearby village of Brightwell-cum-Sotwell, just off the westbound A4130.

▶ Take the A4074 from Wallingford to Reading, which is about 17.75km (11 miles) away.

READING

Visitors to the busy commercial town of Reading might be surprised to find it has a long history. King Henry I was buried in its once famous 13thC abbey, which was almost completely destroyed during the Dissolution of the Monasteries, and it was here that Edward IV announced his marriage to Elizabeth Woodville. Somewhat more recently, Oscar Wilde was imprisoned in Reading Gaol.

Two fascinating museums are located in Reading University at Whiteknights. The Ure Museum of Greek Archaeology has a small but important collection. Although used as a research and teaching resource, it is open to the public during weekdays. The museum's collection includes Stone Age pottery, Egyptian antiquities, ancient Greek vases, and a rare musical instrument – the "Reading Aulos", which is a reed-pipe. In complete contrast, the Museum of English Rural Life shows life in the country before machinery changed it forever.

CLOCKS
The Clock Workshop (LAPADA, TVADA, FBHI), located in Prospect Street in the Caversham area of the town, sells English clocks and French carriage clocks. On Saturdays it is open until 1pm.

COINS
Located in Ravensworth Road, Mortimer, Frank Milward (BNTA, ANA) specializes in English and foreign coins and banknotes. It is open by appointment only – ring 0118 933 2843.

FURNITURE
The town has two antique furniture dealers. The first, Fanny's Antiques in Lynmouth Road, has English and French furniture and is open 7 days a week until 4pm. The second is P D Leatherland Antiques in London Street, which has a large stock of 18th and 19thC furniture as well as porcelain, clocks, paintings, and decorative items.

GENERAL ANTIQUES
Shinfield Antiques is situated just on the outskirts of Reading at Lane End Farm, Shinfield Road, Shinfield, a village on the A327 just to the south of the M4. The shop has a large stock of furniture, china, fireplaces, and architectural antiques and is open 7 days a week.

ANTIQUES CENTRES
Located in Merchants Place, Stables Antiques Centre has 40 dealers selling furniture, silver, china, jewellery, collectables, models, coins, and militaria.

AUCTION HOUSES
The town's only auctioneer is Special Auction Services at The Coach House, Midgham Park. They have special sales of commemoratives, pot lids, Prattware, fairings, Goss and other crested ware, Baxter, and Le Blond prints. The sales are held in March, June, September, and November at the

Courtyard Hotel, Padworth. The office is open by appointment only – ring 0118 971 2949.

▶ Take the A4155 north-westwards to Henley-on-Thames, which is just 13km (8 miles) away.

HENLEY-ON-THAMES
Back in Oxfordshire, Henley-on-Thames is the home of the famous Regatta in July. The twists and bends of the River Thames straighten out for about 1.6km (1 mile) at Henley, making it ideal for racing. The town has literally hundreds of listed buildings with the earliest, the Chantry House, dating back to the 14thC.

ARCHITECTURAL ANTIQUES
In the village of Bix on the A4130, Easy Strip at Old Manor Farm sells Victorian doors and architectural antiques by appointment only – ring 01491 577289. There is also a door stripping service. In the village of Nettlebed, just about 1.6km (1 mile) further north-west on the same road, Nettlebed Antiques Merchants (TVADA), in the High Street, sells garden and architectural items. It also has restoration and upholstery services and is open 7 days a week.

BOOKS
Henley boasts two bookshops. Bromlea and Jonkers (ABA, PBFA) in Hart Street have antiquarian literature, 19th and 20thC first editions, and illustrated children's books. Ways Bookshop (ABA) in Friday Street buys and sells rare and second-hand books. It also has book search, bookbinding, and valuation services.

FURNITURE
Well known for their stylish displays at major fairs, the Country Seat (TVADA, LAPADA) have a large stock of architect-designed, 17th–20thC furniture at their base in Huntercombe Manor Barn. It also has art, pottery, and metalwork. In Friday Street The "Stock" Exchange has period and Victorian furniture as well as porcelain.

GENERAL ANTIQUES
Tudor House Antiques and Collectables in Duke Street has a large stock of antiques and collectables and is open 7 days a week.

MIRRORS
Greys Green is a tiny village on a country road about 3.2km (2 miles) west of Henley. It is the home of The Old French Mirror Company (TVADA). Located in The Nightingales, they have a large stock of decorative gilded and painted French

mirrors from 1720–1920. It is open by appointment only – ring 01491 629913.

ANTIQUES CENTRES

Henley-on-Thames is particularly blessed with antiques centres. There are five in the town, three of which are on the Reading Road. The first of these is the **Henley Antiques Centre**, with 13 dealers selling furniture, glass, china, silver, lace, coins, scientific instruments, and tools. It is open 7 days a week (from 12 noon on Sundays). The second is the **Henley Emporium** with 20 dealers and the third is the **Jackdaw Antiques Centre**. It has a large stock of furniture, ceramics, glass, collectables, and other general antiques. In Friday Street, **The Ferret** (also called the **Friday Street Antiques Centre**) has six dealers selling jewellery, silver, furniture, china, books, and collectables. It is open 7 days a week (from 12 noon on Sundays). **The Worm Home Antiques Centre** in Greys Road has 13 dealers who sell furniture and collectors' items. It is open 7 days a week (also from 12 noon on Sundays).

AUCTION HOUSES

The regional representative of **Bonham & Brooks** is located at the Coach House in Northfield End and is open Monday–Friday, and the first Saturday of each month from 10am–1pm. **Simmons & Sons** in Bell Street have eight sales a year of general antiques. The office is open on Saturday mornings until 12 noon.

▶ From Henley take the A4130 for about 8.5km (5 miles) to its junction with the A404. Turn right and follow the A404, which becomes the A404M. Turn off at the A308, which, after about 10km (6 miles), will take you to Windsor and Eton.

WINDSOR & ETON

The two towns of Windsor and Eton stand side by side, divided only by the River Thames. Most of the antiques shops are in Eton, all conveniently situated in the High Street. Those in Windsor are distributed more widely.

Windsor Castle dominates Windsor. Still used by the Royal Family as a home, it was built by William the Conqueror. Since the 11thC succeeding monarchs have made changes and additions, for example, Edward III built the Round Tower in 1348. Parts of the castle are open to the public, including the State

Apartments (when the Queen is not in residence), Queen Mary's Dolls' House, and the Exhibition of the Queen's Presents and Royal Carriages.

Eton is famous for its school, which stands on the banks of the Thames. Founded by Henry VI in 1440, many of the present buildings date back to the 15thC. Eton has historically provided the nation with some of its most powerful men including the Duke of Wellington, Pitt the Elder, and Harold MacMillan.

ETON

BOXES

Mostly Boxes has a large stock of antique boxes including ivory, tortoiseshell, and decorative ones.

CLOCKS

Times Past Antiques (MBHI) sells clocks, barometers, and small furniture. It is open by appointment only – ring 01753 857018.

FURNITURE

There are three specialist furniture dealers in the High Street. The first, **Eton Antiques**, has 18th and 19thC English furniture. It is open 7 days a week (from 2.30–5pm on Sunday). The next, **Peter J Martin** (TVADA, LAPADA), also has furniture but covers the period from the 18th–20thC and also stocks copper, brass, and mirrors. The shop is open until 1pm on Saturdays. **Woodage Antiques** (LAPADA) also sells 18th–20thC furniture.

GENERAL ANTIQUES

Art and Antiques (Eton Traders) has a large selection of furniture, china, brass, silverplate, jewellery, and collectors' items. It is open 7 days a week (from 2.30–6pm on Sundays). **The Eton Antique Centre Ltd** (TVADA) also has a large range, this time of Victorian and Edwardian furniture, collectors' china, Staffordshire figures, chandeliers, and silver. It is open 7 day a week. Finally, the **Turks Head Antiques** deals in small furniture, porcelain, silver, glass, and pictures.

WINDSOR

FURNITURE

The town has two specialist furniture dealers. **Country Furniture** (TVADA, LAPADA) in St Leonard's Road has a large stock of French provincial furniture, particularly armoires, beds, farm tables, buffets, mirrors, and decorative items. **Dee's Antique Pine** (TVADA), located in Grove Road, sells furniture and decorative antiques and is open Tuesday–Saturday.

GENERAL ANTIQUES

Berkshire Antiques Co. Ltd in Thames Street has a large range of silver, dolls, jewellery, furniture, pictures, porcelain, Art Deco, Art Nouveau, and commemorative ware. Based in the Country Gardens Garden Centre on the Dedworth Road, **Old Barn Antiques** (BSSA) deals in furniture, porcelain, jewellery, garden antiques, militaria, silver, dolls, and glassware. Lastly, **Rule's Antiques** (TVADA) in St Leonard's Road has decorative antiques, brass, lighting, door furniture, and fittings.

▶ Take the A355 from Windsor northbound direct to Amersham, a distance of approximately 19.25km (12 miles). Alternatively, you could visit Cliveden (see below) first. To do so, take the A308 to Maidenhead then the A4094, signposted Cookham, for about 6.5km (4 miles); the turning to Cliveden is on the right.

▶ To reach Amersham from Cliveden, return to the A4094 and continue north to its junction with the A40, just on the north side of the M40. Turn right here and drive for about 3.2km (2 miles). Here the A355 intersects the road – turn left towards Amersham. The total distance from Cliveden to Amersham is about 16km (10 miles).

AMERSHAM

This town is divided into two parts, the old and new. Old Amersham lies in the valley of the River Misbourne and it first gained its charter to hold a market in the 13thC. This part of the town contains many buildings from the 16th and 17thC, although 18thC façades have disguised some of them. New Amersham was built on a hill around the railway station.

GENERAL ANTIQUES

All of the dealers in the town carry a varied and interesting stock. There are two dealers in Whielden Street, the first is **Amersham Antiques and**

Collectors Centre, which sells general antiques and small items. The other is **Sundial Antiques**. It has 19thC copper and brass, small furniture, and ceramics. It is closed on Thursdays and Sundays. **Martony Antiques and Collectables** may be found at Grimsdells Corner, Sycamore Road. It sells general antiques and collectables and is open Tuesday–Saturday. The last of the town's dealers is **Liz Quilter** in the High Street, which has a large stock of pine collectables as well as copper, brass, and rustic furniture. It is open 7 days a week (12 noon–4pm on Sunday).

AUCTION HOUSES

There are two auctioneers in Amersham. The first, **The Amersham Auction Rooms** in Station Road has weekly sales on Thursdays at 10.30am. There is an antiques and collectors sale on the first Thursday of each month. Viewing for all sales is Tuesday 2–5pm, Wednesday 9.30am–7pm, and the morning of the sale from 9am–10.15am. The office is open Saturdays from 9am–11.30am. The other saleroom is **Old Amersham Auctions** in School Lane. They have occasional house sales as well as regular fortnightly auctions of general effects and antiques on Saturdays at 11am. Viewing is on the morning of the sale from 9am.

▶ Leave Amersham on the A416 northbound and continue for 11.25km (7 miles), then turn left onto the A41. Tring is 13km (8 miles) away.

TRING

The Grand Union Canal lies just outside of the town. Here it goes through a series of six locks where the canal climbs to 152.4m (500ft) above sea level.

CARDS

Situated in the village of Wilstone, about 3.2km (2 miles) from Tring on the B488, **W J Hazle** in Grange Road has a large stock of original, reproduction, and modern collectors' cards. It sells by mail order or appointment only – ring 01442 890493.

▶▶ CLIVEDEN

Cliveden (pronounced "clivden" to rhyme with give) is one of England's great mansions and is now owned by the National Trust. Much of the house was rebuilt in 1851 by the architect Sir Charles Barry and is generally acknowledged to be a masterpiece. The grounds are spectacular, with varied gardens set high above the River Thames. Viscount Astor and his wife Nancy once owned Cliveden and it was here they entertained some of the most famous and powerful people of their time, such as Winston Churchill, Henry James, and Rudyard Kipling.

CLOCKS

Country Clocks of Pendley Bridge Cottages, Tring Station, is the town's only specialist clock dealer with a range of 18th and 19thC wall, longcase, and mantel clocks. It is open 7 days a week (from 2–5pm on Sunday).

FURNITURE

John Bly (BADA), situated in The Old Billiards Room, Church Yard, is one of the most famous dealers in the country due to his appearances on programmes like the BBC's *Antiques Roadshow*. His antiques business is also one of the oldest, having been established in 1891. It has a large stock of Georgian furniture as well as porcelain, silver, glass, and other quality antiques. The shop is open Tuesday–Saturday until 4pm. The other two furniture shops are located in the High Street. Farrelly Antiques has antique furniture up to 1900. New England House Antiques displays a large range of Georgian, Victorian, and Edwardian furniture together with silver, glass, paintings, and clocks. It is open Tuesday–Saturday.

▶ Continue along the A41 westbound for about 13km (8 miles) until you arrive in Aylesbury.

AYLESBURY

The town has a wealth of historic buildings, principally in the centre. They include the King's Head (a 15thC coaching inn), the County Hall (built in 1720), and the parish church of St Mary's from the 13thC. Aylesbury also has an award-winning museum, the Buckinghamshire County Museum and Roald Dahl Children's Gallery in Church Street. Among other commendations, it won the Museum of the Year award in 1996/97. The hands-on exhibits show how a number of crafts, like brickmaking, were done in years gone by. The Roald Dahl section uses the author's imaginative creations, such as the Giant Peach, to illustrate natural history, science, technology, and history.

Another attraction, Waddesdon Manor, stands just 6.5km (4 miles) west of the town on the A41. It was built at the end of the 19thC for Baron Ferdinand de Rothschild. This has also won Museum of the Year awards. It houses one of the finest collections of French 18thC antiques in the world. They include Sèvres porcelain, Beauvais tapestries, works by Gainsborough and Reynolds, and fine French furniture. There are also collections of drawings, gold boxes, and buttons.

POTTERY

The town's only dealer is Gillian Neale Antiques, whose owner is a well-known figure at major antiques fairs. It has a large stock of English blue printed pottery dating from 1780–1900. The shop is open by appointment – ring 01296 423754.

▶ Take the A418 northwards to Leighton Buzzard, 17.75 (11 miles) away. Then take the A505 into town. The National Trust property of Ascott (see below) stands at the junction of the two roads and is well worth a visit on the way.

LEIGHTON BUZZARD

Prehistoric and Roman remains have been found in the area as have three Saxon cemeteries, all indicating the ancient origins of the town. There are many historic buildings and a 600-year-old market cross.

BOOKS

Kings Cottage in the little village of Eggington, on the eastern outskirts of the town, is the home of Robert Kirkman Ltd (ABA, PBFA). His small stock of antiquarian books, with an emphasis on English Literature, Churchill, English Bibles, and sets of standard authors, is available by appointment only – ring 01525 210647).

▶ ▶ ASCOTT

In 1876 Leopold de Rothschild bought a small Jacobean farmhouse and converted it into a Tudor mansion. The house contains a collection of English and Dutch paintings, including *Dordrecht on the Maas* by Aelbert Cuyp, a panorama filling one entire wall. There are also collections of French and English furniture and Oriental porcelain.

POTTERY

Nick & Janet's Antiques at Bury Farm, Mill Road, Slapton, which is about 3.2km (2 miles) south of the town, is also open by appointment only – ring 01525 220256. It has a large range of Devon, Torquay, Brannam pottery, Martin Brothers, and modern Moorcroft.

▶ To reach the final stop on the tour, take the A4012 for about 14.5km (9 miles) to Woburn.

WOBURN

The village of Woburn is most associated with Woburn Abbey. On the site of a 13thC Cistercian abbey, the house has been in the Russell family, the Dukes of Bedford, since the 16thC. It has an important collection of art by artists such as Canaletto, Van Dyck, Rembrandt, and Gainsborough. The house also has outstanding collections of 18thC furniture, porcelain, and silver. The award-winning Safari Park is also a major visitor attraction. Here the animals are allowed to roam free while people stay in their cars. There is a range of animals on view including lions, wolves, elephants, tigers, and black bears.

BOOKS & EPHEMERA

Collectors Carbooks in Bedford Street has a large stock of rare, out-of-print, scarce motoring/motor racing books, magazines, posters, autographs, programmes, and new car-related books.

GENERAL ANTIQUES

Back in the village, Town Hall Antiques in the Market Place has a large and varied range of antiques. It is open 7 days a week.

WINE-RELATED ANTIQUES

Also in Bedford Street, Christopher Sykes has a range of corkscrews and wine-related antiques.

ANTIQUES CENTRES

Inside the grounds of the Abbey, Woburn Abbey Antiques Centre has over 50 dealers, including BADA and LAPADA members. These dealers sell a range of antiques, such as English and Continental furniture, oils and watercolours, ceramics, glass, silver, metalware, textiles, jewellery, and antiquities. The centre is open 7 days a week.

LECHLADE ▶ FAIRFORD ▶ CIRENCESTER ▶ MALMESBURY ▶ TETBURY ▶ STROUD ▶
CHELTENHAM ▶ EVESHAM ▶ BROADWAY ▶ MORETON-IN-MARSH ▶ STOW-ON-THE-
WOLD ▶ BURFORD ▶ WITNEY ▶ WOODSTOCK ▶ OXFORD

The Cotswolds make up one of the country's prime antiques buying areas as there are antiques shops in many of the towns and villages. The Cotswolds Antiques Dealers' Association is also one of the biggest and most active of the regional antiques-related associations in Britain.

This is an area of sheep pasture, wooded valleys, and weathered Cotswold stone buildings, many of which appear unaltered since Medieval times. The two major cities here, Cheltenham and Cirencester, have also preserved their historic buildings. Further evidence of the region's long history may be seen in the straight roads that go directly up and down steep hills – these are a legacy of Roman road builders from nearly 2,000 years ago.

The Medieval wool trade shaped the area – wool merchants here were among the wealthiest people in the country and built many of the region's churches.

14 Antiques all the Way

Websites

www.blenheimpalace.com
The official website for Blenheim Palace gives information on the house and grounds as well as details of opening times, admission charges, and directions on how to get there.

www.bourton-on-the-water.co.uk
Bourton-on-the-Water's official website shows current scenes of the village. These neatly transform into pictures of the same spot in days gone by when you pass your mouse across them. Click on any of the images and you will enter the site, from where you can take a virtual walk through the village.

www.cheltenhammuseum.org.uk
Take a virtual tour of the Cheltenham Art Gallery & Museum here.

www.coriniummuseum.cirentown.com
Learn more about Cirencester's museum.

www.oxfordcity.co.uk
If you want to know where to stay or eat, where to go, and what's on in Oxford then visit this site to find the answers.

www.ox.ac.uk
Find out everything you want to know about Oxford University here on its official website.

www.oxlink.co.uk/witney
Take a look at a picture of Witney's butter cross on this site, which is devoted to the town. Also get more information about where to stay and what to do in the area.

▶▶ USEFUL CONTACTS

Tourist Information Centres

Broadway 1 Cotswold Court.
Tel: 01386 852937

Burford Sheep Street.
Tel: 01993 823558

Cheltenham 77 Promenade.
Tel: 01242 522878

Cirencester Corn Hall, Market Place.
Tel: 01285 654180

Evesham The Almonry, Abbey Gate.
Tel: 01386 446944

Malmesbury Town Hall, Market Lane.
Tel: 01666 823748

Oxford The Old School, Gloucester Green.
Tel: 01865 726871

Stow-on-the-Wold The Square.
Tel: 01451 831082

Stroud Subscription Rooms, George Street.
Tel: 01453 765768

Witney Market Square. Tel: 01993 775802

Woodstock Part Street. Tel: 01993 813276

LECHLADE

This pretty town, with its wealth of 17th and 18thC buildings, was the inspiration for Shelley's poem, *Stanzas in a Summer Evening Churchyard*. In the 17thC barges left this town to take stone to London to build St Paul's Cathedral. The Swinford Museum, Filkins, showcases the local trade of stone working.

GENERAL ANTIQUES

Lechlade Arcade in the High Street has 40 rooms of smalls, china, small furniture, cast iron, farm tools and implements, antique pistols, guns, and medals. It is open 7 days a week.

SILVER & JEWELLERY

Located in the High Street, **Corner House Antiques** (LADA) has a large selection of antique silver and jewellery as well as country furniture, porcelain, and objets d'art. It is open Tuesday–Saturday.

ANTIQUES CENTRES

The 30 dealers in **Apsley House Antiques Centre**, Market Place, sell a complete range of antiques. **Jubilee Hall Antiques Centre** in Oak Street has 25 dealers with a large stock of furniture, objets d'art, metalware, and sporting antiques and is open 7 days a week. The **Swan Antiques Centre** in Burford Street has 13 dealers selling Staffordshire china, collectables, furniture, jewellery, books, and glass. It is also open 7 days a week.

▶ The A417 westbound will take you straight to the next stop at Fairford, which is a distance of about 6.5km (4 miles).

FAIRFORD

The town's 15thC church was built by a prosperous local cloth merchant and has 28 beautiful and impressive stained glass windows, magnificent carvings, and an oak-beamed roof.

BOOKS
Located in the village of Kempsford, about 8.5km (5 miles) south of Fairford on a country road, **Ximenes Rare Books Inc.** (ABA, PBFA) sells rare books by appointment only – ring 01285 810640.

FURNITURE
Blenheim Antiques (CADA) in Market Place has 18th and 19thC town and country furniture, clocks, and accessories. Also in the Market Place, **Gloucester House Antiques** (CADA) has a large stock of English and French country furniture, farmhouse tables, chairs, 18th and 19thC French faïence and pottery, and buffets.

▶ Continue westbound on the A417 for about 14.5km (9 miles) to reach Cirencester.

CIRENCESTER

Set on the junction of three Roman roads – Ermin Way, Fosse Way, and Akeman Street – Cirencester was the most important Roman town in Britain after London. Many of the Roman and other artefacts found locally may be seen in the Corinium Museum in Park Street. It also has full-size reconstructions of rooms from a Roman villa and five complete mosaic floors.

After the Romans withdrew from Britain, Cirencester declined in importance until the Middle Ages when it gained renewed prosperity as a centre for the wool trade. Such was the wealth of local merchants that in the 15thC they largely financed the building of an abbey church, which escaped destruction during the Dissolution of the Monasteries by being turned into the town hall. It became a church again in the 18thC.

The late Rosemary Verey was recently one of the country's most eminent gardens. You can see her work in her own garden at Barnsley House, which is 6.5km (4 miles) north-east of Cirencester on the B4425.

ARCHITECTURAL ANTIQUES
Original Architectural Antiques (SALVO) in Elliot Road, Love Lane Estate, has a large stock of architectural antiques including fireplaces, columns, limestone troughs, and oak doors. The shop is open 7 days a week, until 4pm on Sundays.

FURNITURE
Situated at Perrott's Brook, about 8.5km (5 miles) north of Cirencester on the A435, **Forum Antiques** at Springfield Farm sells by appointment only – ring 01285 831821. It has 18thC and earlier veneered walnut, early oak, and French Empire furniture. **Hare's Antiques Ltd** in Black Jack Street has an extensive range of 18th and 19thC English furniture. **Parlour Farm Antiques** in Wilkinson Road, Love Lane Industrial Estate, has antique pine furniture imported from Russia, the Czech Republic, and Germany as well as smalls, kitchenalia, and other furniture. The shop is open 7 days a week. **William H Stokes** (BADA, CADA) in The Cloisters, Dollar Street, has early oak furniture and associated items. **Patrick Waldron Antiques**, also in Dollar Street, has 18th and early 19thC English furniture.

GENERAL ANTIQUES
Still in Dollar Street, **Rankine Taylor Antiques** (LAPADA, CADA, CINOA) has a large stock of 16th–18thC furniture, silver, glass, and rare associated objects. **Silver Street Antiques** in Silver Street sells general antiques and kitchenalia and is open 7 days a week, from 12 noon on Wednesday and Sunday. **Denzil Verey** (CADA) in Barnsley House in the village of Barnsley (6.5km/4 miles north-east of Cirencester on the B4425) has an extensive stock of 18th and 19thC country furniture, copper, brass, glass, lighting, kitchenalia, and decorative accessories.

ANTIQUES CENTRES
There are 60 dealers in **Cirencester Arcade**, Market Place, selling a wide range of furniture, china, glass, jewellery, coins, stamps, and postcards. The centre is open 7 days a week.

AUCTION HOUSES
Corinum Auctions (PTA) in Gloucester Street has quarterly sales of printed ephemera, cigarette cards, books, and postcards held in March, June, September, and December. **The Cotswold Auction Co. Ltd** (RICS) in West Market Place holds monthly sales, both general and specialist, at the Bingham Hall, King Street. The auctions take place on Friday at 10am with viewing on Thursday 10am–8pm and the morning of sale 9–10am. **Moore, Allen & Innocent**, Norcote, have quarterly selective antiques sales on Friday at 10am. Twice yearly, also on Friday at 10am, they have sporting sales and picture sales plus a general monthly sale that takes place on Friday at 10.30am. Viewing is held on the previous day 10.30am–8pm and on the day of sale from 9am. The office is open on Saturday mornings

at 12 noon. In Gloucester Street, **Specialised Postcard Auctions** (PTA) hold sales every six weeks on Mondays at 2pm. Viewing takes place the week prior, Monday–Friday at 10am–1pm and 3–7pm, as well as on the day of the sale from 10am–2pm.

▶ Take the A429 southbound directly to Malmesbury, which is a distance of 19.25km (12 miles).

MALMESBURY

Set between two rivers and built on the site of a fortified Saxon town, Malmesbury was granted its town charter in AD 880 by King Alfred.

Visit the town's church and take a look at a new stained glass. It depicts an 11thC monk called Elmer who tried to fly. He fitted wings to his hands and feet and then jumped off the church tower, thrashing wildly. Legend has it that he flew for about 183m (200 yards), although when he hit the ground he broke both legs and was crippled for life.

Athelstan Museum in the Town Hall is named after the first Saxon king of all England who was probably buried in the abbey. The museum's displays include coins minted in Malmesbury.

CERAMICS
Rene Nicholls in the High Street sells English pottery and porcelain.

FURNITURE
Also in the High Street, **Andrew Britten** has small items of furniture and decorative accessories. Located 11.25km (7 miles) east of Malmesbury in Minety, on the B4040, **Sambourne House Antiques** has a large stock of antique and Continental pine and is open 7 days a week.

GENERAL ANTIQUES
Acorn Antiques in Oxford Street has general antiques including Doulton and furniture. It is open Tuesday–Sunday (on Sundays 11am–2pm). **Athelstan's Attic**, The Cross Hayes, has general house clearance items and is open Monday, Wednesday, Friday, and Saturday.

AUCTION HOUSES
Hilditch Auction (NAVA) in the Gloucester Road Trading Estate, has monthly sales of general

household items on the last Saturday of each month at 10am with viewing on Friday 10am–7pm.

▶ Take the B4014 for 8.5km (5 miles) to Tetbury.

TETBURY

The fine 17th and 18thC buildings reflect the town's prosperous history as a wool-collecting centre. Take a look at the 17th century Market House, which was built on stumpy pillars.

BEDS
Morpheus Beds, New Church Street, has a large selection of antique beds, bedroom furniture, and accessories and is open 7 days a week.

BOOKS
In The Chipping, **Coach House Bookshop** has a large range of antiquarian and second-hand books, Black's colour books and prints as well as English period and Victorian furniture. It is open 7 days a week.

FURNITURE
Balmuir House Antiques (LAPADA) in Long Street has an extensive range of 19thC furniture and paintings. **Breakspeare Antiques** (LAPADA, CADA), also in Long Street, has English period furniture, including mahogany from 1750–1835 and early veneered walnut from 1690–1740. **The Chest of Drawers** (TADA), again in Long Street, also sells English furniture from the 17thC onwards. In New Church Street, **Day Antiques** (BADA, CADA) has early oak and country furniture and related items. Back in Long Street, there are many other dealers. **The Decorator Source** (TADA) has a wide selection of French provincial furniture, accessories, and English country house furniture and objects. **Fiftyone Antiques** (TVADA) sells 18th–19thC decorative furniture together with 19thC pictures. **Bobbie Middleton** (TADA, CADA) has classic country house furniture, mirrors, sconces, and decorative accessories as well as 18th and 19thC upholstered furniture. **Peter Norden Antiques** (LAPADA, TADA) has early oak and country furniture, early woodcarvings, pewter, brass, and treen. **Porch House Antiques** (TADA) has a large range of furniture and decorative items from the 17th–20thC. **Sieff** (LAPADA, TADA) has an extensive choice of 18th and 19thC French provincial fruitwood and 20thC furniture. It is open 7 days a week (until 4pm on Sundays). **Simon Sieff Antiques** (TADA) has a large selection of 18th and 19thC French, fruitwood, and upholstered furniture as well as decorative accessories and objects. **Westwood**

House Antiques (TADA) has a wide range of 17th–19thC oak, elm and ash country furniture, some French fruitwood, decorative pottery, pewter, and treen.

GENERAL ANTIQUES
The following dealers are in Long Street too. BADA dealer **Philip Adler Antiques** has a large eclectic selection of decorative and period antiques. **Ball & Claw Antiques** (TADA) sells 17th and 19thC furniture, Arts and Crafts, engravings, pictures, linens, textiles, children's antique decorative toys, and general antiques. **Anne Fowler** has mirrors, lustres, oil paintings, prints, linen, early garden and painted furniture, faience, and pottery. French items are a speciality.

    Jester Antiques (TADA), this time in Church Street, has exciting, colourful furniture, decorative items, lamps, mirrors, garden and architectural antiques, and specializes in wall, mantel, and longcase clocks. It is open 7 days a week. **Merlin Antiques** in Chipping Court Shopping Mall, Chipping Street, has a large mixed stock of china, pictures, Victorian and Edwardian furniture, costume jewellery, reproduction furniture, and garden stoneware.

ORIENTAL ANTIQUES
Artique in Church Street has an extensive range of Central Asian artefacts, rugs, jewellery, furniture, textiles, and architectural items. It is open 7 days a week (until 8pm on Thursdays and Fridays, and until 4pm on Sundays). **Catherine Hunt** in Long Street has a large stock of Chinese ceramics – Ming, Qing, etc – as well as furniture and textiles from the Ming dynasty onwards. The shop is open 7 days a week.

SILVER & JEWELLERY
Located in Church Street, **Old Mill Market Shop** sells silver, jewellery, china, glass, pine, metalware, and small furniture. It is closed on Thursday afternoons and Sundays.

ANTIQUES CENTRES
All these centres are located in Long Street. **The Antique & Interior Centre** (TADA) has eight dealers selling good-quality furniture, porcelain, silver, and pictures. It opens 7 days a week, including most Bank Holidays. **The Antique Centre** includes dealers offering French furniture and decorative pieces, 19thC Staffordshire pottery, textiles, and Georgian, Victorian, and Edwardian furniture. The centre is open 7 days a week (Sunday afternoons only). Between them, the 40 dealers in the **Antiques Emporium** (TADA) have a large range of fine and country furniture, brass, copper, treen, kitchenalia, paintings, miniatures, silver, jewellery, decorative items, pottery, porcelain, books, glass, and luggage. The centre is open 7 days a week (Sunday afternoons only).

▶ Leave Tetbury on the A4135 westbound. After 6.5km (4 miles) turn right onto the A46 to reach Stroud, which is 13km (8 miles) from the junction.

STROUD
Set astride the River Frome, Stroud's success as one of the most important wool centres in the area during the Middle Ages was due to its plentiful supply of fresh water for washing wool and also minerals for dying it. At the height of the town's prosperity, it had over 150 mills and the area 1.6km (1 mile) east of the town, called the Golden Valley, is said to reflect the wealth that its weaving industry generated.

BOOKS
Ian Hodgkins & Co. Ltd (ABA), The Vatch, sells antiquarian, 19thC art, literature, and children's books by appointment – ring 01453 764270. **Inprint**, in the High Street, has antiquarian, second-hand, and out-of-print books on fine, applied, and performing arts.

GENERAL ANTIQUES
Located about 8.5km (5 miles) east of Stroud, **High Street Antiques** has Oriental rugs, small furniture, and collectables. **Shabby Tiger Antiques** in Nelson Street has a large stock of 19thC smalls, jewellery, furniture, boxes, clocks, china, silver, silverplate, paintings, prints, and decorative objects.

▶ Follow the A46 northbound for 22.5km (14 miles) to arrive in Cheltenham.

CHELTENHAM
Mineral springs were found in the village of Cheltenham in 1716 but it was only in 1788 that a visit by George III transformed it into a fashionable spa town. It has beautiful Regency buildings and continues to thrive as a major centre for tourism. The Pittville Pump Room Museum is housed in one of these elegant Regency buildings. It has exhibitions of costume from the late 18thC and costume accessories from the

mid-19thC. In Clarence Street, the Cheltenham Art Gallery and Museum has a world-famous collection of Arts and Crafts Movement furniture and metalwork. There are also fine collections of Chinese and English pottery and Dutch and British paintings. Music lovers will want to visit Holst's birthplace in Clarence Road. The Regency house recreates the period in decoration and furnishings and you can also see the composer's piano and learn more about his life.

CLOCKS
Montpellier Clocks (BADA, CINOA) in Rotunda Terrace sells longcase, bracket, and carriage clocks, as well as chronometers and barometers.

COSTUMES & CLOTHING
Replay Period Clothing, Well Walk, has a large range of period clothing from 1800–1970, linen, lace, costume, and jewellery. The shop is open Tuesday–Saturday.

DECORATIVE TEXTILES
In Suffolk Parade Catherine Shinn Decorative Textiles sells a wide selection of decorative textiles, antique cushions, furnishings, and accessories.

FURNITURE
Bed of Roses, in Prestbury Road, sells fine stripped pine and is open by appointment only – ring 01242 231918. Giltwood Gallery, Suffolk Parade, has a Edwardian, Georgian, and Victorian furniture as well as mirrors, chandeliers, and pictures. Latchford Antiques in London Road, Charlton Kings, on the south-eastern edge of the city, has Victorian pine and period furniture. Triton Gallery, in Suffolk Parade again, has an extensive stock of Continental and English furniture as well as antique mirrors, chandeliers, and paintings.

GENERAL ANTIQUES
In Montpellier Walk, Art & Antiques (LAPADA) has a large stock of general antiques and is open every day except Thursday and Sunday until 4pm. Tapestry Antiques, Suffolk Parade, has a wide selection of decorative antiques, pine, beds, garden furniture, and mirrors. Troubridge Antiques, Great Norwood Street, has a mixture of general antiques. It is open Tuesday–Saturday.

MILITARIA
Q & C Militaria (OMRS, RSA) in Suffolk Road has an extensive stock of militaria. The shop is open Tuesday–Saturday.

SILVER & JEWELLERY
Greens of Cheltenham Ltd (GTLGB), in Montpellier Walk, sells an extensive selection of jewellery, Oriental works of art, and silver. It is open every day except Wednesday and Sunday. Promenade Antiques, on the Promenade, has a wide range of antique and second-hand jewellery, clocks, watches, silver-plated items, as well as rare, interesting objects.

ANTIQUES CENTRES
Cheltenham Antique Market, Suffolk Road, has a large selection of Victorian–20thC furniture and chandeliers. The 20 dealers in Cheltenham Antiques Centre, also in Suffolk Road, sell an extensive range of furniture, ceramics, jewellery, glass, linen, silver, Art Deco items, toys, and memorabilia. Struwwelpeter in London Road, Charlton Kings, has 6–12 dealers selling period furniture, eclectic decorative items, collectables, and smalls. It is open 7 days a week (until 4pm on Sundays).

AUCTION HOUSES
In Chapel Walk, The Cotswold Auction Co. Ltd started business in 1890. It has fortnightly general sales on Tuesday at 11am with viewing the day before from 10am–5pm and the morning of sale from 9am. Established in 1788, Mallams in Grosvenor Street has antique and general sales monthly on Thursday at 11am with viewing Tuesday 9am–7pm and Wednesday 9am–5pm. There are two ceramics sales each year on Wednesday or Thursday at 11am with viewing two days prior, 9am–5pm, and also two collectors' sales a year on Wednesday at 11am with viewing on Monday and Tuesday 9am–5pm.

▶ Leave Cheltenham on the A435 northbound. About 13km (8 miles) from the town the road joins the A46. Turn onto this and continue going north for a further 13km (8 miles) to Evesham.

EVESHAM
This town is not, in fact, in the Cotswolds – it is set in the Vale of Evesham, which is famous as a fruit-growing area. It was the site of a battle in 1265 where Simon de Montfort was killed, an event that signalled the end of the Barons' Revolt against King John and is commemorated by a stone cross in the town.

BOOKS
Bookworms of Evesham (PBFA) in Port Street sells second-hand and antiquarian books on most

subjects. It specializes in books on Gloucestershire and Worcestershire and is open Tuesday–Saturday.

ANTIQUES CENTRES

The Hayloft Antiques is located at Craycombe Farm, Old Worcester Road in the village of Fladbury, which is just off the A4538 about 8.5km (5 miles) west of Evesham. Its nine dealers sell a range of antique furniture, stripped pine, collectables, china, glass, paintings, prints, books, linen, and textiles. The centre is open 7 days a week from 10.30am, closing at 5pm in the summer and 4pm in winter.

▶ Take the A44 southwards for 10km (6 miles) to Broadway, which is just off the main road.

BROADWAY

One of the Cotswolds' most visited towns, Broadway became prosperous as a staging post on the coach road from Worcester to London. It declined after the advent of the railways but its fortunes changed for the better when it was discovered, in the 19thC, by people like William Morris (a leader of the Arts and Crafts Movement) who was a frequent visitor to the Broadway Tower, an 18thC folly. Visitors today are still charmed by the town – particularly its honey-coloured stone cottages and the grand 17thC coaching inn, the Lygon Arms.

FURNITURE

Fenwick & Fenwick Antiques (CADA), in the High Street, has an extensive range of 17th–early 19thC oak, mahogany, and walnut furniture as well as works of art, treen, boxes, pewter, lace bobbins, Chinese porcelain, corkscrews, and early metalware. BADA dealer H W Keil Ltd, in Tudor House, has a large range of early 17th–early 19thC furniture and works of art.

GENERAL ANTIQUES

Gallimaufry, in the High Street, sells china, glass, furniture, pictures, and collectables and is open 7 days a week.

SILVER & JEWELLERY

Howards of Broadway, again in the High Street, has antique and modern silver and jewellery.

▶ Continue on the A44 for 13km (8 miles) to reach Moreton-in-Marsh.

MORETON-IN-MARSH

Set astride the Fosse Way, Moreton-in-Marsh is made up of the pleasant Cotswold buildings that are typical of the area.

ARCHITECTURAL ANTIQUES

Cox's Architectural Salvage Yard Ltd (SALVO) on the Fosse Way Industrial Estate, Stratford Road, has a large stock of architectural antiques, doors, fireplaces, and Gothic-style windows.

CLOCKS

Open by appointment only, Jeffrey Formby Antiques (LAPADA, BADA) in East Street has English, longcase, bracket, and lantern clocks as well as horological books – ring 01608 650558.

FURNITURE

Berry Antiques (LAPADA) in the High Street sells 18th and 19thC furniture. It is open all week apart from Thursdays (from 11am on Sundays). Dale House, also in the High Street, has a wide selection of 18th–early 20thC furniture and works of art. The shop is open 7 days a week – from 1pm all week apart from Sundays, when it opens at 11am. Gary Wright Antiques Ltd, in the Fosse Way Business Park, has a large stock of furniture: Georgian, mahogany, walnut, marquetry, unusual and decorative objects, and 17th–19thC quality furniture.

GARDEN ANTIQUES

John Fox Antiques (CADA) in the High Street has an extensive range of garden antiques, furniture, and country bygones. It is closed Tuesdays and over the weekend.

GENERAL ANTIQUES

Chandlers Antiques, again in the High Street, has a wide range of small porcelain, glass, jewellery, and silver. It is open by appointment only – ring 01608 651347. Still in the High Street, Seaford House Antiques (LAPADA) sells 18th–early 20thC furniture, porcelain, pictures, and objets d'art. It is open all week apart from Tuesday and Wednesday.

ORIENTAL ANTIQUES

Situated in Longborough, a village about 8.5km (5 miles) west of the town just off the A424, the Oriental Gallery (LAPADA) sells Chinese ceramics and Asian works of art. It is open by appointment only – ring 01451 830944.

ANTIQUES CENTRES

Back to the High Street, London House Antique Centre has a large range of general antiques, Chinese porcelain, furniture, silver, porcelain, and pictures and is open 7 days a week. Windsor House Antiques Centre, still in the High Street, has

109

48 dealers selling high-quality general antiques, porcelain, glass, silver, clocks, paintings, and furniture. The centre is open 7 days a week – on Tuesday and Sunday the shop opens at 12 noon.

▶ The A429 southbound will take you to Stow-on-the-Wold, a distance of 6.5km (4 miles).

STOW-ON-THE-WOLD

Also on the Fosse Way, Stow-on-the-Wold is probably the antiques capital of the Cotswolds. It is an ancient settlement with evidence of habitation from the Iron Age onwards. The town is set on a hill, 244m (800ft) above sea level, at the junction of eight roads. It is the location of the Horse Fair, held twice a year, in May and October. The event attracts travellers from all over the country to buy and sell horses. (During the Horse Fair, many shops in the town are closed.)

BOOKS
The Bookbox (PBFA) in Sheep Street has antiquarian, rare, and second-hand books. It specializes in 19th and 20thC good literature, art, and topography and is open all week except Wednesday and Sunday. In winter it only opens Thursday–Saturday.

CLOCKS
Bryden House Clocks & Antiques (LAPADA) in Sheep Street sells various clocks and barometers as well as Georgian–Victorian furniture. It is closed on Thursdays and Sundays. Grandfather Clock Shop, still in Sheep Street, has a large range of clocks, including longcase, as well as 18th–19thC furniture, 19th and 20thC oil paintings, and watercolours.

DECORATIVE ARTS
Ruskin Decorative Arts (CADA) in Talbot Court sells decorative arts from 1860–1930 covering Arts and Crafts, Art Nouveau, Art Deco, and the Cotswold Movement, including examples of the work of the Guild of Handicraft, Gordon Russell, Gimson, and the Barnsleys.

DOLLS & TEDDY BEARS
Bears on the Wold in Sheep Street has a large selection of old bears from companies such as Steiff, Hermann, Dean's, Merrythought, Hermann Spielwaren, Leebert ,and Tickelpenny. The shop is open every day except Wednesday.

FURNITURE
Baggott Church Street Ltd (BADA, CADA), in Church Street, has a large range of English 17th–19thC furniture, paintings, and objects. It holds an annual exhibition in October. Fosse Way Antiques (CADA) in The Square has a wide selection of 18th–early 19thC furniture, oil paintings, and small period accessories. Simon Nutter and Thomas King-Smith in Wraggs Row, Fosseway, has 18th and 19thC furniture together with silver and porcelain. Priests Antiques & Fine Arts in Digbeth Street has an extensive stock of 17th–early 20thC English furniture and is open Tuesday–Saturday. Michael Rowland in The Square sells 17th and 18thC country furniture, Welsh dressers, tables, bureaux, and sets of chairs. Arthur Seager Antiques, again in Sheep Street, has 16th and 17thC objects, oak furniture, and carvings. It is open Thursday–Saturday until 4pm. Stow Antiques (LAPADA, CADA, CINOA) in The Square has a wide range of 18th–19thC mahogany furniture, large tables, sets of chairs, sideboards, and bookcases and is open Monday–Saturday from 11am. Vanbrugh House Antiques, Park Street, has an extensive selection of early fine furniture, musical boxes, and early maps.

GENERAL ANTIQUES
Duncan J Baggott (LAPADA, CADA) in Sheep Street has a large range of English furniture, portraits, landscape paintings, domestic metalware, fireplace accoutrements, pottery, glass, garden statuary, and ornaments. There is an annual exhibition in October. In Sheep Street, Colin Brand Antiques has a large range of pre-1900 clocks, porcelain, militaria, decorative furniture, and objets d'art. It is closed on Wednesdays and Sundays. Christopher Clarke Antiques (LAPADA, CADA), in the Fosseway, has a wide choice of English furniture, works of art, animal antiques, and unusual decorative items. Country Life Antiques in The Square has an extensive choice of scientific instruments, decorative accessories, metalware, furniture, and paintings. Keith Hockin Antiques (BADA, CADA), again in The Square, sells 17th–early 18thC English oak furniture, pewter, early brass, and 16th–17thC wood carvings. The shop is open Thursday–Saturday. Park House Antiques, Park Street, has a large range of old toys, textiles, small furniture, porcelain, and pottery. It is open every day except Tuesday, but is closed during May.

ORIENTAL ANTIQUES
The Hungry Ghost in Brewery Yard, Sheep Street, has a large stock of Oriental antiques, gifts, and china and is open 7 days a week.

RUGS
Samarkand Galleries (LAPADA, CADA, CINOA), also in Brewery Yard, Sheep Street, has an extensive selection of antique and contemporary

rugs from the Near East and Central Asia, decorative carpets, and nomadic weavings.

ANTIQUES CENTRES

The 15 dealers of the **Church Street Antiques Centre** sell a wide range of general antiques from 1650–early 20thC – furniture, pictures, mirrors, pottery, porcelain, vintage leather goods, silver, Staffordshire animals, blue and white pottery, glass, lacquered furniture, copper, and brass. The centre is open 7 days a week, from 12 noon on Sunday. Still in Sheep Street, **Durham House Antiques Centre** has 36 dealers selling a large range of general antiques, silver, clocks, oak, mahogany, porcelain, Derby, Worcester, Staffordshire, Mason's, linens, prints, and paintings. It is open 7 days a week. **Fox Cottage Antiques** in Digbeth Street has eight dealers selling pottery, porcelain, glassware, silver and plated ware, small furniture, decorative items and country goods, mainly pre-1910.

Take the A424 for 16km (10 miles) to the next stop at Burford.

Bourton-on-the-Water
Alternatively, you can continue on the A429 southbound to Bourton-on-the-Water (see below), just off the main road. To reach Burford, return to Stow-on-the-Wold and follow the directions given.

BURFORD

In the Middle Ages, this lovely town prospered as a centre for cloth, wool, saddlery, and stone from local quarries and, later, from its position on one of the great coach roads. Like Stow, it suffered when the railways bypassed it but its fortunes revived with the growth of tourism. The Tolsey Museum shows the town's social and industrial history.

FURNITURE

In the High Street, **Jonathan Fyson Antiques** (CADA) has a large stock of English and Continental furniture, brass, lighting, fireplaces, accessories, club fenders, papier mâché, tole, treen, porcelain, glass, prints, and jewellery. **Gateway Antiques** (CADA) in Cheltenham Road has an extensive selection of 17th–19thC furniture, Arts and Crafts, decorative objects, and accessories and is open 7 days a week (2–5pm on Sundays). **David Pickup** (BADA, CADA), in the High Street, sells fine English furniture with an emphasis on the Cotswold Arts and Crafts Movement. **Saracen Antiques Ltd** at Upton Downs Farm, has a large stock of predominantly 18th–19thC English furniture. In the High Street, **Swan Antiques** (CADA, LAPADA) sells early country furniture.

GENERAL ANTIQUES

Bygones, in Lower High Street, has general collectables and curios and is open 7 days a week (from 12 noon on Sundays). **Horseshoe Antiques**, also in the High Street, sells 17th–18thC furniture, oil paintings, copper, brass, horse brasses, and clocks, including longcase.

SILVER & JEWELLERY

Still in the High Street, **Boxroom Antiques** has a large stock of jewellery, silver, linen, small furniture, porcelain, glass, collectables, and cutlery. It is open 7 days a week.

SPORTING ANTIQUES

Manfred Schotten Antiques (CADA), again in the High Street, sells sporting antiques as well as library and leather furniture.

ANTIQUES CENTRES

Burford Antiques Centre on The Roundabout, Cheltenham Road, has an extensive stock of 1930s–modern period and reproduction furniture. It is open 7 days a week (from 12 noon on Sundays). **Old George Inn Antique Galleries**, in the High Street, has 20 dealers selling a wide selection of china, glass, furniture, treen, books, pictures, rugs,

▶▶ BOURTON-ON-THE-WATER

This is one of the prettiest and most popular villages in the Cotswolds. There is a stream running right through the middle, crossed by numerous footbridges. The usual mellow Cotswold stone buildings combine to provide one of the most photographed streets in the area. While in the village you may want to visit **Aquarius Books Ltd** in Victoria Street who sells antiquarian and second-hand books. The **Portland Antiques Centre**, also in Victoria Street,

is worth a visit too. It has a range of silver, jewellery, glass, furniture, collectables, and clocks. The local auctioneers, **Tayler and Fletcher**, have been established since 1790 and have monthly sales of furniture on Saturdays at 10am. Viewing takes place on Friday 1–6pm and the morning of the sale from 7.30am. They also have three fine art sales a year on Tuesday at 10.30am with viewing Monday 1–7pm and the morning of the sale from 8am.

and carpets. The centre is open 7 days a week (from 12 noon on Sunday).

▶ The A40 eastbound will take you to Witney, which is just 13km (8 miles) away.

WITNEY

Witney is almost synonymous with blankets, made here since Medieval times. The Cogges Manor Farm Museum in Church Lane is set on a 20 acre site and is a working museum of Victorian life. The farm is stocked with typical Victorian breeds of animals and there are demonstrations of traditional crafts.

BOOKS
In the Market Square, Church Green Books (PBFA) sells general second-hand and antiquarian books – books on bell-ringing are a speciality. The shop shuts at 4pm.

DOLLS & TEDDY BEARS
Teddy Bears of Witney, in the High Street, has a large stock of teddy bears including Steiff, Merrythought, Dean's, Hermann, and artists' bears. It is open 7 days a week.

FURNITURE
Colin Greenway Antiques (CADA) in Corn Street has 17th–early 20thC furniture as well as general antiques and interesting, unusual items.

GENERAL ANTIQUES
W R Harvey & Co. (Antiques) Ltd (BADA, CADA), also in Corn Street, has a large important stock of English furniture, clocks, pictures, mirrors, and works of art from 1680–1830.

SAMPLERS
Among the best-known of antique needlework dealers, Witney Antiques (BADA, LAPADA, CADA) in Corn Street sells needlework and probably has the largest selection of samplers in the country. The shop also has 17th–early 19thC furniture, clocks, and works of art.

▶ Leave Witney on the A4095 to travel direct to Woodstock, 13km (8 miles) away.

WOODSTOCK

Although the town's origins go back to Saxon times, Woodstock is now most associated with the adjacent Blenheim Palace. The estate, as well as some of the cost of building the mansion, was given to Sir John Churchill, first Duke of Marlborough, by Queen Anne in gratitude for his victory at the Battle of Blenheim in 1704. It was designed by Sir John Vanbrugh at the beginning of the 18thC and is set in 2,100 acres of parkland landscaped by Capability Brown. The estate has numerous attractions for visitors, not least the Palace itself, which has been described by many as Vanbrugh's masterpiece. Its magnificent rooms hold many treasures including furniture, paintings, porcelain, and silver as well as carvings by Grinling Gibbons. The Battle of Blenheim is commemorated in a ceiling painting in the Great Hall. Blenheim Palace was also the birthplace of Sir Winston Churchill whose grave lies in Bladon churchyard, a small village just 1.6km (1 mile) away. The room where he was born is now on view. Visitors can see the Temple of Diana, by the lake, where Churchill proposed to Clementine. There are also displays of the great man's letters, pictures, and other memorabilia.

While in Woodstock, it is worth paying a visit to the Oxfordshire Museum in Park Street. It has exhibitions of local history, art, archaeology, landscape, and wildlife as well as information on the county's innovative new industries, such as nanotechnology.

BOOKS
The Woodstock Bookshop (PBFA) in the Market Place sells antiquarian and second-hand books on literature, travel, topography, art, history of art, and prints. It is open 7 days a week.

FURNITURE
Antiques of Woodstock, located in the Market Place, has an extensive range of 17th–19thC oak and country furniture and town and formal period furniture. It is open 7 days a week. In Oxford Street, Chris Baylis Country Chairs (TVADA) has a large stock of English country chairs from 1780–present

day including Windsors, rush-seated, ladder and spindleback chairs, kitchen chairs, etc. It is open Tuesday–Sunday. **The Chair Set**, the Market Place, has 18th–19thC sets of chairs and dining room antiques. The shop is open 7 days a week.

GENERAL ANTIQUES

Located in the High Street, **Bees Antiques** (TVADA) sells fine 18th and 19thC British and Continental ceramics, glass, jewellery, decorative furniture, and metalware. It is open all week apart from Tuesday (on Sunday from 11am–5pm).

ANTIQUES CENTRES

Span Antiques (TVADA), in the Market Place, has 10 dealers selling silver, decorative textiles, furniture, 19th and 20thC pictures, Art Deco, Art Nouveau, porcelain, and books. The centre is open 7 days a week (Sundays from 1pm).

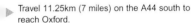 Travel 11.25km (7 miles) on the A44 south to reach Oxford.

OXFORD

The various university colleges are an integral part of the city. Many of the colleges are open to the public and nearly all of them have a long history, some going back to the 13thC. Many of their buildings are also of great architectural importance.

As might be imagined, Oxford has a wealth of museums. Perhaps the best one for first-time visitors is the Oxford Story in Broad Street where 800 years of the town's history is recounted. Also in Broad Street, the Museum of the History of Science holds important collections of scientific instruments.

The Ashmolean Museum in Beaumont Street is probably one of the most famous in the world. Founded in 1683, it is also one of the world's oldest public museums. Its collections include antiquities, paintings and drawings, sculpture, silver, ceramics, musical instruments, coins, and medals. For more musical instruments, visit the Bate Collection of Musical Instruments at the Faculty of Music, St Aldate's, where over

1,000 are on display.

In Pembroke Street, the Museum of Modern Art provides a showcase for temporary exhibitions, many of which are at the cutting edge of modern art. The Pitts River Museum in South Parks Road now has over half a million ethnographic and archaeological artefacts from all over the world. Finally, the Museum of Oxford in St Aldates tells the story of the city from prehistoric times onwards.

BOOKS

In Broad Street, **Blackwell's Rare Books** (ABA, PBFA) has a large stock of modern first editions, private press books, antiquarian English literature, juvenilia, and general antiquarian books. It is open every day except Thursday and Sunday. Open by appointment only, **Robert Clark** (ABA, PBFA) in King Street, Jericho, sells English 17thC books including English literature, history, and theology – ring 01865 552154. **Jericho Books** in Walton Street has rare and second-hand books and is open 7 days a week. **Unsworths Booksellers Ltd** (ABA, PBFA, BA) in Turl Street have antiquarian, second-hand, and remaindered books on humanities. They are open 7 days a week (Sunday from 12 noon–4pm).

FURNITURE

Standing on the Abingdon Road, the **Oxford Furniture Warehouse** has old pine, oak, and general furniture, as well as Continental furniture. It is open 7 days a week. **St Clements Antiques**, in St Clements Street, has a range of town and country pieces.

MAPS & PRINTS

In the High Street, **Magna Gallery** sells maps, prints, and books. In June–August and in December it opens on a Sunday from 11am–4pm.

ANTIQUES CENTRES

Antiques on High Ltd (TVADA), again in the High Street, has 38 dealers selling a large range of smalls and collectables and it is open 7 days a week including Bank Holidays. The five dealers in **Park End Antiques**, Park End Street, sell antique furniture, lighting, vintage costume, Art Deco china, and leather goods. It is also open 7 days a week.

AUCTION HOUSES

Mallams in St Michael's Street has monthly antiques sales on Wednesday at 11am. Viewing takes place on Saturday 9am–1pm and Monday and Tuesday 9am–5pm. They also have jewellery and silver sales in May and November and antique books and pictures in March, June, October, and December.

GREAT MALVERN ▶ WORCESTER ▶ KIDDERMINSTER ▶ BRIDGNORTH ▶ MUCH WENLOCK ▶ SHREWSBURY ▶ CHURCH STRETTON ▶ LUDLOW ▶ LEOMINSTER ▶ HEREFORD

Shropshire, Hereford, and Worcester are good areas to search for antiques in. Many towns and villages have a good selection of different types of dealer and nearly all of the places mentioned in this tour have their own antiquarian bookshops.

The Marches, strictly speaking the western areas of Hereford and Shropshire, make up the border country between Wales and England. Before Wales came under the English Crown, the Marches were the scenes of frequent raids and fierce fighting, which gave the country a legacy of strong castles. In contrast Worcester is a much gentler county of good farmland and contented market towns.

▶ ▶ USEFUL CONTACTS

Websites

www.bridgnorthshropshire.com
What do you need to know about Bridgnorth? Whatever it is, whether where to stay, what's on, sports and leisure activities, this site will have the information you need.

www.hay-on-wye.co.uk
The town's official website gives a good map of the town, a calendar of events, a list of bookshops, as well as information on where to stay and what to do. This is a great site to consult before visiting.

www.royal-worcester.co.uk
Learn about the history of Royal Worcester Porcelain, and also find information on its museum and collectors' society here.

www.svr.co.uk
The Severn Valley Railway's site gives information on its history, the timetable, and special events.

www.virtual-shropshire.co.uk
This site, called Virtual Shropshire, has an enormous amount of useful information on all aspects of Shropshire. If you are taking this tour, make sure you visit this site first.

Tourist Information Centres

Bridgnorth The Library, Listley Street.
Tel: 01746 763257

Church Stretton Church Street.
Tel: 01694 723133

Hay-on-Wye Oxford Road.
Tel: 01497 820144

Hereford 1 King Street.
Tel: 01432 268430

Leominster 1 Corn Street.
Tel: 01568 616460

Ludlow Castle Street.
Tel: 01584 875053

Malvern 21 Church Street.
Tel: 01684 892289

Much Wenlock The Museum, High Street.
Tel: 01952 727679

Shrewsbury The Music Hall, The Square.
Tel: 01743 281200

Worcester The Guildhall, High Street.
Tel: 01905 726311

GREAT MALVERN

There are six towns in the area with Malvern in their name but Great Malvern is the biggest. Best known for its spring water, in the 19thC Malvern was a popular spa town. Its beautiful abbey, founded in 1085 (although most of today's building is 15thC), is said to have the best collection of 15thC stained glass after York Minster.

The Malvern Museum of Local History in Abbey Road, housed in a Medieval gatehouse, covers the geology of the Malvern Hills and local history. This includes informative displays on the composer Sir Edward Elgar.

BOOKS

The Malvern Bookshop in Abbey Road sells antiquarian, rare, and second-hand books. Books on music and sheet music are the specialities. The shop is open 7 days a week. Located in Church Walk, **Priory Books** has a wide range of antiquarian and second-hand books and is open Tuesday–Saturday.

FURNITURE

Foley Furniture, Foley Bank, has furniture of all periods as well as postcards, bottles, die-cast toys, books, etc. Opening days are Wednesday–Sunday. **Great Malvern Antiques** in Abbey Road sells a selection of decorative furniture, furnishings, and paintings by appointment – ring 01684 575490). In Howsell Road, **Kimber & Son Lower** has 18th–early 20thC furniture to suit all tastes. The shop is open all week (until 1pm on Sunday). **Miscellany Antiques**, Cowleigh Road, again open by appointment, has Georgian, Victorian, and Edwardian furniture, some country oak, bronzes, ivories, silver, jewellery, and decorative items. Ring 01684 566671.

GENERAL ANTIQUES

Carlton Antiques in Worcester Road sells furniture, ephemera, postcards, bottles, die-cast toys, second-hand books, etc. The shop is open 7 days a week. Near neighbour **Promenade Antiques & Books** has Victorian and Edwardian furniture, collectables, decorative items, reproduction l amps, and books. In summer, it is open Sunday afternoons as well as the rest of the week. **St James Antiques** in Wells Road has a large range of pine furniture, lighting, and decorative items. It is open all week apart from Wednesday and Sunday.

ANTIQUES CENTRES
The 10 dealers in the Malvern Link Antiques Centre, Worcester Road, have an extensive range of china, glass, Victorian and Edwardian furniture, jewellery, mirrors, pictures, etc. The centre is open 7 days a week.

AUCTION HOUSES
Philip Laney in Portland Road has monthly sales of general antiques and collectables.

▶ Take the A449 for 13km (8 miles) to Worcester.

WORCESTER

The beautiful riverside city of Worcester has had a long and varied history. Although built on the site of a Saxon monastery, the earliest part of the cathedral dates back to Norman times. During the English Civil War, Worcester declared for the King and the city's resulting Royalist Headquarters have now been turned into a museum, the Commandery Civil War Centre in Sidbury. This museum tells the story of the Civil War from the perspective of Oliver Cromwell and Charles I. To see what the citizens of Worcester thought of Cromwell, simply take a look at the façade of the city's Guildhall, where there is an effigy of Cromwell's head – he is nailed by his ears above a doorway!

A wealthy merchant built the Greyfriars, in Friar Street, in 1480. Although it has been altered over the centuries, it is still a good example of a Medieval merchant's house. It contains 16thC tapestries and 17thC furniture and is now owned by the National Trust. Of course, one of the city's most famous products is Royal Worcester Porcelain. Visitors should make time to visit the Dyson Perrins museum in Severn Street.

BOOKS
Watsons Bookshop, Upper Tything, has a large general stock of antiquarian and second-hand books. It is open until 4pm. ABOOKORTWO in Southfield Street sells a general stock of antiquarian and second-hand books by appointment – ring 01905 20816.

CERAMICS
In Cathedral Square, Bygones by the Cathedral (LAPADA, FGA) specializes in Worcester porcelain and also sells decorative antiques, silver, jewellery, porcelain, furniture, paintings, glass, and metalwork.

CLOCKS
The Barbers Clock, Droitwich Road, has clocks from 1840–1930, wind-up gramophones, and Art Deco items. The shop is open on Sunday afternoons as well as the rest of the week.

FURNITURE
Antiques & Curios in Upper Tything has a large stock of Victorian and Edwardian furniture, mirrors, clocks, porcelain, glass, and decorative items. The Antiques Warehouse, in Droitwich Road, has an extensive range of pine furniture, Victorian interior doors, and antique and reproduction fireplaces. It is open from 8am on weekdays. Box Bush Antiques, also in Upper Tything, sells 18th and 19thC pine, mahogany, and walnut furniture as well as decorative items and silver.

Browning & Son, Wylds Lane, established in 1904, has modern and antique general household furniture. It is open every day except Thursday and Sunday. Grays Antiques, in The Tything, has a wide selection of early 19th–early 20thC furniture and furnishings and decorative items including chandeliers. Back in Upper Tything, Heirlooms has a large stock of antique and old reproduction furniture, china, glass, and decorative items. M Lees & Son in Castle Place, Severn Street, sells period furniture, china, pictures, decorative items, and mirrors. On Thursday it is open during the morning only and on Saturday until 4pm. The Old Toll House, located in Droitwich Road, has pine furniture, reclaimed wooden doors, pottery, porcelain, glass, etc.

GENERAL ANTIQUES
Again in Upper Tything, Alexandra Antiques has a wide selection of general antiques. Bygones of Worcester (LAPADA), in Sidbury, sells 17th–20thC furniture, paintings, bronzes, silver, and porcelain. Round the Bend in Deansway has eccentricities and is open 7 days a week.

SILVER & JEWELLERY
P J Hughes Antiques, in Barbourne Road, has a large selection of jewellery, collectables, china, silver, and small furniture and is open Tuesday–Saturday.

ANTIQUES CENTRES
The Tything Antique Centre, in The Tything, has an extensive choice of ceramics, glass, silver, furniture, bedsteads, books, collectables, etc. **Worcester Antiques Centre**, in Reindeer Court, Mealcheapen Street, has 45 dealers selling porcelain, furniture, silver, jewellery, Art Nouveau, Arts and Crafts, and leather.

AUCTION HOUSES
Andrew Grant Fine Art Auctioneers in St Mark's Close has quarterly sales of antiques and fine art on Thursday with viewing the previous day from 10am–7pm. **Philip Serrell** (FSVA) in Sansome Walk has fortnightly general and fine art sales at the Malvern Sale Room.

> The A449 northbound goes directly from Worcester to Kidderminster, which is a distance of about 24km (15 miles).

KIDDERMINSTER
This town hold a treat for railway enthusiasts because it is the southern terminus of the Severn Valley Railway, which runs steam trains between here and Bridgnorth in Shropshire – a distance of 25.75km (16 miles). During the 19thC the town was one of the country's most important carpet-making centres. On the way into Kidderminster, about 6.5km (4 miles) south of the town, you will pass through the village of Hartlebury. This village's castle is home to the Worcestershire County Museum. It contains collections of costume, toys, carriages, bicycles, and archaeological items. There are also fascinating recreations of Victorian rooms including a drawing room, nursery, and scullery.

GENERAL ANTIQUES
Gemini Antiques & Gallery in Offmore Road has a large stock of antique furniture, glass, pictures, mirrors, and porcelain. It is open every day apart from Wednesday and Sunday. On Hoo Farm Industrial Estate, **Retro Products** sells antique and reproduction furniture, handles, knobs, hinges, and accessories.

SILVER & JEWELLERY
BBM Jewellery, Coins & Antiques (BJA) in Lion Street has an extensive range of antique and second-hand jewellery, coins, medals, porcelain, and silver. It is closed Tuesdays and Sundays.

ANTIQUES CENTRES
The Antique Centre, also in Lion Street, has 12 dealers selling a wide variety of furniture, china, glass, silver, jewellery, architectural salvage, and cast-iron fireplaces, surrounds, and tiles.

AUCTION HOUSES
Kidderminster Market Auctions in Comberton Hill has weekly sales of general antiques on Thursday at 10.30am with viewing on Wednesday 4–9pm and the morning of the sale from 7am. The office is open on Saturdays until 1pm. **Phipps & Pritchard Bank**, Exchange Street, holds sales of general antiques and collectables at Hartlebury Village Hall every six weeks. They take place on Saturdays at 10.30am with viewing on Friday 3–6.30pm and the morning of the sale from 8.30am. The office is open until 3.30pm on Saturdays.

> Leave Kidderminster on the A442 and continue on this road for about 21km (13 miles) until you reach Bridgnorth.

BRIDGNORTH
As well as being the northern terminus for the Severn Valley Railway, Kidderminster is also home to an electric funicular railway that takes people up and down the 34km (111ft) high cliffs that separate the Old and New Towns.

ARCHITECTURAL ANTIQUES
Priors Reclamation (SALVO), located on the Ditton Priors Industrial Estate, has a large stock of doors, pine and oak, and antique items for the garden. It is open by appointment only – ring 01746 712450.

BOOKS
The Book Passage in the High Street sells antiquarian and second-hand books. Located in the Harp Yard in St Leonard's Close, the **Bookstack** also has antiquarian and second-hand books.

FURNITURE
Situated in Underhill Street, **Malthouse Antiques** has a large range of Edwardian and Victorian furniture and smalls. It is open every day except Wednesday (open from 2–5pm on Sundays).

GENERAL ANTIQUES
English Heritage, in Whitburn Street, has a range of general antiques, giftware, medals, coins, and silverware.

ANTIQUES CENTRES
The 19 dealers in the Bridgnorth Antiques Centre, Whitburn Street, sell late Victorian, Edwardian, and 1930s furniture and collectables. The centre is open 7 days a week. Old Mill Antique Centre in Mill Street has 90 dealers selling a range of antiques and collectables. It is also open 7 days a week.

AUCTION HOUSES
Also in Mill Street, Perry & Phillips have monthly sales of general antiques on Tuesdays at 10.30am with viewing Saturday–Monday 10am–5pm. They also have occasional special sales.

▶ Travel 13km (8 miles) northward on the A458 to Much Wenlock.

MUCH WENLOCK
Situated on the north side of Wenlock Edge, this ancient market town has many charming and picturesque black and white, half-timbered buildings. The ruins of an 11thC priory may also be seen in the town.

BOOKS
Wenlock Books (BA), in the High Street, is a general bookshop with a wide stock. It is open 7 days a week (Sunday afternoon only).

COLLECTABLES
Also in the High Street, Myra's Antiques has a large stock of collectables, small pieces of furniture, mirrors, and Carltonware. The shop is open Tuesday and Thursday–Saturday until 4pm.

FURNITURE
Open by appointment only, John King (BADA) has an extensive range of period furniture and associated items – ring 01952 727456.

GENERAL ANTIQUES
Wenlock Antiques, again in the High Street, has a wide selection of general antiques.

SILVER & JEWELLERY
Cruck House Antiques in Barrow Street sells silver as well as pictures, small furniture, and collectables.

▶ Take the A458 for 19.25km (12 miles) direct to Shrewsbury.

SHREWSBURY
Standing on the Severn, the centre of Shrewsbury is a jumble of small crooked streets lined with half-timbered buildings. The Norman castle stands high above the River Severn. Thomas Telford converted it into a house in the 18thC. The castle is now home to the Shropshire Regimental Museum, which covers the history of local regiments and contains over 14,000 items including uniforms, medals, weapons, flags, equipment, silver, and china. Located in Barker Street, Rowley's House Museum is a black-and-white-timbered warehouse supported, in part, by pillars. It was once the home of a 17thC merchant, William Rowley who was not only a draper and brewer but also one of Shrewsbury's leading citizens. The displays include pre-Roman, Roman, Medieval, and later exhibits. There is also a collection of costume and Shropshire ceramics.

BOOKS
Candle Lane Books in Princess Street has a large stock of antiquarian and second-hand books. Quarry Books in Claremont Hill also sells antiquarian and second-hand books. The shop is open Tuesday–Saturday.

CLOCKS
The Clock Shop in The Parade, St Mary's Place, is owned by A Donnelly (BHI) and sells clocks, specializing in longcase and barometers. Open by appointment only – call 01743 361388.

COINS & MEDALS
Collectors Gallery (IBNS, IBASS, ANA, BNTA) at Castle Gates has coins, medals, stamps, banknotes, postcards, bonds, and shares.

COLLECTABLES
Collectors Place in Princess Street has a large stock of antique bottles, pot lids, Wade, Beswick, Carltonware, Art Deco, and collectables. Opening hours are Wednesday–Friday 10am–4pm and Saturday 9.30am–5pm.

CUTLERY
Sue Dyer Antiques in St John's Hill has silver collectables, Victorian and Edwardian cutlery, small furniture, Victorian glass, lamps, and unusual items.

FURNITURE
The Green People, The Parade, St Mary's Place, sells antique furniture and collectables. Situated at

Norton Crossroads in the village of Atcham, which is about 5km (3 miles) from the city centre on the southbound A458, **Mytton Antiques** has 18th and 19thC furniture and smalls, longcase clocks, country furniture, and restoration materials. **Quayside Antiques**, Frankwell, has a wide range of Victorian and Edwardian mahogany furniture, large tables, and sets of chairs. The shop is open every day, apart from Thursday and Sunday, until 4pm.

GENERAL ANTIQUES
Expressions in Princess Street sells Art Deco, furniture, pictures, glass, and ceramics and is open until 4pm. Established in 1944, **F C Manser & Son Ltd** (LAPADA) in Wyle Cop has an extensive selection of antiques, furniture, porcelain, glassware, and jewellery.

SILVER & JEWELLERY
Located in Princess Street, **Hutton Antiques** has silver, porcelain, and small furniture. It is open Tuesday–Saturday until 4pm. **The Little Gem** (NAG, Horological Society), St Mary's Street, has antique and second-hand jewellery, modern Waterford crystal, lighting, and handmade jewellery. The shop is open every day except for Thursday and Sunday (and Good Friday).

ANTIQUES CENTRES
Princess Antique Centre in The Square has 100 dealers selling the complete range of antiques and collectables. The 70 dealers at the **Shrewsbury Antique Centre** also in The Square sell a wide range of stock. The **Shrewsbury Antique Market**, Frankwell, has 45 dealers selling antique and period collectables.

AUCTION HOUSES
Halls Fine Art Auctions (ARVA) at Welsh Bridge have antiques sales every six weeks and general and collectors sales every Friday at 10.30am with viewing on Thursday 9.30am–7pm.

▶ Now the tour turns southwards on the A49 to Church Stretton, which is a distance of about 22.5km (14 miles).

CHURCH STRETTON
When you visit this small market town, take a look at the disused North Door of the parish church. Above it you will see a stone carving of a Sheila-na-gig, which is a pagan fertility symbol.

BOOKS
Church Stretton Books (PBFA) in the High Street sells high-quality second-hand and antiquarian

books. Malcolm Saville books are a speciality. The shop shuts at 1pm on Wednesday.

FURNITURE
Longmynd Antiques in Crossways has a large stock of 17th–19thC country oak and mahogany furniture.

GENERAL ANTIQUES
In the High Street, **Cobwebs Antiques & Collectables** has an extensive range of general antiques, collectables, and furniture 1800s–1930s.

ANTIQUES CENTRES
Stretton Antiques Market in Sandford Avenue has 60 dealers selling a wide range of antiques and collectables. The centre is open 7 days a week.

AUCTION HOUSES
Located in the Old Shippon in the village of Wall under Heywood, about 3.2km (2 miles) east of Church Stretton on the B4368, **Mullock Madeley** (ISVA) has sales of sporting memorabilia, vintage fishing tackle, and toys every three months. Sales are held in London, Twickenham, and Ludlow Race Course as well as at other venues.

▶ Continue southbound on the A49 for about 19.25km (12 miles) to the next stop, Ludlow.

LUDLOW
Perched on a cliff overlooking the Rivers Teme and Corve, the 11thC Ludlow Castle is one of 32 built in the Welsh Marches to protect the countryside and towns from marauding bands of Welshmen. The town has some great examples of black and white timber-framed buildings, most notably the Feathers Hotel. In Castle Street, Ludlow Museum has exhibitions of local geology, archaeology, and a detailed history of the area.

BOOKS
K W Swift in Mill Street is a book market with 20 dealers selling around 5,000 volumes (the range of books is frequently changed).

DOLLS & TEDDY BEARS
Little Paws in Castle Street sells traditional teddy bears and dolls.

FURNITURE
Situated in Old Street, **Bayliss Antiques** has oak and mahogany furniture, and paintings. R G Cave

& Sons Ltd (BADA, LAPADA) in Broad Street sells period furniture as well as metalwork and works of art. Also in Broad Street, **Claymore Antiques** has a large stock of English furniture and collectables from Georgian–Edwardian. John M Clegg in Old Street has an extensive range of period oak, mahogany furniture, and associated items. Leon Jones of **Mitre House Antiques** at Corve Bridge has a wide selection of country furniture, mahogany, and clocks. **Ludlow Antique Beds & Fireplaces**, in Corve Street, sells Victorian and Edwardian original fireplaces and brass, and iron and wooden beds of all sizes as well as country furniture and garden furniture. It is open Monday and Friday until 4pm and Saturday.

GENERAL ANTIQUES
The Curiosity Shop in Old Street has a large range of clocks, barometers, furniture, militaria, paintings, music, and boxes. In Corve Street, **Garrard Antiques** has a wide selection of period pine, oak and country furniture, pottery, porcelain, glass, treen, books, and collectables.

SILVER & JEWELLERY
Teme Valley Antiques (NAG, Sothebys.com associates) in The Bull Ring has a large stock of silver as well as porcelain, jewellery, small furniture, and pictures related to porcelain artists.

AUCTION HOUSES
McCartneys in Overton Road has monthly sales of fine art, antiques, and household effects on Friday at 10.30 with viewing Thursday 2–8pm and the morning of the sale from 9–10.30am.

▶ Take the A49 southwards again, this time for 17.75km (11 miles) to Leominster.

LEOMINSTER

Leominster (pronounced "Lemster") has many fine black and white timber-framed houses including Grange Court, which is an excellent example. Standing just off the B4362, 8.5km (5 miles) north-west of the town, Croft Castle is another of the Marches castles. It was mentioned in the *Domesday Book* and it is set in extensive parkland. It also has particularly fine 18thC Gothic interiors.

FURNITURE
Jeffery Hammond Antiques (LAPADA) in Broad Street has good-quality 18th–early 19thC walnut, mahogany, and rosewood furniture with some clocks, paintings, and mirrors.

GENERAL ANTIQUES
Utter Clutter in West Street sells general antiques, collectables, and early toys.

ANTIQUES CENTRES
The 12 dealers in **Leominster Antique Centre**, in Broad Street, sell an extensive range of period furniture, early porcelain, pottery, objets d'art, and antiquarian books. Still in Broad Street, **Leominster Antique Market's** 12 dealers have a large range of glass, china, silver, pine, and other furniture. **Linden House Antiques** in Drapers Lane has 10 dealers with a wide selection of furniture, lighting, glass, silver, porcelain, paintings, early country pewter, and collectables. **Old Merchants House Antiques Centre** in Corn Square has 26 dealers selling an extensive stock of general antiques, collectables, and antiquarian and second-hand books.

AUCTION HOUSES
Brightwells The Fine Art Sale Room in Ryelands Road have three or four general antique sales a month on Wednesdays and Thursdays at 10am. They also have five or six ceramics sales a year on Wednesdays at 11am. Viewing for all sales takes place on Tuesdays 9am–5pm.

▶ Still travelling southbound on the A49, the last stop at Hereford is 21km (13 miles) away.

▶ You might like to break your journey up by stopping at Dinmore Manor (see below), which is about 10km (6 miles) north of Hereford.

HEREFORD

Standing on the River Wye, this city was

▶▶ **DINMORE MANOR**

Situated in a magnificent location on a hillside, the manor house displays a range of architecture from the 14th–20thC. It has a chapel, cloisters, and a great hall. There is also a roof walk, which provides spectacular views across the countryside and beautiful gardens around the house. Do not miss the large and interesting collection of stained glass.

once the capital of West Mercia and has been the seat of the bishop since the 7thC. The present cathedral stands on the site of an earlier Saxon church and contains the famous Mappa Mundi, which shows a view of the world from the 13thC. It also has a chained library with about 1,500 books, including a copy of the Anglo-Saxon *Chronicles* from the 9thC. Sightseeing can be thirsty work so The Cider Museum and King Offa Distillery in Ryelands Street might be a good place to visit. The museum recounts the history of cider making and has displays of various kinds of equipment connected with the business. In the King Offa Distillery you will not only see cider brandy, apple aperitif, and cider liqueur being made, but can also sample the products.

BOOKS
Bourneville Books in White Cross Road sells second-hand, collectable, antiquarian, and rare books as well as prints, watercolours, and books for decoration. **Castle Hill Books** in Church Street has new, antiquarian, out-of-print, and second-hand books. Most subjects are covered here, but the specialist subjects include archaeology and British and Welsh topography.

FURNITURE
In St Owen Street, **Antiques and Country Furniture** has antiques, country furniture, and reproduction furniture. **I and J L Brown Ltd** in Whitestone Park, Whitestone, is the largest source in the UK of English country and French provincial furniture. In addition, the company makes reproduction furniture, especially Windsor chairs.

GENERAL ANTIQUES
The Antique Tea Shop in St Peter's Street sells small items, pastry forks, afternoon tea knives, 1920s–30s jewellery, French furniture, mirrors, and ceramics. **Mulberry's**, located in St Owen Street, has an extensive range of general antiques, silver, furniture, and a large selection of vintage costume. **Waring's Antiques**, again in St Owen Street, has a wide choice of general antiques, collectables, and pine – both old and new.

MAPS & PRINTS
Hereford Map Centre (IMTA) in Church Street has a large stock of old maps of varying scales

including 1:10,000, 1:2,500, 1:500, tythe maps, hand-painted, and County Series maps.

ANTIQUES CENTRES
With 30–35 dealers, **Hereford Antique Centre** in Widemarsh Street has a wide selection of furniture, pictures, fireplaces, china, etc. The centre is open 7 days a week (from 12 noon on Sunday).

AUCTION HOUSES
Sunderlands Sale Rooms in the Cattle Market, Newmarket Street, has fortnightly sales of general furniture on Monday at 5pm. There is an antiques sale every two months on Tuesday at 11am with viewing the day before and the morning of the sale.

▶ Although Hereford is the last official stop on this tour, you might like to turn west to visit Hay-on-Wye (see below). Take the A438 for 35.4km (22 miles) until you reach the village of Clyro. Turn left there onto the B4351 and Hay-on-Wye is less than 1.6km (1 mile) away.

▶▶ HAY-ON-WYE

If you love books you will be in your element here. There are 40 bookshops crammed into what is quite a small town. The shops range from those selling rare antiquarian books to others with modern second-hand paperbacks. There are also specialist bookshops covering subjects from poetry to murder. Even the most discerning reader will find something they like here. If you are planning to visit in May or June, check out the website first (see page 115) because you might be able to time your visit to coincide with the annual *Sunday Times* Hay Festival of Literature and the Arts, which attracts many famous authors.

STRATFORD-UPON-AVON ▶ WARWICK ▶ ROYAL LEAMINGTON SPA ▶ KENILWORTH ▶
COVENTRY ▶ SOLIHULL ▶ BIRMINGHAM ▶ WOLVERHAMPTON ▶ LICHFIELD

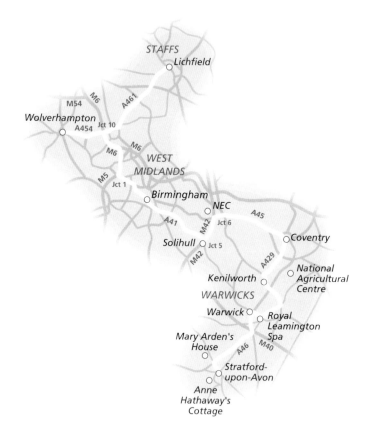

As might be expected in such an historic and picturesque region, there are a great variety of antiques shops in Warwickshire. The city of Birmingham is also a good centre for antiques buyers. Of course, William Shakespeare dominates the area around Stratford-upon-Avon but there is much of interest in the rest of the county too. Many of the villages appear unchanging and stereotypically English. This region has also been the stage for many dramatic events in English history – for example in 1642 the first battle of the Civil War took place at Edgehill, which is about 19.25km (12 miles) south-east of Stratford.

Shakespeare was not the only famous writer to be born in the region. Another, the poet Rupert Brooke, was born in Rugby. He is often seen as a quintessentially English poet. He died from blood poisoning on the way to Gallipoli during World War I.

▶ ▶ USEFUL CONTACTS

▶ ▶ USEFUL CONTACTS

Websites

www.antiquesforeveryone.co.uk
Information on dates, times, other venues, and exhibitors for the Antiques for Everyone Fairs and the LAPADA Fairs, which are mainly held at the NEC in Birmingham, are given on this website.

www.birmingham.org.uk
If you thought Birmingham was only about industry and the Bull Ring, take a look at this site and you will find out how much there is to see and do in England's second largest city.

www.coventry.org
This official Coventry website has extensive information on the city and surrounding area including what to see, where to stay, and places of interest.

www.coventrycathedral.org
For detailed information on the cathedral, visit this website. It not only covers the history but also gives details of services, news, and events.

www.royal-leamington-spa.co.uk
Do you want to know where to stay, eat, shop, or what to visit when you arrive in Leamington Spa? If you do, then check out this website, which provides all such information.

www.shakespeare-country.co.uk
This is the official website for "Shakespeare Country". It is run by South Warwickshire Tourism, and has a wealth of information for visitors to the area.

www.warwick-uk.co.uk
Before visiting Warwick, take a look at the official website to read all the information on the town that you could possibly want.

www.warwick-castle.co.uk
This excellent site provides a huge amount of information on Warwick Castle. It includes everything from a calendar of events to a timeline of the castle's history. You can explore the castle and grounds online and there is also full information on opening times, facilities, and directions.

Tourist Information Centres

Birmingham 2 City Arcade.
Tel: 0121 643 2514

Coventry Bayley Lane.
Tel: 024 7622 7264

Kenilworth The Library, Smalley Place.
Tel: 01926 852595

Leamington Spa The Royal Pump Rooms,
The Parade. Tel: 01926 742762

Lichfield Bore Street. Tel: 01543 308209

Solihull Central Library, Homer Road.
Tel: 0121 704 6130

Stratford-upon-Avon Bridgefoot.
Tel: 01789 293127

Warwick The Court House, Jury Street.
Tel: 01926 492212

Wolverhampton Queen Square.
Tel: 01902 556110

STRATFORD-UPON-AVON

The town has many picturesque buildings, but it is Shakespeare who makes Stratford such a supreme tourist attraction. He was born in 1564 in a house in Henley Street, now restored and furnished in the period style and containing many exhibits. Hall's Croft, the home of the Bard's son-in-law, has a 17thC doctor's dispensary as well as interesting furniture and paintings. The foundations of Shakespeare's last home, New Place, are set in an Elizabethan knot garden and the adjoining Nash's House contains fine Tudor furniture. Mary Arden's House is a Tudor farmhouse where Shakespeare's mother lived as a child. It is at Wilmcote, about 5km (3 miles) north-west of Stratford. Finally, the famous thatched Anne Hathaway's Cottage, home of Shakespeare's wife before her marriage, stands just over 1.6km (1 mile) west of the town.

ARCHITECTURAL ANTIQUES

Iscot Bathroom Company (SALVO) can be found in The Stable Yard, Alscot Park. It has an extensive range of Victorian–Edwardian sanitary ware, Art Deco, and roll-top baths. On Saturday the shop is open until 2.30pm. Thomas Crapper & Co (SALVO, Institute of Plumbing), also in The Stable Yard, was established in 1861. Here you will find Victorian, Edwardian, and unusual bathroom fittings as well as Art Deco and coloured 1930s bathrooms.

ARMS & ARMOUR

Arbour Antiques Ltd in the romantically named Poets Arbour, Sheep Street, has a large stock of 17th–18thC arms and armour.

BOOKS

Located in Chapel Street, Robert Vaughan Antiquarian Booksellers (ABA, PBFA) has a large stock of fine and first editions of English literature, theatre, allied subjects, and Shakespeare.

CERAMICS

Riverside Antiques in Ely Street has a selection of Clarice Cliff as well as antique and designer jewellery. It is open 7 days a week.

SCIENTIFIC INSTRUMENTS

Goodbye to all That in Ely Street sells small firearms and scientific instruments and is open every day.

ANTIQUES CENTRES

Stratford Antiques and Interiors, on the Dodwell Trading Estate, Evesham Road, has 20 dealers selling a variety of antiques and collectables, home furnishings, and decorative items. It is open 7 days a week. The 50 dealers in the Stratford Antiques Centre, Ely Street, also sell a range of antiques and collectables. and are open 7 days a week.

AUCTION HOUSES

Bigwood Auctioneers Ltd (SOFAA), are at The Old School, Tiddington, less than 1.6km (1 mile) east of the town on the B4086. They hold quarterly sales of fine art and antiques, and monthly antiques and collectables and furniture sales. They also have specialist sales of sporting memorabilia in March and September, wine in September and December, and games and toys in April and October. On Saturday the office is open until 12 noon. Steven B Bruce Auctioneers Ltd (NAVA, ANAEA) in Meer Street have monthly antiques sales on Saturday at 11am with viewing the day before from 10am–7pm and on the morning of the sale from 9–11am. The sales are held at various local venues and they also have occasional specialist sales. Situated on the Bearley Road in Snitterfield, about 3.2km (2 miles) north of the town just off the A46, Phillips Brothers (NAVA) have general and antiques sales fortnightly on Saturdays at 10am with viewing from 9am. They also have occasional antiques sales on a Saturday.

▶ Take the A46 for 16km (10 miles) to Warwick.

WARWICK

This historic town possesses the finest Medieval castle in England. In the 11thC, soon after the Norman Invasion, Henry de Newburghe built a motte and bailey on the site of a Saxon defensive mound. In the 14thC the Earl of Warwick built most of the castle seen today. There is much to see in the castle and grounds including dungeons, a Royal Weekend Party housed in the Private Apartments using waxworks, an armoury, the Great Hall, and a Victorian Rose Garden.

The Lord Leycester Hospital, situated by the town's West Gate, was built in 1571 to house 12 retired or disabled soldiers and their wives. It has been used for this purpose ever since. It is a Medieval building containing a chapel, guildhall, The Queen's Own Hussars Museum, and the Master's Garden.

In the Market Place, the 17thC Market Hall contains the Warwickshire Museum of local history, with fossils, the Sheldon Tapestry, and live bees. St John's Museum, located in an early Jacobean house, has a recreated 19thC kitchen and schoolroom. It also contains the Museum of the Royal Warwickshire Regiment. The Warwick Doll Museum, Castle Street, has displays of dolls, toys, and games.

BOOKS

In Jury Street, Warwick Bookshop has a large, general stock of antiquarian and second-hand books. Local topography books are the shop's particular speciality.

CERAMICS

Tango Art Deco & Antiques in Brook Street have an extensive selection of Art Deco ceramics, furniture, and accessories, including items by Clarice Cliff and Susie Cooper. The shop is open Thursday–Saturday.

CLOCKS
Summersons, Emscote Road, sells antique clocks and barometers. On Saturdays it shuts at 1pm.

COLLECTABLES
John Williams Antiques & Collectables, in the High Street, sells cameras, toys, tools, collectables, militaria, and porcelain.

FURNITURE
Located in the High Street, **Tony Curtis Antiques** has period furniture and decorative items. **Emscote Antiques**, in Emscote Road, sells original and reproduction painted pine furniture and is open Thursday–Saturday. Back in the High Street, **English Antiques** has a large stock of 18th and 19thC furniture and decorative items. **Patrick & Gillian Morley** (LAPADA) have two shops, one in West Street, the other on the Cape Industrial Estate, Cattell Road. Both have an extensive selection of period decorative and unusual furniture, and works of art. The shop shuts at weekends. **No. 56 Antiques**, also in West Street, sells a wide range of period and decorative furniture and accessories. **Quinneys of Warwick** in Church Street has been in business since 1865. It has a good stock of 17th and 19thC English furniture. On Saturdays the shop shuts at 1pm. **Don Spencer Antiques**, in the Market Place, sells old desks including oak, mahogany, walnut, Victorian, Edwardian and roll-top, writing tables, and desk chairs.

GENERAL ANTIQUES
Apollo Antiques Ltd (LAPADA, CINOA), The Saltisford, has English 18th–19thC furniture, sculpture, paintings, decorative items, Arts and Crafts items, and Gothic revival items. On Saturdays it shuts at 12.30pm. **Castle Antiques**, located in Swan Street, has small furniture, linen, china, glass, silver, jewellery, and Shelley. **John Goodwin & Sons** in West Street sells general antiques, furniture, pictures, and collectables. In Smith Street, **The Tao Antiques** sells Victorian furniture, copper, brass, china, and general antiques and is open 2–6pm. **Warwick Antiques**, in the High Street, has a range of general antiques.

SILVER & JEWELLERY
Again in the High Street, **Russell Lane Antiques** are official jewellers to the Royal Show. They have a large stock of antique jewellery and silver.

ANTIQUES CENTRES
About 1.6km (1 mile) west of the town, just off the A4177 in Hatton Country World, **The Stables Antique Centre** has 25 dealers. They sell a wide range of old clocks, furniture, curios, china, etc and the centre is open 7 days a week. The 20 dealers in the **Vintage Antiques Centre** (WADA), in the Market Place, sell an extensive selection of Victorian glass, 19thC ceramics, 20thC

colleactables, 1950s items, and smalls. It is open 7 days a week. Back in the High Street, **Warwick Antiques Centre** has over 30 dealers with a large stock of general antiques and collectables.

▶ Take the A445 to the adjoining town centre of Leamington Spa, about 1.6km (1 mile) away.

ROYAL LEAMINGTON SPA
The town received its "Royal" prefix after a visit by Queen Victoria in 1838. It stands on the River Leam and Grand Union Canal and also has natural spring waters, which made it a popular spa town. The Leamington Spa Art Gallery and Museum are housed in the Regency period Royal Pump Rooms.

BOOKS
Portland Books has two shops in the town, one in Spencer Street and the other in Campion Terrace. Both sell antiquarian and second-hand books with Warwickshire history a speciality. The Campion Terrace one is only open Thursday–Saturday.

FURNITURE
In Windsor Street, **Kings Cottage Antiques** (LAPADA) has early oak and country furniture. **The Old Pine House** in Warwick Street has Victorian stripped pine. It is open Tuesday–Saturday.

GENERAL ANTIQUES
Yesterdays, in Portland Street, is a general antiques shop with period furniture, pictures, and bric-a-brac. It is open Thursday–Saturday.

AUCTION HOUSES
BBG Locke & England in Guy Street has weekly sales of household and Victoriana with monthly fine art auctions.

▶ The A452 northbound will take you straight to Kenilworth, which is just 8.5km (5 miles) away.

KENILWORTH
The town's 12th–13thC castle was partly demolished by Parliamentary forces during the English Civil War in the 17thC to prevent its military use by Royalists. The National Agricultural Centre (previously called the Royal Showground), near Stoneleigh, is about 3km (2 miles)

east of the town. It holds many events, including antiques fairs, but is known as being the home of the Royal Show, billed as "Europe's premier exhibition of farming, food & the countryside". This is held annually in July.

CERAMICS
Paull's of Kenilworth (BADA, LAPADA, CINOA) in Warwick Road has a large stock of Masons' ironstone (Janice Paull is one of the best known Masons' dealers in the country). The shop also sells 18th–19thC pottery and Le Bond oval prints. It is open Tuesday–Friday until 4pm.

GENERAL ANTIQUES
Aspidistra, also in Warwick Road, sells antiques, Art Deco, antique, and modern silver.

ANTIQUES FAIRS
The Great British Antiques and Collectors Fairs take place occasionally at the National Agricultural Centre, near Stoneleigh. There are both indoor and outdoor stalls and the event is organized by the legendary Geoffrey Whitaker. He started the giant Newark Antiques and Collectors Fairs, which are now run by DMG Antiques Fairs Ltd.

▶ Leave Kenilworth on the A429, which will take you directly to Coventry – a distance of about 10km (6 miles) into the centre of the city.

COVENTRY

It is amazing, looking at Coventry today, to realize that it started as a small Saxon settlement. Its prosperity came from the wool trade, said to have been introduced here by Leofric, Earl of Mercia. Leofric was the husband of Lady Godiva. Legend says that when she begged him to reduce taxes he said that she could ride through the streets naked before he would do that. So she did and taxes were cut as a result. The city continued to prosper through the centuries, with the industries changing with the times. During World War II the city's factories became a major target for German bombing. On 14th November 1940 there was an air raid, said to have been the heaviest inflicted on any British city or

town. Approximately 40 acres in the city centre were flattened. Out of about 1,000 buildings, only 30 were left undamaged.

The city's Cathedral of St Michael was one of the buildings destroyed that night. All that was left was the spire and outer walls. These were linked to the new cathedral, which was designed by Basil Spence and completed in 1962.

Some Medieval buildings have survived – including the 14thC Guildhall of St Mary, the Tudor almshouses of Ford's Hospital, and the 13thC Cheylestone Manor House.

The city has two notable museums: the Herbert Art Gallery and Museum in Jordan Well and the Coventry Toy Museum in Much Park Street. The former tells the story of 1,000 years of the city's history and includes Graham Sutherland's working drawings for the cathedral's Lady Godiva Tapestry as well as work by Jacob Epstein, Henry Moore, and L S Lowry. The latter, housed in a 14thC monastery gatehouse, contains a collection of toys and games dating from 1740–1951.

BOOKS
A R Price in Walsgrave Road sells antiquarian and second-hand books on all subjects. In Smith Street, Duncan M Allsop (ABA) has a varied stock of books including those with fine bindings.

COLLECTABLES
Armstrong's Books & Collectables in Albany Road sells general second-hand books, special sci-fi comics, annuals, magazines, posters, postcards, and advertisements. The shop is open Tuesday–Saturday. Established in 1890, Luckmans Antiques in Far Gosford Street has small bric-a-brac, books, medals, cigarette cards, and postcards. It is closed on Tuesdays and Sundays.

FURNITURE
Cobwebs, also in Far Gosford Street, has Victorian furniture and antiques and modern wares.

GENERAL ANTIQUES
Situated in Hearsall Lane, Earlsdon Antiques has general antiques and collectables. Opening hours are Friday and Saturday 12 noon–5pm.

ANTIQUES CENTRES

Nicholas Green Antiques, Binley Common Farm, Rugby Road, Binley, on the west side of the city, has 10 dealers selling Victorian to shipping furniture. The centre is open 7 days a week.

AUCTION HOUSES

Warwick Auctions (NAVA), in Queen Victoria Road, has weekly sales of general household goods on Wednesdays at 10am. Viewing takes place the day before from 9am–4.30pm and for the hour before the sale. There are also monthly sales of antiques and collectables on the first Wednesday of each month (except January).

▶ Take the A45 westbound for 14.5km (9 miles) to Junction 6 of the M42. Join the motorway southbound to Junction 5, then the A41 to Solihull.

SOLIHULL

This ancient small town has been swallowed into the Birmingham conurbation but still retains its character.

GENERAL ANTIQUES

Yoxall Antiques & Fine Arts, in Yoxall Road, has a large stock of period furniture, quality porcelain, glassware, clocks, and barometers. The shop is closed Wednesdays and Sundays.

▶ Continue on the A41 until you reach the centre of Birmingham.

BIRMINGHAM

This is England's second largest city and, as such, is hard to successfully navigate without a local map. Birmingham is not often seen as an ideal tourist spot but there is much to do and see in and around this historic city. The Industrial Revolution in the 19thC brought great prosperity to the city as well as the same kind of social problems seen in other great cities at the time. Wartime bombing swept away some of the worst Victorian slums and redevelopment programmes have removed others.

Visit Birmingham Museum and Art Gallery, in the city's magnificent Chamberlain Square. It has international exhibitions of archaeology and ethnography, and also tells the story of Birmingham's history from the 13thC onwards. The museum has one of the country's most important collections of coins and medals and the Pinto Collection of Treen, which contains over 8,000 exhibits. Birmingham's famous Jewellery Quarter has its own museum that tells the history of the trade in the city. There are guided tours around a perfectly preserved 19thC jewellery workshop and a skilled jeweller demonstrates the craft.

Aston Hall, just to the north of the city centre, was built between 1618 and 1635 and is one of the finest Jacobean houses in the country. Some of its rooms are furnished in the style of the 17th and 18thC while others have recreated 19thC life. Dating from almost 1590, Blakesley Hall, to the west of the city centre, is a timber-framed farmhouse, furnished in the style of the mid-17thC. Finally, in 1912 George Cadbury moved the Tudor Selly Manor to its present location. It was in a very dilapidated state so he had it taken down brick by brick and then reconstructed and restored. The interior now reflects life in the 18thC.

ARCHITECTURAL ANTIQUES

Lindsay Architectural Antiques in Hugh Road has architectural salvage, fireplaces, quarry tiles, wrought-iron gates, etc. It is open 7 days a week (until 4pm on Sundays). MDS Ltd, on the Stechford Trading Estate, Lyndon Road, Stechford and Raven Reclaim & Architectural Salvage Ltd, in Stockfield Road, Yardley, are open from 8am.

BEDS

In Poplar Road, Kings Heath, J Girvan Antiques specializes in French beds and also sells pre-1920s and decorative items.

BOOKS

Stephen Wycherley (PBFA), Bristol Road, Selly Oak, is a large, traditional, general, second-hand, and antiquarian bookshop. It is usually just closed on Wednesday and Sunday but during July and August is only open Thursday–Saturday.

COINS
Birmingham Coins, in Shaftmoor Lane, Acocks Green, has a large stock of general, world, and British coins and banknotes, collectors' models, and medals. It is open Tuesday, Thursday, and Friday. Format Coins (IAPN, BNTA) in Bennetts Hill sells coins, medallions, and banknotes.

COLLECTABLES
Situated in Bristol Road, South Northfield, The Good Old Days has a selection of collectables. The Springfield Exchange, Stratford Road, Sparkhill, has an extensive range of collectables, coins, medals, militaria, jewellery, etc. The Midland Football Programme Shop, Oxhill Road, sells football programmes and memorabilia and is open Tuesday–Saturday until 4.15pm.

FURNITURE
Back in the Bristol Road, Selly Oak, Archives has an extensive range of shipping goods, Victorian and Edwardian furniture as well as 1930s–50s small items and general antiques. Birmingham Antiques, Sapcote Trading Estate, Wyrley Road, sells Victorian and period furniture and is open from 8am. In Gravelly Lane, Chesterfield Antiques has a wide selection of Victorian, Edwardian, and 1930s furniture. Moseley Emporium in Alcester Road, Moseley, has a large stock of Victorian, Edwardian, and period furniture together with architectural antiques. Alan Richards Brocante in Gravelly Lane has an extensive range of French furniture, kitchenware, and wood-burning stoves. It is open Thursday–Saturday. Returning to Selly Oak, this time to Katie Road, Roberts Korner sells furniture and collectables and is open 7 days a week from 12 noon–8pm.

GENERAL ANTIQUES
Cambridge House Antiques, situated in Gravelly Lane, has an excellent choice of general antiques. Cross's Curios, in Pershore Road, Selly Park, sells general antiques and old toys. The shop is open Tuesday and Thursday–Saturday. Memory Lane, also in Gravelly Lane, has a stock of 1930s furniture, jewellery, china, and clocks and is open 7 days a week.

SILVER & JEWELLERY
Garratts Antiques (NAG) in the Great Western Arcade has silver, china, glass, pictures, small furniture, and jewellery.

TOYS
Acme Toy Company, Station Road, Erdington, sells antique and collectable toys including TV, sci-fi, and Action Man. On Monday–Thursday it is open until 3pm.

ANTIQUES CENTRES
The Birmingham Antique Centre, located in Pershore Road, Stirchley, has 65 dealers selling a large range of antique furniture, partly used furniture, and bric-a-brac. The centre is open 7 days a week.

ANTIQUES FAIRS
The National Exhibition Centre (NEC), near Junction 6 of the M42, is home to some of the most popular fairs in the country. For example, the Antiques for Everyone Fairs are in April, August, and November, and the LAPADA Fair takes place in January.

AUCTION HOUSES
Biddle & Webb Ltd, Icknield Square, Ladywood Middleway, has pictures and prints sales at 11am on the first Friday of each month. They also have antique and later furnishings, porcelain, and glass sales on the second Friday, toys or decorative arts on the third Friday and, on the fourth Friday, jewellery sales. Viewing for all these takes place on the previous Saturday from 9am–12 noon, and on Wednesday and Thursday 10am–4pm. Fellows & Sons, in Augusta Street, has five antique furniture, porcelain, pictures, clocks, and collectables sales a year. They also have general furniture and household contents sales as well as fortnightly sales of jewellery and watches from pawnbrokers nationwide. Additionally, they hold eight antique and modern jewellery, watches, and silver auctions a year. The office shuts at 4pm on Fridays. Weller & Dufty Ltd (GTA), Bromsgrove Street, has six to eight fine art and antiques sales per year.

▶ Take the A41 again, north-west to Junction 1 of the M5. This is also the junction of the M5 and M6. Follow the signs for the M6 northbound and leave the motorway at Junction 10, which is signposted Wolverhampton. Then take the A454 into the town.

WOLVERHAMPTON
Although Wolverhampton is a distinctive town in its own right, it is also part of the great Birmingham conurbation. The Wolverhampton Art Gallery in Lichfield Street has a large collection of contemporary art and has a number of temporary exhibitions each year.

BOOKS
Bookstack, in Bath Road, has a large stock of antiquarian and second-hand books and is open Tuesday–Saturday.

CLOCKS
Woodward Antique Clocks Ltd (LAPADA) is

ocated in High Street, Tettenhall, to the west of Wolverhampton. The shop's stock includes a range of antique clocks, decorative French mantel clocks, and longcase, bracket, carriage, and wall clocks.

COINS & MEDALS
n Shropshire Street, **West Midlands Collectors** Centre has stamps, coins, medals, banknotes, and a range of curios.

FURNITURE
Doveridge House Antiques (BADA, LAPADA, CINOA) sells its wide range of fine antique furniture, lamps, paintings, silver, and decorative objects by appointment only – ring 01902 312211. n Tettenhall Road, **Martin Quick Antiques** (LAPADA) has a large stock of Georgian, Victorian, and later furniture as well as French furniture. The shop shuts at 2pm on Saturdays. **Martin Taylor Antiques** (LAPADA), also in Tettenhall Road, has an extensive range of furniture c.1800–1930. It opens at 8.30am during weekdays and shuts at 4pm on Saturday.

GENERAL ANTIQUES
Antiquities, in Dudley Road, has a large range of general antiques. To the north-west of the town in Fancourt Avenue, Penn, **Lamb Antique Fine Arts & Craft Originals** (FATG) sells its selection of Arts and Crafts, pottery, pewter, prints, silver, glass, jewellery, copper, and furniture by appointment only – ring 01902 338150. **Newhampton Road Antiques**, n Newhampton Road East, has a large stock of antiques and collectables and is open until 3.30pm. Back in Tettenhall, this time in Upper Green, **No. 9 Antiques** has 19thC furniture, porcelain, silver, and watercolours. It is open Wednesday–Saturday. **Wood "n" Things**, in Penn Road, sells antiques, collectables, Victorian, Edwardian, and 1920s furniture. On Monday and Wednesday it is open mornings only, until 1pm.

AUCTION HOUSES
Walker, Barnett & Hill in Clarence Street has monthly fine art and antiques sales as well as specialist sales of ceramics, jewellery and silver, mirrors and lighting, books, and prints. There are also fortnightly sales of antiques and contemporary furniture at Cosford Auction Rooms.

> Return eastwards back along the A454. Pass under the M6 motorway then, after about 3.2km (2 miles), join the A461, direct to Lichfield. The total distance is about 25.75km (16 miles).

LICHFIELD

The charming, picturesque town of Lichfield is made up of 18thC houses in narrow streets. It was the birthplace of Dr Samuel Johnson and also of Elias Ashmole, founder of the Ashmolean Museum in Oxford. Lichfield Cathedral has three spires, and the West Front contains more than 100 statues.

BOOKS
In Burntwood, **Royden Smith** of Farewell Lane has many antiquarian and second-hand books, and opens at weekends. **The Staffs Bookshop**, in Dam Street, has a wide range of 19thC wooden toys, but chiefly children's, antiquarian, second-hand, and new books. Specialities include Samuel Johnson and 18thC literature.

CLOCKS
The Essence of Time (BHI), Curborough Hall Farm, Watery Lane (off Eastern Avenue Bypass), has a large range of longcase, Vienna, wall, mantel, and novelty clocks. It opens Wednesday–Sunday.

FURNITURE
About 3.2km (2 miles) from Lichfield, in Main Street, Whittington, **Milestone Antiques** (LAPADA) sells Georgian and early Victorian traditional English furniture as well as 19thC English porcelain, including Coalport and decorative items. Opening days are Thursday–Sunday (until 3pm on Sunday).

GENERAL ANTIQUES
Cordelia & Perdy's Antique Shop in Tamworth Street sells a wide range of antiques including furniture, porcelain, and collectables. It is open Tuesday and Thursday–Saturday 10am–4pm.

MAPS & PRINTS
Cathedral Gallery, in Dam Street, has a large selection of antique maps and prints.

SILVER & JEWELLERY
James A Jordan (BHI), Conduit Street, has an extensive stock of jewellery, watches, clocks, and silver. The shop is open every day apart from Wednesday and Sunday.

ANTIQUES CENTRES
The 31 dealers at the **Curborough Hall Farm Antiques Centre**, Curborough Hall Farm (ADA), Watery Lane, sell furniture, china, collectables, jewellery, books, linen, and pictures. The centre is open Tuesday–Sunday.

AUCTION HOUSES
Wintertons Ltd (SOFAA), Fradley Park, has Victorian and general sales every 2–3 weeks on Thursday at 10.30am with viewing on Wednesday 1–7pm. There are also bi-monthly two-day fine art sales on Wednesday and Thursday at 10.30am. View on Tuesdays 12 noon–8pm as well as on day of sale.

NEWPORT ▶ CARDIFF ▶ BARRY ▶ COWBRIDGE ▶ BRIDGEND ▶ NEATH ▶ SWANSEA ▶
MERTHYR TYDFIL ▶ BRECON ▶ ABERDARE ▶ MOUNTAIN ASH

Antiques shops in this area of South Wales are concentrated in Cardiff and, to a lesser extent, Swansea. Others are scattered through the towns and villages, offering a good cross section of all kinds of antiques and collectables.

In the 19thC and for much of the 20thC too, a large proportion of the region was highly industrialized, with coal mining and steel making providing the basis of its economy. The collapse of these activities brought severe economic hardship to many people but the Welsh Development Agency has encouraged some new manufacturing and service industries to move into the area. Tourism has also become more important and some of the old coal mines have been turned into industrial museums in order to give visitors an idea of what life was like for miners.

You cannot visit South Wales without experiencing one of its best and sometimes most moving contributions to culture: the male voice choir. Borne out of the comradeship and community spirit of the coal mines, many of the choirs have survived in spite of the closure of the pits. It is well worth attending a concert if you have the opportunity.

Websites

www.breconbeacons.org
This excellent official website has a complete range of information on the Brecon Beacons – from what to do and where to go to archaeology and job opportunities.

www.castlewales.com/caerphil.html
Take a look at Caerphilly Castle and see for yourself how impressive it is. A view from the air shows its moats and stonewalls, which make it virtually impregnable. The site also recounts the castle's history.

www.cowbridge.co.uk
Cowbridge hardly gets a mention in many guidebooks. This well-illustrated site remedies the oversight with details of the town's history as well as places to eat, stay, and shop.

www.nmgw.ac.uk
The National Museum and Galleries of Wales' website gives detailed information on the collections and exhibitions as well as opening times and directions. Places covered include the Museum of Welsh Life and the National Museum and Gallery in Cardiff.

www.swansea.gov.uk/tourism
The official Swansea site covers all the information a visitor could want including where to stay, events, museums and galleries, activities, etc. All of these are clearly presented and the site is easy to navigate.

www.baynet.co.uk/colliery
Tower Colliery's website recounts the history of the coal mine and the historic workers' buy-out, which saved the colliery and 200 miners' jobs.

www.towy-fairs.co.uk
Check out dates and venues for Towy Antiques Fairs on this site.

NEWPORT

Once called *Gwynllyw*, after an early Christian warrior and saint who ruled it, this is now a busy modern town. It has an excellent museum, The Newport Museum and Art Gallery. This contains displays of prehistoric and Roman artefacts including a mosaic floor

Tourist Information Centres

Brecon Cattle Market Car Park.
Tel: 01874 622485/625692

Bridgend McArthur Glen Design Outlet,
The Derwen. Tel: 01656 664906

Caerphilly Lower Twyn Square.
Tel: 029 2088 0011

Cardiff 16 Wood Street.
Tel: 029 2022 7281

Merthyr Tydfil 14a Glebeland Street.
Tel: 01685 379884

Newport Museum & Art Gallery, John Frost
Square. Tel: 01633 842962

Swansea Plymouth Street. Tel: 01792 468321

removed from a nearby Roman villa. There are also exhibitions of social and industrial history and of the natural history of the area. The Art Gallery has work by Welsh artists and craftspeople – these include the Wait Teapot Collection, the Iris and John Ceramics Collection, and 18th and 19thC watercolours, topographical engravings, studio ceramics, and contemporary prints.

Tredegar House, which is about 5km (3 miles) south-west of Newport just off the A48, is an imposing 16th–17thC mansion. It once stood in 1,000 acres of parkland, which has since been reduced to about 90 acres due to the expansion of the town and the building of the M4. It was owned by one of the great Welsh families, the Morgans, who flourished for many centuries. In the 19th and 20thC their fortunes declined until, in 1951, the house was sold. It became a school and the contents were auctioned. In the early 1970s Newport Borough Council bought the house, which was restored and even some of its original contents were tracked down and brought back.

FIREPLACES

Welsh Salvage Co. (SALVO) in Milman Street has a large stock of fireplaces and flooring. It is open 7 days a week from 8.30am except Sundays, when it is open from 11am–2pm.

GENERAL ANTIQUES

In Chepstow Road, **Antiques of Newport** sells general antiques, period oak and mahogany furniture, and longcase clocks. **Breckwood Antiques**, also in Chepstow Road has a selection of general antiques. **Callie's Curiosity Shop**, Speke Street, Maindee, sells antiques and collectables. It shuts at 2pm on Friday and Saturday.

▶ From the town centre take the A48 westbound to Junction 28 of the M4. You only stay on this motorway for 3.2km (2 miles), then come off at Junction 29 onto the A48(M), which, after a further 3.2km (2 miles), becomes the A48. Follow this into Cardiff, which is another 8.5km (5 miles) away.

CARDIFF

Cardiff is the largest city in Wales and is also the capital and home of the Welsh Assembly. There has been a settlement here since Roman times but it only began to grow during the Industrial Revolution. At the beginning of the 19thC the population of Cardiff was about 1,000, but in just a hundred years this figure had grown to 180,000.

The Glamorganshire Canal, connecting Cardiff to Merthyr Tydfil, was built at the end of the 18thC, then the railways came to the city so docks were also built and later expanded. Cardiff was the world's leading port for the export of coal during the second half of the 19thC. Although the export of coal and iron declined after World War I the city continued to prosper as an administrative and cultural centre.

Cardiff Castle is a beautiful 2,000-year-old castle set in its own grounds in the heart of the city. It has splendid interiors, which were created in the second half of the 19thC by architect William Burges. Within Gothic towers there are opulent interiors with murals, stained glass, marble, gilding, and

elaborate wood carvings and each amazing room has its own individual theme. The castle houses the Regimental Museum of 1st The Queen's Dragoon Guards, which is laid out on a timeline from 1685 onwards. It has displays of weapons, uniforms, medals, and documents relating to the Regiment's history.

In Cathays Park, in the city's Civic Centre, the National Museum and Gallery has a magnificent collection of pictures by many famous artists. There are also exhibitions of coins and medals, ceramics, silver, Bronze Age gold, and early Christian items. In complete contrast, the Museum of Welsh Life at St Fagans, just off the A4232 to the west of the city, recreates life in a bygone age. Thirty buildings have been re-erected here in the grounds of St Fagans Castle and furnished in the style of the originals. The buildings include miners' cottages, farmhouses, a cockpit, and a tollhouse. All the buildings were threatened with demolition on their original sites and were moved here to preserve them.

ARCHITECTURAL ANTIQUES

Cardiff Reclamation on the Tremorfa Industrial Estate, Martin Road, Tremorfa, has architectural antiques and specializes in fireplaces and bathrooms. It is open 7 days a week, shutting at 1pm at weekends. **Holland & Welsh** on the Glay-y-Llyn Industrial Estate, Taffs Well, sells antique flooring and is open at weekends.

BOOKS

In Morgan Arcade, **Capital Bookshop** sells rare and second-hand books including those of Welsh interest. **Pontcanna Old Books, Maps & Prints** (WBA), located in Pontcanna Street, has rare and second-hand books, maps, and prints, specializing in Welsh topography. **Whitchurch Books Ltd** (WBA), Merthyr Road, Whitchurch, in the north-west of the city, sells rare and second-hand books and specializes in archaeology and history.

FURNITURE

Hera Antiques in Whitchurch Road has a large stock of high-quality furniture as well as porcelain and pictures. It is closed Wednesday and Sunday.

GENERAL ANTIQUES
In Penarth Road, **Anchor Antiques (Wales) Ltd** has an extensive range of general antiques, clocks, and ceramics. The shop is open Monday and Thursday–Sunday. **Arcade Antiques**, also in Penarth Road, has general antiques including Mexican furniture. It is open 7 days a week. **Charlotte's Antiques** in Woodville Road has a wide selection of general and period antiques. It shuts at 1pm on Saturday. **Llanishen Antiques**, in Crwys Road, sells general antiques including 19th and 20thC furniture. **Now & Then**, also in Crwys Road, has general antiques. **Roberts Emporium**, located in Salisbury Road, has a large stock of general antiques, collectables, and props for television and theatre.

ANTIQUES CENTRES
In the Royal Arcade, **Cardiff Antique Centre** has a wide range of general antiques and collectables including Welsh china and jewellery. **The Pumping Station**, Penarth Road, has 35 dealers with a large stock of general antiques. It is open 7 days a week.

ANTIQUES FAIRS
Towy Antiques Fairs organizes two events a year at the Cardiff Bowls Club, Sophia Gardens. The fairs have approximately 120 exhibitors covering a wide range of antiques and collectors items.

AUCTION HOUSES
Phillips International Auctioneers & Valuers' regional office is situated in Park Place.

▶ Take the A48 from the city centre to its junction with the A4231 and A4232. Turn left onto the A4231 and Barry is just 8.5km (5 miles) away.

BARRY

This town also benefited from the coal trade – it was exporting six million tons of coal at the beginning of the 20thC.

FURNITURE
Ray Hawkins Antiques Arcade on the Workships Atlantic Trading sells antique shipping furniture and statues. It shuts at 1pm on Saturday.

GENERAL ANTIQUES
Hawkins Brothers, in Romilly Buildings, Woodham Road, has a large stock of general antiques.

▶ Leave Barry on the A4226 northbound (be careful, the A4226 does a dog leg just west of Barry with one part heading west, which you don't want). After about 8.5km (5 miles) the road joins the A48. Turn left here and Cowbridge is about 11.25km (7 miles) west.

COWBRIDGE

This pretty market town has a history going back to the Bronze Age, with archaeological finds from both the Bronze and Iron Ages as well as Roman times. In fact the town's High Street follows the line of a Roman road.

CLOCKS
Castle Clocks in Eastgate sells antique clocks including longcase and wall.

GENERAL ANTIQUES
Eastgate Antiques, in the High Street, has a range of general antiques.

ANTIQUES CENTRES
The Antique Centre, Eastgate, has a large range of general antiques. **Cowbridge Antiques Centre**, also in Eastgate, has nine dealers selling Georgian–Edwardian furniture and smalls.

▶ Continue for another 11.25km (7 miles) westward along the A48 to Bridgend.

BRIDGEND

In days gone by, Bridgend was an important defensive point as it stands on the River Ogmore at a point where three valleys meet. Its ruined Norman castle is positioned on a hillside above the river and there are two other castles nearby, Coity (over 1.6km/1 mile to the north-east) and Ogmore (3.2km/2 miles south of the town). There is an unusual museum housed in Police Headquarters – the South Wales Police Museum has displays telling the history of policing in the area over the centuries.

FURNITURE
Utility, situated in Queen Street, sells late Victorian–Edwardian furniture and decorative items.

GENERAL ANTIQUES
Nolton Antiques & Fine Art, in Nolton Street, has furniture, ceramics, paintings, clocks, ephemera, books, stamps, and decorative reproductions.

TEXTILES
Hart Antiques (Textile Society), Dunraven Place, has an extensive stock of late 18thC–1920s decorative

antiques and period textiles. The shop is open until 2.30pm on weekdays and until 4pm on Saturday.

▶ Take the A48 west to Junction 37 of the M4 where you should join the westbound motorway for about 5km (3 miles). Leave the M4 at Junction 41 and rejoin the A48 for around 1.6km (1 mile) then turn right onto the A474 into Neath.

NEATH

Situated about 3.2km (2 miles) north of this coal mining town just off the A4109, Cefn Coed Colliery Museum uses the mine's old buildings to house its exhibition, which tells the story of mining in the area. As well as recreating a mining gallery it also has a steam winding engine, once used for lifting coal from underground to the surface.

COLLECTABLES
Neath Market Curios (OMRS) in Green Street sells general collectables.

GENERAL ANTIQUES
Neath Antiques, Alford Street, has general antiques, barometers, and clocks.

▶ From the north side of the town, take the A48 for about 3.2km (2 miles) to its junction with the A4217. Join the other road to reach Swansea.

SWANSEA

Swansea, the second city of Wales, has a history going back to the 11thC. Throughout the Middle Ages its economy relied on coal and shipbuilding and, later, its trade as a port. Iron smelting and oil refining also became important industries in the area. During World War II the city centre was heavily bombed and many historic buildings were lost, including the house where Beau Nash, the most fashionable person in Regency Bath, was born.

There are a number of excellent museums and galleries in Swansea. The Glynn Vivian Art Gallery in Alexandra Road has fine collections of work by Welsh, English, and European artists. In Victoria Road, the Swansea Museum, housed in a grand neo-classical building, is gradually updating its displays to bring them more into keeping with expectations in the 21stC. It has done this already with its exhibition of Egyptology, which is set in a recreated tomb and includes a short video on the preservation of an Egyptian mummy. Another interesting display is "The Cabinet of Curiosities", in which there is a recreated Welsh kitchen as well as a Pennyfarthing bicycle and images from the war.

The Swansea Maritime and Industrial Museum, in the city's redeveloped Maritime quarter, is housed in a dockside warehouse that was built in 1904 and is now a Grade II listed building. The museum tells the story of 250 years of the city's industrial history – how it grew and prospered then declined, leaving the largest area of industrial dereliction in Britain. It explains how Swansea coped and recovered. There is also an exhibition covering 100 years of transport history, which includes motorbikes, a steam roller, and a Sinclair C5. Other displays include lifeboats and similar maritime subjects. There are floating exhibits too – a light vessel and a steam tug, which was the last to operate in the Bristol Channel.

EPHEMERA
Collectors' Corner, which is in the High Street, sells enamel badges, postcards, stamps, cigarette cards, and old and new die-cast models. The shop shuts at 4pm during weekdays. However, on Saturdays it it is open mornings only, closing at 1pm.

FIREPLACES
Antique Fireplaces is situated on the John Player Industrial Estate in Clydach, which is just 8.5km (5 miles) from the city centre, north of Junction 45 of the M4. The shop has a large stock of antique fireplaces and is open Wednesday and Saturday from 10am–2pm.

GENERAL ANTIQUES

In Plymouth Street, **Aladdin's Cave** has an extensive range of general antiques and collectables, Doulton Toby jugs, brass, and copper. It is shut at weekends. Back in Clydach, this time in the High Street, **Clydach Antiques** has general antiques (it is also shut at weekends). In Cower Road, Killay, to the west of the city on the A4118, **Killay Antiques** also sells general antiques. On Saturday the shop is open until 1pm. **Sketty Antiques** in Eversley Road, Sketty, again to the west on the A4118, also sells general antiques. The shop shuts at 1pm on Saturday too. **Upstairs Antiques** in St Helen's Road has general antiques.

ANTIQUES FAIRS

Organized by **Towy Antiques Fairs**, a bi-monthly event takes place in the Brangwyn Hall, part of the Guildhall complex. It has about 100 exhibitors that sell a wide range of antiques and collectors' items.

▶ To leave Swansea, retrace your route along the A4217 and A48 back to Neath where you should join the A465 northbound. Continue along the A465 for 38.6km (24 miles) to Merthyr Tydfil.

MERTHYR TYDFIL

Although the smallest borough in Wales, Merthyr Tydfil was once the unofficial capital of the country as it was such an economic force. By 1831 it was the largest coal and steel manufacturing centre in the world and the largest town in Wales. Its population was then 600,000, more than the combined totals of Cardiff, Swansea, and Newport. At its height it had four huge ironworks owned by different families and their products were shipped right round the world, from the railroads of America to the Trans Siberian Railways. While the ironmasters built themselves mansions and lived in luxury, the workers had to tolerate slum housing and dangerous working conditions. In the last half of the 19th and early 20thC, a coal miner was killed every six hours and injured every two minutes, which just shows the situation that was prevalent throughout the South Wales collieries. It is no wonder that the whole area was a hotbed of socialism and radicalism. If you want to see the cost of coal, visit the cemetery and memorial at Aberfan, just 6.5km (4 miles) south of Merthyr where, in 1966, a tip of coal spoil slipped and buried the local school killing 116 children and 28 adults.

The geology of South Wales made its coal expensive and difficult to mine so there came a time when the collieries became uneconomic and were closed. The economy virtually collapsed. Recently, though, there has been a revival in the fortunes of the valleys and, in particular, in Merthyr Tydfil. The despoliation of the valleys by coal has been stopped and they are becoming green again. Tourism is now important, and, with Merthyr right on the edge of the Brecon Beacons National Park, it attracts many visitors to the area.

In Chapel Row, Georgetown, Joseph Parry's Ironworks Cottage is one of a terrace of houses built by the Cyfarthfa Iron Company for its workers. This has been restored to show how a skilled ironworker lived. It was also the birthplace of Joseph Parry, Wales' most distinguished composer. By contrast, Cyfarthfa Castle Museum and Art Gallery is housed in the mansion built by ironmaster and owner of one of Merthyr's ironworks, William Crawshay. The art gallery is reputed to be second only to the National Museum and Art Gallery in Cardiff in the quality of its collection. There are also displays of the town's social and industrial history.

GENERAL ANTIQUES

Halfway Trading, Portmorlais, sells a general range of antiques and new stock. **Paul Williams Antiques** in Warlow Street has a large range of Victorian, Edwardian, and Art Deco furniture as well as china, glass, pictures, and mirrors. The shop shuts at 2pm on Saturday.

▶ Because of the steep valleys to reach the next stop it is necessary to return to the A465 westbound for about 1.6km (1 mile) and then turn

17   Cwm Rhondda

left onto the B4276. (This is a steep road so you may prefer to continue along the A465 for another 1.6km (1 mile) and then take the A4059 southbound instead.) Aberdare is just 1.6km (1 mile) from the junction of the B4276 with the A465.

▶ Alternatively, this is an excellent opportunity to visit Brecon and the National Park. From Merthyr Tydfil take the A470 northwards for 30.5km (19 miles) to arrive in Brecon.

BRECON

This is the administrative centre for the Brecon Beacons National Park and, indeed, the three highest mountains in South Wales loom to the south of the town. Brecon is a charming town with some early buildings, although those from the 18th and 19thC predominate. Brecknock Museum in Captain's Walk recreates a mid-19thC Assize Court in an original courtroom, complete with figures of the judge, barristers, jury, and the accused. There are also exhibitions of local social and rural history in the area as well as archaeology and natural history displays.

The South Wales Borderers and Monmouthshire Regimental Museum of the Royal Regiment of Wales, in the Barracks has an interesting exhibition. This was the regiment that featured in the film *Zulu* and its soldiers also fought with Marlborough in his war against the French as well as against the colonists in the American War of Independence. Its soldiers have won a total of 29 Victoria Crosses, the highest award for gallantry that can be bestowed. Here you can learn more about its mighty battles.

While in the area you should take time to explore the Brecon Beacons – it really is an area of outstanding natural beauty. If you are fit and active, there are some beautiful walks to take. On the other hand, if you are of a more sedentary disposition, you can experience the

breathtaking scenery by taking a steam train belonging to the Brecon Mountain Railway from Merthyr Tydfil northward into the park.

BOOKS, MAPS, & PRINTS
D G & A S Evans in The Street sells books, maps, and prints. It shuts at 1pm on Wednesdays.

GENERAL ANTIQUES
Antiques Etc, in Lion Street, has a large stock of general antiques.

ANTIQUES CENTRES
The 10 dealers in Trecastle Antique Centre, Trecastle, sell a wide range of general antiques.

AUCTION HOUSES
Montague Harris & Co., Ship Street, periodically have sales of general antiques. The office shuts at 1pm on Saturdays. F H Sunderland & Co. (RICS, ISVA) in Wheat Street hold monthly sales of antiques and general effects. (The office is open all day on Saturday as well as weekdays.)

▶ Return along the A470 to Merthyr Tydfil and then follow the directions to Aberdare.

ABERDARE

Once dependent on coal mining, Aberdare produced the best steam coal in the world. However, the town's collieries are all closed now, except for Tower Colliery at Hirwaun, which is 3.2km (2 miles) north on the A465. In 1994 British Coal also closed this colliery down but it reopened in January 1995 after an historic workers' buy-out (the 200 miners contributed £8,000 each). This is now the only worker-owned coal mine in Europe.

The actual town of Aberdare, set at the head of the Cynon Valley, has removed the grime of the collieries and is set amid green and pleasant fields. The dramatic scenery of the Brecon Beacons National Park is just to the north.

GENERAL ANTIQUES
Market Antiques in Duke Street has a large stock of second-hand and antique furniture, collectables, china, glass, pictures, etc. It is open Tuesday,

Wednesday, Friday, and Saturday. In Station Road, **J G Steel** sells china, jewellery, and collectables. It is open every day except Thursday and Sunday.

▶ Mountain Ash is approximately 6.5km (4 miles) away on the B4275.

MOUNTAIN ASH

Further down the Cynon Valley, Mountain Ash is another of the small towns once economically dependent on coal.

GENERAL ANTIQUES

Old Oak Antiques Abercynon, in Margaret Street, has Victorian–Art Deco furniture, decorative items, toys, and collectors' pieces. **The Trading Post**, Oxford Street, has a wide range of stock including furniture, china, glass, silver, jewellery, textiles, books, and continental furniture. The shop is closed Thursday and Sunday.

▶ Although this is the end of the tour, you might like to visit Caerphilly Castle. To do so, take the A4059 southwards for about 5km (3 miles). Then join the A470 southwards for a further 13km (8 miles), before turning left onto the A468. Caerphilly town centre is then 5km (3 miles) away.

▶ ▶ CAERPHILLY CASTLE

This is the second largest castle in Britain (after Windsor Castle). It covers 30 acres and looks imposing. Building started in 1268 but within two years it was attacked by Llwelyn ap Gruffyd, who succeeded in destroying it. Work started again and the castle became almost impregnable, surrounded by high stonewalls and moats. Now its gatehouse contains an exhibition telling the story of the castle together with working, full-sized models of massive siege engines. This is a very impressive castle and well worth visiting.

SAFFRON WALDEN ▶ CAMBRIDGE ▶ NEWMARKET ▶ BURY ST EDMUNDS ▶ LONG MELFORD ▶ CLARE ▶ IPSWICH ▶ WOODBRIDGE ▶ COLCHESTER

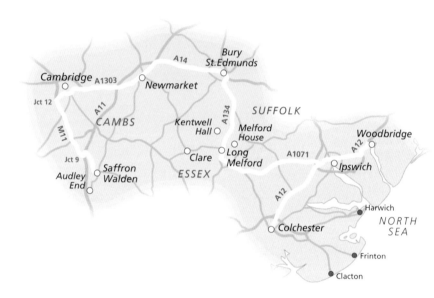

Antique furniture dealers in particular abound in East Anglia and Essex, although antiques of all kinds can be found in shops and centres in the historic and picturesque cities, towns, and villages throughout the region. Much of the area is "Constable Country", as its rural scenes were immortalized in paintings by the master.

In the south of Essex, Southend-on-Sea is a typical British seaside resort. Before package tours brought foreign holidays within the budget of most people, families from London and the surrounding area would come here for their holidays. It is the largest town in the county and also boasts the longest pier in the world. It has great amusement parks, beautiful public parks and gardens, and good live entertainment. By contrast, Frinton-on-Sea is famous for being the absolute antithesis of seaside resorts. It is very quiet and sedate with tree-lined avenues and well-preserved Victorian architecture.

Anybody who remembers the *Lovejoy* series on television, about an antiques dealer who was a lovable rogue, will recognize some of the places on this tour. Belchamp Hall, Sudbury in Suffolk, was used for Lady Jane's house. Other locations used include Long Melford, Saffron Walden, Norwich, and Coggeshall. Essex has had other famous residents including Gustav Holst, who composed his famous *Planets Suite* while living in the county. And author John Fowles was born in Leigh-on-Sea.

Websites

www.aztecevents.co.uk
Aztec Events' website gives information on all their antiques and collectors' fairs, including the ones that take place at the Suffolk Showground, Ipswich.

www.cambridge.gov.uk/leisure/index.htm
The Cambridge website gives basic information to tourists, such as places of interest, events, and where to stay.

www.colchestermuseums.org.uk
With over 2,000 years of history, Colchester's museums have a wealth of artefacts from the Bronze Age onwards. This site gives useful information on the museums together with pictures and details of some of the most popular exhibits.

www.ipswich.gov.uk/tourism
Check out this website on Ipswich and the surrounding area if you are planning a visit.

www.uttlesford.gov.uk/saffire
The Saffron Walden area's official website has a wealth of useful information for visitors. It is well laid out and also has a good search facility on its opening page.

www.cooperantiquesfairs.co.uk/snape.htm
If you are visiting the Ipswich/Woodbridge area in July, you might want to check the date of the Snape Antiques Fair on the organizer's website.

www.woodbridgesuffolk.co.uk
Woodbridge's website has good pictures of the town as well as all the information that visitors will need.

SAFFRON WALDEN

Saffron Walden and the surrounding area was, for 400 years, a centre for growing the saffron crocus. Not only did it give the town its name, the crop also brought it great prosperity too. Although it is no longer grown commercially here, you can still see carvings of the plant in many places in and around the town. The award-winning Saffron Walden Museum,

Tourist Information Centres

Bury St Edmunds 6 Angel Hill.
Tel: 01284 764667

Cambridge Wheeler Street.
Tel: 01223 322640

Colchester 1 Queen Street.
Tel: 01206 282920

Ipswich St Stephen's Church, St Stephen's Lane. Tel: 01473 258070

Newmarket Palace Street.
Tel: 01638 667200

Saffron Walden 1 Market Place.
Tel: 01799 510444

Woodbridge Station Buildings.
Tel: 01394 382240

in Museum Street, has displays of archaeology as well as natural and social history. It also has good collections of furniture, ranging in date from the 15th–18thC, pottery, porcelain and glass, and costume, including a gauntlet said to have belonged to Mary Queen of Scots.

Audley End, just to the west of the town, was one of the largest houses ever built in England. The Earl of Suffolk, Lord Treasurer to James I, started building the house in 1603. It was so big that it was never fully occupied or completely furnished. In 1668 Charles II bought it to turn it into a royal palace but it reverted back to the family in 1701. The sheer size of the mansion made it impractical, so parts of it were demolished (it is now about a third of its original size). The gardens were laid out by Capability Brown and many of the rooms designed by Roberts Adams and Vanbrugh.

DECORATIVE ARTS

In the High Street of Newport, a village that is situated about 5km (3 miles) south of Saffron Walden on the B1383, **Omega Decorative Arts** has

139

stock ranging in date from 1860–1960, which includes Art Deco and Arts and Crafts. The shop is open all week apart from Thursday and Sunday.

FURNITURE
Bowmans Antiques, in George Street, has furniture, pictures, and porcelain. C & J Mortimer & Son in School Street, Great Chesterford, which is just 6.5km (4 miles) north of the town on the B184, sells oak furniture. It is open on Thursday and Saturday afternoons from 2.30–5pm.

GENERAL ANTIQUES
Bush Antiques (EADA), Church Street, has country furniture, copper, brass, treen, ceramics, and glass. It is closed Thursday and Sunday. Market Row Antiques & Collectables, in Market Row, sells general antiques, clocks, and barometers. The shop is shut Thursday mornings and Sundays. Lankester Antiques & Books, again in Church Street, has a large stock of general antiques and antiquarian and second-hand books. Merriechest, Park Lane, sells antiques and collectables and is open on Saturdays only.

MILITARIA
Ickleton Antiques in Gold Street has militaria, postcards, and collectables of World War I and II.

ANTIQUES CENTRES
Situated in the village of Debden, 6.5km (4 miles) south of the town, Debden Antiques (EADA) has 30 dealers with a large range of 17th–19thC furniture, paintings, jewellery, silver, glass, rugs, and garden ornaments. The centre is open 7 days a week (until 4pm on Sundays). There are 40 dealers in the Saffron Walden Antiques Centre, Market Row, that sell a huge range of antiques, collectables, bygones, furniture, silver, jewellery, porcelain, lighting, pictures, and sporting memorabilia. The centre is open 7 days a week.

AUCTION HOUSES
Saffron Walden Auctions, Market Street, holds weekly general sales and antiques and collectables sales every two months on Fridays at 10.30am.

▶ Take the B184 north for 6.5km (4 miles). Then join the M11 motorway at Junction 9, still going north, and head to Cambridge, which is about 13km (8 miles) away.

CAMBRIDGE

As well as having its world-famous university, Cambridge is probably one of the loveliest towns in England. Long before the university was established,

there was a settlement here. Indeed, there is evidence of an Iron Age village on what is now Castle Hill. The first of the university colleges, Peterhouse, was founded in 1284 and the other colleges followed over the centuries.

Cambridge has a number of interesting museums. The Cambridge and County Folk Museum in Castle Street, is housed in the 16thC White Horse Inn. The museum has almost 30,000 exhibits reflecting the history of ordinary people in the area. In contrast, the Fitzwilliam Museum in Trumpington Street has collections of antiquities; applied arts including pottery and glass; furniture, clocks, fans, and armour, Chinese jades, Japanese ceramics, rugs and samplers; illuminated, literary, and music manuscripts and rare printed books; and paintings by Titian, Rubens, Van Dyck, Canaletto, Hogarth, Gainsborough, Constable, Monet, Degas, Renoir, Cézanne, and Picasso. Just off Downing Street, the Sedgwick Museum, which is part of the University of Cambridge Department of Earth Sciences, has collections of fossils, minerals, and rock including decorative and building stones. Another of the University's museums, the Whipple Museum of the History of Science covers all areas of science and has scientific instruments that date back to the 16thC.

ARCHITECTURAL ANTIQUES
Located on the Cambridge Road, Great Shelford, about 6.5km (4 miles) south of the city on the A1301, The Store has a large stock of architectural antiques, furniture, ephemera, collectables, bygones, rural artefacts, and decorative items. It is open Tuesday–Sunday until 4pm.

BOOKS
The Book Shop in Magdalene Street sells antiquarian, second-hand, and out-of-print books. G David (ABA, PBFA, BA), in St Edward's Passage, has a large range of antiquarian books, prints, and

publishers' remainders – fine antiquarian books are their speciality. **The Haunted Bookshop** (PBFA), also in St Edward's Passage, sells second-hand, antiquarian, and children's books – particularly girls' school stories. **Ken Trotman Ltd** (PBFA) in The Old Maltings, Ditton Walk sells their wide range of antiquarian and new books on military history by appointment only – ring 01223 211030. (Catalogues are available.)

CERAMICS
Gabor Cossa Antiques in Trumpington Street has a wide selection of 18th and 19thC ceramics and small items.

COINS
Granta Coins, Collectables and Antiquities (ADPS, SDS), in Magdalene Street, has a large stock of pre-Roman–modern coins. **Valued History**, Benet Street, sells coins and antiquities. It is open Tuesday–Saturday.

COLLECTABLES
Books & Collectables Ltd in the Railway Arches, Coldhams Road, has an extensive range of 16thC–modern books, comics, toys, postcards, cigarette cards, records, pop memorabilia, magazines, china, and furniture. The shop is open 7 days a week (however it shuts early on a Sunday – at 4pm).

FURNITURE
In Lensfield Road, **Jess Applin** (BADA) sells 17th–19thC furniture and works of art. **John Beazor & Sons Ltd** (BADA), Regent Street, has a large range of 18th and 19thC furniture, clocks, and barometers. On Saturday it closes early, at 4pm. **Peter Crabbe Antiques**, in Pembroke Street, has an extensive selection of English furniture, Asian porcelain, and works of art. Located in Station Road, Impington, just outside the northern outskirts of Cambridge, **Woodcock House Antiques** has a wide range of late 19thC decorative furniture, aesthetic items, and smalls.

GENERAL ANTIQUES
Bagatelle Antiques is located at Burwash Manor, Barns New Road, Barton, about 6.5km (4 miles) east of the city centre off the A603. It sells general antiques as well as decorative and garden items. On Saturday it opens at 2pm. **The Old Chemist Shop Antique Centre** in Mill Road has a large stock of general antiques and collectables. **Pembroke Antiques**, Pembroke Street sells furniture, smalls, glass, silver, and jewellery. It is open Tuesday–Saturday until 4pm.

LIGHTING
In Hills Road, **La Belle Epoque** sells period lighting and small items and is open Tuesday–Saturday until 4pm.

ANTIQUES CENTRES
Gwydir Street Antiques in Gwydir Street has 10 dealers selling furniture, silver, bric-a-brac, collectables, and decorative items. **The Hive**, also in Gwydir Street, has 10 dealers with antique pine, kitchenware, collectables, period lighting, pictures, Victorian and Edwardian furniture, and bric-a-brac. It is open 7 days a week; until 7pm on Wednesday. In Mill Road, the 10 dealers in **Those Were The Days** sell furniture, lighting, and fireplaces. The centre is open 7 days a week. **Willroy Antiques Centre**, also in Gwydir Street, has six dealers selling general antiques. It is open 7 days a week (from 12 noon–4pm on Sunday).

AUCTION HOUSES
Cheffins Grain & Comins, in Clifton Road, has 45 sales a year of antiques and later furnishings, specialist fine art, and furniture. **Phillips International Auctioneers & Valuers** have their regional office in Emmanuel Road.

▸ Take the A1303 direct to Newmarket, which is a distance of about 24km (15 miles).

NEWMARKET
The town of Newmarket is synonymous with horse racing. Located here are the headquarters of the Jockey Club, the National Stud, and the National Horseracing Museum – with its collections of exhibits ranging from those connected to jockeys and horses to the famous Ascot hats of Mrs Shilling.

BEDS
Located in Oxford Street, Exning, just to the north of Newmarket, **Exning Antiques & Interiors** sells beds, canopies, covers, drapes, mirrors, and original lighting. It is open Tuesday–Saturday.

GENERAL ANTIQUES
Jemima Godfrey Antiques in Rous Road sells small silver, linen, jewellery, Victorian china fairings, and linen. The shop is open Thursday and Friday.

AUCTION HOUSES
Burwell Auctions, Rous Road, have monthly sales of Victoriana, bric-a-brac, and collectables. **Vost's Fine Art Auctioneers & Valuers Ltd** in Tattersalls, have sales every six to eight weeks of fine art. They also have sales of sporting art and memorabilia in April and September.

▸ Continue eastward, this time on the A14, for 21km (13 miles) to Bury St Edmunds.

BURY ST EDMUNDS

The county town of West Suffolk is named after the last king of East Anglia, who died around AD 870. According to legend he was killed by raiding Danes. First they shot him with arrows then cut off his head. His soldiers found his body but only located his head after following the howls of a she-wolf who was guarding it. His shrine, and the great abbey that grew up around it, were places of pilgrimage throughout the Middle Ages. Although the abbey once occupied about 6 acres, all that is left of it today is a 14thC gateway and the 13thC Abbot's Bridge. When Suffolk became a new separate diocese in 1914, its restored church was promoted to become a cathedral. In Cornhill, Moyse's Hall Museum, housed in a 12thC merchant's house, has collections of archaeology and local history.

FURNITURE
E W Cousins & Son (LAPADA) is located on the Thetford Road, Ixworth, 10km (6 miles) east of Bury St Edmunds on the A143. It has a large stock of 18th and 19thC furniture and is open from 8.30am (open morning only on Saturday). Peppers Period Pieces in Churchgate Street sells 16th–18thC English oak furniture and 15th–19thC metalware. Talisman 2, Out Westgate, has antiques, period furniture, and unusual small collectables. It is open Monday, Wednesdays, and Friday, and Saturday until 3pm.

GENERAL ANTIQUES
Corner Shop Antiques, Guildhall Street, sells china, glass, silver, prints, Victoriana, and collectables. The shop is open until 4pm each day but is closed all day Monday, Thursday, and Sunday.

ANTIQUES CENTRES
Located in South Street, Risby, which is about 5km (3 miles) west of the town just off the A14, The Risby Barn Antique Centre has a large stock of Victorian furniture, china, silver, clocks, and rural bygones. It is open 7 days a week, including Bank Holidays.

AUCTION HOUSES
Lacy Scott & Knight (SOFAA), Risbygate Street, has quarterly sales of fine art and model and collectors' sales. They also have sales of Victoriana

every three to four weeks. Marshall Buck and Casson, Eastgate Street, have sales every three weeks of antiques and general items on Saturdays with viewing on Fridays from 2.30–8pm and the day of the sale from 8–9am.

▶ Take the A134 southwards to Long Melford, a distance of about 27.3km (17 miles).

LONG MELFORD

One of the best-known towns in England for antiques, Long Melford retains its Medieval character with its timbered houses and picturesque village green. If you want to know what a crickle-crankle looks like, visit the churchyard of the 18thC Congregational Church and look at the undulating brick wall. The Elizabethan Melford House, on the edge of the village green, retains a peculiarly English character in spite of having turrets crowned with onion domes. The house contains collections of paintings, ceramics, and Beatrix Potter memorabilia.

Nearby Kentwell Hall, winner of the Heritage Building of the Year 2001, is a moated red brick Tudor mansion set in beautiful grounds. Although still a family home, it has plenty for the visitor including re-creations of Tudor Domestic Life and World War II Life. Visit the great kitchen, dairy, bakery, and forge, which are all fully furnished with the original 16thC equipment.

CLOCKS
Village Clocks, in Little St Marys, has a large stock of antique clocks. It is open every day except Wednesday and Sunday until 4pm.

FURNITURE
Karen Bryan Antiques, Little St Marys, has Georgian and post-Georgian furniture, pictures, and prints. Sandy Cooke Antiques in Hall Street has a large stock of 1700–1830 English furniture and is open Monday, Friday, and Saturday 10am–5pm. Alexander Lyall Antiques, again in Hall Street, sells Georgian and Victorian furniture. The shop is closed Sundays and Bank Holidays. Magpie Antiques (LMTA), still in Hall Street, has an

extensive range of stripped old pine and country collectables. It is shut Monday, Wednesday, and Sunday. **Melford Antiques Warehouse** (LMBA), also in Hall Street, has a wide selection of 17th–20thC furniture, decorative items, a large variety of dining tables, bookcases, chairs, clocks, etc. The shop is open 7 days a week (from 1pm on Sunday). **Noel Mercer Antiques**, Hall Street, has a large choice of early English oak and walnut furniture. **Seabrook Antiques**, Hall Street, has an extensive selection of 17th–19thC decorative and oak furniture. **Suthburgh Antiques**, Hall Street sells a wide range of early oak, walnut, Georgian, and mahogany furniture as well as clocks, barometers, period portraits, early metalware, and maps by appointment only – ring 01787 374818. **Trident Antiques** (LAPADA), again in Hall Street, has an extensive stock of early oak, English furniture, related objects, and barometers. **Tudor Antiques**, this time in Little St Mary's, has furniture, glass, silver, figurines, and paintings. It is open 7 days a week (afternoon only on Sundays).

GENERAL ANTIQUES
Back in Hall Street, **Stable Antiques** sells Victorian–1960s memorabilia and is open 7 days a week (afternoon only on Sundays).

▶ Take the A134 eastbound for about 8.5km (5 miles) then take the A1071 direct to Ipswich.

▶ Alternatively, if you want to visit Clare first, take the A1092 west for about 11.25km (7 miles).

CLARE

This is another of Suffolk's charming villages, which has many Medieval buildings and the remains of a castle.

FURNITURE
F D Salter, in Church Street, sells 18th and 19thC furniture, porcelain, and glass. The shop is open all week apart from Wednesday and Sunday. **Seabrook Antiques** in Mill Lane has a large variety of 18th–20thC furniture and decorative items. The shop is open 7 days a week (afternoons only on Sundays).

TOOLS
Trinder's Fine Tools (PBFA), in Malting Lane, sells woodworking tools including British infill planes by Norris, Spiers, Mathieson, and Preston as well as second-hand and new books on furniture, woodworking, horology, and model engineering. It is shut Wednesday afternoons and Sundays.

ANTIQUES CENTRES
Clare Antique Warehouse, in Malting Lane, has 75 dealers with a large range of general antiques and

pine and oak furniture. It is open 7 days a week (afternoon only on Sunday).

AUCTION HOUSES
Dyson & Son, Church Street, have general antiques sales (600–700 lots) every three weeks on Saturdays with viewing on Fridays 9am–9pm and the day of sale from 9–11am. The office is open until 1pm on Saturdays.

▶ Retrace your route back to Long Melford and then follow the directions above to Ipswich.

IPSWICH

Suffolk's county town of Ipswich has been the site of successive human settlements since the Stone Age. During the Middle Ages the town flourished as a port trading with the Continent. There are over 650 listed historic buildings and 12 Medieval churches here, and much of the street pattern of the centre of the city still follows the original Medieval one. Close to the town centre, the beautiful Tudor Christchurch Mansion was built in 1548 and is set in over 65 acres of lovely parkland. It has good collections of furniture and ceramics as well as the most important collection of works by John Constable and Thomas Gainsborough outside London. There is also a collection of oil paintings, watercolours, drawings, prints, and sculpture by Suffolk artists from the 17thC–present day. The Ipswich Museum has exhibitions of natural history, including: the Bird Gallery that houses the famous Ogilvie collection of British Birds; Suffolk Geology; Ethnography; and Suffolk Archaeology, which includes a reconstructed Roman villa and replicas of the treasure found in the Anglo-Saxon burial site at Sutton Hoo.

ARCHITECTURAL ANTIQUES
Located in the High Street of Spoughton, just outside the western edge of the city on the B1113, **Heritage Reclamations** has interior fittings, stoves, ranges, fireplaces, and garden ornaments.

BOOKS

Claude Cox Books (ABA, PBFA), in Silent Street, has an extensive range of second-hand and antiquarian books, fine printing, and private press. Suffolk maps and prints are its specialities. The shop is open Wednesday–Saturday.

CHINA

Tom Smith Antiques, situated in St Peter's Street, sells antique china.

COINS

Lockdale Coins Ltd (BNTA), Upper Orwell Street, has British and foreign coins, banknotes, metal detectors, and accessories.

COLLECTABLES

Bridge Collectables, in Norwich Road, has a wide selection of mechanical bygones, postcards, Bakelite, coins, curios, and militaria. It is closed Wednesday and Sunday.

EPHEMERA

Suffolk Sci-fi Fantasy (GOMC), on the Norwich Road, has an extensive range of sci-fi collectables, ephemera, and collectable card games, as well as trade cards.

FURNITURE

Hubbard's Antiques, St Margaret's Green, has a large range of 18th–19thC antique furniture, decorative items, and works of art. E F Wall Antiques of Cliff Quay has a wide choice of antique furniture and is open Monday–Friday 7am–6pm.

GENERAL ANTIQUES

A Abbott Antiques in the Woodbridge Road has general antiques, furniture, small, and clocks. The shop is closed Wednesday and Sunday. Andrew Drake Antiques, Spring Road, has a large selection of general antiques. It is open every day except Wednesday and Sunday.

Maud's Attic, St Peter's Street, has a wide range of antiques and collectables. The shop is open Tuesday–Saturday. Memories Antiques, St John's, also sells antiques and collectables and is open Monday–Thursday mornings and Saturday mornings. Merchant House Antiques, St Peter's Street, has antiques and reclamation items. It is open Tuesday–Saturday. Betsan Philipps is on the Norwich Road, selling general antiques.

ANTIQUES FAIRS

The Suffolk Showground Antiques and Collectors Fairs are held at the showground in Bucklesham Road, Ipswich, several times each year. The event is organized by Aztec Events. It is advertised as having hundreds of inside and outside exhibitors and attracts buyers and sellers from a wide area, including mainland Europe.

AUCTION HOUSES

Lockdales, Upper Orwell Street, hold sales alternately between Ipswich and Norwich. Phillips Auctioneers (SOFAA), Boss Hall Road, has general sales every three or four weeks on Tuesdays with viewing on Saturdays 9am–12 noon, Mondays 10am–7.30pm, and on the day of the sale 9–11am. They also have quarterly fine art sales held in March, June, September, and December on Wednesdays and Thursdays in Bury St Edmunds. The office is open until 12 noon on Saturdays.

▶ Join the A12 to the east of Ipswich and follow it north to Woodbridge, just 13km (8 miles) away.

WOODBRIDGE

From the 14thC this town, situated on the River Deben, was a centre of sail making and boat building and it was here that Edward III's warships were built. There are many fine historic buildings in Woodbridge, including the last working tide mill in the country. Standing on the Quayside, there has been a tide mill here since 1170, although the building seen today dates from the end of the 18thC. It was working right up till 1957 when the oak shaft snapped.

The Woodbridge Museum in Market Hill is also well worth a visit. Its displays tell the story of the town and its people. There is also an exhibition on the discovery of the Ship Burial at Sutton Hoo together with a replica of the ship and other archaeological finds at the site. About 1.6km (1 mile) south of the town, the Elizabethan Seckford Hall is now a hotel and restaurant. Thomas Seckford, a great benefactor to the town, built the hall in the 16thC.

AUTOGRAPHS

The Autograph Gallery in Market Hill has a large range of autographs dating from 1562–present day together with other signed items.

BOOKS

Blake's Books (PBFA), The Thoroughfare, sells antiquarian and second-hand books, with Suffolk and sailing books being its specialities. Collectors

Books & CD Centre, also in The Thoroughfare, has some antiquarian books.

CERAMICS
C J C Antiques is located in Station Road, Melton, just on the northern edge of Woodbridge. It has ceramics, furniture, glass, and religious artefacts.

FRENCH ANTIQUES
Dix-Sept Antiques, Station Road, sells French antiques, furniture, glass, pottery, and textiles. The shop is open on Saturdays.

FURNITURE
BADA member, David Gibbins, Market Hill, has 18thC furniture and Lowestoft porcelain. Hamilton Antiques (LAPADA) in Church Street has 18th–20thC furniture. Anthony Hurst (LAPADA), also in Church Street, has 18th and 19thC mahogany and oak furniture. On Wednesday and Saturday, the shop is open mornings only. Raymond Lambert, again in Church Street, sells 19thC furniture. The shop is closed Wednesdays and Sundays. Sarah Meysey-Thompson Antiques, Church Street, sells 19thC and Georgian furniture as well as curios, decorative pieces, and textiles. On Wednesdays, the shop shuts at 1pm. The Old Brewery, this time in Melton Road, Melton, has a large range of furniture and collectables. The shop opens 7 days a week (Wednesday 10am–1pm and Sunday 1–4pm). Isobel Rhodes in Market Hill sells oak and country furniture, pewter, pottery, and brass.

GENERAL ANTIQUES
Bagatelle, Market Hill, sells general antiques, furniture, glass, jewellery, and china. The shop is usually open 10am–3.30pm, has a half day on Wednesday, and is closed Thursday and Sunday.

ANTIQUES CENTRES
Church Street Centre, in Church Street, has 10 dealers selling a wide range of items including small furniture, jewellery, china, glass, silver, ephemera, textiles, pictures, bygones, clocks, and collectables. It has a half day Wednesday. The Woodbridge Gallery, Market Hill, has 30–35 dealers selling an extensive range of general antiques. There is also a fine art gallery. On Wednesdays, it shuts at 1pm.

ANTIQUES FAIRS
If you visit Woodbridge in mid-July, it is worth checking to see if the annual Snape Antiques Fair coincides with your visit. It takes place 27.3km (17 miles) north of Woodbridge at the Snape Maltings near Aldeburgh. It has been running for over 30 years and always attracts quality antiques dealers.

AUCTION HOUSES
Neal Sons & Fletcher, in Church Street, have monthly sales of general antiques. They also have periodic specialist sales of English and Continental furniture, pictures, books, carpets, etc.

▶ Return to the A12, this time travelling south for 10km (6 miles), then turn right onto the A14 around the southern side of Ipswich. Drive for 11.25km (7 miles) until the road meets the A12 again. Turn left onto the A12 and continue southwards for 24km (15 miles) to Colchester.

COLCHESTER
The ancient city of Colchester is among the best known of English Roman settlements, although its history goes back much further – to at least the 5thC BC. After the Roman invasion it soon became an important centre and grew quickly in size, probably aided by the fact that retired Roman soldiers were given grants of land here. When the Iceni, led by Queen Boudica (Boadicea), rebelled in around AD 60, they sacked Colchester. Many of the Roman veterans tried to defend the town but without success. Some survivors fell back to the great Roman temple built to honour the Emperor Claudius. However, this was captured and burnt and the marks of the fire can still be seen on the surviving foundations. After the rebellion was put down, Colchester was rebuilt. In the 11thC, the Normans built a castle on the foundations of the Claudian temple.

As might be expected in a town with such a long history, there are several very good museums here. The Colchester Castle Museum in Ryegate Road has displays covering over 2,000 years of history including Bronze Age gold jewellery, a mosaic floor from a local Roman villa, and the Gosbecks Mercury, which is a bronze statue of the Roman god Mercury – said to be the finest Roman British statue in existence.

Located in a 15thC house, the Tymperleys Clock Museum is home to part of the Bernard Mason Collection of Clocks, which is one of the largest collections in Britain. All the clocks were made in Colchester in 1640–1840, which means the museum is an essential visit for all dealers and collectors of clocks.

ARCHITECTURAL ANTIQUES
Revival, in Drury Road, has a large stock of architectural salvage, furniture, and decorative curios. It is open Tuesday–Saturday until 4pm.

BOOKS
Located in Trinity, Alphabets sells antiquarian and second-hand books. It is open all week apart from Thursday and Sunday. The Castle Book Shop (PBFA), in North Hill, has a wide selection of antiquarian and second-hand books. East Anglia, archaeology, and modern first editions are its specialities. It also sells maps and prints.

COLLECTABLES
Icenimilitaria, Osborne Street, sells wartime memorabilia. It is closed Thursday and Sunday.

FURNITURE
S Bond & Son, in Olivers Lane sells 18th and 19thC mahogany furniture and paintings by appointment only – ring 01206 331175. Colton Antiques, Station Road, has 18th and 19thC Georgian and decorative furniture. It is open from 8am.

GENERAL ANTIQUES
Elizabeth Cannon Antiques, Crouch Street, has a large stock of antique glass, jewellery, silver, porcelain, and furniture.

AUCTION HOUSES
The regional office of Bonhams & Brooks is located in Ford Street, Aldham, which is about 6.5km (4 miles) west of the centre of Colchester, just off the A1124. Reeman, Dansie, Howe & Son, in Headgate, have weekly sales of household goods as well as less frequent antiques sales, held on Wednesdays at 10am with viewing on Tuesdays 9am–7pm and on the day of sale 9–10am. Stanfords, East Hill, also have weekly sales of general goods on Tuesdays at 10am. They also have quarterly sales of antique furniture and collectables, also on Tuesdays but this time at 11am. Viewing takes place on Saturdays, 9am–1pm, Mondays 12 noon–7pm, and the morning of the sale.

DISS ▶ BUNGAY ▶ BECCLES ▶ NORWICH ▶ NORTH WALSHAM ▶ CROMER ▶ HOLT ▶ FAKENHAM ▶ KING'S LYNN

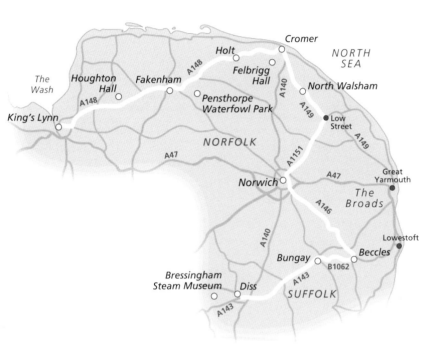

Surprisingly, for a county so steeped in history, there are only two big concentrations of antiques shops on this tour, although all the towns and villages have a good selection.

The tour goes partly into Suffolk, but most of it is within Norfolk. The coast of Norfolk has loomed large in the county's history. The ports along this stretch of coast have traded with Holland for centuries, resulting in a pronounced Dutch influence on the architecture of towns and villages. As in Holland, windmills are common in Norfolk and they were used to drain the farmland,

although many of them are now disused. The famous Norfolk Broads, an area of waterways and lakes, is popular for small boats, birdwatchers, and holidaymakers.

This region has some of the lowest-lying and flattest land in England. It is also some of the most fertile farmland, so much of the county's agricultural land is still being farmed intensively using the latest equipment. In some cases this has been detrimental to wildlife conservation but nowadays the situation has improved greatly with the growing awareness of the problems caused by agricultural chemicals.

19 Broads & Windmills

►► USEFUL CONTACTS

Websites

www.cromer-network.co.uk
This vibrant site contains a wealth of information on Cromer, including attractions, places to stay, eat, and drink. It has useful web links for places of interest.

www.diss.co.uk
According to statistics on the front page, this site is growing in popularity and had over 200,000 hits last year. It is definitely worth looking at as it is full of useful facts.

www.allaboutfakenham.com
If you are visiting the small market town of Fakenham, take a look at its own website first.

www.norfolkcoast.co.uk/FelbriggHall.htm
Learn more about Felbrigg Hall and see pictures of the house on this website.

www.visitnorfolk.co.uk
This official Norfolk site gives all kinds of information on the whole county as well as individual towns.

www.norwich.gov.uk
This informative, official site has all the information that visitors to Norwich could ever want at their fingertips.

Tourist Information Centres

Beccles The Quay, Fen Lane.
Tel: 01502 713196

Cromer Prince of Wales Road.
Tel: 01263 512497

Diss Meres Mouth, Mere Road.
Tel: 01379 650523

King's Lynn Custom House, Purfleet Quay.
Tel: 01553 763044

Norwich The Guildhall, Gaol Hill.
Tel: 01603 666071

DISS

This town is full of 16thC buildings that follow a Medieval street plan, all centred on the church. The Bressingham Steam Museum, which is just over 3.2km (2 miles) west of Diss off the A1066, is said to have the most comprehensive collection of steam engines in Europe. There are four separate working railways

as well as stationary and traction engines. There is also a collection of fire engines and other equipment.

FURNITURE
Brockdish Antiques is situated in Scole Road, Brockdish, which is about 6.5km (4 miles) east of Diss on the A143 to Bungay. The shop sells Edwardian and Victorian furniture (it is closed Wednesday and Sunday). **Diss Antiques & Interiors** (LAPADA, GOMC), in the Market Place, has Tudor–Edwardian furniture together with ceramics and silver.

ANTIQUES CENTRES
Antique and Collectors' Centre Diss, in Cobbs Yard, St Nicholas Street, has 28 dealers with a large range of 1850–1970 general antiques, Art Deco china and glass, commemoratives, and militaria.

AUCTION HOUSES
Thos Wm Gaze & Son (RICS), Roydon Road, has weekly sales of antiques, collectables, Victorian pine, and modern furniture and effects on Fridays. They have periodic sales of decorative arts, paintings, books, and ephemera, which also take place on Fridays. Additionally, there are periodic sales on Saturdays of toys, nostalgia, architectural salvage, statuary, rural and domestic bygones, automobilia, and collectors' cars. The office is open until 1pm on Saturday as well as weekdays.

► Take the A143 for 24km (15 miles) east to reach the next stop, Bungay.

BUNGAY

The ruins of its 12thC castle dominate this pretty village, which is set just over the county border in Suffolk.

GENERAL ANTIQUES
In Earsham Street, **Black Dog Antiques** has general antiques, collectables, and pine furniture. It is open 7 days a week. **Broadly Antiques**, Broad Street, sell general antiques, country furniture, costume, and jewellery (it is closed Wednesday and Sunday). **Friend or Faux**, again in Earsham Street, has antiques, decorative objects, murals, paintings, and hand-painted furniture. It is open Friday and Saturday. Also in Earsham Street, **One Step Back** sells general antiques and furniture. The shop is open all week apart from Wednesday and Sunday.

AUCTION HOUSES
Bungay Auction Rooms, Trinity Street, has fortnightly or monthly sales of antiques and collectables. In summer they take place on

USEFUL CONTACTS

Saturday evenings, but in winter are on Sundays. Viewing takes place the day of the sale in summer and the day before in winter. Office hours are Monday–Friday 10am–12noon.

▶ The B1062 eastbound will take you directly to Beccles, which is about 8km (5 miles) away.

BECCLES

Situated on the River Waveney, still in Suffolk, Beccles has some lovely Georgian houses. Its church has a separate 14thC bell tower with a peal of 10 bells.

BOOKS
Besley's Books (ABA PBFA), Blyburgate, sells antiquarian books with gardening, natural history, art, and private press being their specialities. It is closed Wednesday and Sunday.

FURNITURE
Fauconberges in Smallgate has 17th–19thC furniture as well as pictures and glass.

GENERAL ANTIQUES
Blyburgate Antiques in Blyburgate sells general antiques and furniture. It is closed Monday, Wednesday, and Sunday. M & A Ratcliffe, Saltgate, has general antiques and 18th and 19thC furniture. It closes early on Wednesdays.

AUCTION HOUSES
Durrants Auction Rooms, Gresham Road, have weekly sales of antiques every Friday with a special sale every six weeks. Viewing takes place the day before and on the morning of the sale. The office is open weekdays and until 12 noon on Saturdays.

▶ Take the A146 to Norwich, which is 27.3km (17 miles) away.

NORWICH

Dominated by its cathedral and castle, Norwich caters for all tastes (it is said to have a church for every week of the year and a pub for every day!). The heart of this historic city still follows the Medieval street plan and has about 1,000 listed buildings. No visit to Norwich would be complete without a visit to the cathedral. Building started in 1098 using Caen

stone brought from Normandy, although local flint was also used. The cathedral's spire is second only to the one on Salisbury Cathedral and rises to 96m (315ft). Take a look at the beautiful and intricate fan-vaulted roof and the magnificent stained glass windows. Behind the High Altar, there are the remains of a Saxon bishop's throne, still visible below the later wooden one. There are numerous other beautiful, interesting, and historic features to see in the cathedral so it really should not be missed when visiting the city.

As might be expected in such an historic city, there are many fascinating and varied museums. In the heart of the city, Norwich Castle Museum has fine displays of work by the Norwich School of Painters as well as the Twining Teapot collection, archaeology, and natural history including the bones of the prehistoric West Runton Elephant. Housed in a Medieval church, the St Peter Hungate Museum in Princes Street has exhibits telling the story of life in the parish over the centuries. There is also a brass-rubbing centre with over 40 replica brasses for enthusiasts to rub. In the Shire Hall, Market Avenue, the Royal Norfolk Regimental Museum recounts the history of the regiment from the late 17thC onwards and includes details of its campaigns in countries worldwide.

The Bridewell Museum, in Bridewell Alley, is located in a merchant's house dating from 1325. It houses displays that show the lives of some of the people who have lived in the house. It also shows the industries that have made Norwich prosperous, including the making of chocolates, shoes, textiles, and mustard. There are also reconstructions of a smithy and pharmacy from the 1930s, which includes over 5,000 items.

ARCHITECTURAL ANTIQUES

Harvey's Architectural Reclaim, in Raynham Street, has an extensive range of fireplaces, surrounds, sinks, doors, gates, and chimney pots. It shuts at 4pm on weekdays and is also shut all day Monday and Sunday.

BOOKS

Crowe's Antiquarian Books (PBFA), Upper St Giles Street, sells antiquarian books, including local history and prints. In Surrey Street, Peter J Hadley (ABA, PBFA) has antiquarian books, especially covering English, architectural history, art reference, and literature. The shop is open Friday and Saturday. The Movie Shop, St Gregory's Alley, has a large stock of general and antiquarian books. Tombland Bookshop, in Tombland, has a wide range of antiquarian books.

COINS

Clive Dennett (BNTA, IBNS), St Benedict's Street, has a large selection of coins, medals, banknotes, and currency. The shop is open all week except Thursday and Sunday.

COLLECTABLES

The Collectors' Shop, situated in Angel Road, has a wide range of stamps, postcards, coins, models, small items, and collectables. It is closed Thursday and Sunday.

FURNITURE

In Elm Hill, Antiques & Interiors sells furniture and porcelain. Arthur Brett & Sons (BADA), St Giles Street, has 17th–18thC furniture and fine art. Barry Craske Antiques, in Magdalen Street, sells country and pine furniture and bygones. It is open until 4pm on weekdays. Nicholas Fowle Antiques (BADA) in Websdales Court, Bedford Street, has 18th and 19thC furniture. It shuts at 1pm on Saturday. John Howkins Antiques Ltd, Dereham Road, sells Victorian and Georgian furniture.

GENERAL ANTIQUES

Black Horse Gallery (BADA, LAPADA), Wensum Street, sells a complete range of antiques and collectables. Déjà Vu, Magdalen Street, has a large stock of general antiques and furniture and is open 7 days a week. St Michael at Plea Antiques and Collectors Centre, Redwell Street Bank, has a wide range of china, silver, toys, brass, prints, small items of furniture, books, coins, and medals. Silvermans, Upper St Giles Street, has an extensive selection of general antiques. Malcolm Turner, St Giles Street, has a large collection of mixed porcelain, bronze figures, silver, and jewellery, and is open Tuesday–Saturday.

SILVER & JEWELLERY

In Lower Goat Lane, Maddermarket Antiques (NAG) has a wide range of antique, second-hand, and modern jewellery and silverware. Timgems Jewellers, Elm Hill, sells antique jewellery and silverware and is open Tuesday–Saturday.

AUCTION HOUSES

The regional office of Phillips International Auctioneers & Valuers is located in Fishergate.

▶ Take the A1151 from Norwich for 21km (13 miles) to the village of Low Street. Turn left there onto the A149 and the next stop, North Walsham, is only 10km (6 miles) away.

NORTH WALSHAM

Because of a disastrous fire in 1600, much of the town was destroyed and later rebuilt, which has left a legacy of mostly Georgian and Victorian buildings.

BOOKS

The Angel Bookshop, Aylsham Road, sells general antiquarian books with those on Norfolk and natural history being specialities. The shop shuts at 1pm except on Saturdays, when it shuts at 4pm.

GENERAL ANTIQUES

Eric Bates & Sons, in Bacton Road, has general 19thC antiques as well as Victorian chairs.

AUCTION HOUSES

In Market Place, Nigel F Hedge has quarterly sales of antiques on Saturdays at 10.30am at Hoveton Village Hall with viewing the previous day from 3–8pm and the morning of the sale from 8am. The office shuts at 1pm on Saturdays. Horners Auctioneers, Midland Road, has weekly general sales on Fridays at 10am with viewing on Thursdays 2–8pm. The office shuts at 12 noon on Saturdays.

▶ Continue for a further 14.5km (9 miles) on the A149 to Cromer.

CROMER

Norfolk reaches its highest point, 103.6km (340ft) above sea level, at West Runton, which is about 5km (3 miles) west of the seaside town of Cromer. There are also high cliffs at Cromer that rise above good, safe bathing beaches. Felbrigg Hall, standing just 3.2km (2 miles) to the south-west of the town, is said to be one of the finest

17thC houses in the region. Much of the house was redecorated in the mid-18thC following the owner's return from a Grand Tour of Europe. As a result, it also has one of the best Grand Tour collections in the country.

BOOKS

Books Etc, in Church Street, has a large stock of antiquarian and second-hand books. From Easter–September it is open 11am–4pm Monday–Saturday, from October–Easter the shop is open 11am–4pm Wednesday–Saturday.

CERAMICS

On the Promenade, Collectors' Cabin has a wide range of ceramics and glass, including Crown Derby. It is open Tuesday–Sunday.

FURNITURE

Collectors' World, New Parade, has an extensive selection of furniture, general antiques, and collectables. It is open Tuesday–Saturday.

SILVER & JEWELLERY

Bond Street Antiques (NAG, FGA), unsurprisingly in Bond Street, sells silver and jewellery.

▶ Take the A148 for 16km (10 miles) to Holt.

HOLT

The large village of Holt is the centre for a varied range of antiques shops. It was destroyed by fire in the early 18thC but was rebuilt to the original Medieval street pattern.

BEDS

Trinities, in Bull Street, sells fully restored Victorian beds, antiques, collectables, artefacts, and memorabilia. It is open every day except Thursday and Sunday, until 4pm.

BOOKS

Baron Art has two shops, one in The Old Reading Room, the other in Chapel Yard, Albert Street. Both have antiquarian books, paintings, and ceramics. The shop in Albert Street is open Monday–Saturday, the other opens 7 days a week. In Fish Hill, Simon Gough Books Ltd has antiquarian books.

CERAMICS

In the High Street, Richard Scott Antiques has a wide selection of ceramics, studio pottery, and oil lamps. The shop is closed on Thursdays and Sundays.

COLLECTABLES

Cobwebs, in Fish Hill, has a large range of bygones and collectables as well as woodworking and agricultural tools. Holt Antique Centre, Albert Street, has a wide selection of collectables and is open 7 days a week.

COSTUME & TEXTILES

Past Caring, in Chapel Yard, Albert Street, has a wide choice of linen, lace, vintage clothing, accessories, and costume jewellery from 1800s–1950. It is closed Thursday and Sunday.

FURNITURE

Heathfield Country Pine, Hempstead Road, has a big selection of antique pine and country items. It opens at 8am. Maura Henry Antiques & Interiors, again in Chapel Yard, Albert Street, sells a wide range of Georgian furniture and is open on Fridays and Saturdays.

GENERAL ANTIQUES

Back in Fish Hill, Cottage Collectables has general antiques and jewellery. It is open 7 days a week. Langhams, in Bull Street, has an extensive collection of general antiques and collectables.

ANTIQUES CENTRES

The 14 dealers at the Mews Antique Emporium in the High Street sell a wide range of furniture, pictures, pottery, and china. The centre is open 7 days a week (until 4pm on Saturdays).

▶ Continue westwards on the A148 for 19.25km (12 miles) to Fakenham.

FAKENHAM

This pleasant market town stands on the River Wensum. The Penshurst Waterfowl Park is just 3.2km (2 miles) south of the town, and Houghton Hall is about 11.25km (7 miles) west, off the A148. Surrounded by beautiful parkland, this magnificent mansion is considered to be one of the finest examples of Palladian architecture in the country. It was built in the 18thC for the Prime Minister, Robert Walpole. As well as lavish furnishings and paintings, it boasts an outstanding collection of militaria, including over 20,000 model soldiers.

GENERAL ANTIQUES
Sue Rivett Antiques, Norwich Road, sells general antiques and pre-Victorian–Victorian items. The shop is closed Wednesday and Sunday.

ANTIQUES CENTRES
Fakenham Antiques Centre, also in the Norwich Road, has 20 dealers selling a large range of period furniture, antiques, curios, and collectables.

AUCTION HOUSES
Hugh Beck Auctions, in Cattle Market Street, holds weekly sales of general antiques on Thursdays at 11am with occasional specialist sales. Viewing takes place on Wednesdays 2–5pm and on the morning of the sale from 9–11am. Office hours are Tuesday 10am–1pm, Thursday 10am–5pm, and Friday 10am–2pm.

▶ Take the A148 westward again – this time to King's Lynn, which is 32km (20 miles) away.

KING'S LYNN

Once called Bishop's Lynn, until the king seized the town in 1536, King's Lynn was a prosperous port, trading with Europe throughout the centuries. The town's prosperity depended on its position on the River Ouse, which is navigable to large ships.

Standing on the quay, the historic 15thC Hanseatic Warehouse, once belonging to the Hanseatic League of merchants, is a reminder of the town's past. It is made up of a brick and timber construction and has an overhanging upper storey. Downriver, the ornate Customs House was built in the late 17thC and, nearby, the Guildhall, built in 1421, has a striking chequerboard façade and, inside, an open-timbered roof. King's Lynn has another Guildhall, that of St George, which was also built in the early 15thC and is said to be the largest surviving guildhall in Europe.

If you want to learn more of the town's past, visit the Lynn Museum in Market Street, where there are displays recounting the history of the area. These displays include a range of Nelson's

memorabilia, fairground gallopers, and a recreated Victorian ironmonger's shop together with information on other shops of the time.

COINS
Roderick Richardson, Kings Staithe Lane, has a large stock of English hammered, early milled, gold, and silver coins.

GENERAL ANTIQUES
The Old Curiosity Shop, in St James Street, sells general antiques, collectables, and furniture.

ANTIQUES CENTRES
The Old Granary Antique Centre, Kings Staithe Lane, has general antiques and collectables.

AUCTION HOUSES
Holt & Company (GTA) is situated in Church Lane, East Winch, which is a village about 8.5km (5 miles) from King's Lynn on the A47. It has six sales a year of modern and antique guns at the Duke of York's Barracks, King's Road, London.

When you look at the beautiful buildings of Cambridge University, you can imagine scholars in days gone by using a pewter inkwell and quill pen. Punts, like the Goss piece shown below, are still used by undergraduates on the River Cam – maybe you will want to try punting yourself if the weather is warm and sunny. You should also visit the Cambridge and County Folk Museum, which is housed in a 16thC inn. It contains more than 30,000 objects, including the doll's house illustrated here.

You will probably see a lot of windmills, many of them disused, on your tour round the region, because they were once used to drain the land. Take time to visit the Norwich Castle Museum where, among many other exhibits, there is the world's largest collection of teapots. The Lynn Museum in King's Lynn is also worth visiting for its Nelson memorabilia, displays of Victorian high street shopping, and fairground gallopers.

This is Oliver Cromwell country, the Lord Protector who became head of state after the execution of King Charles I at the end of the English Civil War. You can visit the Cromwell Museum in Huntingdon or see his home, the Old Vicarage, in Ely. While in Ely, visit the Stained Glass Museum housed in the Cathedral. It has one of the most important collections of stained glass in the country with exhibits from the Middle Ages onwards. Further west, towards the end of the tour, Stamford is home to one of England's most imposing mansions, Burghley House. It has outstanding collections of paintings, furniture, and ceramics including the striking Japanese porcelain cockerel shown here.

Make sure you are hungry when you start this tour in Melton Mowbray so that you can sample its famous pork pies. As you approach Grantham, imagine the old stagecoaches that used to enter the town to stop and change horses at one of the coaching inns there. Finally, don't forget to visit the Lace Hall in Nottingham, where you can see exhibitions on the city's association with lace making. Its exhibits include everything from lace-making machines to demonstrations of small-scale bobbin lace.

Staffordshire, in the southern part of this tour, is famous for its potteries and coal mines. The mines have closed but the potteries are still going strong today. You should visit the fascinating museums in Stoke-on-Trent, which include the Gladstone Pottery Museum – a complete working 19thC pottery. Leave yourself time to walk around and enjoy the Peak District National Park too, which is an area of outstanding natural beauty.

This region was at the heart of the 19thC Industrial Revolution, and so contains a wealth of industrial history. The railways were instrumental in the economic development of the area – Crewe has the second largest railway junction in the country. One of its major industries was cotton weaving, and so it is fitting that Manchester is home to one of Britain's largest collections of costume in Platt Hall, Rusholme. Cheshire also has many notable fine houses including Eaton Hall, illustrated on the blue-and-white soup tureen above.

A Great Cathedral to Health Spa

The Spirit of Yorkshire is a good title for a book on the county as its people are known for their individualistic spirit. If you have the time, visit the National Railway Museum on the outskirts of York. The city's great cathedral is also unmissable as are many of its other museums. Visitors to Yorkshire often overlook its holiday resorts like Bridlington, which is illustrated on the paperweight below. At Harrogate, visit the Royal Pump Room Museum, which tells the story of the spa, and look out for more Goss crested souvenir ware like the piece shown here, commemorating the sulphur baths.

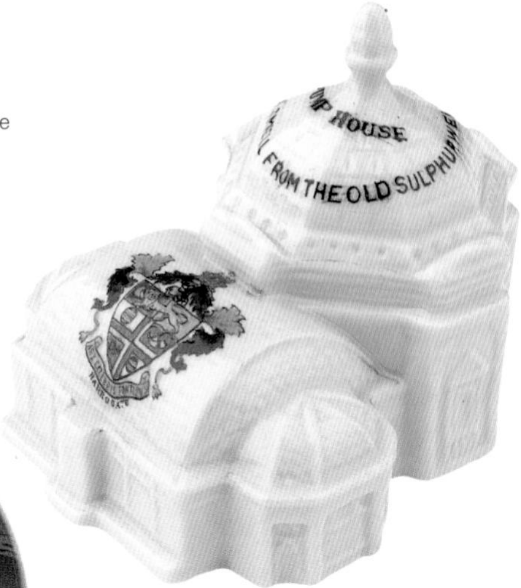

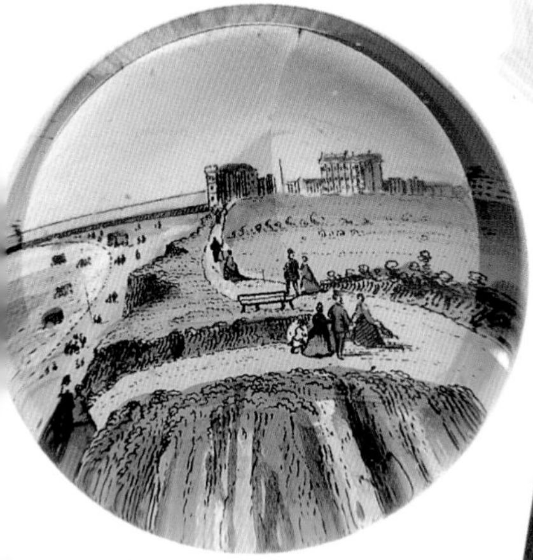

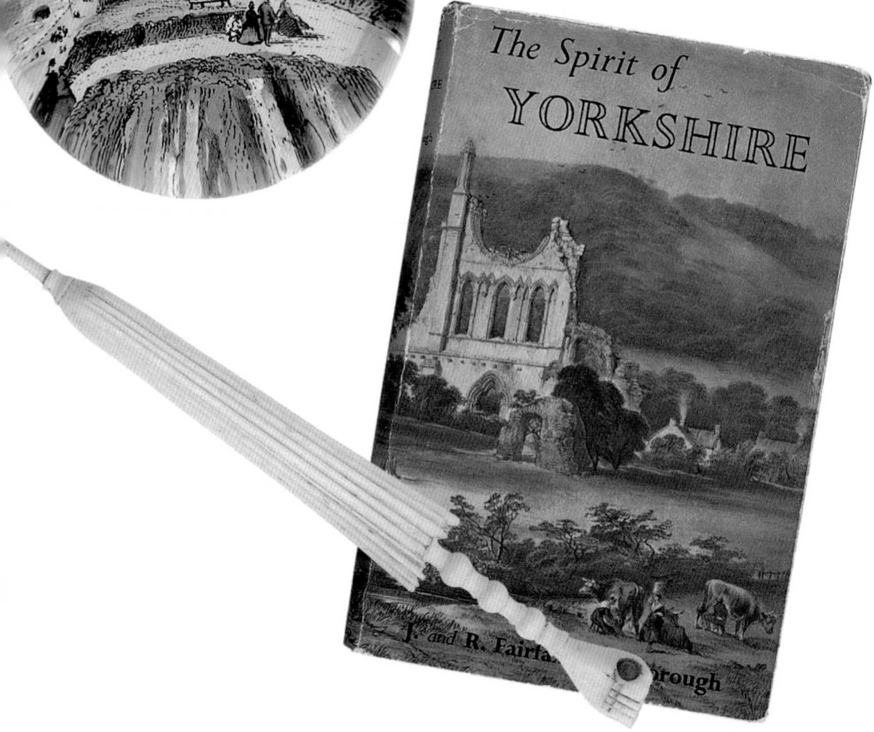

When visiting Scotland you will find many great collectable Scottish souvenirs, such as the tartan Gwenda compact and the Scotsman bottle opener illustrated here. Glasgow has many museums, and one of the most interesting is the recreated Mackintosh House, with interiors and furniture from the great designer and architect's own home. Edinburgh also has an enormous number of museums that recount the history of the city as well as illustrate its great contribution to the arts.

WISBECH ▶ ELY ▶ ST IVES ▶ GODMANCHESTER ▶ PETERBOROUGH ▶ STAMFORD ▶ MARKET DEEPING ▶ SPALDING ▶ HOLBEACH ▶ LONG SUTTON

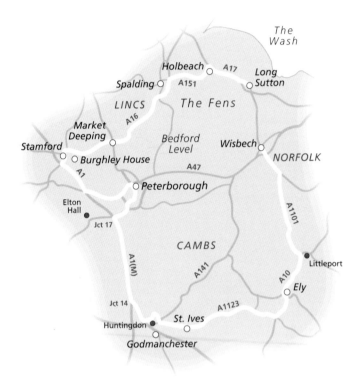

This relatively short tour does not have any big concentrations of antiques shops, but there are antiques centres in almost every town to guarantee a good range of dealers.

Much of the region is made up of fenland with ditches to drain the land. It is prime bulb growing country – if you buy British tulips, daffodils, or other flowering bulbs for your garden, they probably came from this area.

The Fens were formed after the last Ice Age, 10,000 years ago, when Britain was split off from Europe and the land

here sank and was, from time to time, covered by the sea. After the sea finally receded, it left a large area of swamp. The Romans tried to drain it but were largely unsuccessful. In the 17thC Dutch engineers came to the area and dug drains to take the water to the sea. Wind and later steam pumps made the work of draining the Fens easier.

This is an area dedicated to wildlife conservation and there are many nature reserves including Moulton Marsh. It is entirely manmade and encompasses a range of habitat important for birds.

Websites

www.cathedral.ely.anglican.org
Ely Cathedral's official site has an online virtual tour as well as useful facts.

www.stainedglassmuseum.org
If you love the beauty of stained glass, this website, which belongs to the Stained Glass Museum in Ely Cathedral, is ideal. There are pictures of beautiful glass as well as information on stained glass and about the museum itself.

www.peterborough.gov.uk
As might be expected from the city's official site, there is all the information here that a visitor to Peterborough might need.

www.peterboroughheritage.org.uk
Peterborough Museum and Art Gallery has an extensive and interesting collection of artefacts relating to the history of the city. Take a look at some of these online.

www.spaldingnet.com
Find out more about Spalding and, in particular, its Flower Parade on this informative and well-illustrated website.

www.stamford.co.uk
Take the virtual tour at this Stamford website and you will see why visitors love the town and find it beautiful.

Tourist Information Centres

Ely Oliver Cromwell's House, St Mary's Street.
Tel: 01353 662062

Huntingdon The Library, Prince's Street.
Tel: 01480 388588

Peterborough 3–5 Minster Precincts.
Tel: 01733 452336

Spalding Ayscoughfee Hall, Churchgate.
Tel: 01775 725468

Stamford Arts Centre, St Mary's Street.
Tel: 01780 755611

Wisbech 2–3 Bridge Street.
Tel: 01945 583263

WISBECH

Incredibly, Wisbech used to be a thriving port on the River Nene, once navigable right into the centre of the town. The shifting coastline of the Wash has since marooned Wisbech 19.25km (12 miles) inland and it is now inaccessible to ships. Its prosperous past may be seen in the many fine Georgian merchants' houses and in its Dutch-influenced architecture. One of these, Peckover House, was built in 1777 by Jonathan Peckover. Together with two partners, he started a bank here which, a century later, merged with Barclays. Peckover House is interesting but it is the garden that attracts most visitors. The Victorian-style garden has some superb and unusual specimen plants including a tulip tree, a ginkgo, and a Chusan palm.

CERAMICS

Granny's Cupboard Antiques in the Old Market sells Victorian and Edwardian china, glass, and furniture from various periods up to the 1950s. It is open Tuesday and Thursday 10.30am–4pm and Saturday 10.30am–3pm.

FURNITURE

Steve Carpenter, Norfolk Street, has longcase clocks, 18th and 19thC country furniture, and quality smalls. The shop is open every day except Wednesday and Sunday.

GENERAL ANTIQUES

BADA dealer Peter A Crofts, in the High Road, has general antiques, furniture, silver, and china. The shop is open all week apart from Saturday.

AUCTION HOUSES

Grounds & Co., on Nene Quay, holds antiques and collectors' sale three times a year. The office is open on Saturday as well as weekdays. Maxey & Son, in the Cattle Market Chase, has antiques sales two to four times a year. On Saturday, the office shuts at 12 noon.

▶ Take the A1101 direct to Ely, which is a distance of about 29km (18 miles).

ELY

This city was named Ely, it is said, because of the large number of eels found in the area. Ely's magnificent cathedral dominates the surrounding fenland. Originally part of a monastery, building started on the cathedral in 1083 when Ely was an island. This splendid building has numerous features of interest and is simply unmissable if you visit the area. The Stained Glass Museum is one of the most interesting parts of the cathedral. Its exhibits date from the Middle Ages onwards and it contains one of the most important stained glass collections in the country.

There are other places of interest, including the 15thC Bishop's Palace, a late 17thC house called The Chantry, the beautiful Prior Crauden's Chapel (now the school chapel for the grammar school), and the Old Vicarage, which was once the home of Oliver Cromwell and his family.

In the 11thC the surrounding marshland, treacherous for strangers, provided a haven for the last resistance led by Hereward the Wake to the Norman Invasion. He and his men held out until 1071 when the Normans built a road across the marshes and were finally able to crush Saxon resistance to their rule.

GENERAL ANTIQUES
n Forehill, **Jus' Perfick** has an extensive range of furniture, smalls, clocks, postcards, jewellery, and linen. It is open Thursday–Sunday. **Mrs Mills' Antiques Etc** in St Mary's Street has a large stock of porcelain, silver, and jewellery. The shop is closed Tuesday and Sunday.

ANTIQUES CENTRES
The 68 dealers in **Waterside Antiques**, The Wharf, Waterside, sell furniture and collectables. The centre is open 7 days a week.

▶ Leave Ely on the A10 southbound. When you reach the village of Stretham, which is about 8.5km (5 miles) from Ely, turn right onto the A1123. Follow this road for 24km (15 miles) and you will arrive in St Ives.

ST IVES

This market town on the River Ouse has strong associations with Oliver Cromwell, who was churchwarden here. The Norris Museum in the Broadway covers the

history of Huntingdonshire, a county that disappeared in local government changes. Exhibits range from 160 million-year-old fossils to the Civil War and Oliver Cromwell.

GENERAL ANTIQUES
Quay Court Antiques, Bull Lane, Bridge Street, sells a range of pottery, porcelain, pictures, and jewellery and is open Monday and Friday 11am–2pm, Wednesday 10.30am–3pm, and Saturdays, 11am–4pm.

ANTIQUES CENTRES
Hyperion Antique Centre (ICOM) in Station Road has 20 dealers selling a wide range of antiques and collectables.

AUCTION HOUSES
Hyperion Auction Centre (ICOM), also in Station Road, holds general antiques sales on the second Monday of each month. Viewing takes place on the previous Saturday 9.30am–5pm and the day of sale from 9.30–10.30am. The office is open Saturday.

▶ Take the A1123 to Huntingdon, which is just 8.5km (5 miles) away. Then take the B1514 for about 1.6km (1 mile) and turn left onto the A14. Godmanchester is right by the junction, almost adjoining Huntingdon.

GODMANCHESTER

There has been a settlement on this site by the River Ouse for 2,000 years but its neighbour, Huntingdon, far outstripped Godmanchester in population growth and prosperity. While in the area you can visit the neighbouring town, which was once the administrative centre of Huntingdonshire (this county has now been absorbed into the county of Cambridgeshire). Both Oliver Cromwell and Samuel Pepys went to school in Huntingdon and the Cromwell Museum in Grammar School Walk has exhibitions on the life of the Lord Protector.

BOOKS
Located in Post Street, **The Bookshop Godmanchester** (BA) has second-hand, antiquarian, and new books – particularly children's books. It is open Tuesday–Saturday.

20 Bulbs & Ditches

Leave Godmanchester (or Huntingdon, if you visit the museum there) on the A14, which you should take for 6.5km (4 miles) to Junction 14 of the A1(M). After 21km (13 miles) on the A1(M), come off at Junction 17 and take the A1139 to drive into Peterborough.

PETERBOROUGH

This city is on the River Nene and it grew up around a Medieval monastery, although only a few of those historic buildings survive today. While Peterborough Cathedral might not have the breathtaking beauty of Salisbury or Ely cathedrals, it is an excellent example of Norman architecture. Both Catherine of Aragon, Henry VIII's first wife, and Mary, Queen of Scots were buried here, although Mary was later moved to Westminster Abbey. Peterborough Museum in Priestgate recounts the history of the city with displays ranging from prehistory to the present day. There is also an exhibition relating to Mary, Queen of Scots who was executed at nearby Fotheringay Castle.

The Art Gallery has a changing programme of exhibitions of contemporary arts and crafts. A completely different kind of exhibition may be seen at Railworld in Oundle Road. Displays here relate to the benefits to the environment of rail travel as opposed to using the motorcar. It has external displays of real rail engines and internal ones of railway-related material, like posters. On the western edge of Peterborough, Longthorpe Tower in Thorpe Road, Longthorpe, is a fortified 14thC tower. It is said to have the finest Medieval secular wall paintings in the country. Finally, the romantic Elton Hall stands about 8.5km (5 miles) west of the city, just off the A605. It has been in the same family for nearly 350 years and has a pleasing mixture of Medieval, Gothic,

and Classical architecture. It appears that, through the centuries, the family had a real passion for collecting because the house contains over 12,000 books, including Henry VIII's prayer book, superb furniture, and paintings by Gainsborough, Reynolds, Constable, and Millais, among others.

BOOKS
T V Coles in Lincoln Road sells out-of-print, antiquarian, and second-hand books as well as militaria, ephemera, postcards, etc. Old Soke Bookshop, Burghley Road, sells small antiques, pictures, prints, and maps as well as books, and is open Tuesday–Saturday.

FURNITURE
Antiques & Curios Shop, located in Lincoln Road, Millfield, just to the north of the city centre, has mahogany, oak, pine, and country furniture and fireplaces. G Smith & Son (Peterborough) Ltd, also in Lincoln Road but this time in Werrington, further to the north of the centre, sells 18th and 19thC furniture and clocks.

ANTIQUES CENTRES
The dealers in the Fitzwilliam Antiques Centre, on Fitzwilliam Street, have a large selection of general antiques and collectables.

Leave Peterborough on the A47 westbound and continue for 13km (8 miles). Then turn right onto the A1 for 10km (6 miles) to Stamford.

STAMFORD

Stamford is lovely stone-built town with many fine Georgian houses. In Norman times it was a centre for great religious houses and their schools. From the 12thC it was also an important centre for wool, which brought great prosperity to the town.

Just 1.6km (1 mile) east of the town stands Burghley House, one of the country's great Elizabethan mansions. It was built by William Cecil, the first Lord Burghley and Elizabeth I's Lord Chancellor. The breathtakingly beautiful staterooms contain outstanding collections of paintings, furniture, works of art, and ceramics. The paintings include one of the best collections of 17thC Italian art outside of Italy while the furniture includes stunning and unique 18thC examples. Among the ceramics are the earliest examples of Japanese porcelain and Blanc de Chine in the country as well as many other unique and beautiful objects. Whatever else you do on this tour, make sure you do not miss Burghley House.

BOOKS

St Mary's Books & Prints, in St Mary's Hill, has a large stock of antiquarian, rare, and second-hand books, with Wisden's Cricket Almanac being a speciality. It is open 7 days a week from 8am. **St Paul's Street Bookshop** (PBFA), St Paul's Street, sells antique, rare, and second-hand books and specializes in motoring books. It is open all week apart from Wednesday and Sunday. **Staniland Booksellers** (PBFA), St George's Street, has a wide range of antiquarian, rare, and second-hand scholarly books, especially on architecture, applied art, philosophy, music, history, and literature. **Undercover Books** in Scotgate has an extensive selection of antiquarian, rare, and second-hand books with law enforcement being its speciality. The shop is open Tuesday–Saturday.

FURNITURE

Claire Langley Antiques, again in St Mary's Hill, sells general antique mahogany and oak furniture. **Graham Pickett Antiques** in the High Street, St Martins, has a range of English and French provincial furniture and beds. The shop shuts at 4pm on Thursday. In Broad Street, **Vaughan Antiques** (LAPADA) has English furniture, clocks, and decorative items. 8th and 19thC furniture are their specialities.

GENERAL ANTIQUES

St George's Antiques in St George's Square has a wide range of general antiques and furniture. It is open Monday–Friday. **Andrew Thomas**, North Street, has an extensive selection of general antiques and antique painted furniture.

ANTIQUES CENTRES

The 58 plus dealers in the **St Martin's Antique Centre**, in the High Street, St Martins, sell a large range of general antiques, collectables, objets d'art, and 20thC items. The centre is open 7 days a week.

> The next stop at Market Deeping is 13km (8 miles) away on the eastbound A16.

MARKET DEEPING

This charming town on the River Welland was once an important staging post on the coach road. Take a look around the triangular Market Place and you will see inns with archways leading to what was once the stable yards.

ANTIQUES CENTRES

In the High Street, **Market Deeping Antiques and Crafts Centre** has a large stock of general antiques, collectables, and crafts. It is open 7 days a week.

> Take the A16 eastbound just over 16km (10 miles) to Spalding.

SPALDING

Spalding was once a flourishing Medieval port on the Wash. Then the surrounding fenland was drained, leaving the town several miles inland. Today it is an important bulb-growing centre – in May this is celebrated in the spectacular Flower Parade where floats decorated with flowers parade through the town.

Ayscoughfee Hall Museum in Churchgate is housed in the former home of a 15thC wool merchant. Its exhibitions show life in the area and also cover the draining of the fens as well as the history of the Hall. It is set in five acres of gardens, part of which date back to the early 18thC, so there's something here for the gardeners too.

CLOCKS

Penman Clockcare (BWCG) in Pied Calf Yard sells antique clocks.

GENERAL ANTIQUES

Spalding Antiques in Abbey Path has general antiques, clocks, and watches.

AUCTION HOUSES

A P Sales in the High Street have monthly general auctions on the third Friday of the month. **R Longstaff & Co.**, New Road, holds bi-monthly sales of general antiques. The office is open 7 days a week (shutting at 3pm at weekends). **Munton & Russell** (ISVA) in Sheep Market has periodic sales of general antiques.

▶ Take the A151 eastbound for 10km (6 miles) then turn right onto the A17 and Holbeach is located just past the junction.

HOLBEACH

Although a small market town, Holbeach is one of the largest parishes in England. It is also situated in the bulb-growing area of Lincolnshire.

BOOKS

Situated in Boston Road, P J Cassidy has a large stock of antiquarian books, maps, prints, and Lincolnshire topography.

▶ Continue on the A17 eastward for 11.25km (7 miles) to reach Long Sutton.

LONG SUTTON

During the Middle Ages–19thC, Long Sutton was a thriving market town, as can be seen from the fine Georgian houses in the town. The famous highwayman, Dick Turpin, lived here in 1737 and it was testimony from a local man that helped to convict him.

CARPETS

In the Market Place, J B Galleries has a large range of antique carpets and is open by appointment – ring 01406 362762.

FURNITURE

Old Barn Antiques has two shops, one in Bridge Road and the other in New Road. These are both in the village of Sutton Bridge, which is just 3.2km (2 miles) further east on the B1359. Both shops have a large stock of Victorian, Edwardian, and 1920s furniture. The former is open 7 days a week (until 4pm on Sundays), and the New Road shop is open Monday–Friday from 8.30am.

GENERAL ANTIQUES

Chapel Emporium, London Road, has a wide range of general antiques and is open 7 days a week.

ANTIQUES CENTRES

In London Road, Long Sutton Antique and Craft Centre has a large stock of general antiques, collectables, and crafts. It is open 7 days a week.

MELTON MOWBRAY ▶ GRANTHAM ▶ NEWARK-ON-TRENT ▶ LINCOLN ▶ GAINSBOROUGH
▶ RETFORD ▶ MANSFIELD ▶ SUTTON IN ASHFIELD ▶ NOTTINGHAM ▶ LOUGHBOROUGH

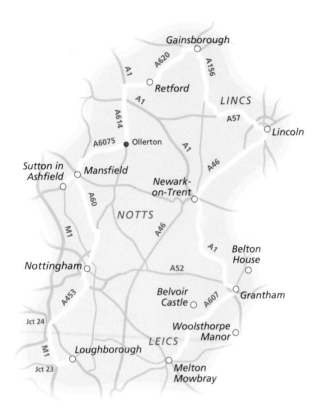

On this tour cities like Nottingham and Lincoln, which have large concentrations of a variety of antiques shops, are ideal whether you are just browsing or know exactly the type of antique you want to buy. Most of the other towns and villages in the area also have a good selection.

Most of the tour is in Nottinghamshire. This county is usually associated with Robin Hood and Sherwood Forest (most of which has long since disappeared).

In fact, by King John's time in the 13thC, when Robin Hood was supposed to have lived there, Sherwood Forest was no longer dense woodland.

After the English Civil War in the 17thC, much of the royal forest of Sherwood passed into private hands. By Victorian times it was owned by members of the aristocracy. Coal was found on a number of the resulting estates, which led to villages becoming dependent on mining.

159

▶ ▶ USEFUL CONTACTS

Websites

www.belvoircastle.com
Whatever you want to know about Belvoir
Castle, the answer will be here on the castle's
well-illustrated website.

www.lincoln-info.org.uk
Lincoln council's website shows a wealth
of places to visit that you should try and go
to while you are in the city. It also provides
essential information on where to stay and
eat as well as forthcoming events.

www.not-online.co.uk/virtual
This site shows a "virtual" Newark, with all the
places of interest marked on a map. Click on
a spot and a picture will appear.

www.dmgantiquefairs.com
For information on the Newark Antiques and
Collectables Fair, as well as their other events,
consult DMG Antiques Fairs' website.

www.nottinghamcity.gov.uk
Nottingham City Council's website has all the
information you could possibly need when
visiting the city.

Tourist Information Centres

Grantham St Peter's Hill. Tel: 01476 406166

Lincoln Castle Square. Tel: 01522 873213

Loughborough Market Place.
Tel: 01509 218113

Melton Mowbray Thorpe End.
Tel: 01664 480992

Newark Castlegate. Tel: 01636 655765

Nottingham Smithy Road. Tel: 0115 915 5330

Retford Grove Street. Tel: 01777 860780

MELTON MOWBRAY

This town is synonymous with pork pies
and Stilton cheese, which were originally
produced on local farms. One of the
town's bakers started making pork pies
in 1831. They proved so popular that a
factory to produce them in bulk was
started in 1840. However, if you want
to taste a real Melton Mowbray pork pie,
there is still a shop in the town that has
been making them by hand since 1851.

ANTIQUITIES
Ancient and Oriental Ltd (ADA) is located in Park
View in the village of Grimston, which is about
8.5km (5 miles) to the west of the town. It sells
ancient art and items of archaeological interest
from major world cultures. It is open 7 days a week
from 8am–8pm.

ARCHITECTURAL ANTIQUES
The Old Bakery Antiques Main Street is situated
in another nearby village, this time Wymondham,
which is about 13km (8 miles) to the east of the
town. It sells antique kitchenware, pine, stained
glass, door hardware, chimney pots, tiles,
decorative items, garden items, and architectural
antiques. The shop is open every day except
Thursday and Sunday.

FURNITURE
Berlea Antiques is on Six Hills Road in Wartnaby,
which is about 5km (3 miles) north of Melton
Mowbray off the A606. The shop sells general
antique furniture and collectables by appointment
only – ring 01664 812044. Flagstones Pine and
Country Furniture in Burton Street has pine and
country furniture – old and reproduction – as well
as lighting and accessories.

GENERAL ANTIQUES
Lotties, in the High Street, has general antiques
and collectables and it is open Tuesday–Saturday.
Parkside Antiques, Leicester Street, sells general
antiques. It is open Tuesday, Friday, and Saturday.

▶ Take the A607 northbound directly to Grantham,
a distance of 24km (15 miles).

GRANTHAM

Historic Grantham, on the River Witham,
was the birthplace of Isaac Newton and
Margaret Thatcher. Because the town is
situated on the Great North Road it has
been an important stop for centuries.
It has one of the oldest inns in the
country, the Angel and Royal, where,
according to legend, King John once
held court and Richard III signed the
Duke of Buckingham's death warrant.
Woolsthorpe Manor, the birthplace of Sir
Isaac Newton, stands on the A1 about
11.25km (7 miles) south of Melton
Mowbray. The 17thC farmhouse contains
a copy of his famous *Principia* and there
is also a descendent of the apple tree

under which he was lying when an apple fell and led to Newton formulating the Theory of Gravity.

In contrast, Belton House, which is 5km (3 miles) north-east of Grantham, is quite a grand house built in the latter half of the 17thC. It contains fine furniture, mirrors, silver, Oriental porcelain, tapestries, Old Master paintings, and Duke of Windsor memorabilia. There are also carvings of the Grinling Gibbons School and a baroque plaster ceiling by Edward Goudge in the North Chapel.

Finally, Belvoir (pronounced "beever") Castle, owned by the Duke of Rutland, stands about 11.25km (7 miles) west of Grantham, on the site of a Norman castle. The current house was first built in Tudor times and then rebuilt in the early 19thC. It contains fine French furniture; paintings by Reynolds and Gainsborough, among others; silks and tapestries; as well as sculpture and porcelain. All of this is displayed in beautiful, elegant rooms.

CLOCKS

Grantham Clocks (BHI), in Lodge Way sells clocks by appointment – ring 01476 561784. Pinfold-Wilkinson Antiques (BHI, AHS), Guildhall Street, also sells clocks as well as a range of watches and jewellery.

FURNITURE

Grantham Furniture Emporium in Wharf Road has a large stock of Victorian–Edwardian furniture and 1920s shipping furniture. The shop is open Tuesday and Thursday–Sunday until 4pm.

GENERAL ANTIQUES

In Swinegate, Harlequin Antiques has general antiques. Heritage Antiques, also in Swinegate, has a wide range of general antiques, country furniture, and collectables. It is closed Thursday afternoon, Tuesday, and Sunday. Notions Antiques, in the Market Place, sells general antiques.

AUCTION HOUSES

Golding, Young & Co. (NAVA) in Old Wharf Road has fortnightly sales of general antiques, and bi-monthly antique and fine art auctions. Marilyn

Swain Auctions (SOFAA), in Sandon, has fortnightly sales of general antiques.

▶ The A1 north will take you directly to Newark, which is about 21km (13 miles) away.

NEWARK-ON-TRENT

For anybody connected with the antiques trade, Newark-on-Trent is synonymous with the giant antiques and collectors fair that takes place at the Newark and Notts Showground. It was started by Geoffrey Whitaker in the 1980s and was really the forerunner of the giant showground events that are so widespread today. He sold the fair to DMG Antiques Fairs Ltd and, since then, it has grown enormously, with some events having as many as 4,500 stallholders.

One of the town's most famous attractions is the ruins of its Norman castle, where King John died in 1216. During the Civil War, Newark was a Royalist stronghold and the castle was besieged three times by Parliamentary forces. On the third occasion, Charles I was on his way to relieve the siege when he encountered enemy troops and so fought the Battle of Naseby, where he was finally defeated. Newark Castle was slighted (rendered indefensible by demolishing key defences) and was never rebuilt.

Newark Town Hall is also worth seeing because it is one of the finest Georgian town halls in the country and contains a good collection of civic plate, mostly from the 17th and 18thC, as well as paintings and historical records. Another of the town's attractions is The Vina Cooke Museum of Dolls and Bygone Childhood. It has a large collection of dolls from the 18thC onwards. It also houses displays of dolls' houses, books, games, model railways, Christening robes, and other costume.

BOOKS

Lawrence Books in Lombard Street has a wide range of antiquarian, rare, and second-hand books and it is open 7 days a week (until 4pm on Sunday).

FURNITURE

No 1 Castlegate Antiques, in Castlegate, has a large stock of 18th and 19thC antique furniture, clocks, barometers, and decorative items.

GENERAL ANTIQUES

In North Gate, R R Limb Antiques has a wide range of general antiques and they are also piano exporters. They are open by appointment only – ring 01636 674546. Portland Antiques, Portland Street, has an extensive selection of general antiques and is open Tuesday, Wednesday, Friday, and Saturday.

SILVER & JEWELLERY

M B G Antiques (BGA), again in Castlegate, sells period jewellery, diamond rings, quality pictures, and general antiques. The shop is open Wednesday–Saturday until 4pm.

ANTIQUES CENTRES

Castlegate Antique Centre, in Castlegate, has nine dealers with a large range of general antiques. The centre is open 7 days a week. The very big Newark Antiques Centre, in Lombard Street, has 101 dealers with an extensive selection of general antiques. It is also open 7 days a week, including Bank Holidays (on Sundays and Bank Holidays it is open until 4pm). In Kelham Road, the 80 dealers in Newark Antiques Warehouse Ltd sell a wide assortment of good furniture, collectables, and smalls. They are open Monday–Saturday (from 8.30am on weekdays), and on the Sunday before Newark Antiques Fair from 9am–7pm.

Portland Street Antique Centre, Portland Street, has 100 dealers selling a great variety of general antiques. Tudor Rose Antiques Centre, in the Market Place, has 30 dealers with a good range of small collectable antiques, antique furniture, silver, metalware, treen, and country items. The centre is open Monday–Saturday and on the Sundays prior to Newark Antiques Fair from 12 noon–5pm.

ANTIQUES FAIRS

The Giant Newark International Antiques and Collectors Fair takes place bi-monthly throughout the year at the Newark and Notts Showground and, with up to 4,500 stalls, it is said to be the largest event of its kind in Europe. The fair takes place over two days, Monday and Tuesday. It is made up of both indoor and outdoor stalls that provide every type of antique and collectable imaginable.

▶ Lincoln is just 25.75km (16 miles) away from Newark on the A46.

LINCOLN

The historic city of Lincoln was once a *colonia* where veteran Roman legionaries were given grants of land when they retired. Its beautiful 12thC cathedral, standing on a hill 61m (200ft) above the city, dominates the skyline. The present cathedral was started in 1140 on the site of one built in the previous century that had been destroyed by fire. The cathedral's fine West Front is said to symbolize Heaven's Gate and the magnificent Angel Choir has the largest eight-light window in the country.

The Greyfriars Exhibition Centre, housed in a lovely 13thC building in Broadgate, is used for annual exhibitions of the City and County Museum's extensive collections dating from prehistory to 1750. In Lindum Road, Usher Gallery displays a nationally important collection of paintings and drawings by Peter DeWint. It also has topographical works, portraits, Chinese export porcelain, and 18th and 19thC English and Continental porcelain.

BOOKS, MAPS, & PRINTS

Harlequin Gallery (PBFA), in Steep Hill, has a large stock of antiquarian and second-hand books, maps, and prints. The shop opens and shuts early on Wednesdays.

CLOCKS

Eric A Bird Jewellers (BHI), St Mary's Street, sells antique and modern clocks and pocket watches.

FURNITURE

In Castle Hill, Rebecca Calvert Antiques (LAPADA) sells English oak furniture and associated objects. C & K Dring, in the High Street, has Victorian and Edwardian inlaid furniture, clocks, musical boxes, and tinplate toys. The shop is closed Wednesday and Sunday. David J Hansord and Son (BADA), again in Castle Hill, has a large stock of 18thC English furniture, works of art, and objects.

GENERAL ANTIQUES

Dorrian Lamberts sells general antiques and is in Steep Hill. Whatnots in St Paul's Lane, Bailgate, has a range of general antiques and collectables. It is open 7 days a week.

AUCTION HOUSES

Thomas Mawer & Son Ltd in Portland Street has quarterly sales of general antiques. Naylors Auctions, Meadow Lane, South Hykeham, which is about 6.5km (4 miles) to the south of the city, has monthly sales of general antiques.

▶ Leave Lincoln on the A57 westbound. Continue on that road to the village of Drinsey Nock, where you should turn right onto the A156. Gainsborough is 16km (10 miles) from the junction.

GAINSBOROUGH

The buildings in this town, on the River Trent, date principally from the 17thC and later. However, right in the centre of Gainsborough stands the Old Hall, built between 1460 and 1480, which is said to be the largest Medieval building open to the public in the country.

GENERAL ANTIQUES

R M Antiques, in Tennyson Street, has a large stock of general antiques and is open until 4pm.

ANTIQUES CENTRES

Pilgrims Antiques Centre, Church Street, has a large range of general antiques. It is open Tuesday–Saturday.

AUCTION HOUSES

Drewery and Wheeldon are situated on Trinity Street. They have periodic sales of general antiques. The office is open on Saturday mornings as well as during weekdays.

▶ Leave Gainsborough on the A631 and, after about 3.2km (2 miles), turn left onto the A620. Retford is 17.75km (11 miles) away.

RETFORD

Set in farming country, Retford is a handsome market town containing many fine Georgian houses.

GENERAL ANTIQUES

Lynn Guest Antiques is in Mill Lane, Rockley, on the A1, which is just 8.5km (5 miles) south of the town. It has general antiques and collectables.

AUCTION HOUSES

The regional office of Phillips International Auctioneers & Valuers is located in The Square.

▶ Take the A620 westbound to leave Retford. At Ranby, turn left onto the A1 and follow this for just over 1.6km (1 mile) to the next roundabout. Here, you should take the A614 for 11.25km (7 miles) to Ollerton. At Ollerton turn right onto the A6075. This road will take you into Mansfield, which is a further 14.5km (9 miles) away.

MANSFIELD

This town stands in the heart of what was once Sherwood Forest. The centre oak of the forest stood in the town's Westgate until the 1940s when it had to be felled. Now a plaque marks the spot. In Leeming Street, the Mansfield Museum and Art Gallery has exhibitions of local and social history, which includes fine and decorative arts.

GENERAL ANTIQUES

Antiques & Clock Shop (BWCG), Bancroft Lane, has a large stock of general antiques. It shuts at 3pm on Saturdays. Fair Deal Antiques, in Chesterfield Road North, has an extensive range of general antiques and is open 7 days a week.

ANTIQUES CENTRES

Mansfield Antique Centre, Yorke Street, in Mansfield Woodhouse on the northern edge of the town, has general antiques. It is open Thursday–Sunday.

▶ Take the A38 westbound to reach the almost adjoining town of Sutton in Ashfield.

SUTTON IN ASHFIELD

The long history of Sutton in Ashfield goes back to Saxon times although, until the 19thC, it was little more than a village. During the 19thC a factory for making stockings was built and it was so successful that the hosiery industry still continues there today.

COLLECTABLES

Yesterday and Today in Station Road sells collectables from the 1920s–30s and oak furniture.

GENERAL ANTIQUES

In the High Street, Station Hill, Carols Curiosity Shop has general antiques and is open Tuesday–Saturday (closing at 4pm on Saturday). ▶

AUCTION HOUSES

C B Sheppard & Son, Chatworth Street, has monthly sales of general antiques.

▶ Retrace your route to the centre of Mansfield and then take the A60 southbound for 22.5km (14 miles) to reach Nottingham.

NOTTINGHAM

Almost everybody associates Nottingham with Robin Hood and his long-running battle with the Sheriff. It is such a romantic story of good triumphing over evil that it is a pity there is no evidence that Robin or his Merry Men ever existed.

Nottingham Castle is one of the city's most notable features. It was built by William the Conqueror soon after the Norman Invasion and it has been the scene of much English history. Among many other episodes, Richard III waited there for news of Henry Tudor's arrival in the country and Charles I used the castle to gather forces to fight and win the Battle of Edgehill. Later Parliamentary forces demolished much of the castle it was rebuilt in an Italian style in 1679. It was then burnt down by Luddites in the early 19thC but was rebuilt again. It now houses a museum and art gallery with a fine collection of 18th–20thC art.

The city's Roman Catholic cathedral was designed by Augustus Welby Pugin, who also designed the interior of the Houses of Parliament. Nottingham's Natural History collection can be found in one of the most splendid Elizabethan houses in the country. Wollaton Hall, to the west of the city, was built in the 1580s and is set in 500 acres of parkland and flower gardens. One of Nottingham's most famous industries is lace making, which developed in the city in the 19thC. If you want to know more about this industry then visit the Lace Hall, High Pavement, where you can see

how it developed. You can then view the great factory lace-making machines as well as watch demonstrations of the small-scale bobbin lace.

ARMS & ARMOUR

Michael D Long Ltd (GTA), Derby Road, has a large stock of fine antique arms and armour. On Saturday it closes at 4pm.

ARCHITECTURAL ANTIQUES

In Castle Boulevard, **Gatehouse Workshops** has architectural antiques including stained glass. During the week it closes at 4pm.

AUTOGRAPHS

Richard Davie Autographs in Lenton Avenue, The Park, sells his wide selection of autographs, letters, and signed photographs by appointment only – ring 0115 950 8828. **John Priestley** in Avenue B, Sneinton Market, sells a large variety of football programmes, autographs, and postcards.

BOOKS

Andy Holmes (PBFA) is in Highbury Avenue, Bulwell, in the north-east of the city. He sells a large range of antique, rare, and second-hand books, which cover 19thC travel, gypsies, folklore, and general topics, by appointment only – ring 0115 979 5603. **Jeremy & Westerman**, Mansfield Road, has antique and second-hand books.

COINS & MEDALS

Collectors World, Wollaton Road, Wollaton, has an extensive selection of coins, banknotes, cigarette cards, and postcards. The shop is open Tuesday–Saturday. In Derby Road, **Dutton and Smith Medal Collectors** sells campaign medals by appointment – ring 0115 987 6949. **N S E Medal Department** (OMRS) in Derby Road has a wide variety of antique coins, medals, and cap badges. It shuts at 3.30pm. **Nottingham Coin Centre**, Alfreton Road, sells coins, medals, and collectables and is open until 2pm.

COLLECTABLES

Lights, Camera, Action (UACC), in Cyril Avenue, sells by appointment only – ring 0115 913 1116. It has an extensive range of collectors' items, autographs, and Titanic memorabilia.

FURNITURE

Antiques Across the World (LAPADA) in London Road, Manvers Street, has a large stock of Georgian, Victorian, and Edwardian furniture. The shop shuts at 2pm on Saturdays. **Corn Exchange Antiques** in the Cattle Market has a wide range of general antique furniture and is open Monday–Friday. **The Glory Hole** is located in Station Road, Sandiacre, right on the south-west edge of

Nottingham. It sells antique furniture. **Harlequin Antique Pine Co.**, Mansfield Road, has an extensive selection of antique pine furniture. In Derby Road, **David & Carole Potter** (LAPADA) sells general antiques, 18th and 19thC furniture, and quality decorative items by appointment only – ring 0115 941 7911.

GENERAL ANTIQUES
Acanthus Antiques & Collectables, again in Derby Road, has general antiques and is open Tuesday–Friday from 10am–3pm and Saturday from 12 noon–4pm. **Dave Buckley Antiques** in the British Rail Goods Yard, London Road, sells a range of general antiques and is open Monday–Friday. **Castle Antiques**, Derby Road, has a stock of general antiques, pictures, maps, and prints. **Fourways Antiques**, Owen Avenue has general antiques for sale by appointment only – ring 0115 972 1830.

D D & A Ingle (ORMS, FSE), Carlton Hill, Carlton, has general antiques. **Ivory Gate Antiques**, again in Derby Road, has a large stock of general antiques. **Luna** in George Street sells 1950s–70s objects for the home. **P & P Antiques**, Gregory Street, has a wide variety of general antiques and shipping goods. Back in Derby Road, **Pegasus Antiques** (NAG) sells general antiques and 18th and 19thC furniture.

ANTIQUES CENTRES
Also situated in Derby Road, the **Top Hat Antique Centre** has 15 dealers that sell a range of general antiques.

AUCTION HOUSES
Bonhams & Brooks have their regional office in Mansfield Road. **Arthur Johnson & Sons**, Meadow Lane, have weekly sales of antique and export furniture on Saturdays at 10am with viewing on Fridays from 2–6.45pm and the morning of the sale from 9am. **Mellors & Kirk** (RICS), The Auction House, have weekly general sales on Tuesdays with a fine art sale every six weeks. The office is open until 12 noon on Saturdays (as well as being open from 8.30am on weekdays).

In Mansfield Road, **Neales Auctioneers** (SOFAA, ARVA) have specialist antique and fine art sales plus general antiques and later sales every week. The office is open on Saturday mornings until 12.30pm as well as weekdays. **John Pye & Sons Ltd** (NAVA), Radford Road, have fortnightly general sales. The office is open on weekdays from 8am.

▶ Leave Nottingham on the A453 and follow this road for 17.75km (11 miles) until you reach Junction 24 of the M1. Join the southbound section of the motorway to Junction 23, which is a distance of about 10km (6 miles). Then turn east on the A512 and drive to Loughborough, which is another 5km (3 miles) away.

LOUGHBOROUGH
This is the second largest town in Leicestershire. It has a most unusual war memorial – a Carillon Tower with 47 bells, all of which were cast locally at John Taylor Bellfounders. The company has been in Loughborough since 1839 but, amazingly, it can trace its history back to the 14thC.

BOOKS
Malcolm Hornsby in Church Gate has a large stock of antique, rare, and second-hand books; eastern Mediterranean travel books are a speciality.

FURNITURE
N F Bryan-Peach Antiques is located in Far Street, Wymeswold, which is about 10km (6 miles) east of the town on the A6006. He sells 18th and 19thC furniture as well as clocks and barometers. The shop is closed Thursday and Sunday.

GENERAL ANTIQUES
Loughborough Antiques Centre in Market Street has general antiques, jewellery, and clocks. The shop is open Tuesday and Thursday–Saturday.

STAFFORD ▶ STOKE-ON-TRENT ▶ NEWCASTLE-UNDER-LYME ▶ LEEK ▶ BUXTON ▶ BAKEWELL ▶ CHESTERFIELD ▶ MATLOCK ▶ ASHBOURNE ▶ DERBY

With Stoke-on-Trent on this tour pottery has to be a major theme of it, although there are not as many specialist ceramic dealers as you might expect. However, the wealth of pottery and porcelain museums in Stoke more than compensates for this. As far as the antiques shops are concerned, the major speciality on this tour seems to be furniture, with the main concentration of antique furniture dealers being in Leek.

The Peak District, in the northern part of the tour, is an area of outstanding and dramatic beauty and is well worth visiting. The Peak District National Park was set up in 1951 and was the first National Park in Britain. The Park covers an area of 1,437sq km (555sq miles) and parts of three counties: Derbyshire, Staffordshire, and Cheshire. The area encompasses a range of landscapes from pleasant farmland to stark crags, and pretty villages to historic market towns. There are also some exceptional houses with stunning collections of furniture, paintings, etc. If you are visiting in the winter, be aware that roads around Buxton can become impassable – it is not unusual for the town to be completely cut off from the outside world.

▶ ▶ USEFUL CONTACTS

Websites

www.buxtonfestival.co.uk
Check out this site if you want to visit Buxton during its annual music festival.

www.chatsworth-house.co.uk
Find out more about Chatsworth, one of the most outstanding historic houses in Britain.

www.jaguarfairs.com
Jaguar Fairs' website gives the dates and other information on their two fairs in the Derby area (as well as other events).

www.haddonhall.co.uk
Take a "virtual" tour of this 12thC manor house near Bakewell.

www.staffordbc.gov.uk
This, the official Stafford website, has an enormous amount of useful information for visitors to the town.

www.antiquesfairs.com
The long-established antiques fair organized by Bowman Fairs in the Bingley Hall, Stafford Showground, has its own website with information and dates.

www.antiques-stafford.co.uk
If you want to visit the Stafford Antiques Fair, organized by West Midland Antiques Fairs, check out the dates listed here.

www.stoke.gov.uk/museums
Stoke-on-Trent is famous for pottery and porcelain manufacture. Find out about the town's museums, many of which are devoted to ceramics.

www.royal-doulton.co.uk
Royal Doulton is one of Stoke's best-known names. Learn more about the company's history and their current activities here.

▶ ▶ USEFUL CONTACTS

Tourist Information Centres

Ashbourne Market Place.
Tel: 01335 343666

Bakewell Bridge Street.
Tel: 01629 813227

Buxton The Crescent. Tel: 01298 25106

Chesterfield Low Pavement.
Tel: 01246 345777

Derby Market Place. Tel: 01332 255802

Leek Market Place. Tel: 01538 483741

Matlock Crown Square.
Tel: 01629 583388

Stafford Market Street.
Tel: 01785 619619

Stoke-on-Trent Quadrant Road.
Tel: 01782 236000

STAFFORD

This ancient town is the administrative centre of Staffordshire and is set on the edge of Cannock Chase, a designated Area of Outstanding Natural Beauty. Stafford retains much of it Medieval layout, although many of the original black and white timber-framed houses have now gone. In spite of that, the Ancient High House in Green Gate Street is the largest timber-framed house in England. The Tudor black and white building contains a fine collection of furniture and it is also home to the Staffordshire Yeomanry Museum.

If you are a keen angler, you might also want to visit Izaak Walton's Cottage, who was the author of *The Compleat Angler*. The 16thC cottage is situated about 8.5km (5 miles) north-west of Stafford, just off the A5013. It offers displays on the history of angling as well as a Medieval rose and herb garden. Finally, Shugborough Hall, 10km (6 miles) east of Stafford on the A513, is the ancestral home of the Earls of Lichfield. The grand 18thC house contains fine collections of ceramics, silver, paintings, and French furniture. The servants' quarters are also on display complete with restored brew house, laundry, kitchens, and coach houses. The house is set in Grade 1 gardens on the National Register of Historic Gardens, which means that they are of exceptional national interest and well worth a visit for that reason alone.

GENERAL ANTIQUES

Browse Antiques, in Lichfield Road, has a large stock of antiques, quality second-hand and reproduction furniture, collectables, and giftware. Bookcases are also made to order. It is open all week apart from Wednesday (closing at 4pm on Sundays). Windmill Antiques, Castle Hill, Broad Eye, has antiques and decorative items.

ANTIQUES FAIRS

The long-established Bowman Fairs organize a three-day fair with 400 exhibitors six times a year, in the Bingley Hall, Stafford County Showground. Also at Stafford County Showground, The Stafford Antiques Fair, this time organized by West Midland Antiques Fairs, takes place seven times a year in the Prestwood Complex. It has 350 exhibitors in three halls.

AUCTION HOUSES

Hall & Lloyd, South Street, holds fortnightly sales of Victorian and Edwardian shipping furniture as well as contemporary furniture and collectables on Saturdays at 10am. Viewing takes place on Fridays 9am–6pm.

▶ Take the A5013 to the edge of Stafford and Junction 14 of the M6 motorway. Then take the M6 northbound for 17.75km (11 miles) to Junction 15, where you should leave the motorway and take the A500 to Stoke-on-Trent. The centre of the town is only 3.2km (2 miles) away from this point.

STOKE-ON-TRENT

Famous as the centre of "The Potteries", Stoke-on-Trent was also the centre for the *Five Towns* novels of Arnold Bennett. Most famously, though, it is the home of some of England's major pottery and porcelain makers including Wedgwood, Minton, Doulton, and Spode. As might be expected, there is a variety of museums devoted to ceramics. Among them, the Gladstone Pottery Museum is the only one set in a complete working Victorian pottery. It has working bottle ovens and potters demonstrating the ways potters worked 100 years ago.

Many of the major pottery and porcelain companies have their own museums. The Wedgwood Visitor Centre in Barlaston contains the most complete range of Wedgwood ceramics, including the trial pieces for Catherine the Great's 900 piece dinner service. As well as ceramics, there are paintings and sketches by Reynolds, John Singer Sergeant, Thomas Allen, Graham Sutherland, and David Shepherd.

The Sir Henry Doulton Gallery has exhibits dating right back to the early 19thC and the days of the Lambeth factory. Doulton also give tours of their factory on weekdays (they say pre-booking is advisable). There are also tours of the Minton Studio where the hand gilding of pieces is done.

The Etruria Industrial Museum in Lower Bedford Street is housed in a flint and bone mill. Its displays include a beam engine and a working blacksmith.

BOOKS

Abacus Gallery, Millrise Road in Milton, on the north-eastern side of the town, has antiquarian and second-hand books, prints, and engravings. Local history is its speciality. On Saturdays the shop shuts at 4pm.

CERAMICS

David J Cope, Halliseahead Lane, Dales Green, sells Moorcroft, Royal Worcester, Royal Doulton, and other porcelain. It is open 7 days a week.

FURNITURE

In Hartshill Road, On the Hill Antiques has 1930s oak furniture, pottery, and collectables. Wooden Heart, Stoke Road, Shelton, has a wide range of Edwardian and Victorian mahogany furniture and decorative items. It is open from 8.30am on weekdays and shuts at 3.30pm on Saturdays.

GENERAL ANTIQUES

Ann's Antiques in Leek Road, Stockton Brook, has jewellery, linen, toys, furniture, and architectural antiques, etc. It is closed Thursday and Sunday.

▶ The centres of Stoke and Newcastle-under-Lyme are only a couple of miles apart so you can reach Newcastle from almost anywhere in Stoke. The A53 is probably the easiest.

NEWCASTLE-UNDER-LYME

Stoke's adjoining neighbour, Newcastle-under-Lyme, is a much quieter and more residential town, although for centuries it was the largest town in Staffordshire and the main market for the north of the county. Situated on the Brampton Road, the Borough Museum and Art Gallery has a good collection of 19thC figures as well as pottery excavated from the 18thC factory of Samuel Bell in Lower Street, Newcastle. The museum also has collections of weapons, medals, and other militaria including a Victoria Cross from 1857, teddy bears, Dutch dolls, and other toys.

CERAMICS

Basford Park Road Antiques, Basford Park Road, Basford, sells fine ceramics, collectables, Royal Doulton, Moorcroft, Beswick, and small furniture. It is open until 4pm.

FURNITURE

Richard Midwinter Antiques, in Bridge Street, has a selection of 16th–19thC oak, mahogany, and walnut furniture.

GENERAL ANTIQUES

In King Street, Windsor House Antiques has a wide range of antiques including furniture, silver, glass, linen, pictures, ceramics, and kitchenware.

▶ Take the A53 direct to Leek, which is a distance of approximately 17.75km (11 miles).

LEEK

Situated just outside the Peak District National Park, Leek was once important for its silk mills, most of which date from the 19thC. For an earlier building, take a look at the Church of St Edward the Confessor. This dates from 1297 and was possibly built on the site of an earlier Saxon church.

BOOKS

Leek Old Books in King Street sells antiquarian and second-hand books on ornithology, natural history, local history, military, and transport history. It is open Tuesday, Wednesday, Friday, and Saturday.

CLOCKS

K Grosvenor, St Edward Street, has a large stock of clocks, barometers, and scientific instruments. It is open until 4pm.

FURNITURE

In Clerk Bank, The Antique Store has a range of painted furniture, decorative items, gardenalia, and architectural antiques. It is open Monday, Wednesday, Friday, and Saturday until 4pm. Antiques & Objets d'Art of Leek in St Edward Street has Georgian and Victorian furniture, porcelain, and paintings. The shop is open all week except for Thursday and Sunday. Antiques Within in Compton has an extensive stock of pine, oak, and mahogany furniture as well as Continental furniture. It also sells brass, copper, mirrors, and collectables.

Anvil Antiques, Cross Street, has reproduction and old pine furniture and old French mahogany furniture. The shop is open 7 days a week (until 4pm on Sundays). Johnsons, Mill Street, sells English and French country furniture, decorative accessories, and unique objects. Jonathan Charles Antiques, Broad Street, has pine and country furniture, iron and brass bedsteads, and collectables. Odeon Designs Ltd (Lighting Association), again in St Edward Street, has a wide variety of pine furniture, antique and reproduction lighting, and small decorative objects. In Britannia Street, Roberts & Mudd Antiques has an extensive range of pine and country furniture, decorative items, and French furniture. The shop opens at 8am weekdays and shuts at 12 noon on Saturday. Back in St Edward Street, Simpsons has original decorative, painted, and pine furniture for both the home and garden. Southbank Antiques, Southbank Street, sells period mahogany, oak, and walnut furniture and decorative items.

GENERAL ANTIQUES

Sylvia Chapman Antiques, in St Edward Street, sells quality furniture, porcelain, pottery, decorative items, oil lamps, and Victorian coloured glass. The shop is open all week except Thursday and Sunday. Cornerhouse Antiques, Brook Street, has Georgian, Victorian, pine, and mahogany furniture as well as brass, copper, iron, steel, kitchenware, country items, and 1920s antiques. Decorative Antiques, again in St Edward Street, sells 19th– early 20thC English and European decorative antiques, soft furnishings, lighting, and tapestries.

Roger Haynes Antique Finder, in Compton, sells a large range of decorative English and French items, pine, and country small items and collectables by appointment only – ring 01538 385161. Stephen Hibberts Antiques, St Edward Street, has an extensive selection of Lalique, Galle, tapestries, carved furniture, chandeliers, carpets, beds, furniture, and clocks.

MIRRORS

Molland Antique Mirrors, Compton, has a wide variety of 19thC French and English mirrors and is open from 8am.

ANTIQUES CENTRES

Compton Mill Antique Emporium, Compton, has 25 dealers selling a wide range of antiques. The centre is open 7 days a week (afternoons only on Sundays). Leek Antiques Centre, in Brook Street, has seven or eight dealers with a large variety of antiques including dining tables, sets of chairs, bedroom furniture, chests of drawers, pottery, watercolours, oil paintings, and pine.

AUCTION HOUSES

Bury & Hilton in Market Street holds sales of antiques on the first Thursday of each month with special antiques sales in April and October.

▶ Continue on the A53 for 19.25km (12 miles) to the next stop in Buxton.

BUXTON

This is possibly the most famous of Peak District towns. At 305m (1,000ft) above sea level, it is the highest town in England and when travelling to it you could be in bright warm sunshine one moment and in cold, damp fog the next. Buxton is a pretty market town, most notable for its annual music festival, which is centred around its little jewel of an opera house.

The Buxton Museum and Art Gallery has an award-winning display, The Wonders of the Peak, which tells the story of the area from the "Big Bang" through to the 19thC. There is also a complete Victorian study, which was left to the museum by the eminent archaeologist Boyd-Dawkins. There are also collections of furniture, scientific instruments, and Oriental items.

To the south-west of the town, Poole's Cavern received its name from a robber called Poole, who is said to have lived in the cave in the 15thC. However, man has used the cave since Neolithic times and archaeological digs have uncovered

Stone Age, Bronze Age, and Roman artefacts. The cavern is famous for its stalactites and stalagmites, rimstone pools, and beautiful formations coloured by minerals leached out of the ground above.

Buxton is an ideal centre for exploring the surrounding Peak District and is a place of beautiful and dramatic scenery.

GENERAL ANTIQUES

Antiques Warehouse, Lighthouse Road, has a large range of general antiques and is open until 3pm on weekdays and 4pm on Saturdays. Royles of Buxton, in the Cavendish Arcade, The Crescent, is open Tuesday–Sunday.

TEXTILES

Back to Front, in Market Street, has antique textiles, which it sells 7 days a week until 8pm.

▶ Take the A6 westbound for 19.25km (12 miles) to Bakewell.

BAKEWELL

Most people probably think of Bakewell tarts when they hear of this town. The tarts were said to have originated in the Rutland Hotel in Bakewell when a cook misunderstood some instructions! Bakewell Old House Museum is located in a Tudor tax collector's house. Its 14 rooms reflect different periods and its collections include costume, lace, samplers, toys, furniture, and ceramics.

Haddon Hall stands just 3.2km (2 miles) south of the town on the A6. This perfectly preserved 12thC manor house contains outstanding collections of tapestries, woodcarvings, and wall paintings. It is set in beautiful terraced gardens that are famous for their roses.

You cannot visit Bakewell without also visiting Chatsworth, which is 6.5km (4 miles) east of the town. This is one of the most outstanding historic houses in Britain and is the home of the Duke and Duchess of Devonshire. Building started in 1687 and it was completed

20 years later. It is set in a 1,000 acre park containing magnificent gardens with elaborate fountains and water features. The mansion itself is a treasure house with superb collections of pictures, drawings, furniture, silver, ceramics, and books. Its collection of "Curiosities" includes a Turkish barge from the 1830s, a late 17thC jewelled hawk, a carving of a lace cravat from around 1700, and a "colossal foot".

FURNITURE
In Harthill Hall, Alport, about 6.5km (4 miles) south of Bakewell, **Peter Bunting** (BADA, LAPADA, CINOA) sells English oak and country furniture, tapestries, and portraits. He asks that people call before visiting – ring 01629 636203. **G W Ford & Son Ltd** (LAPADA) in King Street has 18thC and 19thC mahogany and country furniture as well as 19thC–early 20thC sculpture, silver, Sheffield plate, treen, and decorative items. It is open 7 days a week.

GENERAL ANTIQUES
Lewis Antiques, also in King Street, sells general antiques, 18th and 19thC furniture, and clocks. It is open all week apart from Thursday and Sunday. **Thornbridge Antiques** (LAPADA), again in King Street, has a large stock of general antiques. It is open 7 days a week (until 4pm on Sundays).

MAPS & PRINTS
J Dickinson, King Street, sells antique maps and prints from the 16th–19thC, as well as Derbyshire books and related items, by appointment only – ring 01246 551370.

SCIENTIFIC INSTRUMENTS
Ganymede Antiques, King Street, has scientific instruments, clocks, silver, and metalwork and is open 7 days a week.

ANTIQUES CENTRES
Chappells & The Antiques Centre Bakewell (BADA, LAPADA) in King Street has period antiques from 17th–20thC. It is open 7 days a week.

The A619 eastbound will take you direct to Chesterfield, which is 21km (13 miles) away.

CHESTERFIELD

Chesterfield is most famous for the twisted spire on All Saints Church. It was once the home of 19thC railway engineer, George Stephenson, and his grave may be seen in Trinity Church.

BOOKS & MAGAZINES
In Hoole Street, Hasland, just outside the south eastern edge of the town, **Caroline Hartley Books** sells antiquarian, rare, and second-hand books and is open Monday–Friday until 4pm. **Alan Hill Books** (PBFA), Beetwell Street, has a large stock of second-hand and antiquarian books as well as maps, prints, and local topography.

EPHEMERA
Tilleys Vintage Magazines Shop, Derby Road, sells its large stock of antiquarian magazines and printed collectables from the 19th–20thC by appointment only – ring 01246 454270.

GENERAL ANTIQUES
Arkwrights Emporium, in South Street, has a wide range of general antiques and is open until 4pm. **Haslam Antiques**, Chatsworth Road, sells general antiques, both period and decorative. It is open Thursday–Saturday. **Ian Morris**, also in Chatsworth Road, has general antiques. **Marlene Rutherford Antiques**, Sheffield Road, Whittington Moor, in the north of Chesterfield, has a selection of general antiques, upholstered furniture, oil lamps, and clocks. It is open Monday, Tuesday, Friday, and Saturday 1–4pm and Thursday 10am–4pm.

Take the A632 for 16km (10 miles) to Matlock.

MATLOCK

The town of Matlock is confined to the River Derwent Valley beneath steep wooded hillsides. In the 19thC it was popular for its warm spa water but gradually the fashion for taking the waters declined. The former pump room, the Pavilion, is now used to house the Peak District Mining Museum, which contains a fine collection of mining equipment from the former lead mines in the area. Parts of a lead mine have been recreated, complete with sound effects. There are also displays recounting the history of lead mining and what it was like to be a miner.

To get a good view of the town and the surrounding country, visit the Heights of Abraham, which are situated high above

Matlock and opposite High Tor – a lofty cliff that also gives excellent views. There is a cable car service to the Heights, starting near the railway station. Apart from the view, the main attractions of the Heights are two show caves, partly natural and partly old lead mines. One of these is thought to have been worked in Roman times and contains a spring known as Jacob's Wishing Well.

The National Tramway Museum, which is about 10km (6 miles) south of Matlock, off the A6, has over 70 trams from all over the world including steam, electric, and horse-drawn examples. These are not static exhibits – you can ride on them and they have one specially converted to lift and carry wheelchairs.

BOOKS
R F Barrett, Dale Road, sells antique, rare, and second-hand books. It is open 7 days a week.

GENERAL ANTIQUES
Country Cottage Antiques, Matlock Green, sells general antiques and upholstered chairs and is open Tuesday and Thursday–Friday 1–5pm, Wednesday 2–5pm, and Saturday 11am–4.30pm.

ANTIQUES CENTRES
Matlock Antiques & Collectables, in Dale Road, has a large range of general antiques. The centre is open 7 days a week until 4pm (5pm on Saturdays).

AUCTION HOUSES
Also in Dale Road, Noel Wheatcroft & Son (FNAEA) has monthly sales. The office closes at 4pm (but is closed all day Thursday).

▶ Take the A6 south for just 5km (3 miles) from Matlock to the village of Cromford, where you should turn right onto the B5023. After about 1.6km (1 mile) there is a fork in the road. Take the right-hand fork, which is the B5035. This goes direct to Ashbourne, approximately 16km (10 miles) away.

ASHBOURNE

On the edge of the Peak District, Ashbourne has a number of interesting buildings including the 15thC Gingerbread Shop. The town's most notable feature is its traditional annual

Shrove Tuesday and Ash Wednesday game of football. The goals are 5km (3 miles) apart and the teams consist of hundreds of men. As there are very few rules, wise local shopkeepers board up their windows so it is pointless trying to window shop on those days.

Happily for people who do not want to walk too far, all the antiques dealers in the town are in Church Street.

FURNITURE
J H S Antiques (LAPADA, CINOA, Pewter Society, Metalware Society) sells period oak, metalware, carving, and treen. It is open Tuesday and Thursday–Saturday. Watson & Watson, has 18th and 19thC French country furniture.

GENERAL ANTIQUES
M G Bassett has a wide range of general antiques. It is open all week except Wednesday and Sunday. Pamela Elsom Antiques (LAPADA) also sells general antiques. It is open Thursday–Saturday. Prestwood Antiques has a large stock of general antiques and it is closed Wednesday and Sunday. Rose Antiques sells general antiques. The shop is also closed Wednesday and Sunday. Spurrier-Smith Antiques (LAPADA, CINOA) has an extensive selection of general antiques, furniture, and decorative items. It too is closed Wednesday and Sunday. Top Drawer Antiques has a wide variety of general antiques, pine, kitchenware, and decorative items. Again, it is closed Wednesday and Sunday.

▶ Take the A52 for 21km (13 miles) to arrive at the next stop, Derby.

DERBY

Originally the site of a Roman fort, Derby, which is on the River Derwent, had developed into a busy market town by Norman times and later became an industrial centre.

The country's first silk mill started here in the early 18thC in Silk Mill Lane, off Full Street. The building now houses the Derby Industrial Museum and has exhibitions of local industries, which include details of the development of the railways and the finest collection in the world of Rolls Royce Aero engines from 1915 onwards. In Friargate, the

Georgian Pickford's House Museum has collections of furniture, furnishings, and costume.

Nearby Kedleston Hall, which is 6.5km (4 miles) north-west of the town on the A52, was designed by Robert Adam and is one of the best examples of neo-classical architecture in the country. It houses fine collections of furniture, portraits, and tapestries and is also the venue of a large antiques and collectors' fair.

ARCHITECTURAL ANTIQUES

Finishing Touches, Uttoxeter Old Road, sells Victorian and Georgian fireplaces and fire surrounds, pine doors, locks, handles, and window catches. It is open Tuesday–Saturday.

BOOKS

Derventio Books in Monk Street has antiquarian and second-hand books and antiquarian topographical prints. Derbyshire books are its particular speciality.

FURNITURE

Friargate Pine and Antique Co., Stafford Street, sells antique and reproduction pine.

GENERAL ANTIQUES

Friargate Antiques Company, Friargate, has a large stock of general antiques including Royal Crown Derby. It is open until 4pm each day (5pm on Saturdays). In Monk Street, Rummages also sells general antiques.

ANTIQUES CENTRES

Derby Antique Centre, also in Friargate, has an extensive range of general antiques. The centre is open all week, except Wednesday and Sunday, until 4pm.

ANTIQUES FAIRS

Jaguar Fairs organize two different antiques and collectors' fairs in the area. The first takes place at Kedleston Hall, 6.5km (4 miles) north-west of Derby on the A52. The other is held in Derby University.

AUCTION HOUSES

In Becket Street, Neales Auctioneers (ARVA, SOFAA) has fortnightly sales of general antiques with specialist auctions of antiques and toys every 12 weeks.

NANTWICH ▶ CREWE ▶ KNUTSFORD ▶ WILMSLOW ▶ STOCKPORT ▶ MANCHESTER ▶
ALTRINCHAM ▶ BOWDON ▶ CHESTER

Cheshire and Greater Manchester are particularly well endowed with a variety of antiques shops, especially in towns like Nantwich, Knutsford, and Chester. Over the last few years, Cheshire and Manchester have also attracted many more high-quality antiques fairs with dealers from all over the country.

The county of Cheshire is a beautiful, largely agricultural region dotted with pretty market towns that are worth exploring in more detail. You can also visit the foothills of the Pennine Hills in the east side of the county near Macclesfield. In the west the Cheshire plain stretches to the mountains in North Wales. And if you are the outdoor type, Cheshire presents many opportunities for energetic pursuits including horse riding, walking, and water sports on the many lakes and reservoirs.

In contrast, Manchester was one of the powerhouses of the Industrial Revolution and its 19thC legacy predominates much of the city, although it has lost much of its original industrial base. Nowadays many of its 19thC mills have been put to other uses, to create sought-after loft apartments and offices.

▶▶ USEFUL CONTACTS

Websites

www.chester.org
If you are visiting Chester, do not miss this official website, which contains all you need to know about the city.

www.penman-fairs.co.uk
For information and a list of dates of the Chester Antiques Fair consult this, the organizers' website.

www.virtual-knutsford.co.uk
If you have never been to Knutsford, take a "virtual" tour of the picturesque Cheshire town here. You can also find out about B & Bs, hotels, restaurants, and local attractions.

www.manchester.com
Manchester's official website includes a "guidebook" as well as just about everything else you could ever want to know about one of England's premier cities.

www.tattonpark.org.uk
Take a look at this website for information on all the attractions of Tatton Park.

Tourist Information Centres

Altrincham Stamford New Road. Tel: 0161 912 5931

Chester Northgate Street. Tel: 01244 402111

Knutsford Toft Road. Tel: 01565 632611

Manchester Town Hall Extension, Lloyd Street. Tel: 0161 234 3157

Nantwich Church Walk. Tel: 01270 610983

Stockport Chestergate. Tel: 0161 474 4444

NANTWICH

From Roman times right up to the 19thC, Nantwich was a centre for salt production. Unfortunately the town has not had the happiest or luckiest history. During the Middle Ages it suffered repeated attacks by the Welsh and it was also besieged by Royalists during the Civil War. It has also been through two devastating fires – one in 1438 and the other in 1583. In spite of all this, its 14thC church is fine enough, both inside and out, to be called the "Cathedral of South Cheshire". For more information on the town's history, visit Nantwich Museum in Pillory Street, which recounts the development of the town and also has a special Cheshire Cheese room showing how the cheese was made.

CLOCKS
Clock Corner (BHI), Audlem Road, sells its large stock of antique clocks of all types – bracket, Vienna, longcase, mantel, etc – by appointment only. Ring 01270 6244481.

FURNITURE
In Welsh Row, **Adams Antiques** (BADA, LAPADA) has an extensive range of early oak, walnut, and country furniture as well as Welsh dressers, Mason's ironstone, and longcase clocks. **Chapel Antiques** in Hospital Road has Georgian and Victorian furniture, decorative items, and mirrors. The shop is open Tuesday–Saturday. **Roderick Gibson**, Hospital Street, has antique and reproduction furniture and small collectables.

GENERAL ANTIQUES
Barn Antiques, The Cocoa Yard, Pillory Street, has a wide range of china, small furniture, copper, brass, and collectables including Carltonware and Beswick. The shop is open all week apart from Wednesday and Sunday (closing at 4pm on Mondays and Tuesdays). **Love Lane Antiques**, Love Lane, sells general antiques and is also closed on Wednesdays and Sundays. **Nantwich Antiques**, Beam Street, has a large selection of period and reproduction furniture, Oriental rugs, silver, prints, paintings, jewellery, and Indian furniture.

ANTIQUES CENTRES
Dagfields Crafts & Antiques Centre, Dagfields Farm, Crewe Road is situated in the village of Walgherton, which is 6.5km (4 miles) south-east of Nantwich on the A51. It is a large centre with 150 dealers and 25 workshops selling collectables and furniture of all periods. The centre is open 7 days a week.

AUCTION HOUSES
The regional office of **Bonhams & Brooks** is located in Pall Mall. **Peter Wilson** (SOFAA) in Market Street has five two-day sales per year on Wednesdays and Thursdays at 10.30am with viewing on the previous Sunday 2–4pm, and Monday and Tuesday

10am–4pm. There is also a weekly uncatalogued fast sale on Thursdays at 11am with viewing on Wednesdays 10am–4pm. The office is open on Saturday mornings as well as weekdays.

▶ Take the A534 for about 3.2km (2 miles) to reach Crewe.

CREWE

This town is strongly associated with the railways and is said to have the second biggest rail junction after Clapham Junction in London.

ARCHITECTURAL ANTIQUES
Cheshire Cast Company, Crewe Hall, Weston Road, sells its large stock of original cast-iron radiators by appointment – ring 01270 585885.

BOOKS
Copnal Books, Meredith Street, has a wide variety of second-hand and antiquarian books and is open Monday, Friday, and Saturday.

FURNITURE
Antique & Country Pine in Edleston Road sells English and Continental original and stripped pine as well as handmade reproductions. It is closed Wednesday and Sunday. The Buying Centre, Nantwich Road is open by appointment only to sell furniture, clocks, watches, and jewellery – ring 01270 258241.

▶ Take the A534 north-east for about 10km (6 miles) to Junction 17 of the M6, which is just past Sandbach. Turn onto the northbound carriageway of the motorway and continue on it to Junction 19, which is 19.25km (12 miles) away. Come off the motorway and follow the signs to Knutsford, less than 3.2km (2 miles) from the M6.

KNUTSFORD

This lovely market town was the *Cranford* of Elizabeth Gaskell's novel of the same name. She was married in the town's parish church and buried in the churchyard of the Unitarian chapel. The town contains a number of picturesque black and white timbered houses that are typical of Cheshire. About 3.2km (2 miles) north of the town, there are two great houses in the 1,000 acres of

Tatton Park. Building on the mansion started in the late 18thC and it is now a prime example of Georgian architecture. It contains many fine paintings, furniture, and furnishings – including over 200 pieces of Willow and Gillow furniture that were specially made for the house. Nearby, the Tudor Old Hall was built in the early 16thC but, when the mansion was built, the hall was converted into farm labourers' cottages. Robert Bailey now organizes an antiques fair there.

There is another notable house 3.2km (2 miles) west of Knutsford. Tabley House is a fine Palladian mansion – built in 1761 it contains excellent collections of furniture and paintings as well as musical instruments.

CLOCKS
Coppelia Antiques is situated about 8.5km (5 miles) south-west of Knutsford in Plumley Moor. The shop has a large collection of grandfather clocks and fine Georgian furniture and is open 7 days a week.

FURNITURE
King Street Antiques, King Street, sells furniture as well as porcelain and silver (it is closed Monday, Wednesday, and Sunday). The Lemon Tree, also in King Street, sells English country furniture in satin walnut and stripped pine. The shop is open 7 days a week (from 12 noon on Sundays).

GENERAL ANTIQUES
Past & Presents, again in King Street, has a large stock of general antiques, model ships, a wide range of clocks, collectables, and furniture. It is open 7 days a week (Sunday afternoons only).

ANTIQUES FAIRS
The Tatton Park Antiques Fair, organized by Robert Bailey, is a periodic high-quality event. Further details can be obtained from Bailey Fairs Information Line – ring 01277 213139.

AUCTION HOUSES
Frank R Marshall & Co., in Church Hill, has five general antiques and collectors' sales a year on Tuesdays at 10am. There are also fortnightly sales of household effects, again on Tuesdays at 10am with viewing on Mondays 9am–6.30pm.

▶ Take the B5085 direct to Wilmslow, which is situated about 11.25km (7 miles) east of the previous stop.

WILMSLOW

Although Wilmslow is now largely a residential suburb of Manchester, you can see what life was like in days gone by at the Quarry Bank Mill. Situated about 1.6km (1 mile) north of the town on the B5166, this Georgian cotton mill recreates life in a mill. You can see what being an apprentice was like in the Apprentice House or learn about steam and waterpower in the Power Galleries. As well as having a beam engine from the first half of the 19thC, it also still has its original water wheel, which dates from 1784.

FURNITURE

The Old Sofa Warehouse in Hawthorn Lane has a large stock of Victorian, Edwardian, and later furniture – sofas, winged armchairs, chaise longues, etc. It is open Thursday–Saturday.

ANTIQUES CENTRES

The 20 dealers at Wilmslow Antiques in Church Street have a wide range of stock including furniture, silver, copper, brass, pottery, china, and pictures.

▶ Leave Wilmslow northbound on the A34 until it reaches Junction 3 of the M60. Join the motorway eastbound for 5km (3 miles) to Junction 1. Turn off and Stockport is right by the motorway.

STOCKPORT

Although an ancient market town, Stockport expanded rapidly with the 19thC cotton industry. However, even though it changed a lot the charms of the earlier town can still be seen in the merchants' houses around the Market Place. Well worth a visit, Lyme Park is located about 11.25km (7 miles) south of Stockport off the A6. It is the largest house in Cheshire and was originally Tudor, although there were many changes carried out in the 18th and 19thC. The house contains an important collection of clocks as well as carvings by Grinling Gibbons.

ARCHITECTURAL ANTIQUES

Nostalgia, in Shaw Heath, has a large stock of antique fireplaces as well as 1780–1900 sanitary ware. It is open Tuesday–Saturday.

FURNITURE

Hole in the Wall Antiques in Buxton Road, Heavaley to the south of Stockport, has an extensive selection of 1850–1920 American, Victorian, Georgian, and Edwardian furniture. The shop is open 7 days a week. Limited Editions, King Street, has a wide range of antiques that are mostly furniture, especially dining tables and chairs.

GENERAL ANTIQUES

Antique Furniture Warehouse, Cooper Street, has a large range of antiques from Georgian–1940s including porcelain, English inlay furniture, decorative items, and architectural antiques. Michael Long Antiques in Wellington Road North sells general antiques, mainly to trade. Manchester Antique Company, St Thomas's Place, has an extensive stock of general antiques as well as some second-hand and Continental European furniture. It is open from 8am on weekdays and until 4pm on Saturdays, mainly for trade. Page Antiques, Buxton Road, sells general antiques and Georgian, Victorian, and Edwardian furniture.

SCIENTIFIC INSTRUMENTS

In Bramhall Lane, Flintlock Antiques sells scientific instruments, telescopes, military items, paintings, marine models, and furniture.

ANTIQUES CENTRES

E R Antiques Centre, in Wellington Street, has six dealers that have a wide range of glass, china, pottery, scent bottles, silver plate, and costume jewellery. It is open Monday–Saturday 12 noon–7pm.

AUCTION HOUSES

Bonhams & Brooks North has its regional office in St Thomas's Place.

▶ Take the A6 northbound right into the centre of Manchester.

MANCHESTER

This is one of the great 19thC industrial cities and it still retains many of its magnificent Victorian commercial and industrial buildings. Many of them have been put to new uses but have kept their splendid façades. Manchester grew during the 18th and 19thC, bringing great prosperity to the few and misery and poverty to many. With no way for the poor to voice their protests at their conditions, their discontent culminated in the Peterloo Massacre. On 16th August 1819 around 80,000 people gathered on St Peter's Fields in Manchester to hear a radical speaker. Although the crowd was peaceful and contained many women and children, the local magistrates panicked at the size of the crowd and read the Riot Act. They then ordered the yeomanry to arrest the speaker. The soldiers also panicked and charged the crowd with sabres, which resulted in 11 deaths and hundreds of injured.

Although the city was bombed during World War II, much of its industrial and earlier heritage survives. Based in one of the world's oldest passenger railway stations, the Museum of Science and Industry in Manchester has the largest collection of working steam mill engines in the world as well as historic aeroplanes and exhibitions that recount the history of the cotton industry in the city. In complete contrast, the Gallery of Costume in Platt Hall, Rusholme, was the first museum in the country to specialize in costume. It has one of the largest collections in Britain and the items date from 1600 onwards. The Central Art Gallery is in Old Street, Ashton-under-Lyne, which is on the eastern side of the city. It is housed in a Victorian Gothic building, and has three galleries featuring temporary exhibitions.

BOOKS
The Beech Road Bookshop, Beech Road, M21, sells second-hand and antiquarian books. It is open all week except Wednesday and Sunday. Forest Books of Cheshire, located in Lloyd Street, M2, has a large stock of second-hand, antiquarian, rare, new books, pictures, and prints. The Old Book Shop, Paton Street, M1, has a general stock of second-hand and rare books. The shop is open Tuesday–Saturday. Secondhand & Rare Books, Church Street, M4, has antiquarian and second-

hand books, including some topography and special interest. The shop is open Monday–Saturday from 12 noon–4pm.

FURNITURE
In Slade Lane, M13, **Malik Antiques** has a large stock of antique furniture, porcelain, architectural items, and garden furniture. **Select**, Claremont Road, M14, sells mostly furniture with some general antiques.

GENERAL ANTIQUES
Didsbury Antiques, School Lane, M20, sells general antiques and it is open Tuesday–Saturday.

SILVER & JEWELLERY
St James Antiques, South King Street, M2, has an extensive range of jewellery, silver, and paintings. The shop shuts at weekends.

TEDDY BEARS
Teddy Bear Shop, in the Royal Exchange Arcade, M2, has a wide selection of Steiff, Dean's, Merrythought, and Artist bears. It is open 7 days a week.

ANTIQUES CENTRES
Empire Exchange, Charles Street, M1, has a large range of collectors' items, old and new books, toys, football memorabilia, dolls, teddy bears, jewellery, and military. It is open 7 days a week until 7.30pm. The Ginnell Gallery in Lloyd Street, M2, has 30 dealers selling a wide selection of general antiques, decorative arts (1900–present day), and antiquarian and second-hand books. **The Levenshulme Antiques Village**, Stockport Road, M19, has 12 furniture dealers situated in Old Town Hall. It is open 7 days a week (closing at 4pm on Sundays).

AUCTION HOUSES
Capes, Dunn & Co. (ISVA), in Charles Street, M1, has sales twice weekly. On Mondays at 12 noon there are sales of Victorian and later period furniture and effects. Viewing takes place on the day of the sale from 10am. There are also specialist sales on Tuesdays at 12 noon with viewing on Mondays 10am–4pm and on the day of the sale from 10am–12 noon.

▶ Take the A56 southbound to Altrincham, which is on the outskirts of the city.

ALTRINCHAM
Now a pleasant suburb of Manchester, Altrincham was granted its town charter in 1290. There is little left to see of its ancient past but 5km (3 miles) to the west

is a fine 18thC house, Dunham Massey. This is set in beautiful gardens and a deer park. The house contains an outstanding collection of furniture, paintings, and silver.

BOOKS
Abacus Books, Regent Road, sells antiquarian and second-hand books with arts, gardening, and crafts books being specialities. The shop is closed Wednesday afternoon and weekends.

FURNITURE
Church Street Antiques Ltd, in Old Market Place, has a large stock of fine Georgian and Victorian furniture as well as art, objets d'art, carpets, and decorative items. It is open 7 days a week (from 12 noon–4pm on Sundays).

GAMES
Greenwood Street Antiques, Greenwood Street, sells its large selection of antique chess sets and games by appointment only – ring 0161 941 6978.

GENERAL ANTIQUES
Altrincham Antiques, Tipping Street, is open by appointment to sell a wide range of general antiques – ring 0161 941 3554. In Regent Road, **Squires Antiques** has an extensive stock of silver, jewellery, porcelain, brass, copper, lighting, and small fine furniture. The shop is closed Monday, Wednesday, and Sunday.

AUCTION HOUSES
Patrick Cheyne Auctions (FSVA), Hale Road, holds bi-monthly sales at the Assembly Rooms, Hale.

▶ Follow the local signs to adjoining Bowdon.

BOWDON
This pretty village was mentioned in the *Domesday Book*. It appears so rural that it is hard to believe that today it is really a suburb of Manchester.

FURNITURE
Richmond Antiques in Richmond Road has a wide range of decorative furniture, chandeliers, and mirrors including 19thC French and English examples. The shop is open Tuesday–Saturday 12 noon–6pm.

GARDEN ANTIQUES
Rural Heritage Garden Antiques, Church Brow, has a large stock of English garden antiques including stone troughs, sundials, bird baths,

cast-iron urns, straddle stones, and gargoyles. It is open 10am–5pm but they ask you to contact them before visiting – ring 0161 929 8081.

▶ Join the M56 westbound at Junction 7 and continue on it for 35.4km (22 miles) until you reach its junction with the M53 – Junction 15 (Junction 11 of the M53). Turn left onto the M53 for 5km (3 miles), to its next junction, Junction 12, and you will then be right on the edge of Chester.

CHESTER
The city of Chester is unique, because it is the only one in England to have preserved all its city walls. Two thousand years ago, it was the site of a Roman fort, which was home to legions for the duration of the 300 years of occupation. The city has prospered throughout the centuries, first as a successful port until the 15thC when the River Dee silted up. Then it became a commercial centre for the region. The two-tier Medieval shopping arcades are among Chester's most famous landmarks; another is the 12thC sandstone cathedral. The 12thC Chester Castle is home to the Cheshire Military Museum, whose displays feature the county's regiments with exhibits including weapons, medals, and badges. Nearby Eaton Hall, the palace of the Duke of Westminster, is set in beautiful gardens.

BOOKS
More Books, Lower Bridge Street, sells rare and second-hand books and has a stock of local Welsh history books. It is open Monday–Saturday, and also opens on Sundays during the summer months. **Stothert Old Books** (PBFA), Nicholas Street, has a wide range of antiquarian and second-hand books including local history, topography, natural history, and good illustrated books, etc.

CERAMICS
Made of Honour, City Walls, sells 18th and 19thC British pottery and porcelain as well as decorative items, boxes, caddies, and Staffordshire figures.

DECORATIVE ANTIQUES
Objets d'Art, Watergate Row, sells decorative items.

FURNITURE

Chester Antique Furniture Cave, Boughton, has an extensive selection of furniture of all periods and types including large dining tables, desks, bureaux, chairs, etc. In the High Street, Saltney, in the south-west of Chester, **DKR Refurbishers** has a large stock of original pine and oak furniture. The shop is open 7 days a week, but from 2–4pm only on Sundays. **Mansion House Antiques**, Watergate Row, has a wide range of Georgian and Victorian oak furniture, coffers, four-poster beds, and soft furnishings. **Melody's Antique Galleries** (LAPADA), City Road, has an extensive selection of 17th–20thC furniture, varied small items, and paintings. **Moor Hall Antiques**, again in Watergate Row, sells 18th and 19thC British furniture.

The Old Warehouse Antiques, Delamere Street, has Victorian and Edwardian furniture, beds, and soft furnishings. **Richmond Galleries** in New Crane Street has a large range of new and old country pine furniture and decorative items. There are two shops called **Second Time Around** – the first is in Spital Walk and the second is in Christleton Road. Both are in Boughton, in the eastern part of the city, and both have a large stock of Victorian, Georgian, and Edwardian furniture.

GENERAL ANTIQUES

Adams Antiques of Chester (LAPADA), Watergate Row, sells 18th and 19thC furniture, clocks, glass, 19th–early 20thC small silver, mechanical devices, and lighting. **Ask Simon**, Christleton Road, has a wide range of decorative antiques, domestic paraphernalia, sporting and farming items, pictures, collectables, and furniture. **Borg's Antiques**, also in Christleton Road, sells silver, furniture, porcelain, Royal Doulton, and small decorative items, etc. **Cestrian Antiques**, Watergate Street, has an extensive range of small items of furniture, oak coffers, boxes, silver, glass, ceramics, longcase clocks, mantel clocks, wall clocks, pictures, and lighting. Back in Christleton Road, **Dales of Chester** has a wide selection of antique stock including furniture, china, copper, and brass. **K D Antiques**, City Walls, sells boxes, Staffordshire figures, prints, collectables, and glass. **Saltney Restoration Services**, in St Mark's Road, sells its lighting, sanitary ware, furniture, and ironware by appointment only – ring 01244 312529.

METALWARE

The Antique Shop, Watergate Street, sells small items – mainly brass, copper, and pewter. It is open Monday–Saturday and also on Sundays from Easter–Christmas.

SCIENTIFIC INSTRUMENTS

Antique Scientific Instruments sells slide rules, calculators, early scientific instruments, and drawing equipment by appointment only – ring 01244 318395.

SILVER

Watergate Antiques, Watergate Street, has a large stock of silver, silverplate, and ceramics.

ANTIQUES CENTRES

Again in Christleton Road, Boughton, **Wheatsheaf Antiques Centre** has a wide range of general antiques from the 17thC until the early 20thC. It is open 7 days a week (from 12 noon on Sundays).

ANTIQUES FAIRS

Penman Antiques Fairs holds two events a year, in February and October, in the County Grandstand, Chester Racecourse. The vetted fair has been running since 1988 and has 60 exhibitors from all over the UK.

AUCTION HOUSES

Halls Fine Art (Chester) Ltd (ARVA), Watergate Street, has fortnightly general sales on Wednesday at 11am, with viewing two days prior. There are also bi-annual wine sales as well as sales of collectors' models, toys, scientific instruments, and juvenilia three times a year.

Phillips International Auctioneers and Valuers have their regional office in Christleton Road.

YORK ▶ MALTON ▶ SCARBOROUGH ▶ PICKERING ▶ THIRSK ▶ RIPON ▶ HARROGATE

All the towns on this Yorkshire tour have a good selection of antiques shops but there are particularly large concentrations in both York and Harrogate. The latter also has a large number of specialist furniture dealers.

The county of North Yorkshire stretches across Northern England from its spectacular coastline in the East, across moors and fertile valleys to the Dales in the West. It attracts millions of tourists, who flock to see its traditional market towns, beautiful countryside, and historic sites.

Yorkshire, England's largest county, encompasses a diverse range of landscapes from the spectacular North Yorkshire Moors, beautiful valleys, to the traditional seaside towns. Then there are industrial towns like Leeds, Bradford, and Sheffield in the southern part.

Perhaps the most famous of Yorkshire's range of landscapes are the Yorkshire Dales and the North Yorkshire Moors, both National Parks. The beautiful scenery of the Dales and the Moors has provided locations for television series like *Heartbeat, All Creatures Great and Small*, and *Last of the Summer Wine*.

The North Yorkshire Moors has the largest area of woodland in any of the country's National Parks. The Yorkshire Dales National Park contains moorland scenery and its limestone caverns are popular with potholers. The Dales have a kinder, softer face too, which is shown in its peaceful farmland with fields bordered by drystone walls.

YORK

This city started as the Roman settlement *Eboracum*. There was a Roman fort here and it was the military headquarters for the region. Its main purpose was to repress any signs of rebellion and to repel attacks from the north.

Nowadays the cathedral, York Minster, dominates the city. It is the largest Medieval cathedral in the country. Building started on it in 1220 on the site of an earlier Saxon church. It has some magnificent features including its stained glass windows, many of which still have their original Norman glass. In the North Nave the Five Sisters Window dominates the area. It is made up of glazed coloured glass dating from the mid-13thC. Manufactured in Europe it is the largest window of this type in the world. During the Civil War, when many churches were badly damaged or destroyed by Parliamentary forces, York Minster was spared because the city surrendered on the condition that its churches were left undamaged.

The city has many interesting museums. The Archaeological Resource Centre (The ARC), in Saviourgate, allows you to assume the role of archaeologist. You can handle real artefacts and try to identify them with the help of staff. In the Jorvik Viking Centre, in Coppergate, life in AD 948 is recreated with every detail as accurately reconstructed as possible using archaeological evidence. In Coxwold, Shandy Hall was once the home of Laurence Sterne, the 18thC author of *Tristram Shandy*. The house dates from the 15thC, with later additions, and contains the world's most important collection of Sterne's work together with contemporary pictures. The Merchant Adventurers Hall dates from the mid-14thC and is one of the largest buildings of this date in Britain.

The National Railway Museum in Leeman Road has a large collection of full-scale railway engines and it tells the story of rail from Stephenson's Rocket up to the present day. The Yorkshire Museum of Farming is in Murton Lane, Murton Park, which is just 3.2km (2 miles) to the east of York. The place houses four different attractions – Yorkshire Museum of Farming, Danelaw Dark Age Village, Brigantium: The Roman Fort, and the Derwent Valley Light Railway.

BOOKS
Jack Duncan, in Fossgate, sells antique, scholarly, and second-hand books, with English literature being his speciality. **Minstergate** (PBFA), Minster Gates, specializes in children's and illustrated books. The shop is open 7 days a week. **Janette Ray Rare Books** (ABA, PBFA), Bootham, has rare and second-hand books, architectural and decorative arts, as well as those on landscape design and gardens. The shop specializes in books on 19thC Arts and Crafts, Art Deco, and Modernism. It is open Friday and Saturday. In Micklegate, **Ken Spelman** (ABA, PBFA, ILAB) has a large stock of antique, rare, and second-hand books.

COINS & MEDALS
Ancient World (ADA), High Petergate, sells ancient coins and antiquities. It is open 7 days a week. **J Smith** (BNTA), in The Shambles, has a large range of coins, stamps, and medals.

EPHEMERA
Mike Fineron Cigarette Cards & Postcards is situated in The Pastures, Dringhouses, in the south-west of the city. The shop sells cigarette cards and postcards by appointment only – ring 01904 703911. Yorkshire postcards are its speciality.

FURNITURE
The French House Ltd, Micklegate, has a wide selection of 18th–19thC French furniture and decorative items. In Vine Street, **Now & Then** sells small antique furniture and collectables. It is open Thursday–Saturday.

GENERAL ANTIQUES
Bishopgate Antiques, in Bishopgate, sells general antiques and is open 7 days a week (on Sundays from 12 noon–5pm). **Hudsons of York**, The Stonebow, has a large range of general antiques and European furniture. The shop is open 7 days a week (until 4pm on Sundays). In Clarence Street, **Laurel Bank Antiques** has general antiques,

collectables, Edwardian, Victorian, Georgian, and William IV furniture as well as longcase, wall, and mantle clocks. It is open all week apart from Tuesday and Sunday. **Minster Antiques**, Goodramgate, sells general antiques. **The Mulberry Bush Antique Shop**, also in Goodramgate, has general antiques, watercolours, oils, and clocks. **Stable Antiques**, Stonegate, sells general antiques and porcelain. It is open 7 days a week from 8.30am. **Taikoo Books Ltd**, in Bootham, sells general antiques and antiquities, including African and Oriental. The shop is shut at weekends. **York Vale Antiques** (GADR) is in Water Lane.

RAILWAYANA
Collectors Corner, George Hudson Street, has a large stock of railway antiquities and memorabilia.

SILVER & JEWELLERY
Advena Antiques & Fairs, Stonegate, sells antique silver and jewellery. It is open 7 days a week, but shuts at 4pm on Sundays. **Harpers Jewellers Ltd**, Minster Gates, has an extensive range of jewellery.

ANTIQUES CENTRES
In Stonegate, **Cavendish Antiques & Collectors Centre** (BSSA) has 60 dealers selling a large selection of general antiques. The centre is open 7 days a week. Also with 60 dealers, **The Red House Antique Centre**, Duncombe Place, has datelined stock and is open 7 days a week in summer (open until 8pm Thursday–Saturday all-year-round). **Stonegate Antiques Centre** (BSSA), again in Stonegate, has 120 dealers selling a large range of general antiques. It is open 7 days a week. The 15 dealers in **York Antiques Centre**, Lendal, have an extensive stock of antiques.

AUCTION HOUSES
John Simpson (ASVA), Forest Grove, has quarterly sales of general antiques and is open by appointment only – ring 01904 424797.

▶ The A64, going north-east, will take you straight to Malton, which is 32km (20 miles) from York.

MALTON
Once the site of a Roman fort, Malton is the meeting point of roads from all directions, which reveals the importance it had in earlier times. Standing 10km (6 miles) west of Malton, the world-famous Castle Howard is a magnificent early 18thC house designed by Vanbrugh. If it looks familiar, it may be because it was used as a location in the

television series *Brideshead Revisited*. The house contains over 300 pieces of rare china including Crown Derby, Meissen, and Chelsea. There is also an outstanding collection of pictures including works by Gainsborough, Holbein, Canaletto, and Rubens.

BOOKS

Old Talbot Gallery, Market Street sells books, prints, pictures, and maps. It is open by appointment only – ring 01653 696142.

FURNITURE

Northern Antiques Co., Parliament Street, in the adjoining town of Norton, has Georgian and Victorian furniture as well as decorative accessories. The shop is shut Saturday afternoons.

GENERAL ANTIQUES

In The Shambles, **Magpie Antiques** sells general antiques, kitchenalia, and small collectables. The shop is open until 4pm each day but is closed Thursday and Sunday. **Matthew Maw**, Castlegate, has general antiques.

AUCTION HOUSES

Boulton & Cooper Fine Art (SOFAA), Market Place, has sales of general antiques on alternate months. **Cundalls**, also in the Market Place, has eight to ten sales of general antiques a year.

▶ Continue onto Scarborough via the eastbound A64, which is a distance of 37km (23 miles).

SCARBOROUGH

Although it lives up to its image of a typical English seaside resort, Scarborough's history actually goes right back to the Bronze Age. Its 12thC castle was built on a headland between two bays, 91m (300ft) above sea level. Skeletons showing signs of violence have been found here and experts think they were a result of Saxon raids on the town. The castle was also besieged by Parliamentary troops during the Civil War. Its defence was so impressive that, on its eventual surrender, its defenders were allowed to march out with drums beating and flags flying. After that, the castle saw no more action until two German cruisers

fired upon it during World War I, which meant it became one of the few English castles to be shelled by Germans.

BOOKS

Hanover Art & Book Gallery, Hanover Road, sells antique, rare, and second-hand books as well as antique and modern prints. **Bar Bookstore** (The Antiquary Ltd.) (PBFA), in Swan Hill Road, has antiquarian, rare, and second-hand books and is open Tuesday–Saturday.

GENERAL ANTIQUES

Bar Street Antiques, in Bar Street, sells general antiques and is open until 4pm. **Allen Reed**, Victoria Road, has a large stock of general antiques. The shop is open until 3.30pm. In Ramshill Road, **Charles Smith & Son** has an extensive range of general antiques and 19thC watercolours.

ANTIQUES CENTRES

Antique and Collector's Centre (PTA), St Nicholas Cliff, sells general antique jewellery, ephemera, cigarette cards, coins, postcards, antiques, commemorative ware, etc.

AUCTION HOUSES

David Duggleby Fine Art, Vine Street, has fortnightly 500 lot sales of house contents and Victoriana, and every eight weeks 700 lot sales of fine art and antiques. **Ian Peace & Co.** (RICS), Falconers Road, has periodic sales of general antiques and house contents. **Ward Price Ltd** (ASVA), in Queen Street, has sales of general antiques on alternate months. The office is open on Saturdays until 2pm as well as weekdays.

▶ Take the A170 westbound direct to the next stop in Pickering, 27.3km (17 miles) away.

PICKERING

The history of the ancient town of Pickering goes back to the 2ndC BC when a Celtic settlement was located here. The town stands on the edge of the North Yorkshire moors and reigning monarchs on hunting expeditions frequently used its now ruined 12thC castle.

In Bridge Street, the Beck Isle Museum of Rural Life is located in a Regency mansion. Each room has a different theme including: printing, a dairy, a cobblers, a chemist's shop, and a

Victorian parlour.

BOOKS

Inchs Books (ABA, PBFA), in Westgate sells antique and second-hand books by appointment only – ring 01751 474928.

CERAMICS

Stable Antiques is in Pickering Road, in Thornton Dale, which is 3.2km (2 miles) east of Pickering on the A170. The shop has a large range of porcelain and is open 7 days a week 2–5pm.

GENERAL ANTIQUES

Country Collector, in Birdgate, sells ceramics, blue and white china, glass, silver, metalware, collectables, and antiquities. It is closed Wednesday and Sunday. C H & D M Reynolds, Eastgate, has a wide selection of general antiques including furniture and curios.

ANTIQUES CENTRES

The 30 dealers in the Pickering Antique Centre, Southgate, sell general antiques, books, postcards, and pictures and are open 7 days a week.

▶ Take the A170 for 43.4km (27 miles) to Thirsk.

THIRSK

The pretty market town of Thirsk was the birthplace of Thomas Lord, the founder of Lord's Cricket Ground. It is ideally situated for exploring the North York Moors National Park, just to the east.

BOOKS

In Westgate, The Book & Stamp Shop, sells antiquarian, rare, and second-hand books as well as prints and British and Commonwealth stamps. It is closed Wednesday and Sunday. Hambleton Books, in the Market Place, sells antique, rare, and second-hand books – books on cricket a speciality. It is open 7 days a week (until 4pm on Sundays).

GENERAL ANTIQUES

Squiffy's, again in the Market Place, has antiques, collectables, and gifts.

▶ Take the A61 eastbound for 21km (13 miles) to reach Ripon.

RIPON

Standing on the confluence of the Rivers Cover, Skell, and Ure, Ripon was first granted its charter in AD 886 by Alfred the Great. Its present cathedral is the fourth church to stand on the spot. St Wilfrid built the first in the 7thC and its crypt may be seen beneath the present 13thC building. It was designated as a cathedral (the seat of a bishop) in 1836 when the diocese of Ripon was created.

Standing in the market place there is an obelisk surmounted by a weather vane in the shape of a huntsman's horn. In Medieval times the Wakeman sounded a horn to summon the Town Watch to their duty. Although the office of Wakeman was replaced by the mayor in 1617, a hornblower still sounds his horn every evening in the Market Square. You may see the Wakeman's House in the corner of the Market Square.

The ruins of Fountains Abbey, 6.5km (4 miles) south-west of Ripon, are a popular destination, receiving over 300,000 visitors a year. They are the remains of one of the richest Cistercian abbeys in England and are considered so important that they were made into a World Heritage Site in 1987.

GENERAL ANTIQUES

Hornsey's of Ripon, in Kirkgate, has a large stock of antiques, collectables, rare books, fine linen, and lace. Hug & Plum, also in Kirkgate, sells general antiques and collectables and it is also a stockist for Lorna Bailey. Kindon Antiques is found on the Melmerby Industrial Estate, in the village of Melmerby, 8.5km (5 miles) north-east of Ripon, just off the A1. The shop sells general antiques and large pieces of unusual pine. It is open Monday–Friday. Judy Richards & Son, North Street, has general antiques, longcase clocks, Victorian beds, and Staffordshire figures. It is closed Wednesday afternoon and Sunday. Sigma Antiques in Water Skellgate has a large stock of general antiques. Skellgate Curios, Low Skellgate, sells general antiques. It is open 11am–5pm every day apart from Wednesday.

AUCTION HOUSES

Crown Auctions in St Wilfrid's Road is open Monday–Friday 9–10.30am and Saturday 10–11.30am.

▶ Continue southwards on the A61 to Harrogate, a distance of 25.75km (16 miles).

HARROGATE

Until the 16thC this area had a few scattered farming settlements. Then, in 1571, medicinal springs were discovered in High Harrogate and, later, sulphur springs were found in Low Harrogate. These all attracted many visitors to the area, and the two small villages grew into the town of Harrogate. A pump room was built in 1842. Visit the Royal Pump Room Museum in Crown Place to find out more about Harrogate's spa.

The Mercer Art Gallery in Swan Road has a series of temporary exhibitions. The War Room and Motor House Collection in Park Parade has collections of war-related memorabilia and models – there are about 12,000 die-cast model vehicles in the Motor House Collection.

BOOKS
Richard Axe Books, Cheltenham Crescent, has a large stock of antiquarian, rare, and second-hand books. Yorkshire topics are its speciality.

CERAMICS
Paul M Peters (LAPADA), Bower Road, has an extensive range of Chinese, Japanese, and European ceramics as well as Oriental works of art. It is open Monday–Friday.

FURNITURE
In Montpellier Parade, Armstrong Antiques (BADA, LAPADA) sells fine 18th and 19thC English furniture. Derbyshire Antiques Ltd, also in Montpellier Parade, sells early oak pieces, associated items, and furniture from Georgian–1820. Haworth Antiques (BWCG), Cold Bath Road, has furniture and clocks. It is shut Sunday and Monday. Charles Lumb & Sons Ltd (BADA), in Montpellier Gardens, has 18th and 19thC English furniture and works of art. Kate Marshall Decorative Antiques, Cheltenham Crescent, has a large stock of antique French country furniture and is open Tuesday–Saturday 11am–5pm. Elaine Phillips Antiques Ltd (BADA), Royal Parade, sells 17th and 18thC oak furniture, metalware, treen, and some mahogany. Thorntons of Harrogate (LAPADA), again in Montpellier Gardens, has 18th and 19thC furniture, clocks, barometers, and decorative items. Back in Montpellier Parade, Weatherells Antiques

(LAPADA) has a wide range of 18th–early 20thC English and Continental furniture, paintings, and objets d'art. Chris Wilde Antiques (LAPADA), in The Courtyard, Mowbray Square, has an extensive selection of Victorian and Georgian furniture, longcase clocks, and pictures. It is open Tuesday–Saturday. Year Dot Interiors, Regent Parade, sells painted, pine, oak, and country furniture.

GENERAL ANTIQUES
Dragon Antiques, in Dragon Road, has general antiques, ephemera, and postcards. The shop is open 11am–6pm. Garth Antiques, Montpellier Mews, sells general antiques. Havelocks Pine and Antiques, Westmoreland Street, has a large stock of general antiques. It is open 7 days a week (until 4pm on Sundays).

LIGHTING
St Julien (MCG), Royal Parade, has an extensive range of antique and period lighting as well as door furniture and fireplaces.

TOOLS
Grandads Attic in Granville Road sells antique, usable tools, garden tools, and kitchenalia. It is open Thursday–Saturday.

ANTIQUES CENTRES
The 50 dealers in The Ginnel Antiques Centre, The Ginnel, sell a very large range of quality datelined antiques.

ANTIQUES FAIRS
Robert Bailey organizes three fairs a year with about 100 exhibitors in Harrogate at the Pavilions of Harrogate on the outskirts of the town. Louise Walker, well-known dealer and fairs organizer, puts on two events in the town in the spring and autumn, both in the Harrogate International Centre.

AUCTION HOUSES
Christopher Matthews, Mount Street, has quarterly sales of antiques. Morphets of Harrogate (SOFAA), Albert Street, have quarterly sales of fine art and antiques on Thursdays at 10am with viewing on Tuesdays 2–7pm, Wednesdays 10am–5pm, and Thursdays 8.30–10am. Furniture and effects are auctioned on Thursdays at 10am with viewing on Wednesdays 10am–7pm and Thursdays 8.30–10am. The office shuts at 12 noon on Saturdays. Tennants Auctioneers, in Montpellier Parade, have three general antiques sales a month with quarterly fine art sales and two books and collectors' sales each year. The office is open on Saturday until 3.30pm as well as weekdays. Thompson Auctioneers, located on Hollins Lane, Hampsthwaite, about 6.5km (4 miles) north-west of Harrogate, have sales of general antiques on Fridays at 6.30pm. The office is closed on Friday and Saturday afternoons.

GLASGOW ▶ EDINBURGH ▶ DUNFERMLINE ▶ KIRKCALDY ▶ KINROSS ▶ PERTH ▶
STIRLING ▶ FALKIRK

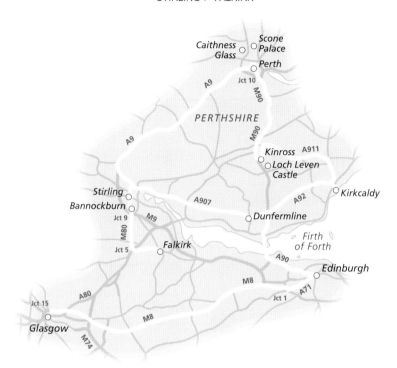

You will probably be surprised at the enormous number of antiques shops in Edinburgh and Glasgow, particularly the number of specialist book and furniture dealers. If you have time to take the extra leg on this trip, Perth also has a good selection of shops and has the bonus of some stunning countryside.

The area around Glasgow suffered in the 1970s, 80s, and 90s as traditional heavy industries like coal mining, steelmaking, and ship building declined. Now Glasgow has shaken off its image of being a grim industrial city, and has revealed itself as a beautiful city containing many magnificent buildings. Oil has, to some extent, replaced the old heavy industries in its importance to Scotland's economy, with the majority of British offshore oil now being found in Scottish waters. Aberdeen has become home to the headquarters of the oil companies' offices as well as providing services to the oil rigs.

The region around Glasgow and Edinburgh has the highest population, although the most magnificent scenery is found to the north, in the Highlands. Whichever part of the country you visit, Scotland's heritage and strong national identity shines through. It is famous as the home of golf as well as the Highland Games, which are held throughout the summer all over Scotland.

Websites

www.dunfermlineonline.net
Dunfermline was once the capital of Scotland.
Find out more about this ancient city from its
home page.

www.edinburgh.org
There is so much to see and do in Edinburgh
so, particularly if you are visiting for the first
time, you really should consult the city's
official website first. There is extensive
information on hotels, B & Bs, places to eat,
and much more.

www.falkirkweb.co.uk
Look here for places to visit once you are in
Falkirk, including where to shop and eat. The
site also has pictures of the town.

www.glasgow.gov.uk
Glasgow's website gives a good detailed
account of its history as well as information
on all aspects of the city.

www.antiquesforeveryone.co.uk
Check here for forthcoming Antiques for
Everyone Fairs in Glasgow, organized by the
same team who present the events at the
National Exhibition Centre in Birmingham.

www.scone-palace.co.uk/tourism
Learn about ancient Scone Palace, where
Scottish kings were once crowned.

www.whisky-heritage.co.uk
One of Scotland's most famous exports,
Scotch whisky is popular throughout the world.
Learn more about it here.

Tourist Information Centres

Dunfermline Maygate. Tel: 01383 720999

Edinburgh Princes Street.
Tel: 0131 473 3800

Falkirk Glebe Street. Tel: 01324 620244

Glasgow George Square.
Tel: 0141 204 4772

Kinross Junction 6 of the M90 motorway.
Tel: 01577 863680

Kirkcaldy Whytescauseway.
Tel: 01592 203154

Perth West Mill Street. Tel: 01738 627958

Stirling St John's Street. Tel: 01786 471301

GLASGOW

For many years Glasgow had a
reputation as a grim city full of slum
tenements. Nowadays that image has
become outdated as it was designated
European City of Culture in 1990 and UK
City of Architecture and Design in 1999.

Evidence of Stone Age settlements
has been found on the banks of the
Clyde. Glasgow first entered recorded
history in the 6thC when St Mungo
arrived and established his church here
on the site of the present cathedral. It
was established as the seat of the
bishop in the early 12thC and 300 years
later its university was founded, which
is now the second oldest in Scotland.
Over the following centuries the city
prospered, especially through trade with
the New World and again during the
Industrial Revolution when shipping and
heavy engineering became important.

With the decline of traditional
industries, Glasgow suffered huge
unemployment. However, years of
grime began to be removed from its
buildings, which revealed an astounding
architectural heritage. It was against this
background that the city has been reborn
as a centre for art and culture.

Glasgow has a large number of good
museums and art galleries. One of the
most striking is the Gallery of Modern Art
in Queen Street. It has four floors – each
has a theme of fire, earth, water, or air.
Exhibits include works by David Hockney,
Andy Warhol, Sebastiao Salgado, and
Eduard Bersudsky as well as Scottish
artists such as John Bellany and Ken
Curry. Nearby in Richmond Street the
Collins Gallery, which is part of the
University of Strathclyde, presents a

programme of exhibitions including contemporary fine and applied art, sculpture, photography, local history, and architecture. The famous Burrell Collection, in Pollok Country Park, has over 8,000 objects that were collected by Sir William Burrell and given to the city in 1944. The collection includes stained glass, Impressionist paintings, Medieval tapestries, and ancient art. The Hunterian Art Gallery, part of the University of Glasgow in Hillhead Street, has the largest display of work by Whistler in the world as well as 19th and 20thC Scottish works by Guthrie, McTaggart, and Peploe, and paintings by 19thC French Impressionists such as Pissarro and Rodin. It also includes the Mackintosh House, where rooms from the home of Charles Rennie Mackintosh have been recreated (one of Glasgow's most famous designers and architects).

On a completely different note, a first floor flat in the Tenement House in Buccleuch Street recreates a Victorian tenement home. A Miss Agnes Toward lived here from 1911–75 and made few changes apart from installing electricity. The National Trust for Scotland bought the house in 1982 and reinstalled the original gas lighting but made few other changes. An exhibition on the ground floor explains more about Glasgow life during the 19thC.

BOOKS

Cooper Hay Rare Books (SAA), Bath Street, sells books and prints, specializing in Scottish art and juvenile books. It shuts at 1pm on Saturdays. In Gibson Street, Downside Books (PBFA) sells antiquarian, out-of-print,and second-hand books, specializing in academic and Scottish topics. Gillmorehill Books, Bank Street, has rare and second-hand books. Voltaire & Rousseau, in Otago Lane, has a large stock of second-hand and rare books. The shop specializes in books on Scotland and foreign languages.

CLOCKS

Browns Clocks, Radnor Street, sells longcase clocks. It shuts at 1pm on Saturdays

COSTUMES & CLOTHING

Saratoga Trunk Yesteryear Costume & Textiles, Hyde Park Street, has a wide range of Victorian–1990s vintage clothing, linens, lace, etc. It is open Monday–Friday.

FIREPLACES

Rusty Grates, Niddrie Road, Queens Park, sells antique fireplaces – Victorian, Georgian, and Art Nouveau. The shop opens at 12 noon on Saturdays.

FURNITURE

In Torrisdale Street, Butler's Furniture Galleries sells Georgian, Victorian, and Edwardian furnishings. It is open Monday–Friday. Canning Antiques, Millbrae Road, Langside, has Georgian, Victorian, and Edwardian furniture together with small mirrors. It is open 7 days a week (from 12 noon on Sundays). Den of Antiquity, Langside Lane, Victoria Road, Queens Park, has antique and shipping furniture and is open 7 days a week (from 12 noon on Sundays). Muirhead Moffatt & Co., West Regent Street, sells antique furniture, jewellery, and porcelain. The shop is open Monday–Friday. The Renaissance Furniture Store, Niddrie Road, sells furniture, silver, and Arts and Crafts items. The shop is open 7 days a week.

GENERAL ANTIQUES

In Park Road, Kelvin Bridge, All Our Yesterdays has a large stock of general antiques. It is open from 12 noon on Saturdays. E A Alvarino, in Radnor Street, Kelvingrove, has a large stock of general antiques and is open Monday to Friday 1–5pm. Antique City, Fernleigh Road, sells general antiques including architectural objects. It is open 7 days a week. The Antiques Warehouse, Yorkhill Quay Estate, has an extensive range of general antiques. It is open 7 days a week (from 12 noon on Sundays). Back in Niddrie Road, Finnie Antiques has a wide selection of general antiques, furniture, Arts and Crafts and lighting. The shop is open 7 days a week (from 12 noon at weekends). Flying Dutchman Antiques, in Yorkhill Way, sells a large variety of general antiques, including Continental European furniture. It is open 7 days a week (from 12 noon on Sundays). Lansdowne Antiques in Park Road sells general antiques and closes at 4pm on Saturdays. Lovejoy Antiques, again in Yorkhill Quay, has general antiques. It is open 7 days a week (from 12 noon on Sundays). Restore-It, in Cambuslang Road, Rutherglen, has a range of general antiques. Stuart Mylers, in West Regent Street, also sells general antiques. Quinns Antique Arcade, London Road, has general antiques. It is open at weekends 10am–4pm. Relics, in Dowanside Lane, sells general antiques and collectables including 1960s wares. It is open 7 days a week (from 12.30pm on Sundays). R Rutherford, West Regent Street, has general antiques and Scottish agates. Victoria Antiques Ltd,

Pollockshaws Road, has a wide range of general antiques. **Tim Wright Antiques** (LAPADA) is in Bath Street. The shop shuts at 2.30pm on Saturdays. In Kildrostan Street, **Yesteryear** has general antiques. It shuts at 1pm on Saturdays.

LIGHTING

Luma Lighting, in The Square Yard, has an extensive selection of Victorian–1920s house lighting. It opens at weekends.

MILITARIA

The Treasure Bunker Militaria Shop, King Street, has a wide range of military antiques from the Battle of Waterloo–World War II. It is open Tuesday–Saturday.

SILVER & JEWELLERY

Jeremy Sniders Antiques, Bath Street, is a Georg Jensen silver specialist and also sells general antiques, Scandinavian antiques, silverware, and jewellery.

ANTIQUES FAIRS

The management that made **Antiques for Everyone** an outstanding success at the NEC in Birmingham has brought its winning formula north of the border. The annual event is held at The Scottish Exhibition & Conference Centre (SECC) and it has around 200 good-quality exhibitors.

AUCTION HOUSES

Carpet Auctioneers Ltd (SAA) is situated on Washington Street. As well as Monday–Friday, the office is open every second Saturday 9.30am–1.30pm. **Arthur E Collins & Son** (SAA), Trongatem, has two pawnbrokers' sales per week. **Great Western Auctions**, in Otago Street also has two sales a week, this time of general antiques. **Kerr & McAllister** (SAA), Niddrie Road, has auctions of household goods every Thursday evening. **Robert McTear & Co.** (IAA), Elliot Place, has weekly sales of general antiques. **Patersons Auctioneers & Valuers**, Orchard Street, in Paisley, has fortnightly sales of general antiques. **Phillips Fine Art Auctioneers**, St Vincent's Street, holds weekly sales of general antiques in Edinburgh.

▶ Leave Glasgow on the M8 and follow the motorway to the outskirts of Edinburgh. Leave the M8 at Junction 1 on the ring road and take the A71 into the city centre. The distance from Glasgow to Edinburgh is about 64.3km (40 miles).

EDINBURGH

This beautiful and imposing city is Scotland's capital and the home of the new Scottish Parliament. The city is dominated by it historic castle, which was built on a volcanic plug of rock. It was here that Mary Queen of Scots gave birth to James VI of Scotland, who later became James I of England. It is also home to the Scottish Crown Jewels and the Scottish United Services Museum, with its exhibitions of uniforms, weapons, and medals.

The world-famous Royal Mile runs from Edinburgh Castle to Holyrood Abbey and has many places to visit along its length, including the Scotch Whisky Heritage Centre.

Edinburgh, as might be expected from any city of such historic significance, has a large number of interesting museums and galleries. Among them, the Scottish National Portrait Gallery in Queen Street has portraits of many important Scottish people. There are also works by Gainsborough, Van Dyck, and Rodin. The City Centre in Market Street has a permanent collection of some 3,500 Scottish works of art including oils, watercolours, prints, drawings, and photographs from some of the country's leading artists. It also hosts temporary exhibitions from all over the world.

In Belford Road, the Scottish National Gallery of Modern Art has work by Henry Moore, Barbara Hepworth, William Turnbull, and Eduardo Paolozzi, among many others. Also in Belford Road, the Dean Gallery has galleries for temporary exhibitions as well as important archive material, which is particularly centred on Dada and the Surrealists. The National Gallery of Scotland, on The Mound, holds one of the country's greatest collections of art including masterpieces by El Greco, Titian, Rembrandt, Van Dyck, Monet, Gauguin, and Raphael.

In the heart of Edinburgh's New Town, The Georgian House, Charlotte Square, is furnished exactly as it would have

been at the end of the 18thC. It displays
a fine collection of silver, furniture,
paintings, and pottery and porcelain.
The National Library of Scotland, on
George IV Bridge, was founded in the
late 17thC and it has over 7 million items
of printed material. On the Royal Mile, in
Canongate, the People's Story recounts
the histories of ordinary people from the
18thC onwards. Not only does it use
conventional written resources to do this,
but it also draws on oral history sources.
The reconstructions include a prison cell,
a cooper's workshop, and a 1940s
kitchen. Nearby, Huntly House Museum
has collections relating to Scottish history
ranging from prehistoric times onwards.
Among its most impressive exhibits
are the 17thC National Covenant and
a nationally important collection of
Scottish pottery.

In complete contrast, Lauriston Castle,
in Davidson's Main, is a 16thC tower
house that was extended in the early
19thC. Its perfectly preserved Edwardian
interiors reflect the tastes and lives of its
last private owners. Back on the Royal
Mile, in Lawnmarket, The Writers'
Museum is housed in an early 17thC
building. It documents the lives and work
of great Scottish writers like Robert
Burns, Sir Walter Scott, and Robert Louis
Stevenson. Nearby, Gladstone's Land
shows a typical 17thC Edinburgh
tenement. It was built in 1620 and was
the home of a merchant. It is now
furnished in the style of the time.

Also in the Royal Mile, The Museum
of Childhood has collections of dolls,
teddies, toys, and games from all over
the world. It also documents a range of
Edinburgh children's street games and
shows how children have dressed
through different periods. Finally, still in
the Royal Mile, the Brass Rubbing Centre
in Chalmers Close is housed in Trinity

Aspe, which is a small surviving piece
of a Gothic church built in 1460. Inside
are replica brasses of all types. The staff
will help you if you have never tried your
hand at brass rubbing before so why not
give it a go?

ANTIQUITIES
Bow-Well Antiques, in West Row, has a large stock
of general and Scottish antiquities.

ARCHITECTURAL ANTIQUES
EASY Edinburgh & Glasgow Architectural Salvage
Yard (SALVO), Couper Street, sells architectural
antiques, fireplaces, doors, ranges, pews, etc.
Holyrood Architectural Salvage, Holyrood Business
Park, Duddingston Road West, has a wide range
of period fireplaces, baths, radiators, panelled
doors, brassware, and stained glass. T & J W
Neilson Ltd (National Fireplace Association)
in Coburg Street has an extensive selection of
antique chimneypieces, dog grates, register grates,
fenders, and fireplace accessories.

BOOKS
In Dalkeith Road, The Bookworm sells antique and
second-hand books. Armchair Books, West Port,
has a wide range of books, especially Victorian
illustrated books. The shop is open 12 noon–5pm.
Broughton Books, Broughton Place, has rare and
second-hand books. It is open Tuesday– Friday
from12 noon and on Saturdays from 10.30am.
Castle Books in Rankeillor Street sells rare and
second-hand books. Grant & Shaw Ltd (ABA),
again in West Port, sells its antiquarian books –
on literature and travel – by appointment only.
Ring 0131 229 9339. McNaughtan's Bookshop
(ABA), Haddington Place, has general antiquarian
and second-hand books covering architecture,
children's, and Scottish topics. The shop is open
Tuesday–Saturday. The Old Children's Bookshelf
(PBFA), Canongate, Royal Mile, sells children's
novels, annuals, prints, and comics. In Victoria
Street, The Old Town Bookshop sells antiquarian
and second-hand books, maps, and prints. It
specializes in antiquarian art books.

Past & Present (PBFA), Clerk Street, sells
general antiques, antiquarian children's books, and
Art Deco items. It is open 7 days a week (2–6pm
on Sundays). Second Edition, in Howard Street, has
a large range of quality books, militaria, arts, and
Scottish books. It is open Monday–Friday from
12 noon and all day Saturday.

Till's Bookshop, Hope Park Crescent, has
literature, fantasy, mystery, humanities, poetry,
drama, cinema, general, and first edition books. It
is open Monday–Friday 12 noon–7.30pm, Saturday
all day, and Sunday from 12 noon. West Port
Books, West Port, has a wide range of antiquarian

and second-hand books – especially fine art books and Indian imports.

COINS & MEDALS
ECS (LANA), West Cross, Causeway, has a large stock of antique coins and medals, stamps, ephemera, and cigarette cards.

COSTUME & CLOTHING
In Henderson Row, Gladrags has a wide and unique selection of exquisite period clothes, accessories, jewellery, and linen. The shop is open Tuesday–Saturday.

DOLLS & TOYS
Bébés et Jouets sells antique French bébés and German dolls, teddy bears, juvenilia, and related items by appointment only – ring 0131 332 5650.

FURNITURE
Laurance Black Ltd (BADA), in Thistle Street, sells Scottish furniture as well as glass, pottery, clocks, and treen. It shuts at 1pm on Saturdays. Buccleuch Antiques, Bruntsfield Place, sells mainly Victorian and Edwardian furniture. Dunedin Antiques Ltd, in North West Circus Place, has a large stock of furniture and decorative items. Tim Hardie, Bruntfield Place, has 19thC furniture, including desks, bookcases, and military chests. The shop shuts at 1pm on Saturdays. Kaimes Smithy Antiques, in Howdenhall Road, sells 18th and 19thC furniture, clocks, paintings, and Chinese ceramics. It is open Tuesday, Wednesday, Friday, and Saturday afternoons. London Road Antiques, in Earlston Place, has an extensive range of 19thC furniture, Victorian and Georgian wares, and stripped pine. It is open 7 days a week (Sunday afternoon only). In Stanley Road, Trinity Curios has a wide range of quality furniture, porcelain, silver, linen, and collectables. The shop is open Wednesday–Sunday afternoons.

GENERAL ANTIQUES
Auckinleck, West Port, sells general antiques from Georgian–Victorian times. It is open Tuesday–Saturday. Causewayside Antiques, Causewayside, has general antiques, reproduction china, and furniture. The shop is open 7 days a week (afternoon only on Sundays). Bobby Clyde Antiques in Grange Road sells general antiques and is open Monday, Thursday, Friday, and Saturday. Collector Centre, Gilmore Place, has a large stock of general antiques, mostly collectables and books, silver, and militaria. It is open all week except Wednesday and Sunday. It has special summer hours in July, August, and part of September – Monday–Saturday until 9pm and Sunday 1–6pm. Duncan & Reid, Canon Mills, has 18th–early 19thC pottery, porcelain, glass, and second-hand and antiquarian books. It is open Tuesday–Saturday afternoons. Donald Ellis Antiques, Bruntsfield Place, sells

general antiques. It is open Monday–Tuesday and Thursday–Friday. Georgian Antiques (LAPADA), in Pattison Street, Leith, has a very large collection of general antiques. The shop shuts at 2pm on Saturdays. Goodwin's Antiques Ltd in Queensferry Street has an extensive range of general antiques. Back in Bruntsfield Place, Harlequin Antiques sells general antiques. Hawkins & Hawkins, Atholl Crescent, has a wide variety of general antiques, which it sells by appointment only – ring 0131 229 2128. Gordon Inglis Antiques, in Barclay Terrace, sells quality UK art, studio pottery, ceramics from c.1900, Scottish hand-painted pottery, linen, books, ephemera, collectables, and Scottish art-glass. It is open Monday, Wednesday, Friday, and Saturday afternoon. Allan K L Jackson, Causewayside, sells general antiques and is open Tuesday–Saturday. Alan Lawson & Son, also in Causewayside, has general antiques and reproduction items. J D Loue, Jane Street, has general antiques and opens at 8.30am. J Martinez Antiques, Brandon Terrace, sells general antiques, jewellery, and clocks. Millers Antiques, again in Causewayside, has general antiques, original pine, hand-stripped oak, advertising, and unusual collectables.

Now & Then, West Cross, Causeway, sells old toys, antiques, telephones, old clocks, cameras, and small items of furniture. It is open Tuesday–Saturday, but mostly by appointment – ring 0131 668 2926. Reid & Reid, in St Stephen Street, has general antiques and books and is open Tuesday–Saturday. James Scott, Dundas Street, has general antiques. It closes on Thursday and Sunday. Still Life, Candlemaker Row, has a large range of general antiques, china, glass, and pictures. The shop is open Monday–Saturday afternoons. The Talish Gallery, Canongate, has a wide variety of small general antiques, Oriental wares, and silver and is open until 4pm. The Thursday Shop in Clermiston Road, Corstorphine, sells general antiques, small china, glass, and silver. It is open Tuesday, Thursday, Friday, and Saturday – shutting early, at 2pm, on Saturday. In Dundas Street, Unicorn Antiques has general antiques and bric-a-brac.

MAPS & PRINTS
In Canongate, the Royal Mile Gallery has a large stock of antiquarian maps and prints.

PICTURES
Calton Gallery (BADA), Royal Terrace, has a wide selection of fine art – Scottish, marine, 19th–early 20thC paintings, and watercolours. It is open on Saturday mornings from 10am–1pm as well as weekdays during exhibitions.

SILVER & JEWELLERY
D L Cavanagh Antiques, Cockburn Street, has an extensive range of silver and jewellery as well as coins, medals, and collectors' items. Chit Chat

Antiques, St Stephen Street, sells flatware, silverplate, and silver. The shop is open Tuesday–Saturday. **Royal Mile Curios**, High Street, has a large range of antique jewellery and Scottish jewellery. It is open 7 days a week. **Wild Rose Antiques**, Henderson Row, has a wide selection of decorative table silver, ladies' and gent's jewellery, porcelain, pottery, and glass. Opening days are Thursday–Saturday.

STAMPS

In West Crosscauseway, **Lothian Stamps** sells all world stamps and cigarette cards and is open Tuesday–Saturday.

AUCTION HOUSES

Bonhams & Brooks Scotland regional office is located in Melville Street. **Finlays Auctioneers Ltd** (NAVA), in Jane Street, has weekly sales of general antiques on Saturdays. The office is open until 8pm on Fridays, and from 8am–4pm on Saturday. **Phillips Fine Art Auctioneers** (SOFAA), George Street, has weekly sales of antiques and collectables. The office is open from 8.30am, including Saturday. It closes at 12 noon on Saturdays. **Thomson, Roddick & Medcalf**, Harden Green Business Park, Eskbank, has weekly sales of antiques, fine art, and general furnishings.

▶ Take the A90 directly to Dunfermline. This route takes you over the Forth Road Bridge. The next city is a total distance of about 27.3km (17 miles) from the centre of Edinburgh.

DUNFERMLINE

This ancient city was, for six centuries, the capital of Scotland and is also the burial place of seven Scottish kings, including Robert the Bruce. In Moodie Street, you can pay a visit to the Andrew Carnegie Birthplace Museum, which tells the story of the locally-born millionaire's life before he left the town. In an adjoining cottage, you can learn about how he rose from being a telegraph operator in Scotland to finding his fortune in the USA.

AUCTION HOUSES

Dunfermline Auction Company Ltd, Castleblair Lane, has three sales a month of antiques and collectables. The office is open on Saturday mornings as well as weekdays. **Premier Auctions**, Rumblingwell, has weekly antiques and general household sales on Saturdays at 10am with viewing from 10am–8pm on Fridays. The office is closed Friday but open Saturday.

▶ Take the A92 east for 17.75km (11 miles) to reach Kirkcaldy.

KIRKCALDY

This town is sometimes known as "Lang Toun" because of its mile-long promenade on the Firth of Forth. Kirkcaldy still has some 15thC houses near its harbour. It was the birthplace of Adam Smith, the author of *Wealth of Nations*, and also of the architect Robert Adam. Kirkcaldy Museum and Art Gallery in the War Memorial Gardens has an excellent collection of 19th and 20thC Scottish paintings, in addition to an impressive exhibition of local history.

BOOKS

Book-ends, in Sailor's Walk, High Street, has a range of rare and second-hand books, and specializes in Scottish topics. It is open Tuesday–Saturday.

GENERAL ANTIQUES

A K Campbell & Son, in the High Street, sells general antiques, militaria, furniture, bric-a-brac, postcards, and banknotes. **The Golden Past**, Rosslyn Street, has general antiques and pine furniture. It is open Tuesday–Sunday.

SILVER & JEWELLERY

In the High Street, **A K Campbell & Son** sells antique jewellery and silver.

AUCTION HOUSES

M D's Auction Co., Smeaton Industrial Estate, Hayfield Road, have weekly sales of 500 lots on Thursdays at 6.30pm. The office is open on Saturday mornings as well as all week.

▶ At this point you can retrace your route back to Dunfermline and take the A907 to Stirling, which is about 22.5km (14 miles) from Dunfermline.

▶ Alternatively, go further north to visit Kinross and Perth. To do this, take the A92 for 6.5km (4 miles) to the town of Glenrothes where you should turn left onto the A911 for 17.75km (11 miles). At the village of Milnathort turn left onto the A922 – Kinross is less than 1.6km (1 mile) from the junction.

KINROSS

Kinross is on the shores of Loch Leven, the biggest of Scotland's lowland lochs. Mary Queen of Scots once escaped from Loch Leven castle, which is a short ferry ride from the town's western shore.

GENERAL ANTIQUES

Bridge Bygones Antiques, Rumbling Bridge, sells general antiques, Victorian and later furniture, and effects. It is open at weekends 12 noon–5pm. Miles Antiques (LAPADA), in Mill Street, has a large stock of general antiques and is open Monday–Friday afternoons. Tudor House, South Street, Milnathort, which you will have passed on your route into Kinross, sells general antiques. It is open Tuesday and Wednesday 1–5pm and Friday–Saturday 10am–5pm.

▶ Take the M90 northbound at Junction 6, which runs alongside Kinross, and continue for 24km (15 miles) to Junction 10, where you should leave the motorway. The centre of Perth is less than 3.2km (2 miles) north of this point.

PERTH

Nearby Scone (pronounced "Skoon") was the ancient capital of Scotland and Scottish kings were crowned in Scone Palace. The palace is now open to visitors during the summer and it contains superb collections of clocks, French furniture, pottery and porcelain, ivories, Vernis Martin papier mâché, and objets d'art.

Sir Walter Scott wrote about "The Fair Maid of Perth", whose house you can see in North Port. The Perth Museum and Art Gallery in George Street has a wide ranging collection of local history, natural history, and art, including a Tahitian mourner's cloak as well as silver and glassware. The world-famous Caithness Glass is situated just a couple of miles north of the city. It has a visitor centre, which allows you to see how glass is made today. You can also view their impressive, historic collection of paperweights, and you could be tempted by one of their limited edition items.

CERAMICS

Yesterdays Today, Old High Street, sells Scottish pottery and glass, jewellery, silver, Royal Doulton, and Beswick.

GENERAL ANTIQUES

Ainslie's Antiques, Gray Street, has a large stock of general antiques including Victorian and Edwardian furniture. It is open Monday–Friday. Design Interiors, South Street, has general antiques and collectables. Also in South Street, Alexander S Deuchar & Son sells general antiques. It is open Monday–Friday. Henderson Antiques, North Methuen Street, has general antiques. Imrie Antiques & Interiors, Back Street, Bridge of Barn, has a wide range of general antiques. The Tay Street Gallery, in Tay Street, sells general antiques and Georgian furniture. It is open Tuesday, Thursday, and Friday mornings.

SILVER & JEWELLERY

In St Paul's Square, Gallery One has Scottish silver, pictures, and Monart glass. It is open until 4pm on weekdays and until 1pm on Saturdays.

AUCTION HOUSES

Lindsay Burns & Co. (SAA), King Street, has bi-weekly sales of household effects on Thursdays at 10.30am, with viewing on the previous day. The office is open on Saturday mornings as well as weekdays. Loves Auction Rooms (SAA), Canal Street, has weekly sales of household effects and quarterly sales of antiques. The office is also open Saturday mornings. Ian M Smith Auctioneers & Valuers, Perth Airport Business Park, Scone, has fortnightly sales of general antiques. The office is open Saturday mornings as well as weekdays.

▶ Take the A9 westbound for 37km (23 miles) direct to Stirling.

STIRLING

Stirling Castle stands on top of a 76m (250ft) rock, which is an ideal defensive position, and the town grew up around it. The original castle was a timber fortress, which was rebuilt in stone in the 13thC. The present-day castle dates mostly from the 15th and 16thC and it contains the Regimental Museum of the Argyll and Sutherland Highlanders. There is another museum in the town, the Stirling Smith Art Gallery and Museum in Dumbarton Road, which is situated right next to the castle. It contains an important collection of Scottish paintings and other Scottish-related exhibits. These include the oldest football (from the mid-16thC), the oldest curling stone (from the early 16thC), and ancient tartans. It is also home to temporary exhibitions, which have, in the past, included quilting, watercolours, children's photography, and work from the Embroiders' Guild.

The battlefield of Bannockburn, the turning point in Robert the Bruce's fight for the independent throne of Scotland, lies to the south-east of Stirling, and just to the west of the M9 motorway.

GENERAL ANTIQUES

Abbey Antiques, Friars Street, sells general antiques. **Stewart Sales Rooms** in Dumbarton Road has a large stock of general antiques. It is open all week except Wednesday and Sunday.

Join the M80 at the southern end of the town at Junction 9 and continue southwards for 8.5km (5 miles) to Junction 5, where you transfer to the M876 for 3.2km (2 miles). Leave the M876 at Junction 1 and the A883 will take you into Falkirk, which is just another 3.2km (2 miles) away.

FALKIRK

Falkirk's great Carron Ironworks made cannons for the navy when Nelson was an admiral. Callendar House, on the south-east of the town, has a history going back over 900 years. Now it has been restored to its Georgian splendour and it has a working kitchen of the period, recreations of a general store, a printer's shop, as well as a clock and watchmaker's workshop.

COLLECTABLES

Rairweathers, Vicars Street, sells collectors' items and curios.

AUCTION HOUSES

Finlays Auctioneers Ltd (NAVA), Bankside, holds weekly sales of general antiques. Its office is open from early until late on Tuesdays and Wednesdays.

Index

Index

Index

Picture Credits

Trade Associations

ABA	Antiquarian Booksellers' Association	GMC	Guild and Master Craftsmen	NMTA	National Market Trade Federation
ADA	Antique Dealers' Association	GOMC	Guild of Master Craftsmen	NPA	National Pawnbroking Association
ADPS	Approval Dealers' Protection Society	GTLGB	Gem Testing Laboratory of Great Britain	OMRS	Orders & Medals Research Society
AHS	Antiquarian Horological Society	GTA	Gun Trade Association	OMSA	Orders & Medals Society of America
ANA	American Numismatic Association	IADA	Irish Antique Dealers' Association	PADA	Petworth Antique Dealers' Association
ARVA	Association of Regional Valuers & Auctioneers	IADAA	International Association of Dealers in Ancient Art	PBFA	Provincial Book Fair Association
BA	Booksellers' Association	IAPN	International Association of Professional Numismatists	PTA	Postcard Traders' Association
BABADA	Bath & Bradford on Avon Antique Dealers' Association	IBNS	International Bank Note Society	RADS	Registered Antique Dealers' Association
BADA	British Antique Dealers' Association	ICOM	International Council of Museums	RICS	Royal Institute of Chartered Surveyors
BGA	British Gemologists' Association	ILAB	International League of Antiquarian Booksellers	RWHA	Royal Warrant Holders' Association
BHI	British Horological Insititute	IMCOS	International Map Collectors' Society	SAA	Scottish Association of Auctioneers
BJA	British Jewellers Association	ISVA	Incorporated Society of Valuers & Auctioneers	SAADA	Sherborne Art & Antique Dealers' Association
BNTA	British Numismatic Trade Association	KCSADA	Kensington Church Street Antique Dealers' Association	SALVO	Association for dealers in architectural salvage
BWCG	British Watch & Clockmakers' Guild	LADA	Lechlade Antique Dealers' Association	SLAD	Society of London Dealers
CADA	Cotswold Antique Dealers' Association	LANA	Life Member of the American Numismatic Association	SOFAA	Society of Fine Art Auctioneers
CC	Clockmakers' Company	LAPADA	London & Provincial Antique Dealers' Association	TADA	Tetbury Antique Dealers' Association
CINOA	Confederation Internationale des Negotiants en Oeuvres d'Art	LMTA	Long Melford Trade Association	TVADA	Thames Valley Antique Dealers' Association
EADA	Essex Antique Dealers' Association	MBHI	Member of British Horological Society	UACC	United Autograph Collectors' Club
ESoc	Ephemera Society	NAG	National Association of Goldsmiths	WADA	Warwick Art Dealers' Association
FATG	Fine Art Trade Guild	NAVA	National Association of Auctioneers & Valuers	WKADA	West Kent Antique Dealers' Association
FBHI	Fellow of the British Horological Institute	NAWCC	National Association of Watch & Clock Collectors		
FGA	Fellow of the Gemological Association				
FSVA	Fellow of the Society of Valuers & Auctioneers				